D1133468

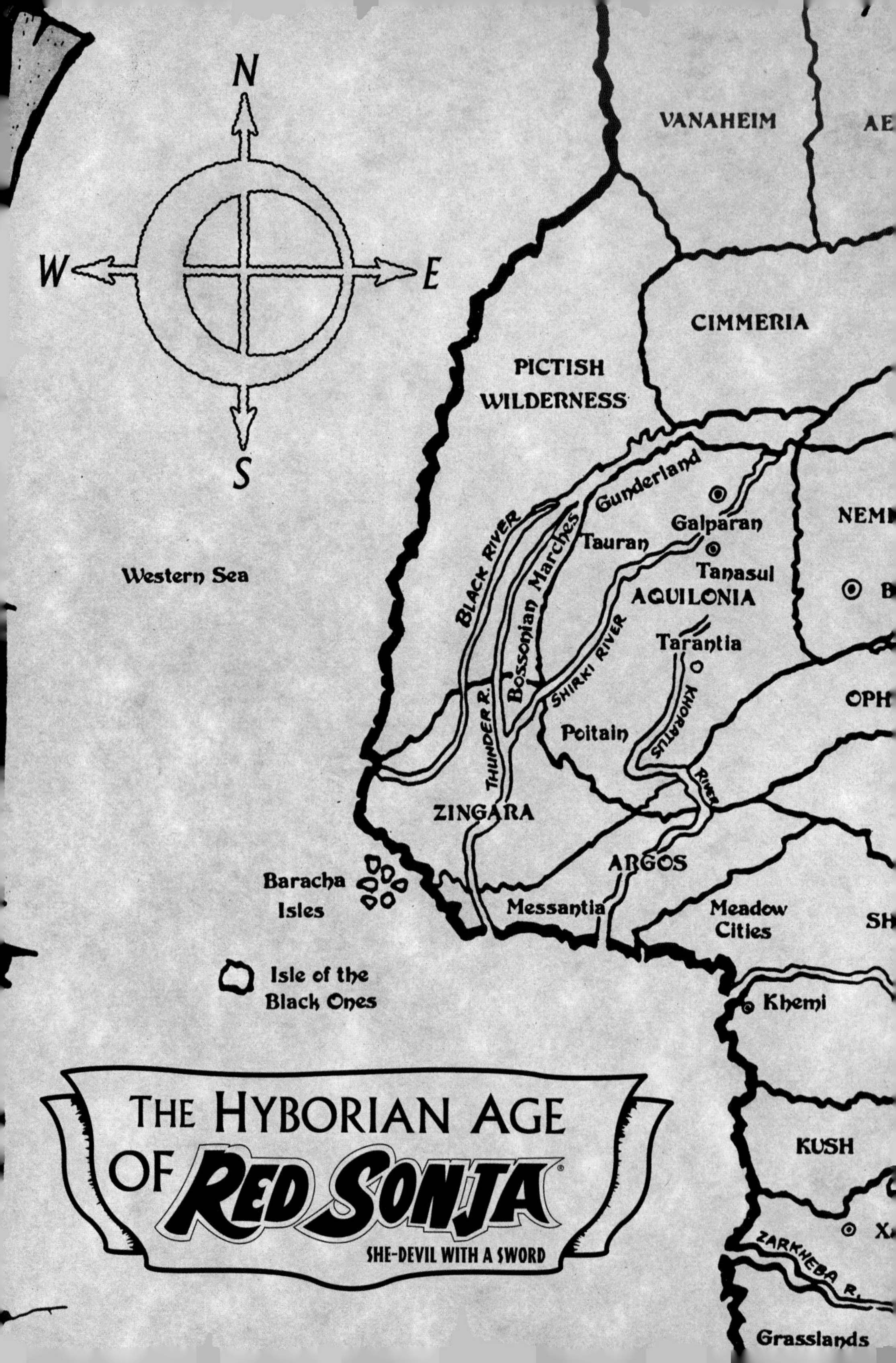
N
W
E
S
VANAHEIM
AE
CIMMERIA
PICTISH WILDERNESS
Gunderland
Galparan
Tauran
Tanasul
AQUILONIA
NEM
B
Western Sea
BLACK RIVER
Bossonian Marches
SHIRKI RIVER
Tarantia
KHORATUS RIVER
OPH
THUNDER R.
Poitain
ZINGARA
ARGOS
Baracha Isles
Messantia
Meadow Cities
SH
Isle of the Black Ones
Khemi
THE HYBORIAN AGE OF RED SONJA
SHE-DEVIL WITH A SWORD
KUSH
X
ZARKHEBA R.
Grasslands

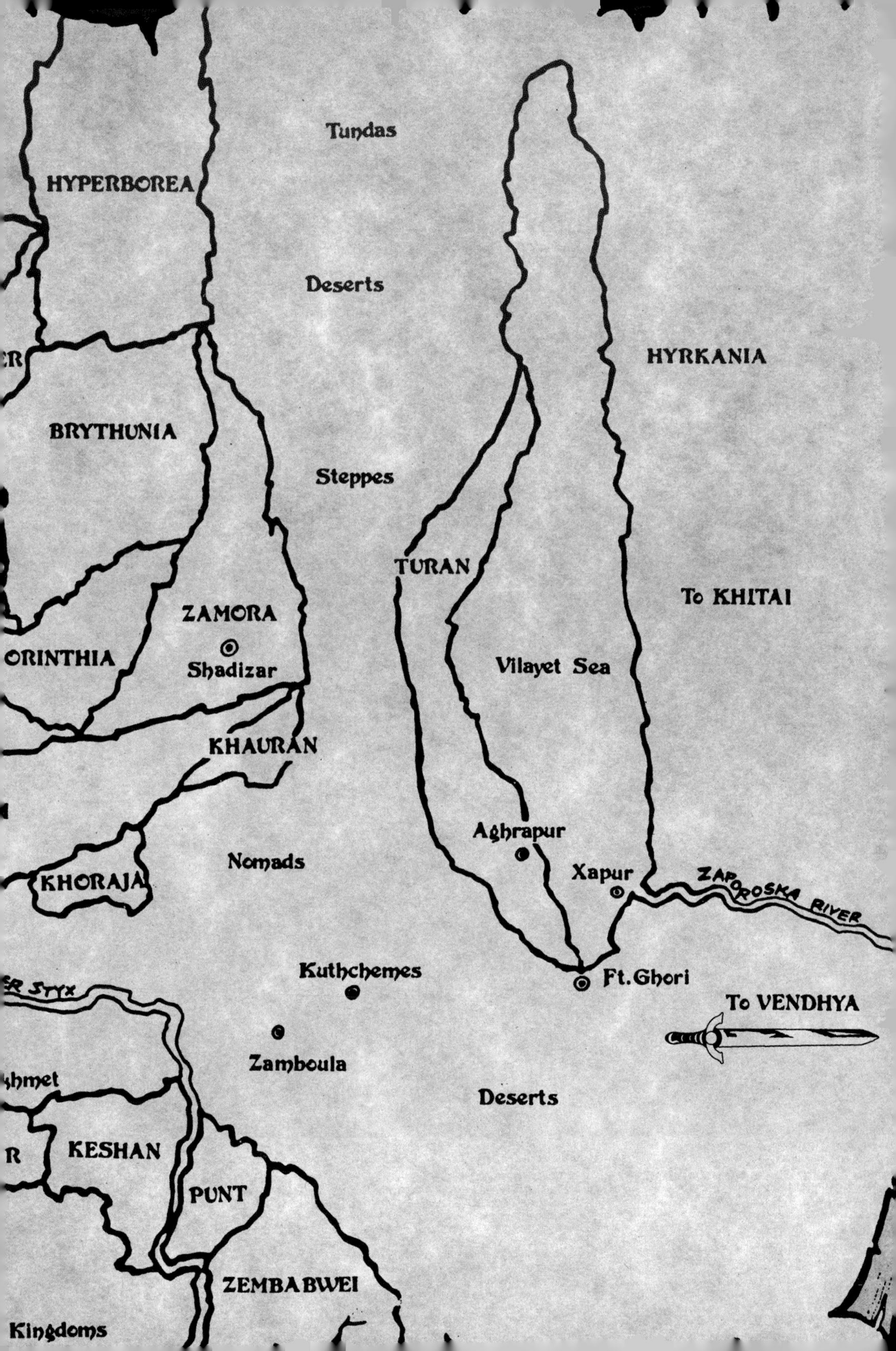

Tundas
HYPERBOREA
Deserts
HYRKANIA
BRYTHUNIA
Steppes
TURAN
To KHITAI
ZAMORA
Shadizar
ORINTHIA
Vilayet Sea
KHAURAN
Aghrapur
Nomads
Xapur
ZAPOROSKA RIVER
KHORAJA
Kuthchemes
Ft. Ghori
To VENDHYA
Zamboula
Deserts
KESHAN
PUNT
ZEMBABWEI
Kingdoms

Dynamite Entertainment Presents

RED SONJA®

SHE-DEVIL WITH A SWORD

Dedicated to Robert E. Howard

Volume VIII: The Blood Dynasty

- WRITTEN BY
  BRIAN REED
- ART BY
  WALTER GEOVANI (ISSUES 41-47, 49)
  DIEGO BERNARD (ISSUE 48)
- COLORS BY
  VINICIUS ANDRADE (ISSUES 41-47, 49)
  ADRIANO LUCAS (ISSUE 48)
- LETTERING BY
  SIMON BOWLAND (ISSUES 41-48)
  BILL TORTOLINI (ISSUE 49)
- COVER BY
  PAUL RENAUD
- BASED ON THE HEROINE CREATED BY
  ROBERT E. HOWARD

THIS VOLUME COLLECTS RED SONJA: SHE-DEVIL WITH A SWORD ISSUES FORTY-ONE THROUGH FORTY-NINE BY DYNAMITE ENTERTAINMENT.

EXECUTIVE EDITOR - RED SONJA
LUKE LIEBERMAN

SPECIAL THANKS TO ARTHUR LIEBERMAN
AT RED SONJA LLC.

DYNAMITE ENTERTAINMENT
NICK BARRUCCI PRESIDENT
JUAN COLLADO CHIEF OPERATING OFFICER
JOSEPH RYBANDT EDITOR
JOSH JOHNSON CREATIVE DIRECTOR
JASON ULLMEYER GRAPHIC DESIGNER

DYNAMITE® ENTERTAINMENT
WWW.DYNAMITEENTERTAINMENT.COM

To find a comic shop in your area, call the comic shop locator service toll-free 1-888-266-4226

For information regarding press, media rights, foreign rights, licensing, promotions, and advertising e-mail:
marketing@dynamiteentertainment.com

Printed in Canada

First Edition
SOFTCOVER ISBN-10: 1-60690-063-3 ISBN-13: 978-1-60690-063-5
HARDCOVER ISBN-10: 1-60690-062-5 ISBN-13: 978-1-60690-062-8
10 9 8 7 6 5 4 3 2 1

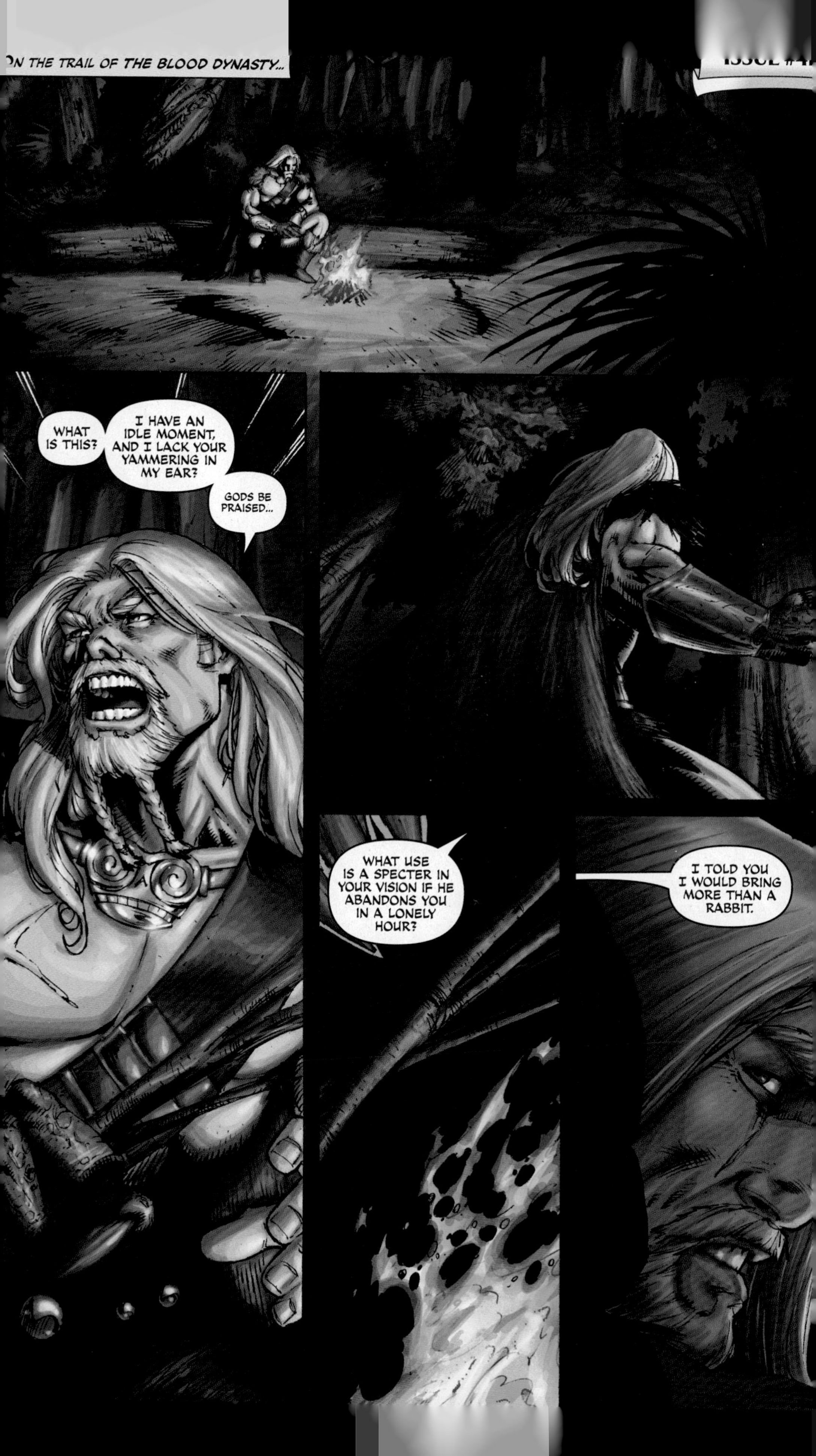

ON THE TRAIL OF THE BLOOD DYNASTY...
WHAT IS THIS?
I HAVE AN IDLE MOMENT, AND I LACK YOUR YAMMERING IN MY EAR?
GODS BE PRAISED...
WHAT USE IS A SPECTER IN YOUR VISION IF HE ABANDONS YOU IN A LONELY HOUR?
I TOLD YOU I WOULD BRING MORE THAN A RABBIT.

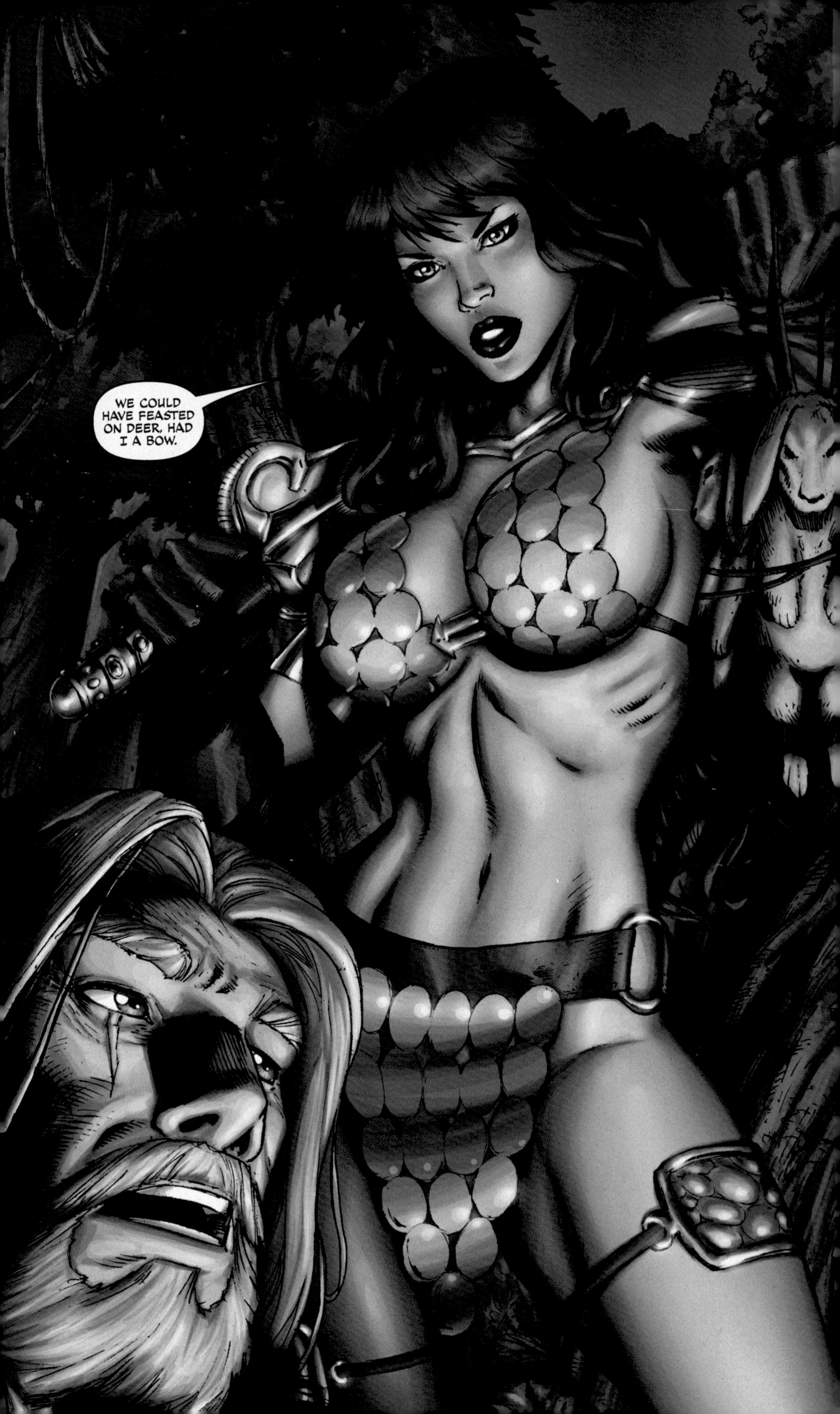
WE COULD HAVE FEASTED ON DEER, HAD I A BOW.

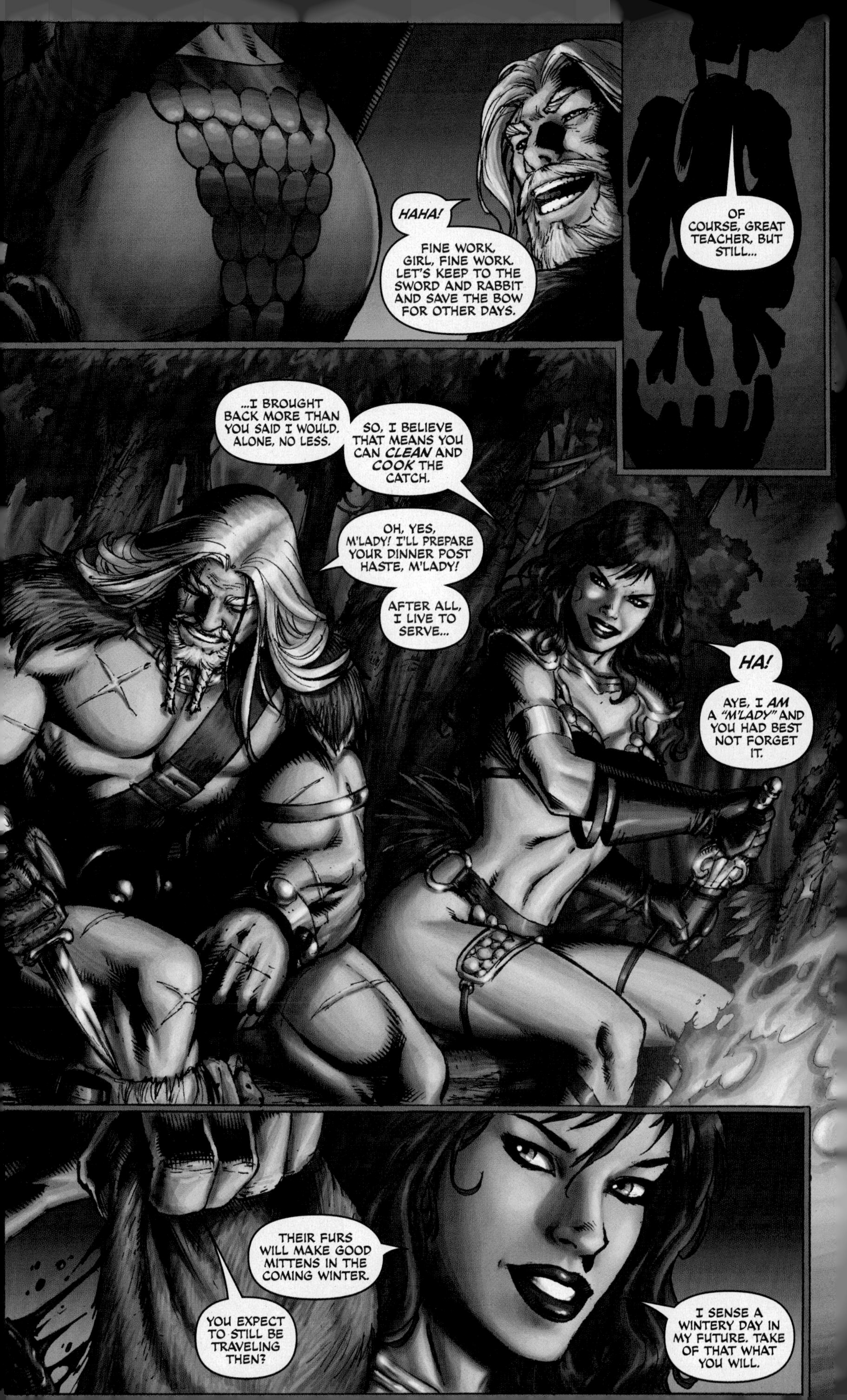
HAHA!
FINE WORK, GIRL, FINE WORK. LET'S KEEP TO THE SWORD AND RABBIT AND SAVE THE BOW FOR OTHER DAYS.
OF COURSE, GREAT TEACHER, BUT STILL...
...I BROUGHT BACK MORE THAN YOU SAID I WOULD. ALONE, NO LESS.
SO, I BELIEVE THAT MEANS YOU CAN CLEAN AND COOK THE CATCH.
OH, YES, M'LADY! I'LL PREPARE YOUR DINNER POST HASTE, M'LADY!
AFTER ALL, I LIVE TO SERVE...
HA!
AYE, I AM A "M'LADY" AND YOU HAD BEST NOT FORGET IT.
THEIR FURS WILL MAKE GOOD MITTENS IN THE COMING WINTER.
YOU EXPECT TO STILL BE TRAVELING THEN?
I SENSE A WINTERY DAY IN MY FUTURE. TAKE OF THAT WHAT YOU WILL.

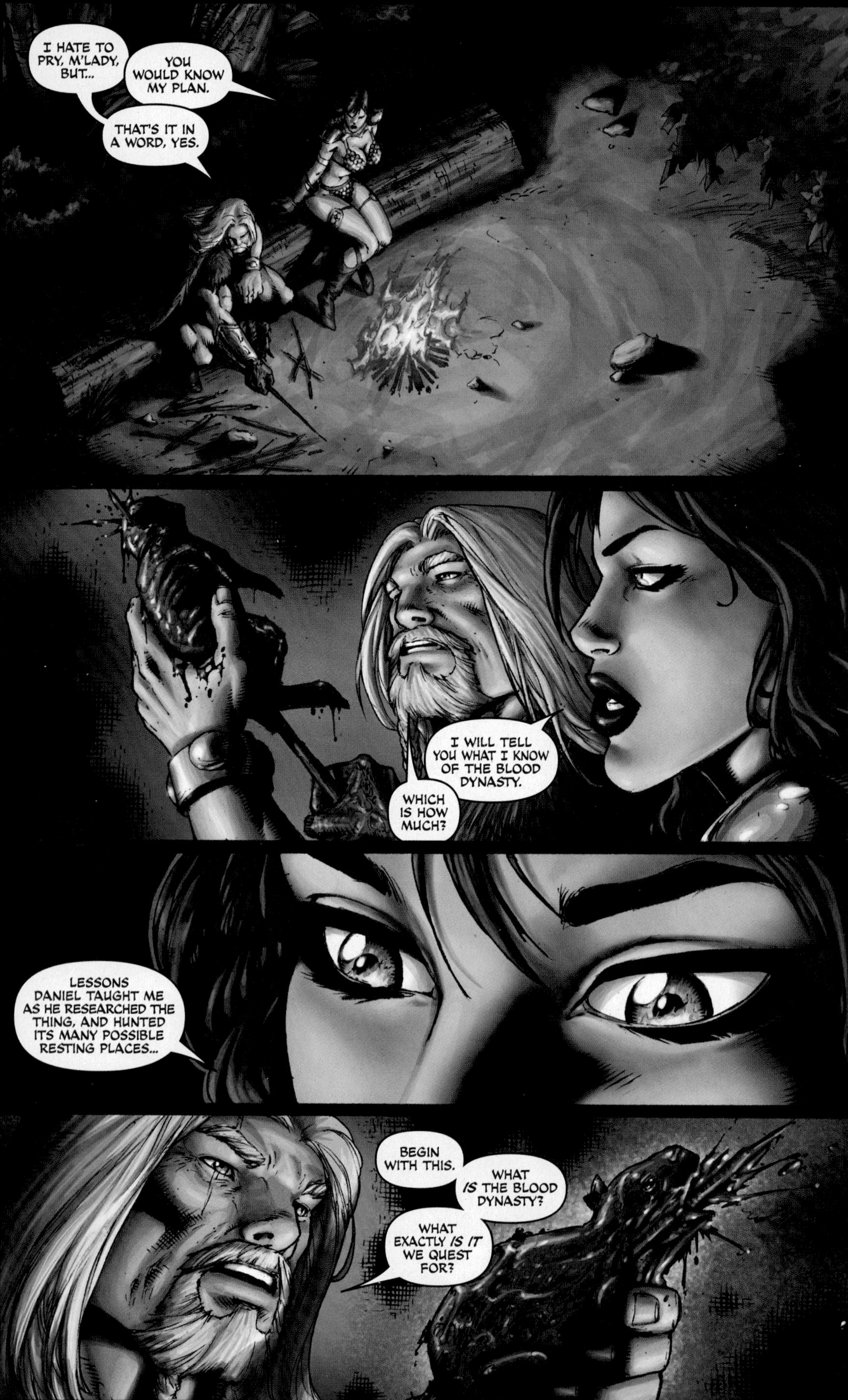
I HATE TO PRY, M'LADY, BUT...
YOU WOULD KNOW MY PLAN.
THAT'S IT IN A WORD, YES.
I WILL TELL YOU WHAT I KNOW OF THE BLOOD DYNASTY.
WHICH IS HOW MUCH?
LESSONS DANIEL TAUGHT ME AS HE RESEARCHED THE THING, AND HUNTED ITS MANY POSSIBLE RESTING PLACES...
BEGIN WITH THIS.
WHAT *IS* THE BLOOD DYNASTY?
WHAT EXACTLY *IS IT* WE QUEST FOR?

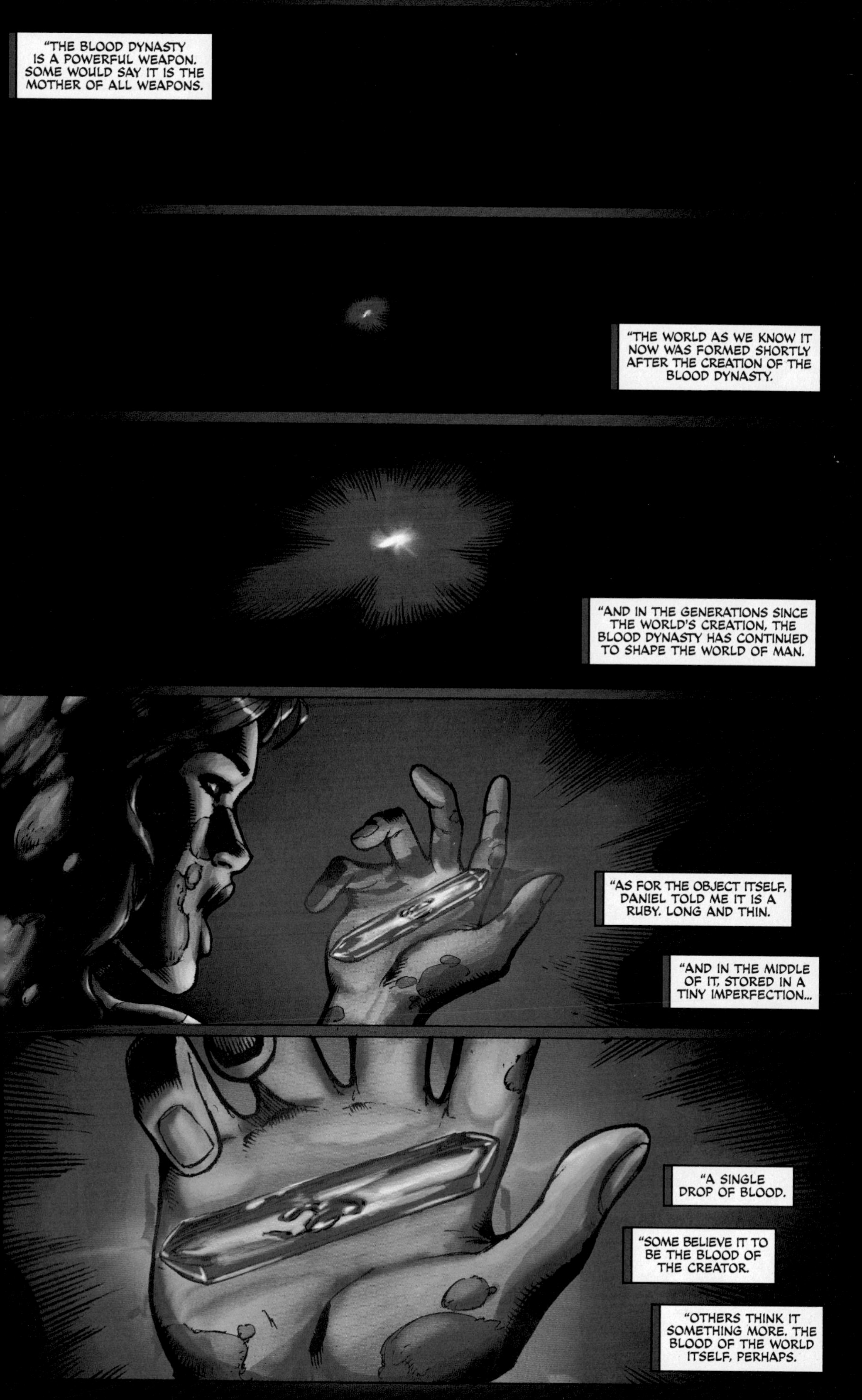
"THE BLOOD DYNASTY IS A POWERFUL WEAPON. SOME WOULD SAY IT IS THE MOTHER OF ALL WEAPONS.
"THE WORLD AS WE KNOW IT NOW WAS FORMED SHORTLY AFTER THE CREATION OF THE BLOOD DYNASTY.
"AND IN THE GENERATIONS SINCE THE WORLD'S CREATION, THE BLOOD DYNASTY HAS CONTINUED TO SHAPE THE WORLD OF MAN.
"AS FOR THE OBJECT ITSELF, DANIEL TOLD ME IT IS A RUBY. LONG AND THIN.
"AND IN THE MIDDLE OF IT, STORED IN A TINY IMPERFECTION...
"A SINGLE DROP OF BLOOD.
"SOME BELIEVE IT TO BE THE BLOOD OF THE CREATOR.
"OTHERS THINK IT SOMETHING MORE. THE BLOOD OF THE WORLD ITSELF, PERHAPS.

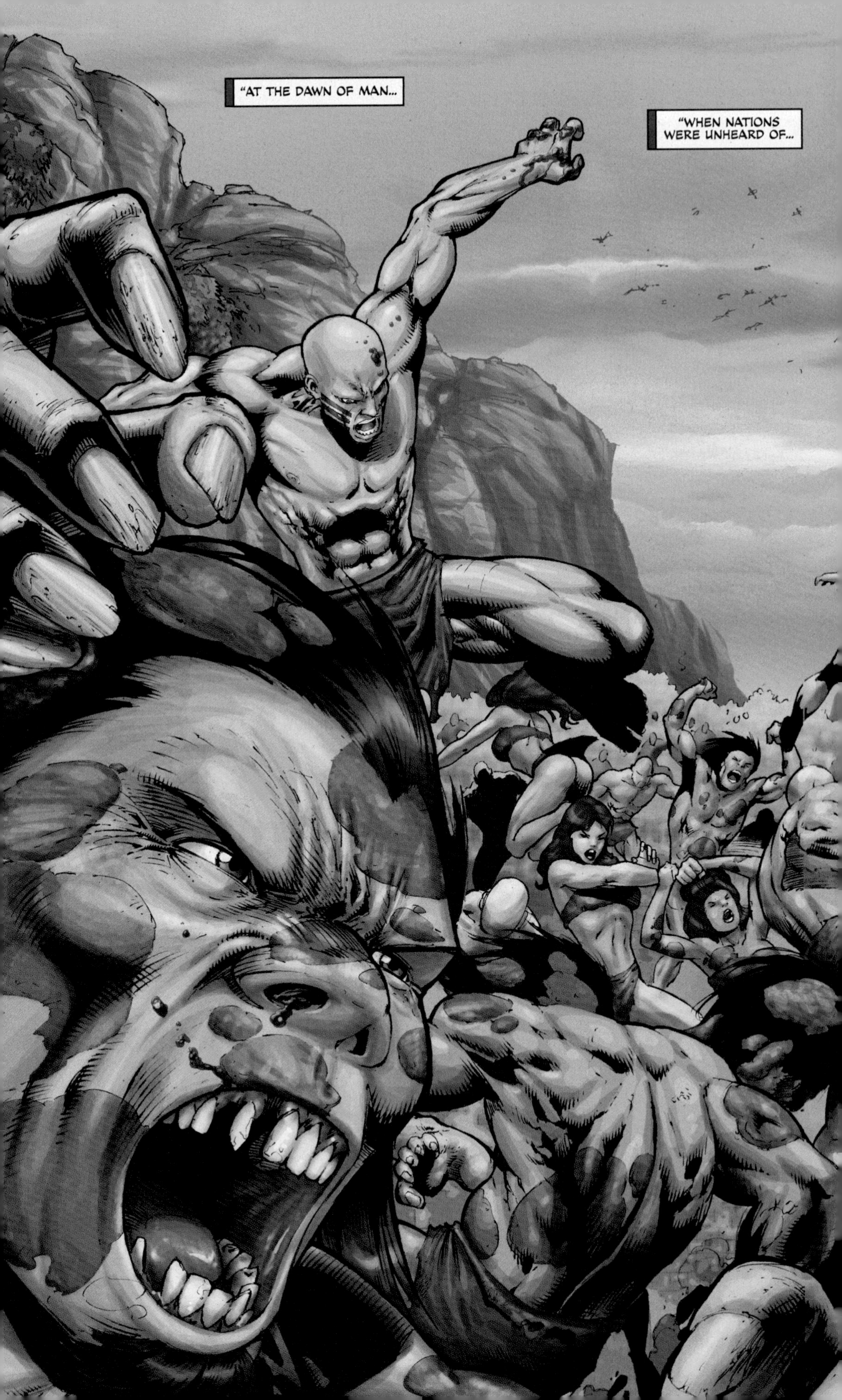
"AT THE DAWN OF MAN...
"WHEN NATIONS WERE UNHEARD OF...

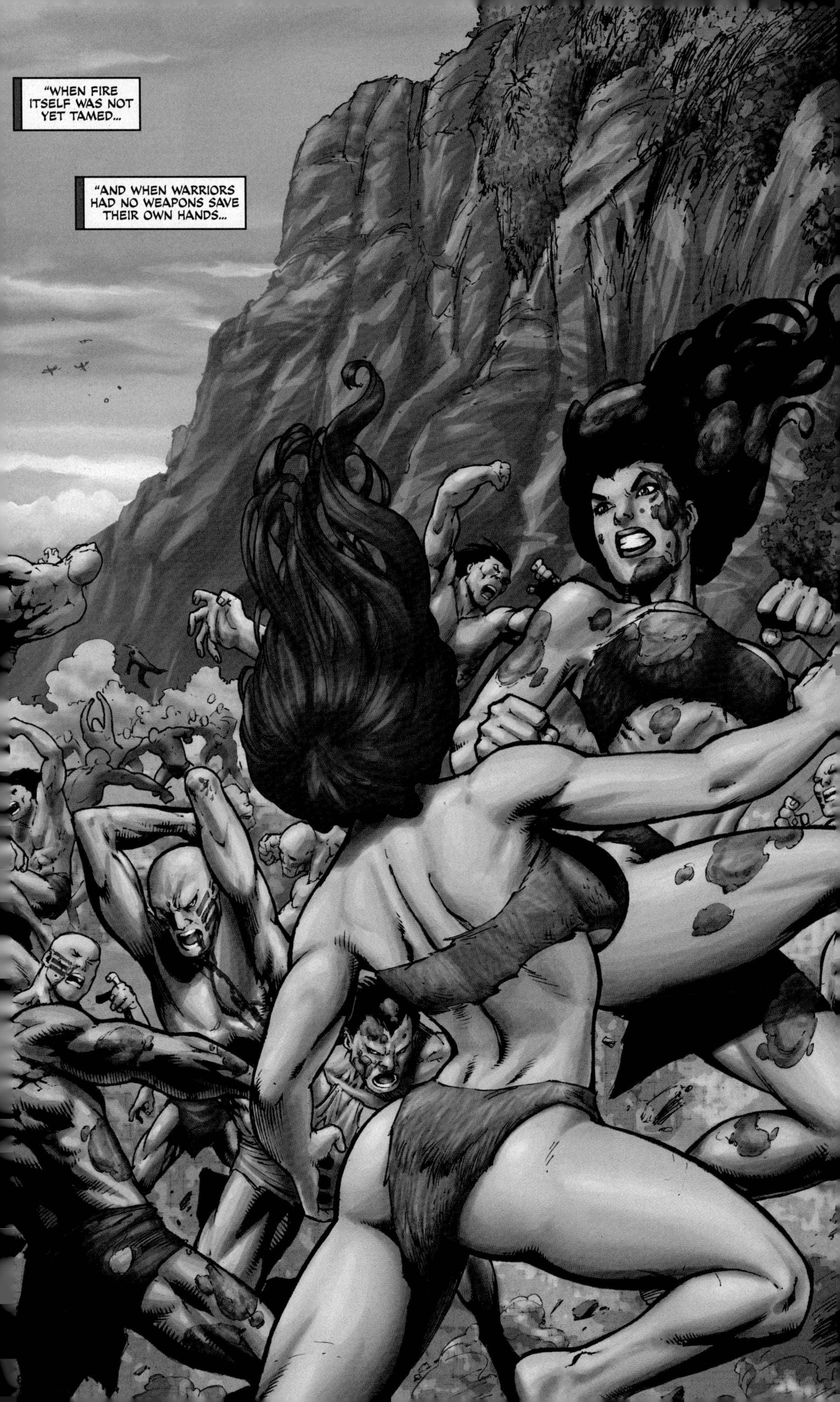
"WHEN FIRE ITSELF WAS NOT YET TAMED...
"AND WHEN WARRIORS HAD NO WEAPONS SAVE THEIR OWN HANDS...

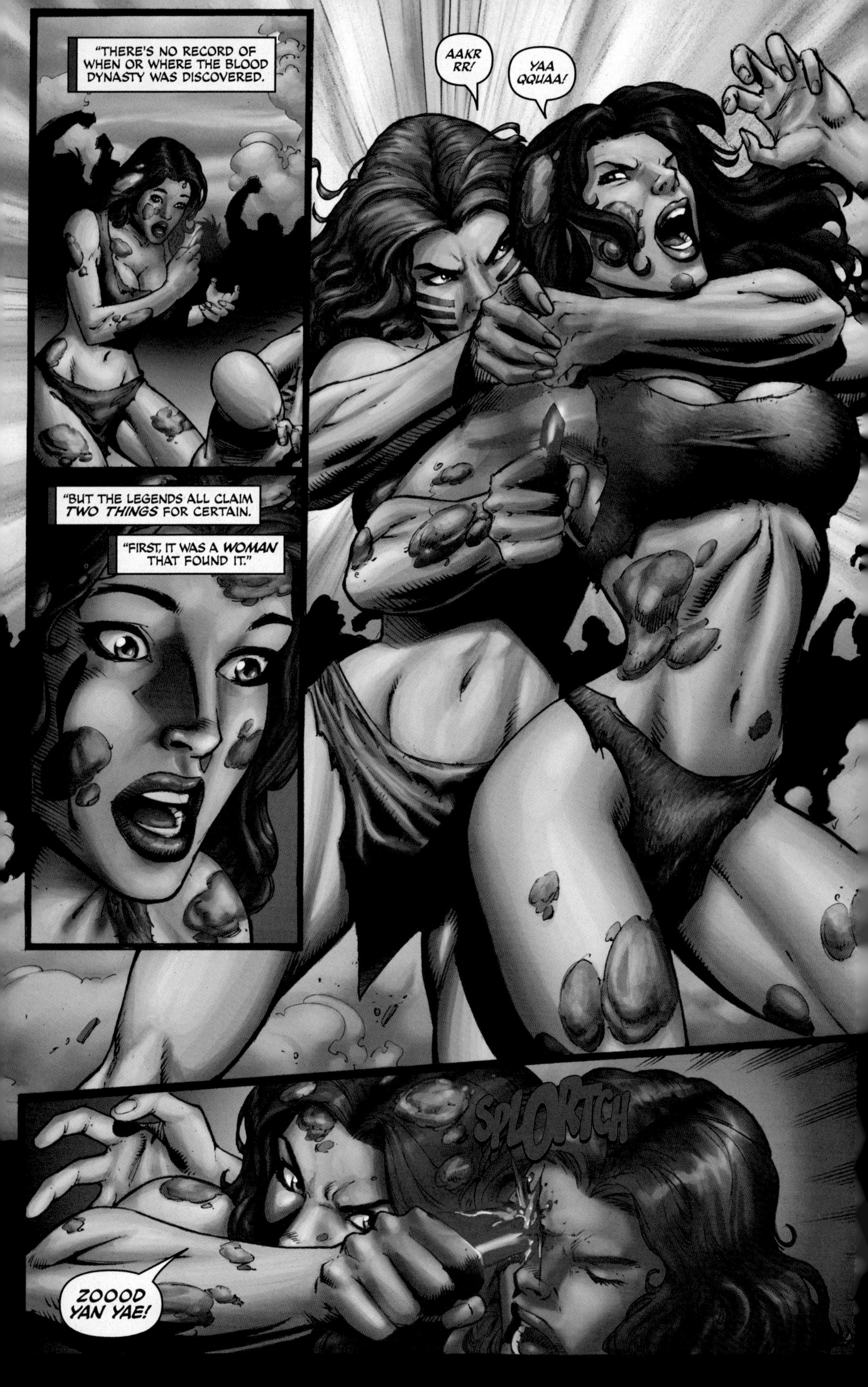
"THERE'S NO RECORD OF WHEN OR WHERE THE BLOOD DYNASTY WAS DISCOVERED.
AAKR RR!
YAA QQUAA!
"BUT THE LEGENDS ALL CLAIM *TWO THINGS* FOR CERTAIN.
"FIRST, IT WAS A *WOMAN* THAT FOUND IT."
SPLORTCH
ZOOOD YAN YAE!

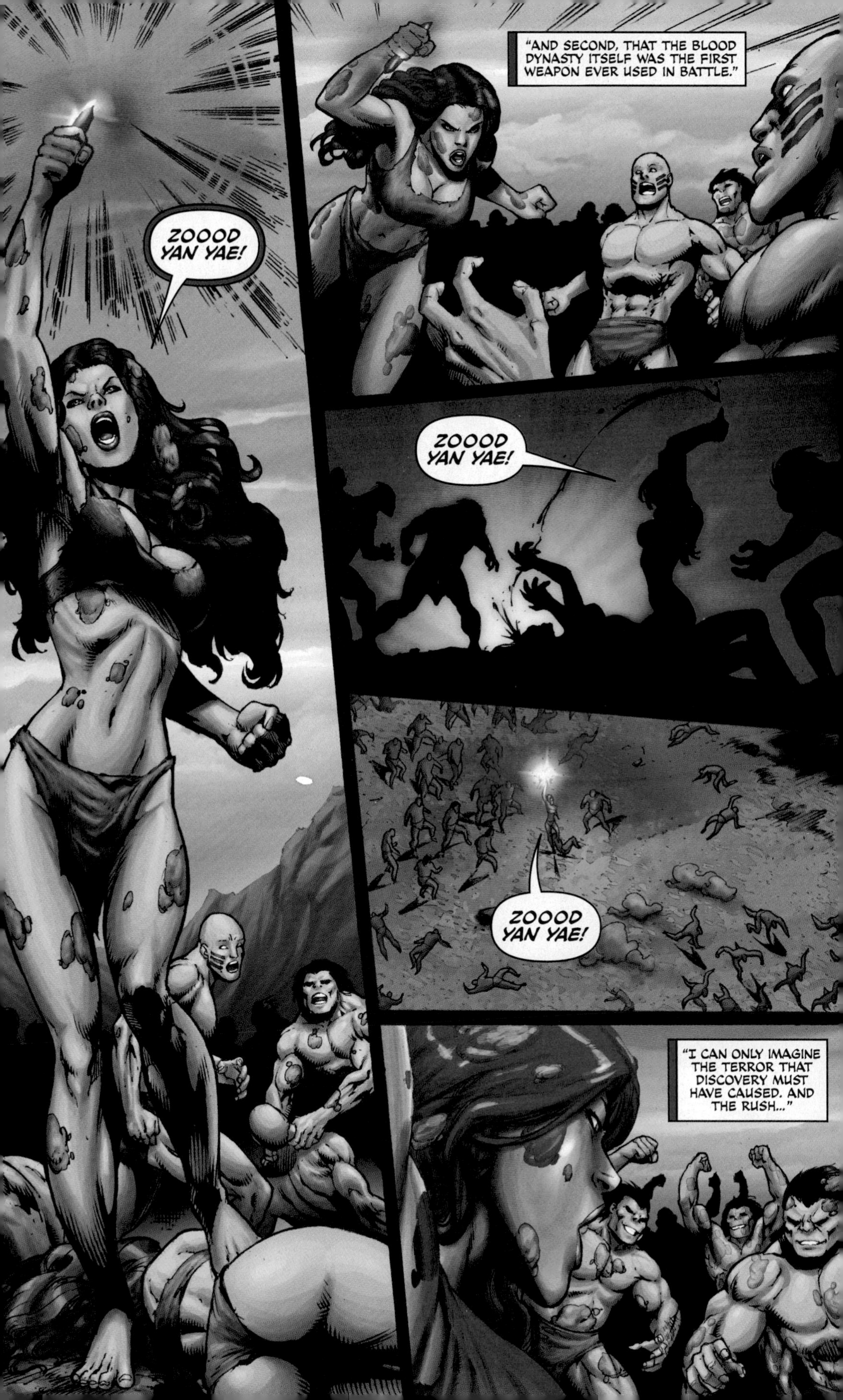
ZOOOD YAN YAE!
"AND SECOND, THAT THE BLOOD DYNASTY ITSELF WAS THE FIRST WEAPON EVER USED IN BATTLE."
ZOOOD YAN YAE!
ZOOOD YAN YAE!
"I CAN ONLY IMAGINE THE TERROR THAT DISCOVERY MUST HAVE CAUSED. AND THE RUSH..."

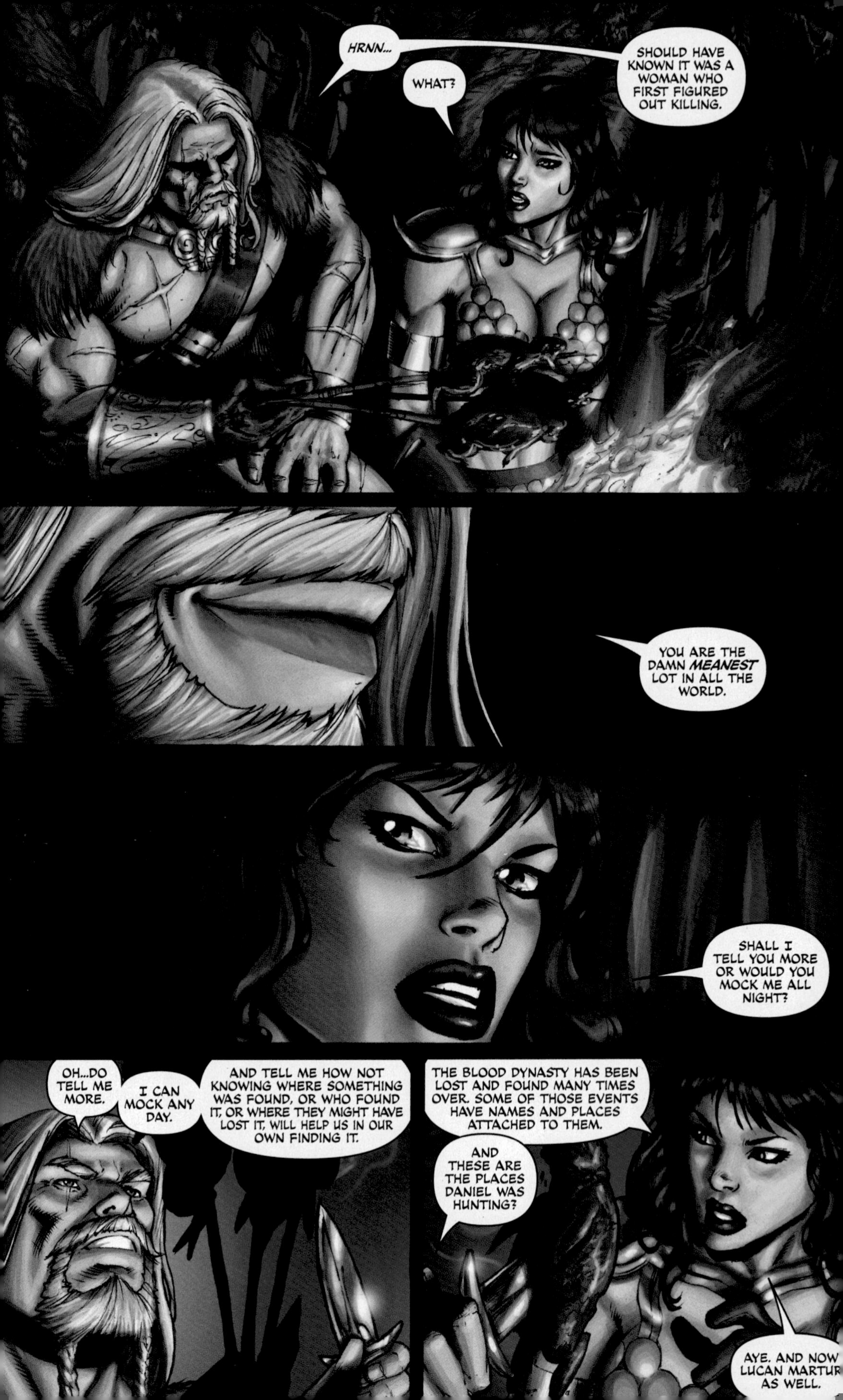
HRNN...
WHAT?
SHOULD HAVE KNOWN IT WAS A WOMAN WHO FIRST FIGURED OUT KILLING.
YOU ARE THE DAMN *MEANEST* LOT IN ALL THE WORLD.
SHALL I TELL YOU MORE OR WOULD YOU MOCK ME ALL NIGHT?
OH...DO TELL ME MORE.
I CAN MOCK ANY DAY.
AND TELL ME HOW NOT KNOWING WHERE SOMETHING WAS FOUND, OR WHO FOUND IT, OR WHERE THEY MIGHT HAVE LOST IT, WILL HELP US IN OUR OWN FINDING IT.
THE BLOOD DYNASTY HAS BEEN LOST AND FOUND MANY TIMES OVER. SOME OF THOSE EVENTS HAVE NAMES AND PLACES ATTACHED TO THEM.
AND THESE ARE THE PLACES DANIEL WAS HUNTING?
AYE. AND NOW LUCAN MARTUR AS WELL.

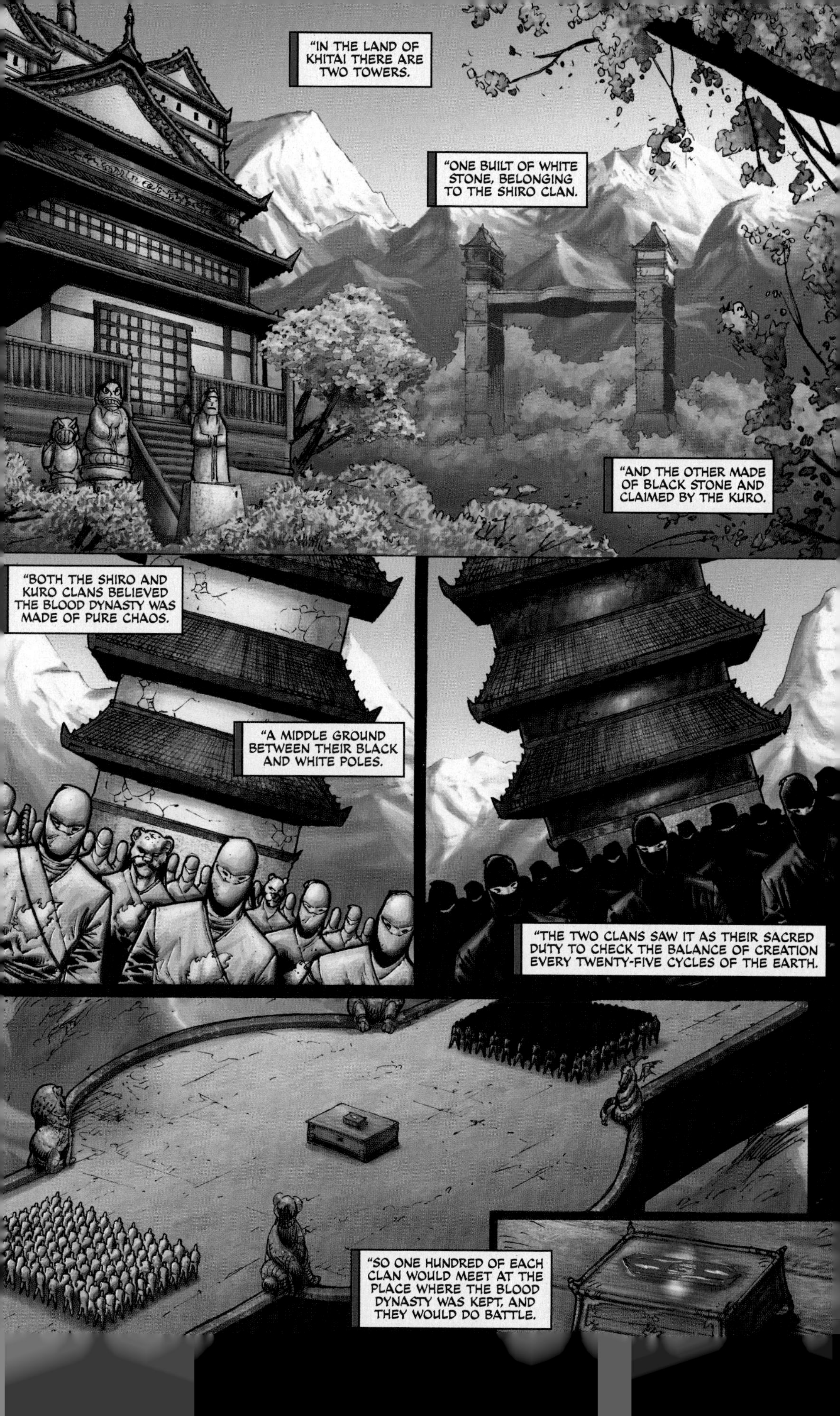
"IN THE LAND OF KHITAI THERE ARE TWO TOWERS.
"ONE BUILT OF WHITE STONE, BELONGING TO THE SHIRO CLAN.
"AND THE OTHER MADE OF BLACK STONE AND CLAIMED BY THE KURO.
"BOTH THE SHIRO AND KURO CLANS BELIEVED THE BLOOD DYNASTY WAS MADE OF PURE CHAOS.
"A MIDDLE GROUND BETWEEN THEIR BLACK AND WHITE POLES.
"THE TWO CLANS SAW IT AS THEIR SACRED DUTY TO CHECK THE BALANCE OF CREATION EVERY TWENTY-FIVE CYCLES OF THE EARTH.
"SO ONE HUNDRED OF EACH CLAN WOULD MEET AT THE PLACE WHERE THE BLOOD DYNASTY WAS KEPT, AND THEY WOULD DO BATTLE.

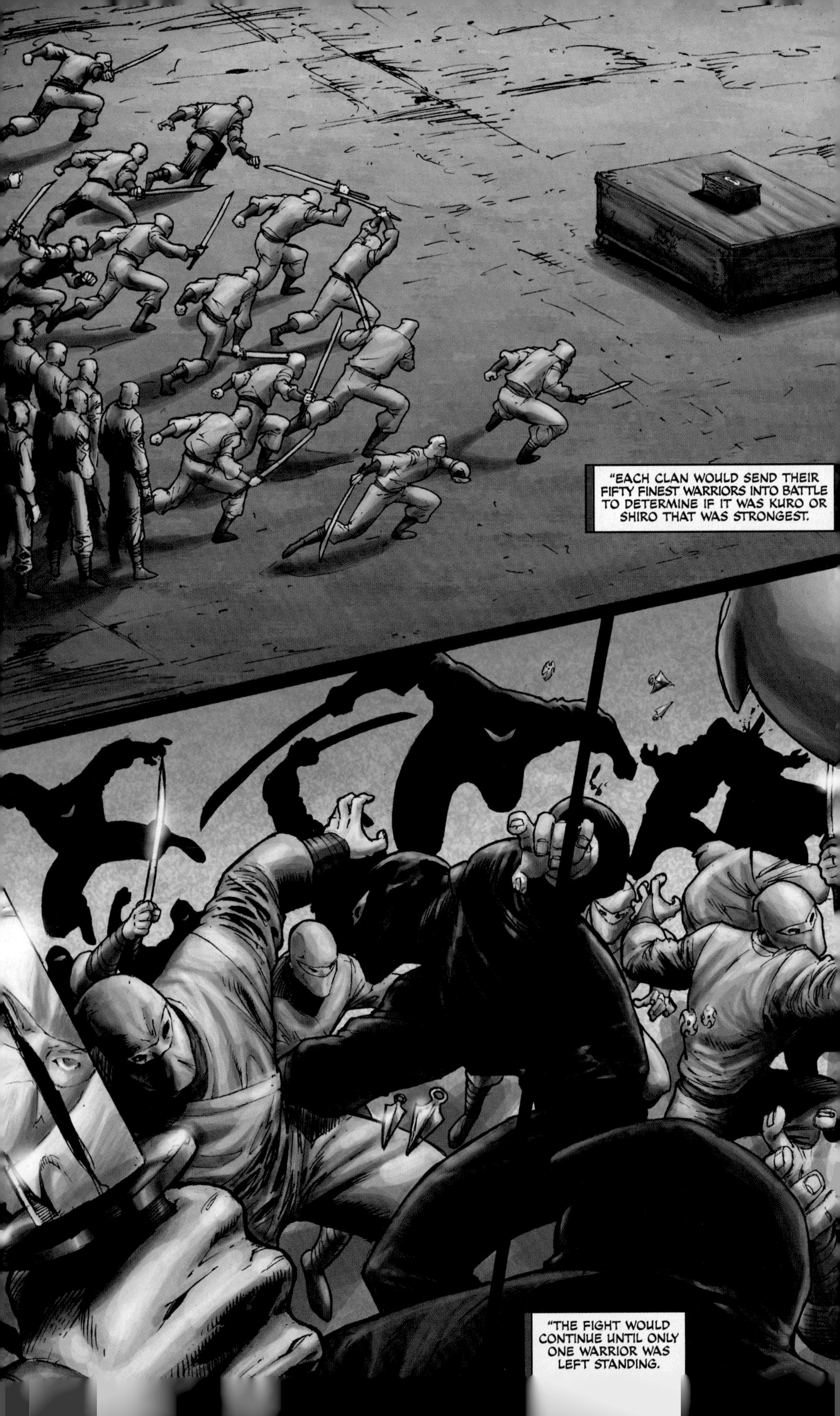
"EACH CLAN WOULD SEND THEIR FIFTY FINEST WARRIORS INTO BATTLE TO DETERMINE IF IT WAS KURO OR SHIRO THAT WAS STRONGEST.
"THE FIGHT WOULD CONTINUE UNTIL ONLY ONE WARRIOR WAS LEFT STANDING.

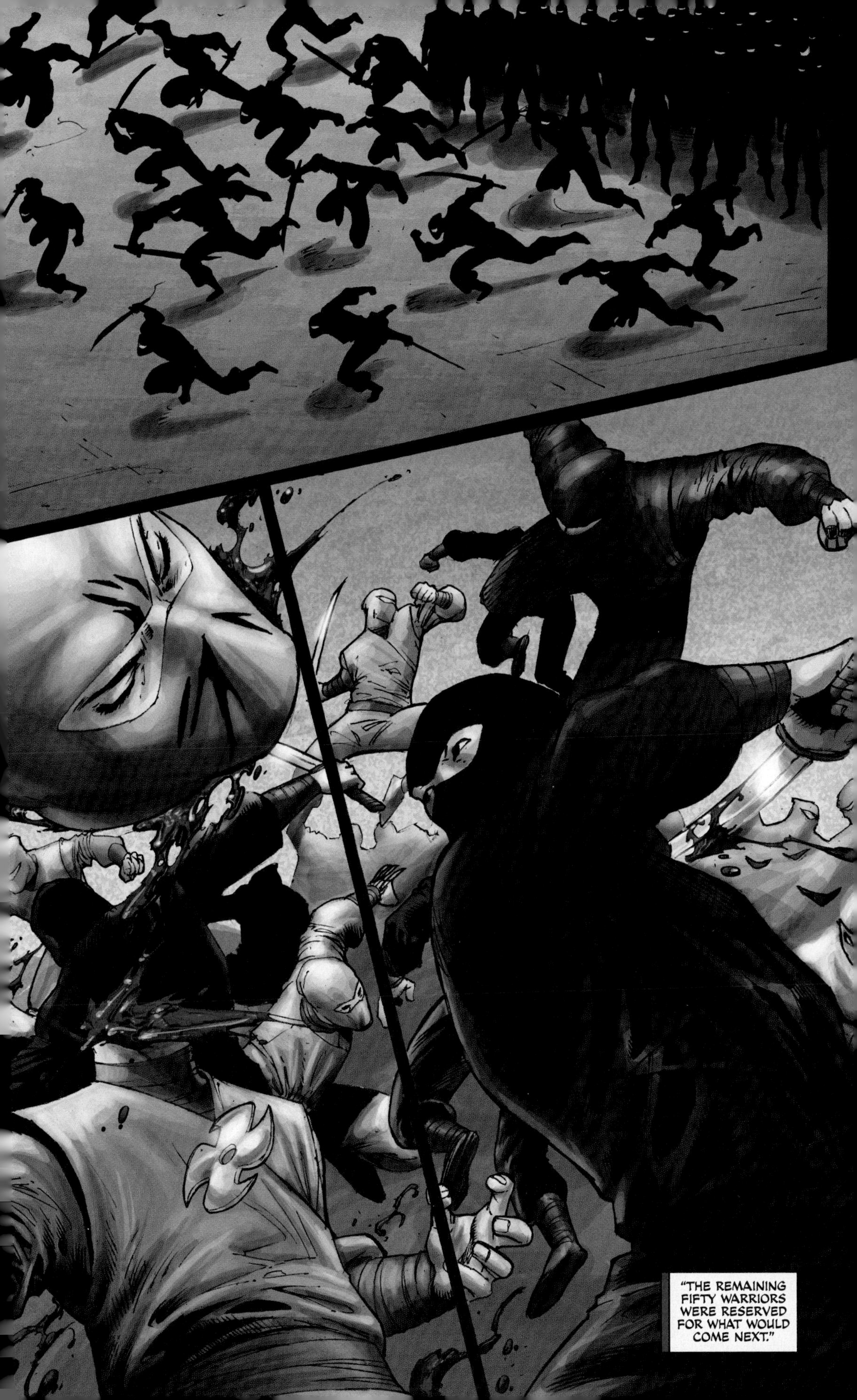
"THE REMAINING FIFTY WARRIORS WERE RESERVED FOR WHAT WOULD COME NEXT."

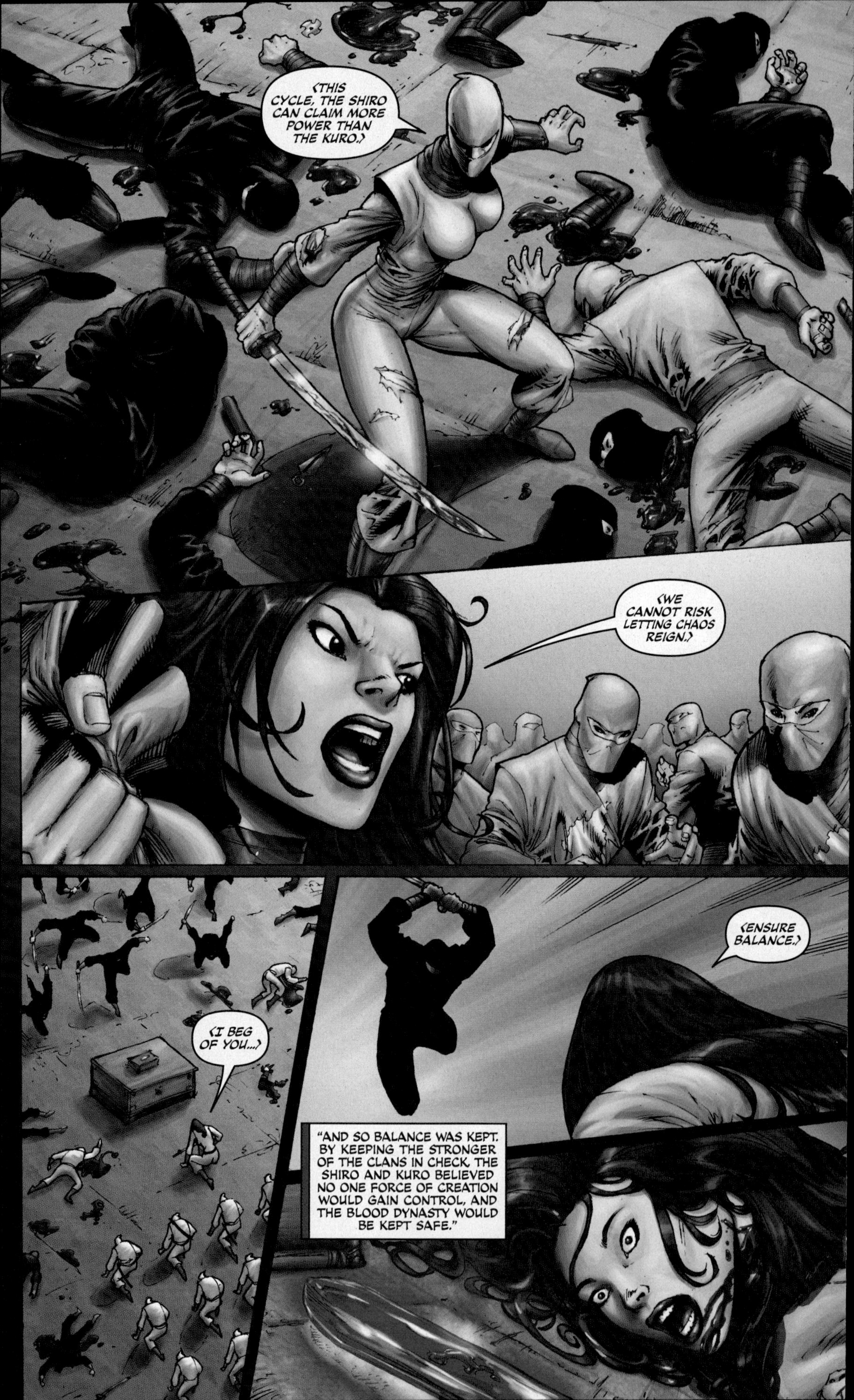

<THIS CYCLE, THE SHIRO CAN CLAIM MORE POWER THAN THE KURO.>
<WE CANNOT RISK LETTING CHAOS REIGN.>
<I BEG OF YOU...>
<ENSURE BALANCE.>
"AND SO BALANCE WAS KEPT. BY KEEPING THE STRONGER OF THE CLANS IN CHECK, THE SHIRO AND KURO BELIEVED NO ONE FORCE OF CREATION WOULD GAIN CONTROL, AND THE BLOOD DYNASTY WOULD BE KEPT SAFE."

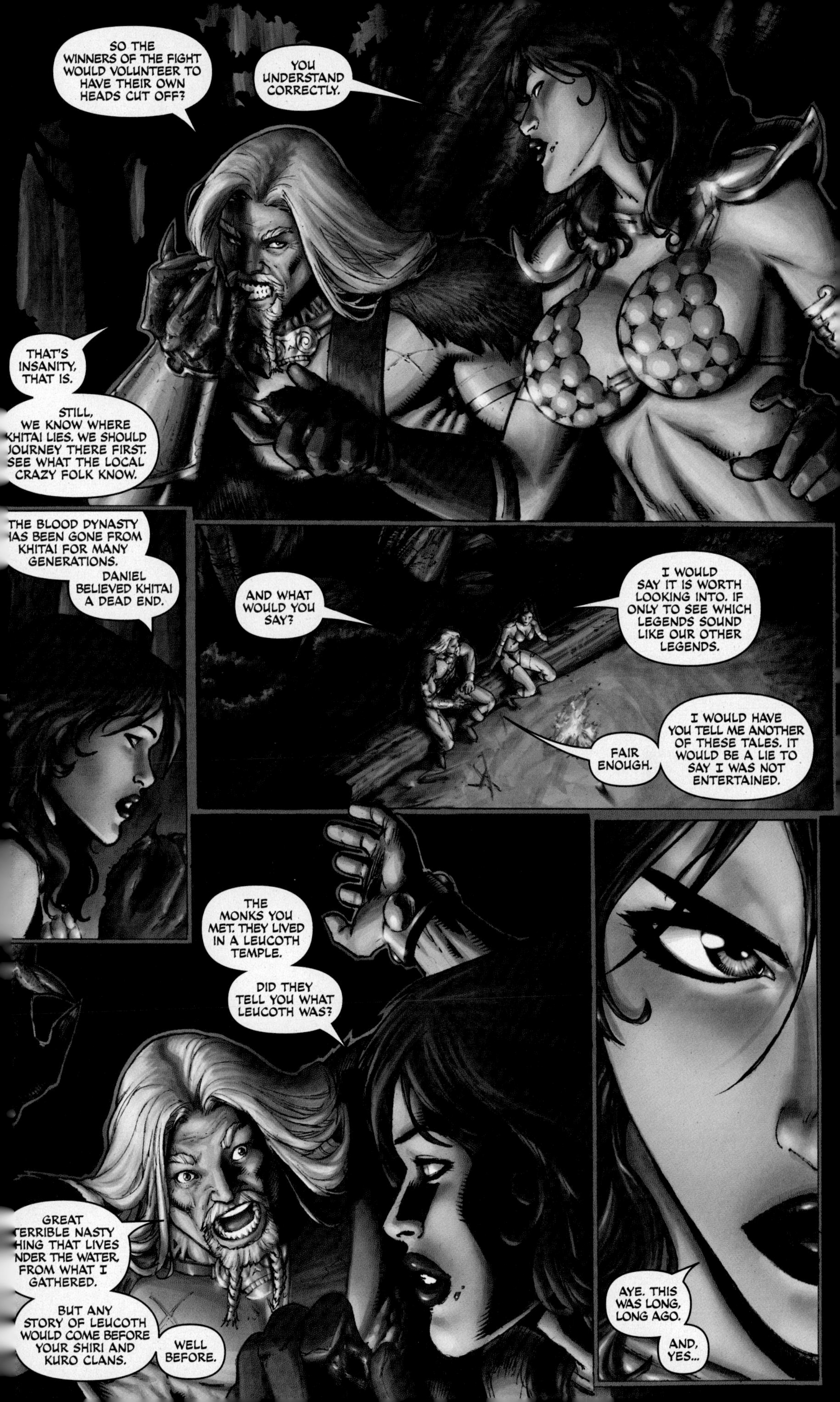

SO THE WINNERS OF THE FIGHT WOULD VOLUNTEER TO HAVE THEIR OWN HEADS CUT OFF?
YOU UNDERSTAND CORRECTLY.
THAT'S INSANITY, THAT IS.
STILL, WE KNOW WHERE KHITAI LIES. WE SHOULD JOURNEY THERE FIRST. SEE WHAT THE LOCAL CRAZY FOLK KNOW.
THE BLOOD DYNASTY IAS BEEN GONE FROM KHITAI FOR MANY GENERATIONS.
DANIEL BELIEVED KHITAI A DEAD END.
AND WHAT WOULD YOU SAY?
I WOULD SAY IT IS WORTH LOOKING INTO. IF ONLY TO SEE WHICH LEGENDS SOUND LIKE OUR OTHER LEGENDS.
FAIR ENOUGH.
I WOULD HAVE YOU TELL ME ANOTHER OF THESE TALES. IT WOULD BE A LIE TO SAY I WAS NOT ENTERTAINED.
THE MONKS YOU MET. THEY LIVED IN A LEUCOTH TEMPLE.
DID THEY TELL YOU WHAT LEUCOTH WAS?
GREAT TERRIBLE NASTY HING THAT LIVES NDER THE WATER, FROM WHAT I GATHERED.
BUT ANY STORY OF LEUCOTH WOULD COME BEFORE YOUR SHIRI AND KURO CLANS.
WELL BEFORE.
AYE. THIS WAS LONG, LONG AGO.
AND, YES...

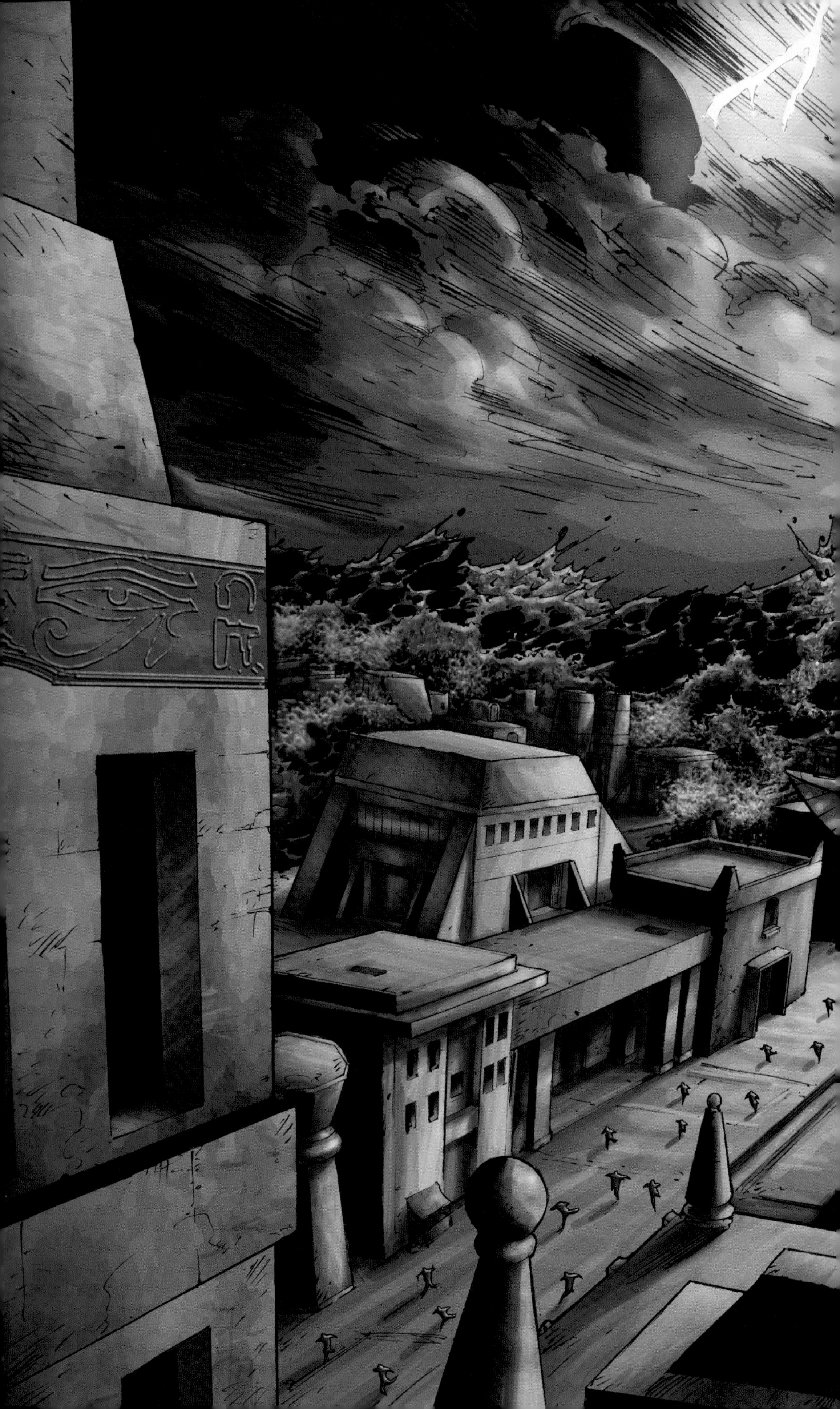

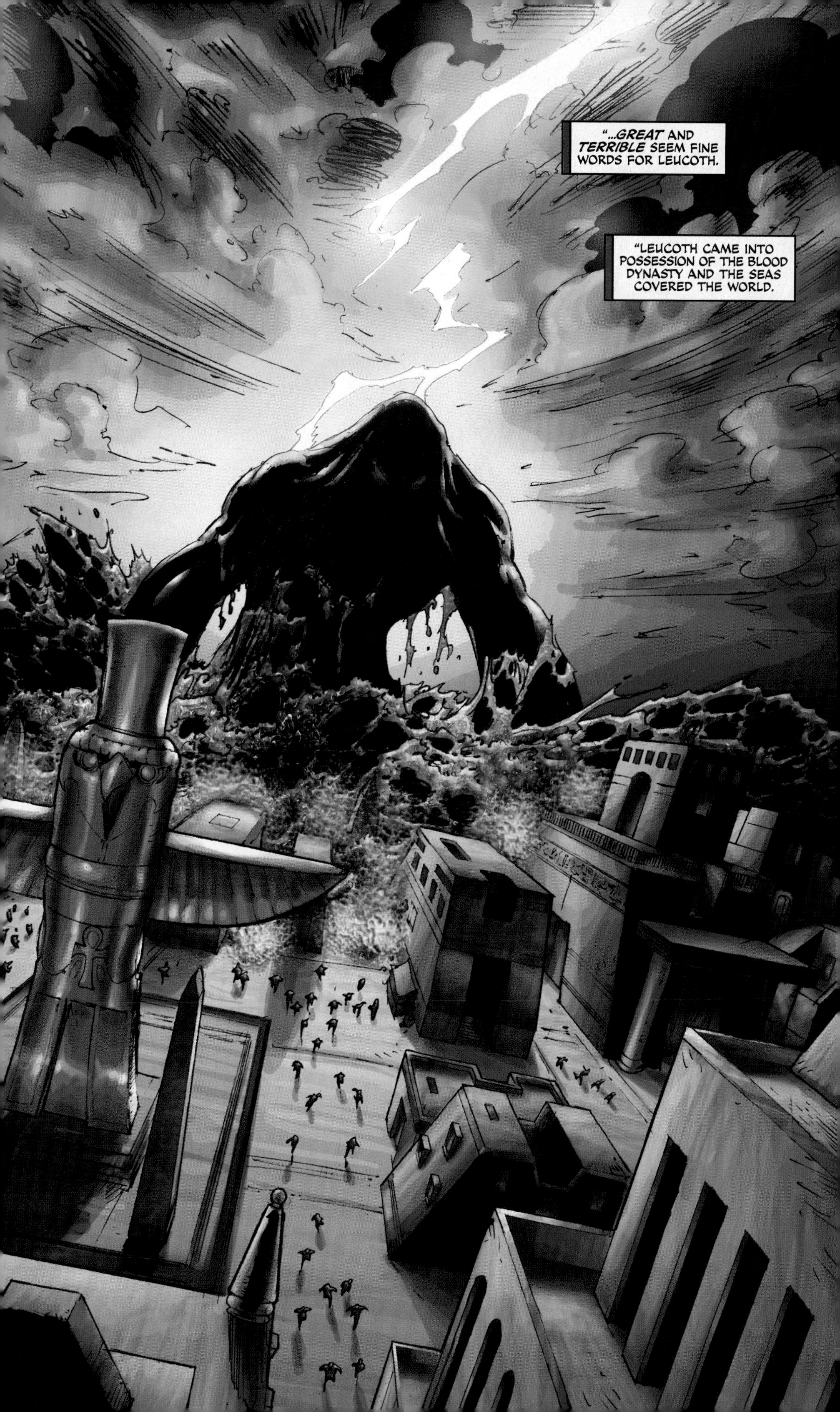
"...GREAT AND TERRIBLE SEEM FINE WORDS FOR LEUCOTH.
"LEUCOTH CAME INTO POSSESSION OF THE BLOOD DYNASTY AND THE SEAS COVERED THE WORLD.

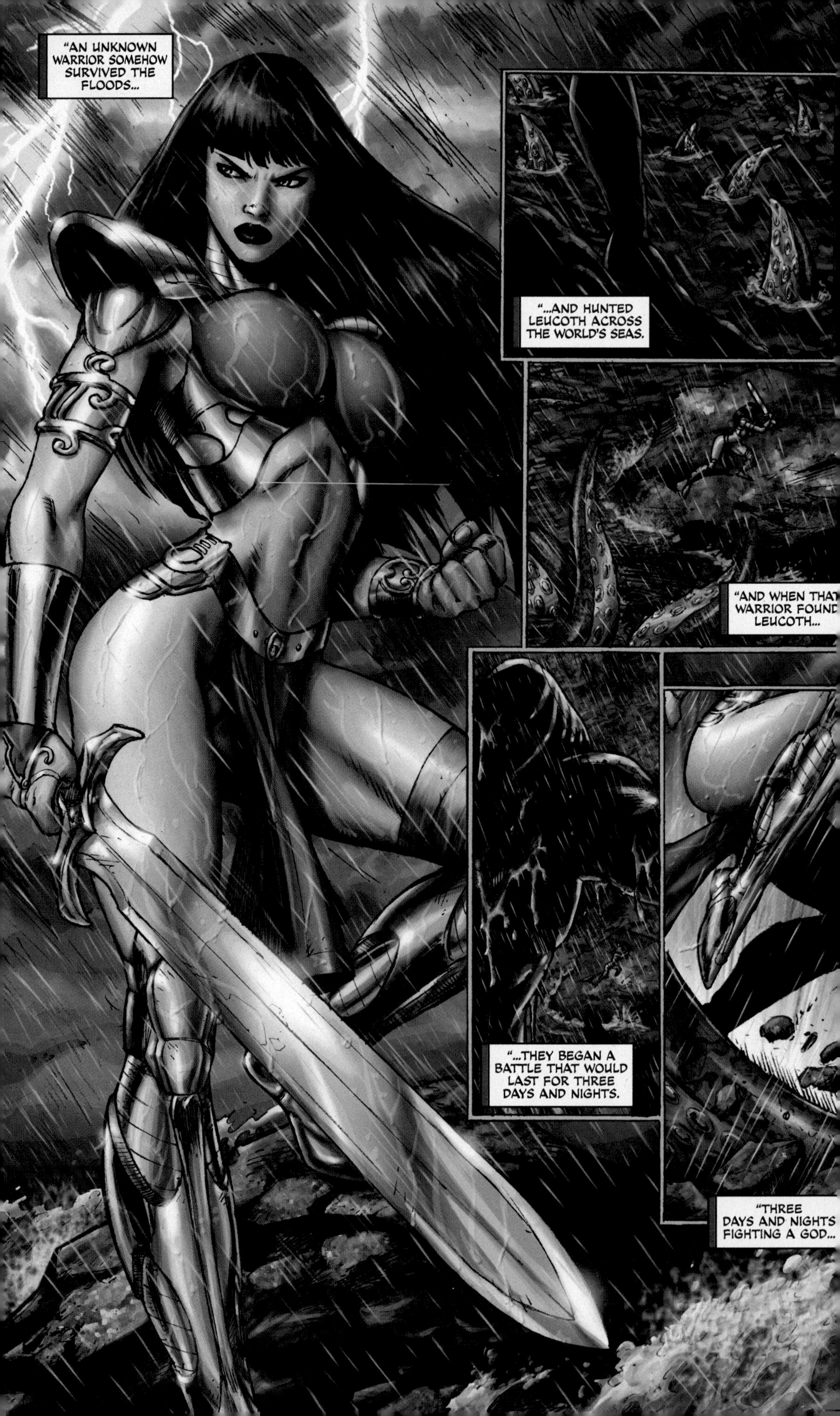
"AN UNKNOWN WARRIOR SOMEHOW SURVIVED THE FLOODS...
"...AND HUNTED LEUCOTH ACROSS THE WORLD'S SEAS.
"AND WHEN THAT WARRIOR FOUND LEUCOTH...
"...THEY BEGAN A BATTLE THAT WOULD LAST FOR THREE DAYS AND NIGHTS.
"THREE DAYS AND NIGHTS FIGHTING A GOD...

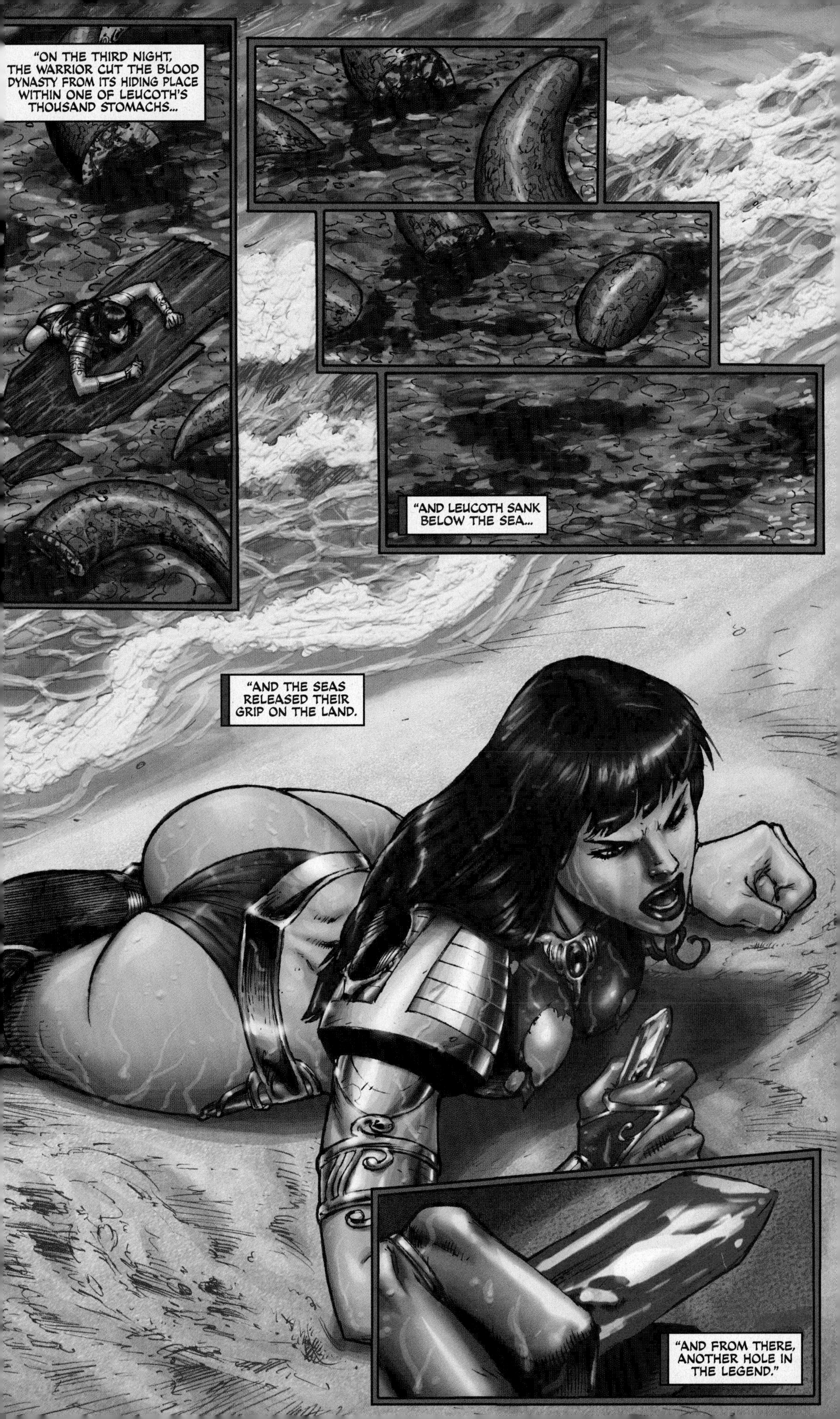
"ON THE THIRD NIGHT, THE WARRIOR CUT THE BLOOD DYNASTY FROM ITS HIDING PLACE WITHIN ONE OF LEUCOTH'S THOUSAND STOMACHS...
"AND LEUCOTH SANK BELOW THE SEA...
"AND THE SEAS RELEASED THEIR GRIP ON THE LAND.
"AND FROM THERE, ANOTHER HOLE IN THE LEGEND."

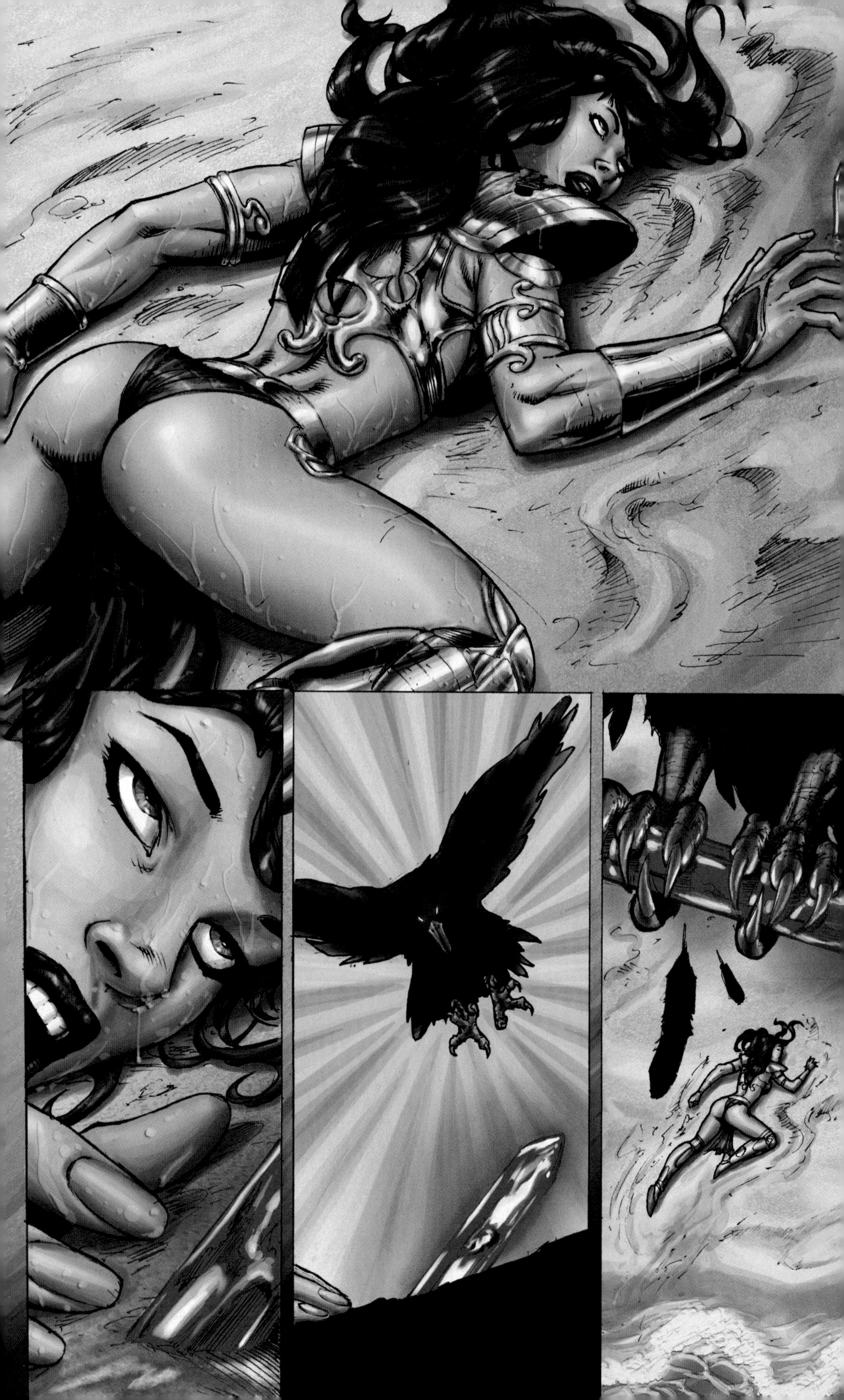

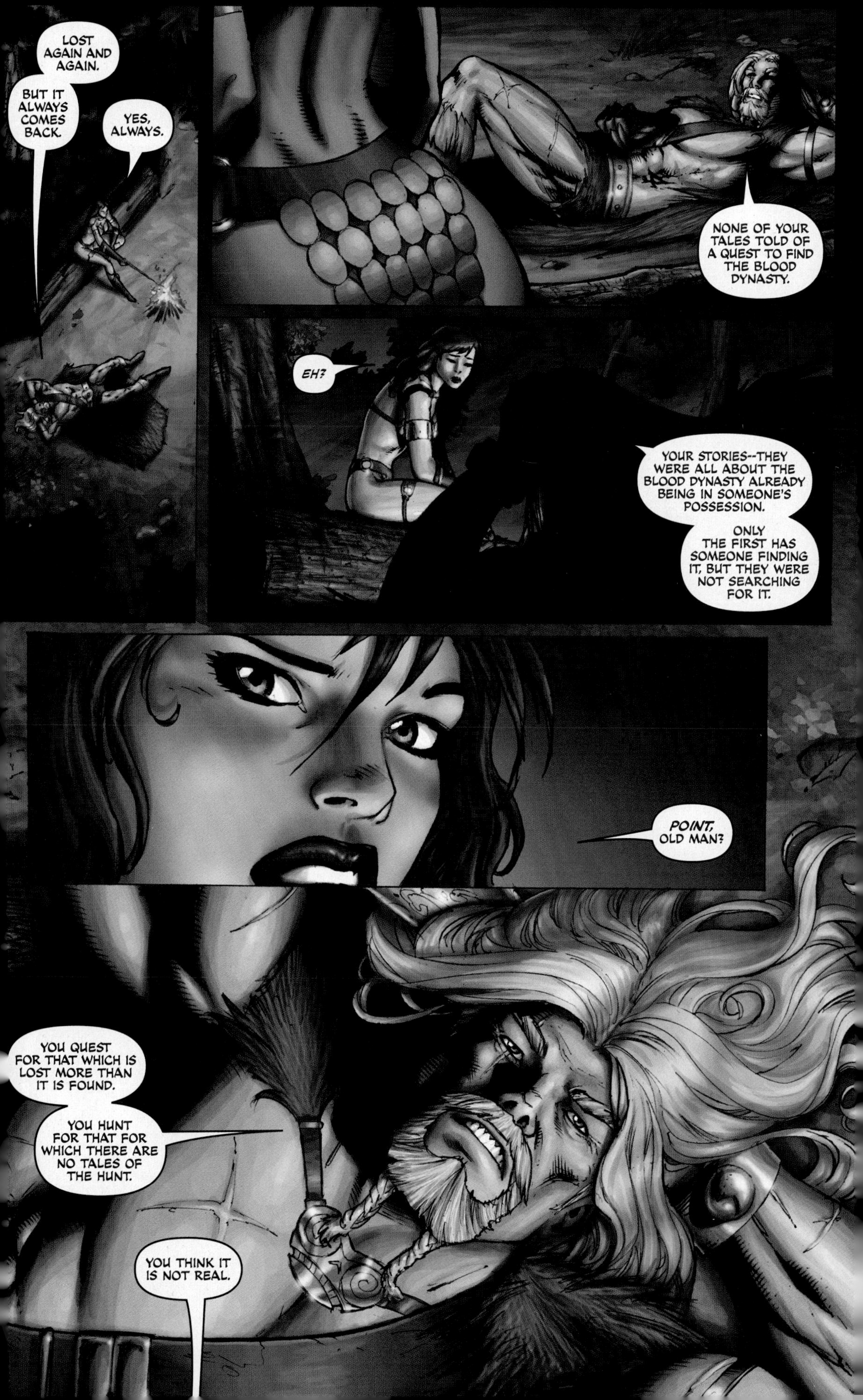

LOST AGAIN AND AGAIN.
BUT IT ALWAYS COMES BACK.
YES, ALWAYS.
NONE OF YOUR TALES TOLD OF A QUEST TO FIND THE BLOOD DYNASTY.
EH?
YOUR STORIES--THEY WERE ALL ABOUT THE BLOOD DYNASTY ALREADY BEING IN SOMEONE'S POSSESSION.
ONLY THE FIRST HAS SOMEONE FINDING IT, BUT THEY WERE NOT SEARCHING FOR IT.
POINT, OLD MAN?
YOU QUEST FOR THAT WHICH IS LOST MORE THAN IT IS FOUND.
YOU HUNT FOR THAT FOR WHICH THERE ARE NO TALES OF THE HUNT.
YOU THINK IT IS NOT REAL.

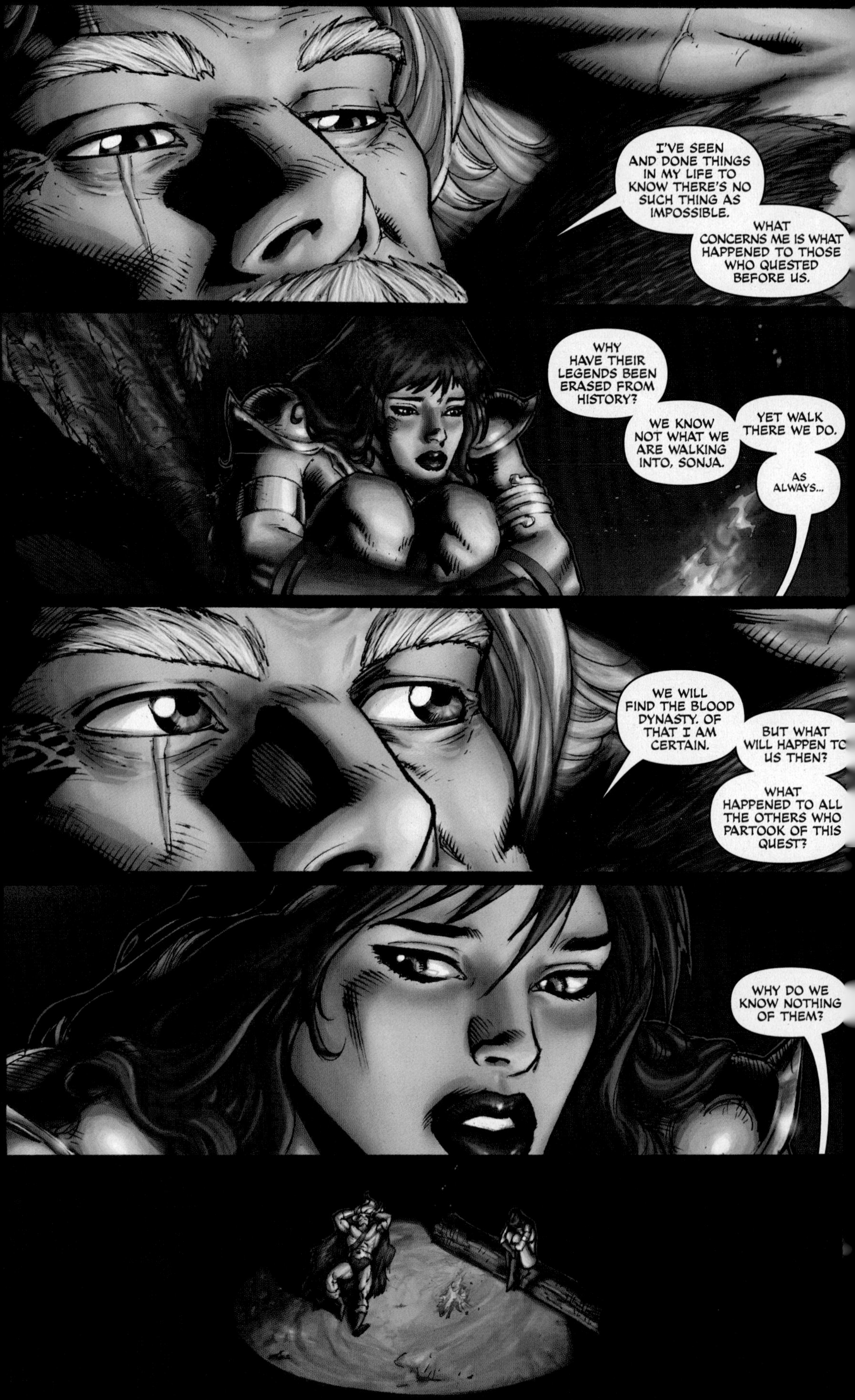
I'VE SEEN AND DONE THINGS IN MY LIFE TO KNOW THERE'S NO SUCH THING AS IMPOSSIBLE.
WHAT CONCERNS ME IS WHAT HAPPENED TO THOSE WHO QUESTED BEFORE US.
WHY HAVE THEIR LEGENDS BEEN ERASED FROM HISTORY?
WE KNOW NOT WHAT WE ARE WALKING INTO, SONJA.
YET WALK THERE WE DO.
AS ALWAYS...
WE WILL FIND THE BLOOD DYNASTY. OF THAT I AM CERTAIN.
BUT WHAT WILL HAPPEN TO US THEN?
WHAT HAPPENED TO ALL THE OTHERS WHO PARTOOK OF THIS QUEST?
WHY DO WE KNOW NOTHING OF THEM?

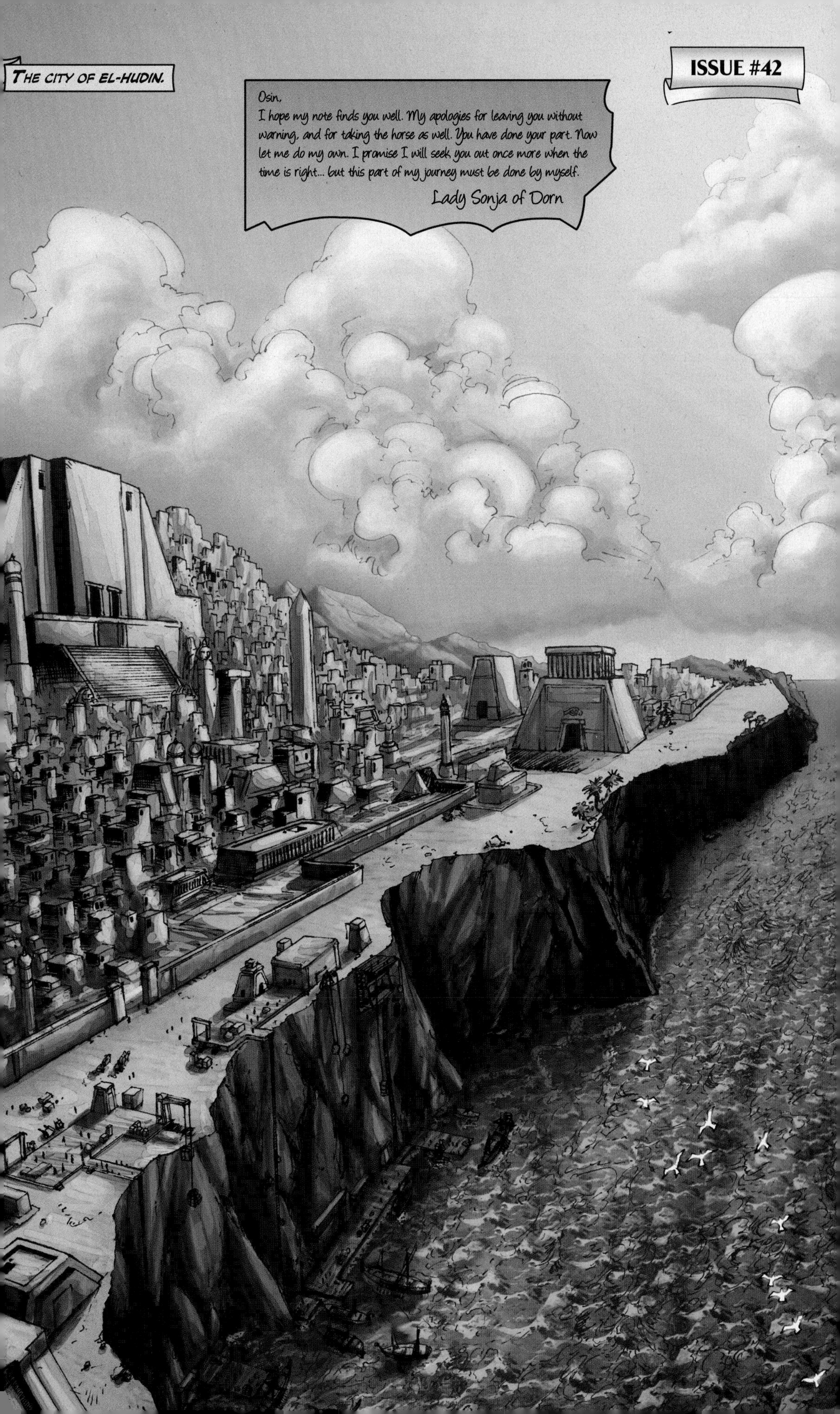
THE CITY OF EL-HUDIN.
ISSUE #42
Osin,
I hope my note finds you well. My apologies for leaving you without warning, and for taking the horse as well. You have done your part. Now let me do my own. I promise I will seek you out once more when the time is right... but this part of my journey must be done by myself.
Lady Sonja of Dorn

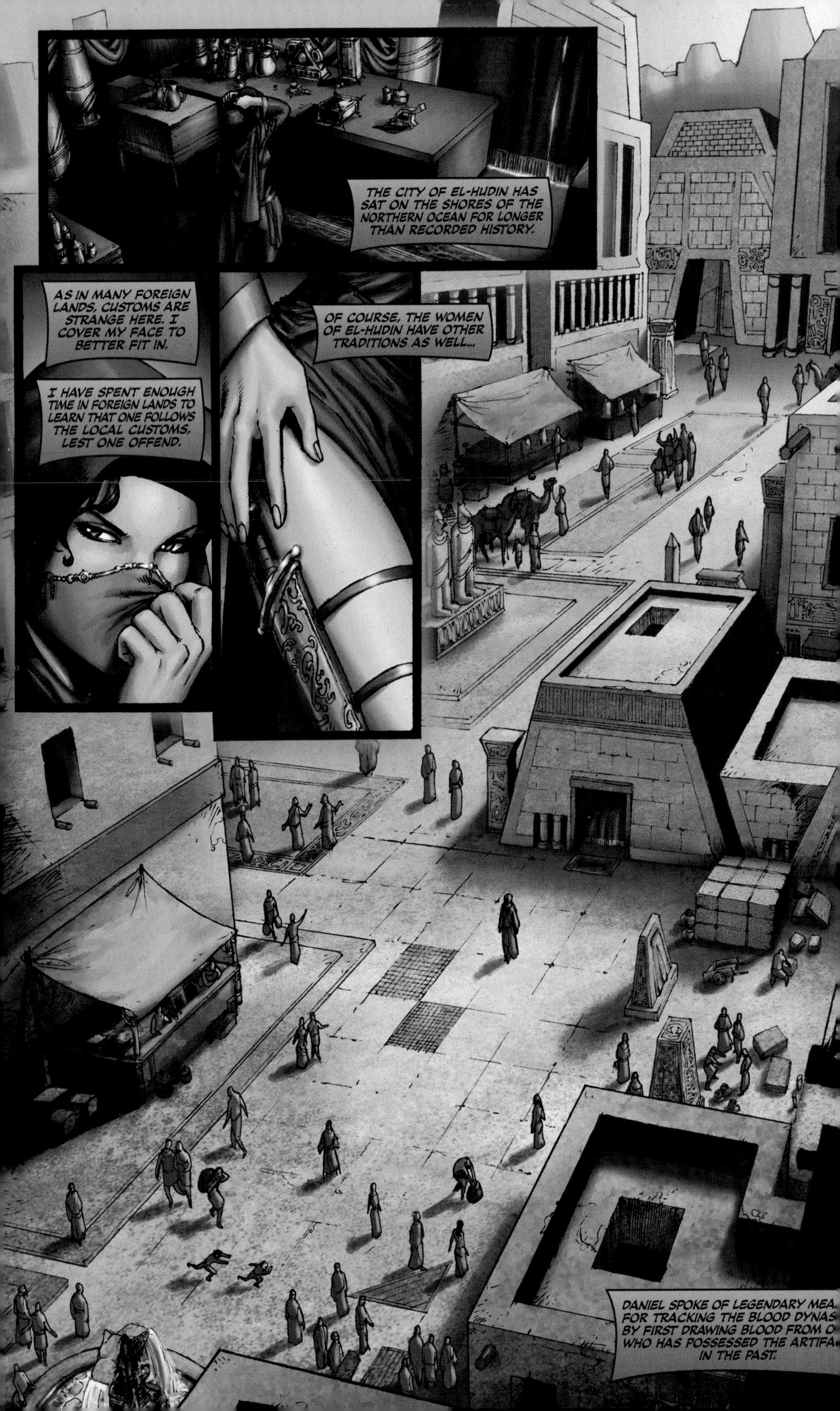
THE CITY OF EL-HUDIN HAS SAT ON THE SHORES OF THE NORTHERN OCEAN FOR LONGER THAN RECORDED HISTORY.
AS IN MANY FOREIGN LANDS, CUSTOMS ARE STRANGE HERE. I COVER MY FACE TO BETTER FIT IN.
I HAVE SPENT ENOUGH TIME IN FOREIGN LANDS TO LEARN THAT ONE FOLLOWS THE LOCAL CUSTOMS, LEST ONE OFFEND.
OF COURSE, THE WOMEN OF EL-HUDIN HAVE OTHER TRADITIONS AS WELL...
DANIEL SPOKE OF LEGENDARY MEA
FOR TRACKING THE BLOOD DYNAS
BY FIRST DRAWING BLOOD FROM O
WHO HAS POSSESSED THE ARTIFA
IN THE PAST.

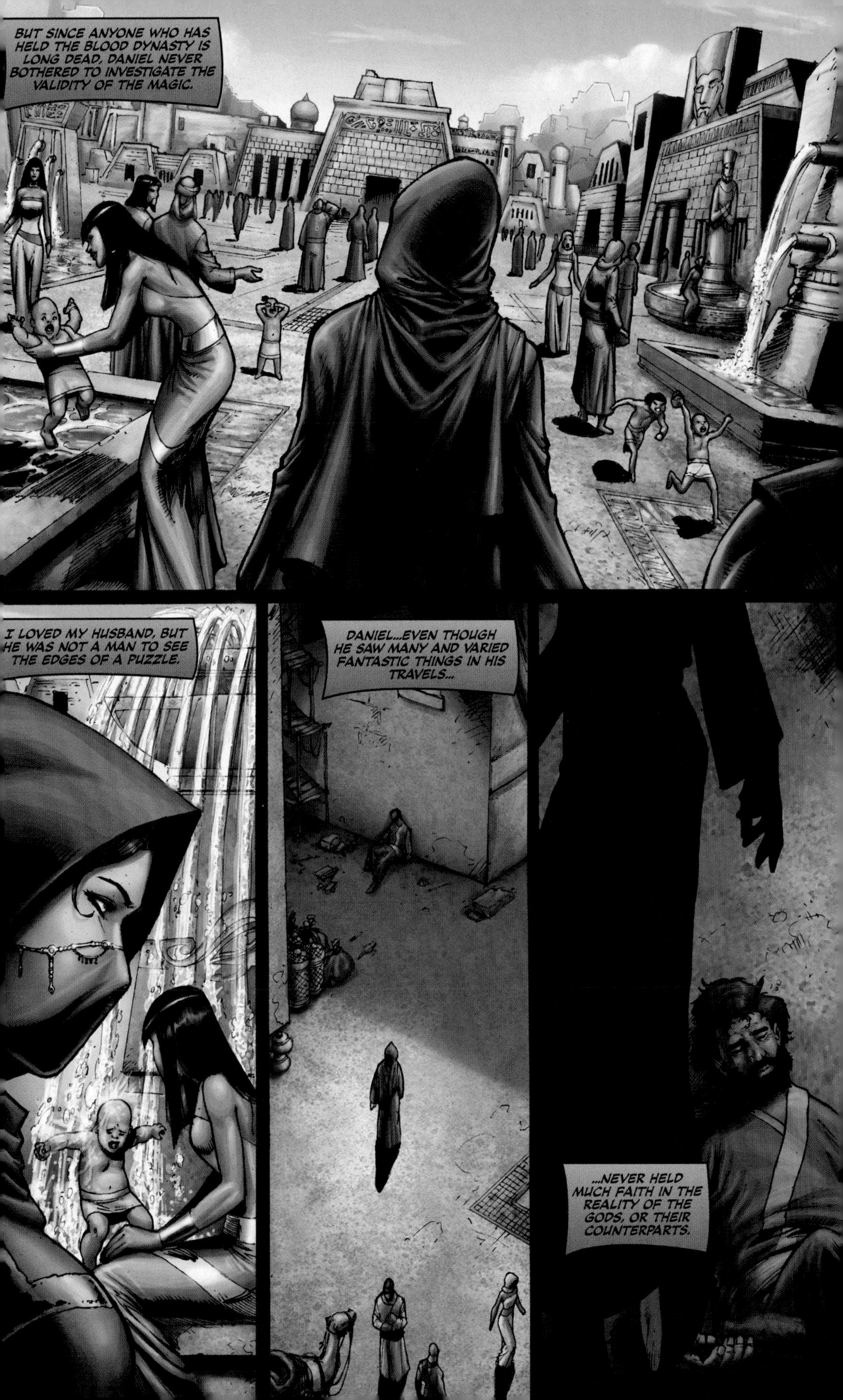
BUT SINCE ANYONE WHO HAS HELD THE BLOOD DYNASTY IS LONG DEAD, DANIEL NEVER BOTHERED TO INVESTIGATE THE VALIDITY OF THE MAGIC.
I LOVED MY HUSBAND, BUT HE WAS NOT A MAN TO SEE THE EDGES OF A PUZZLE.
DANIEL...EVEN THOUGH HE SAW MANY AND VARIED FANTASTIC THINGS IN HIS TRAVELS...
...NEVER HELD MUCH FAITH IN THE REALITY OF THE GODS, OR THEIR COUNTERPARTS.

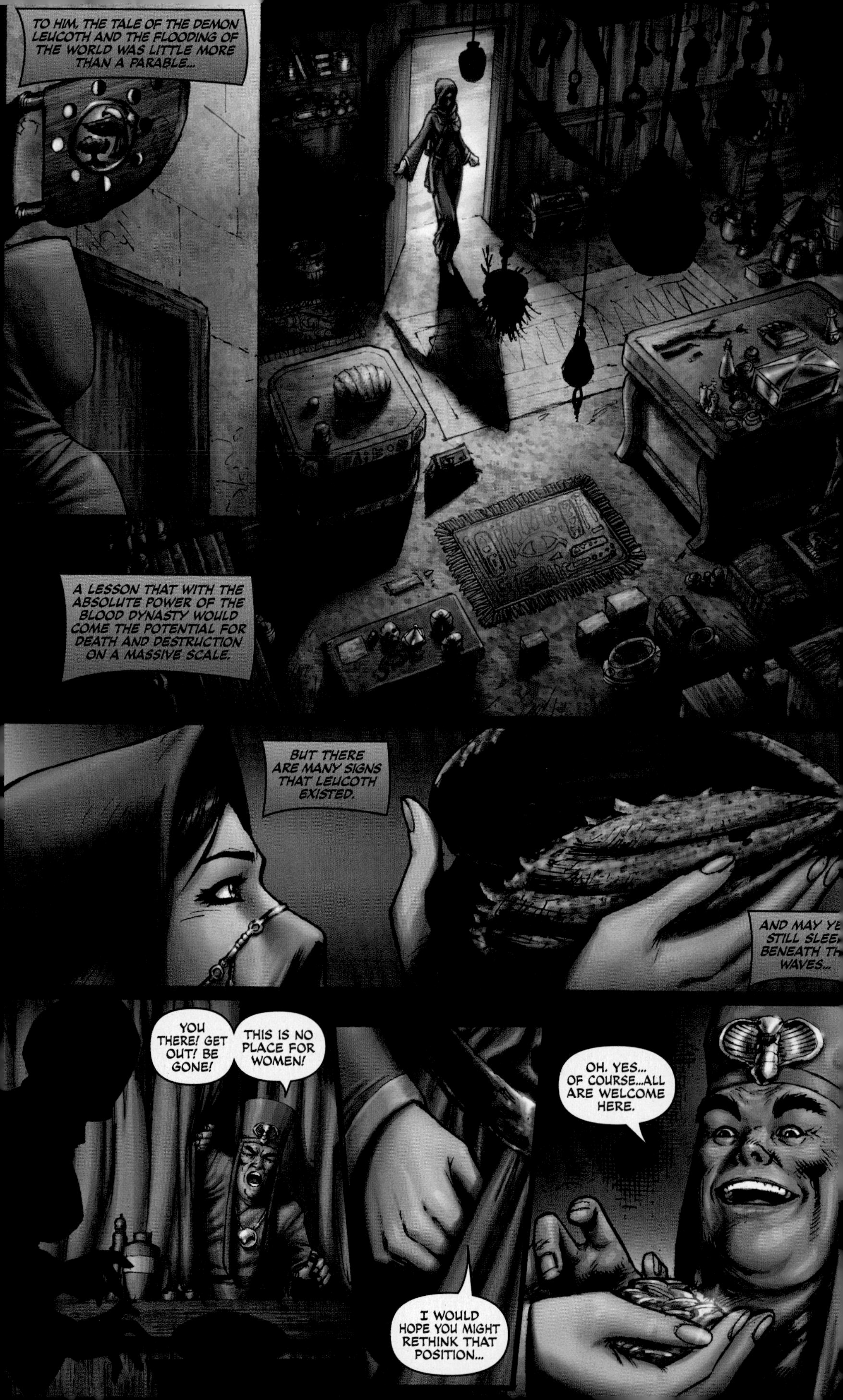
TO HIM, THE TALE OF THE DEMON LEUCOTH AND THE FLOODING OF THE WORLD WAS LITTLE MORE THAN A PARABLE...
A LESSON THAT WITH THE ABSOLUTE POWER OF THE BLOOD DYNASTY WOULD COME THE POTENTIAL FOR DEATH AND DESTRUCTION ON A MASSIVE SCALE.
BUT THERE ARE MANY SIGNS THAT LEUCOTH EXISTED.
AND MAY YE STILL SLEE BENEATH TH WAVES...
YOU THERE! GET OUT! BE GONE!
THIS IS NO PLACE FOR WOMEN!
I WOULD HOPE YOU MIGHT RETHINK THAT POSITION...
OH. YES... OF COURSE...ALL ARE WELCOME HERE.

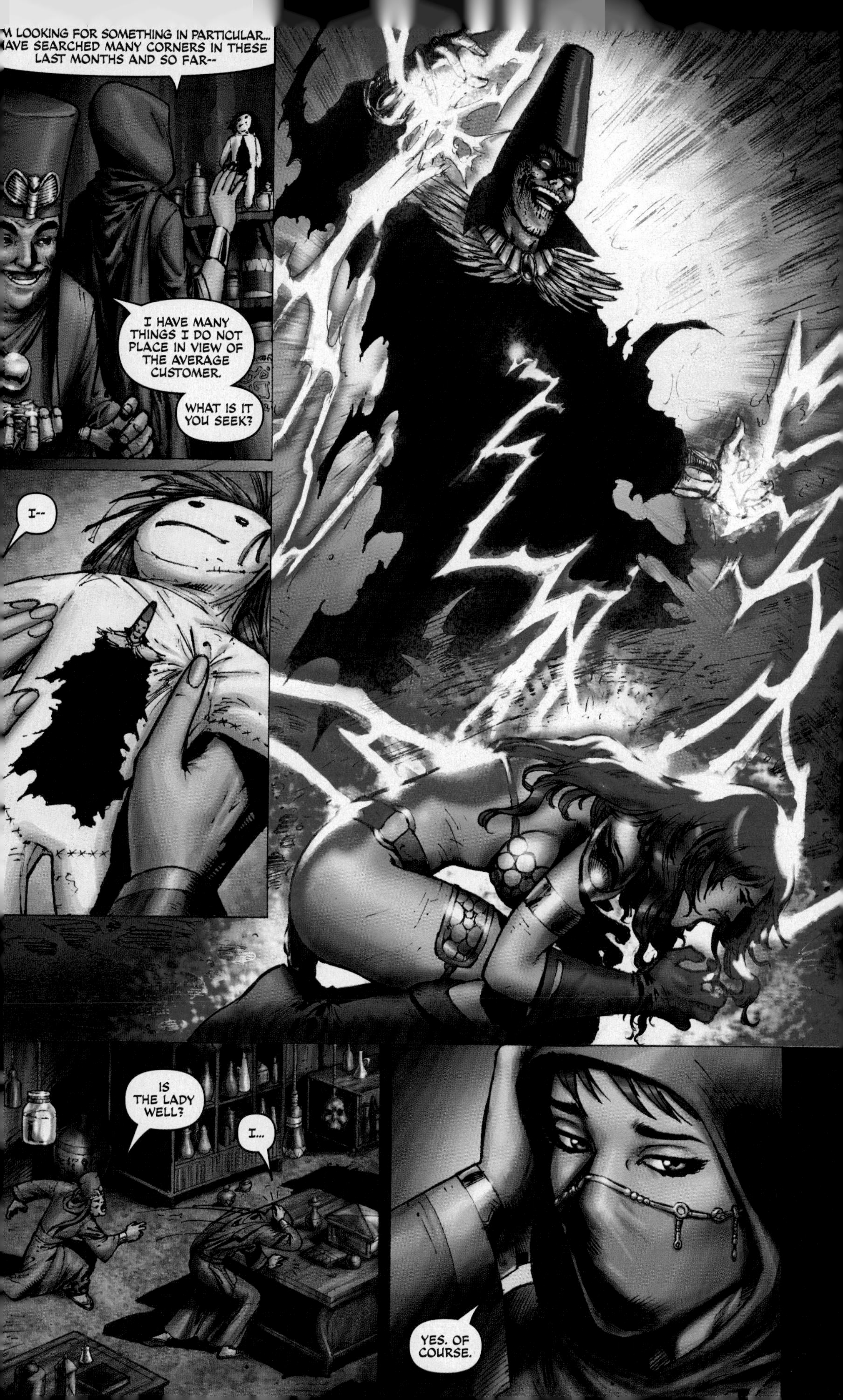
'M LOOKING FOR SOMETHING IN PARTICULAR... HAVE SEARCHED MANY CORNERS IN THESE LAST MONTHS AND SO FAR--
I HAVE MANY THINGS I DO NOT PLACE IN VIEW OF THE AVERAGE CUSTOMER.
WHAT IS IT YOU SEEK?
I--
IS THE LADY WELL?
I...
YES. OF COURSE.

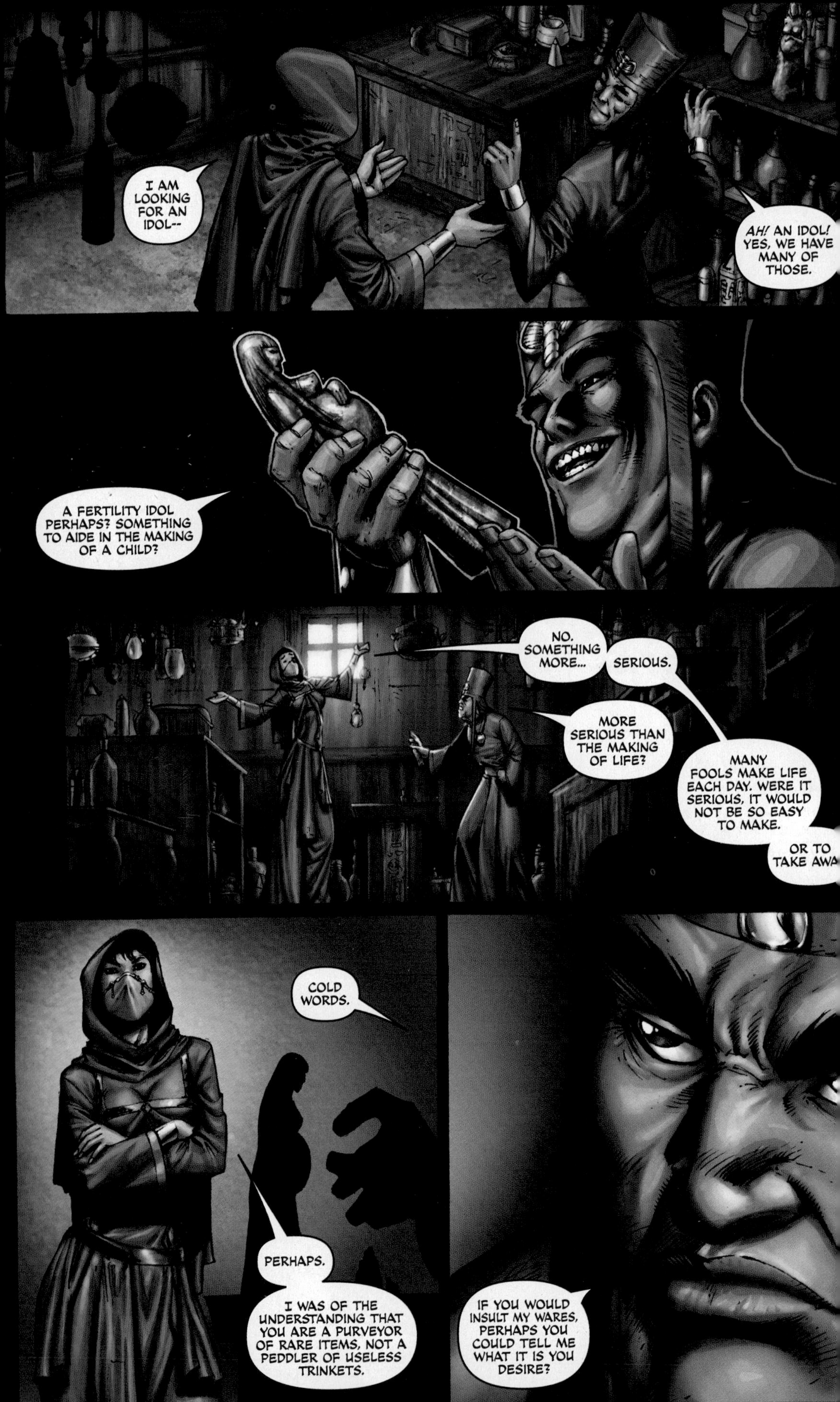
I AM LOOKING FOR AN IDOL--
AH! AN IDOL! YES, WE HAVE MANY OF THOSE.
A FERTILITY IDOL PERHAPS? SOMETHING TO AIDE IN THE MAKING OF A CHILD?
NO. SOMETHING MORE...
SERIOUS.
MORE SERIOUS THAN THE MAKING OF LIFE?
MANY FOOLS MAKE LIFE EACH DAY. WERE IT SERIOUS, IT WOULD NOT BE SO EASY TO MAKE.
OR TO TAKE AWA
COLD WORDS.
PERHAPS.
I WAS OF THE UNDERSTANDING THAT YOU ARE A PURVEYOR OF RARE ITEMS, NOT A PEDDLER OF USELESS TRINKETS.
IF YOU WOULD INSULT MY WARES, PERHAPS YOU COULD TELL ME WHAT IT IS YOU DESIRE?

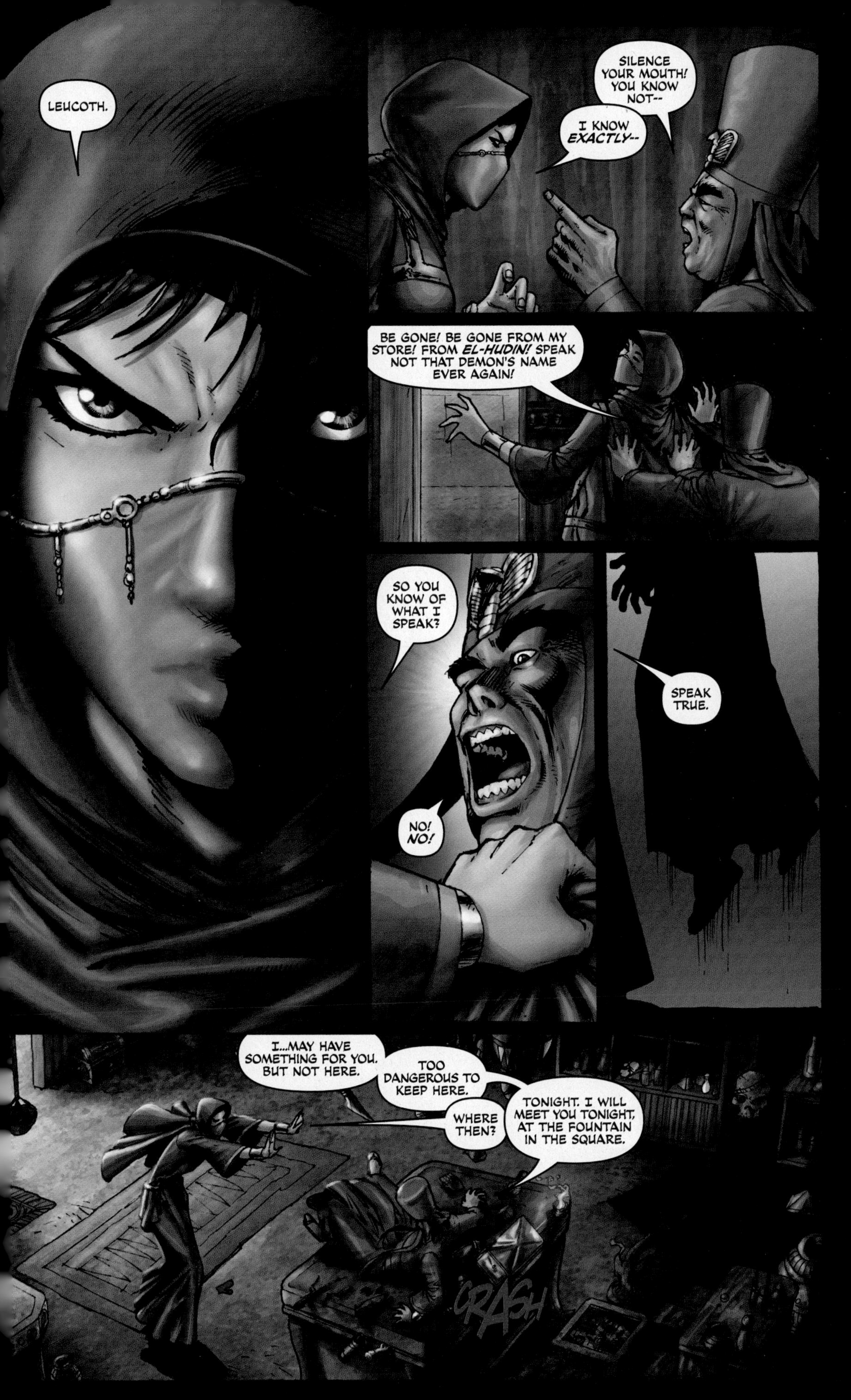
LEUCOTH.
SILENCE YOUR MOUTH! YOU KNOW NOT--
I KNOW *EXACTLY*--
BE GONE! BE GONE FROM MY STORE! FROM *EL-HUDIN!* SPEAK NOT THAT DEMON'S NAME EVER AGAIN!
SO YOU KNOW OF WHAT I SPEAK?
NO! *NO!*
SPEAK TRUE.
I...MAY HAVE SOMETHING FOR YOU. BUT NOT HERE.
TOO DANGEROUS TO KEEP HERE.
WHERE THEN?
TONIGHT. I WILL MEET YOU TONIGHT, AT THE FOUNTAIN IN THE SQUARE.
CRASH

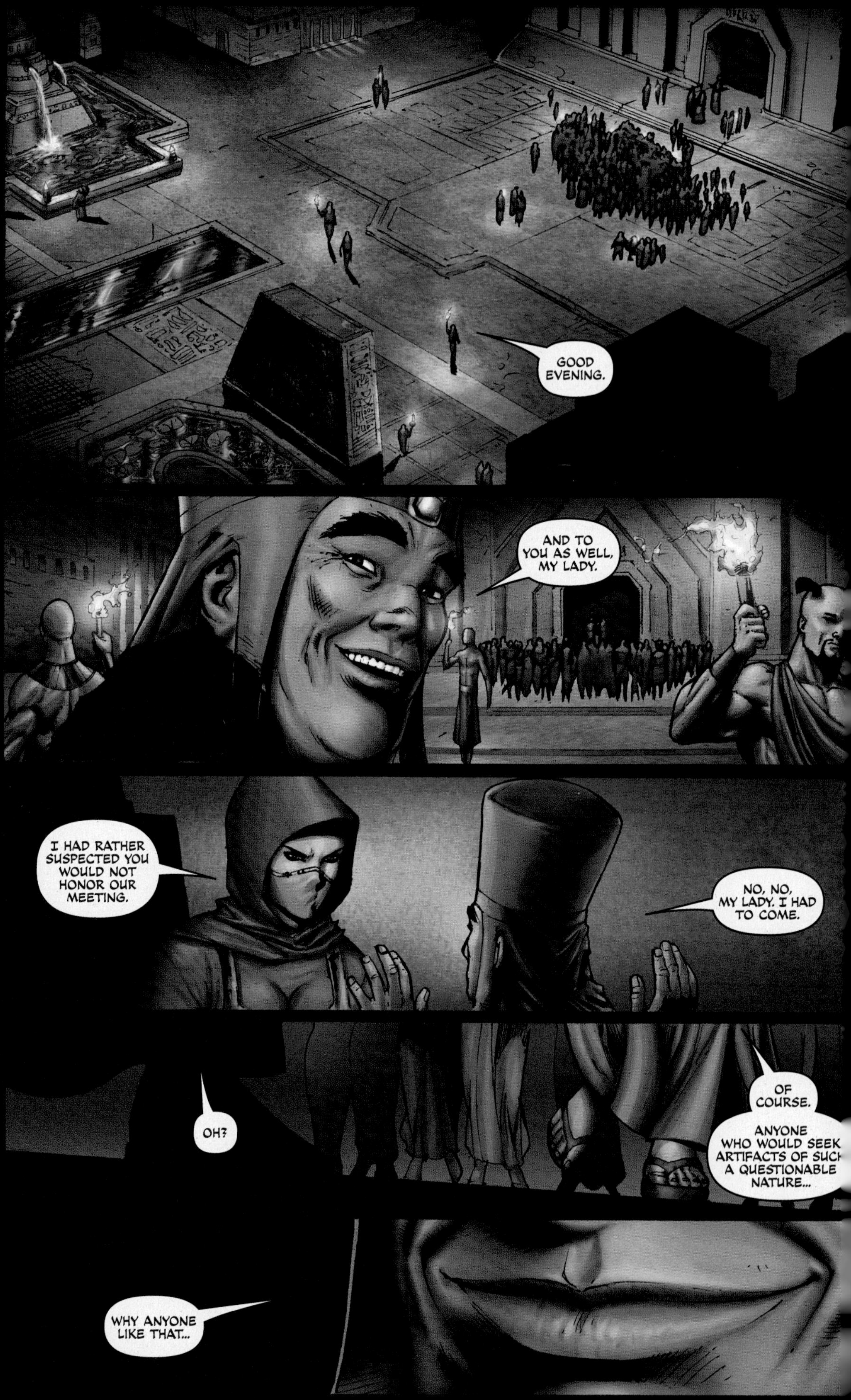
GOOD EVENING.
AND TO YOU AS WELL, MY LADY.
I HAD RATHER SUSPECTED YOU WOULD NOT HONOR OUR MEETING.
NO, NO, MY LADY. I HAD TO COME.
OH?
OF COURSE.
ANYONE WHO WOULD SEEK ARTIFACTS OF SUCH A QUESTIONABLE NATURE...
WHY ANYONE LIKE THAT...

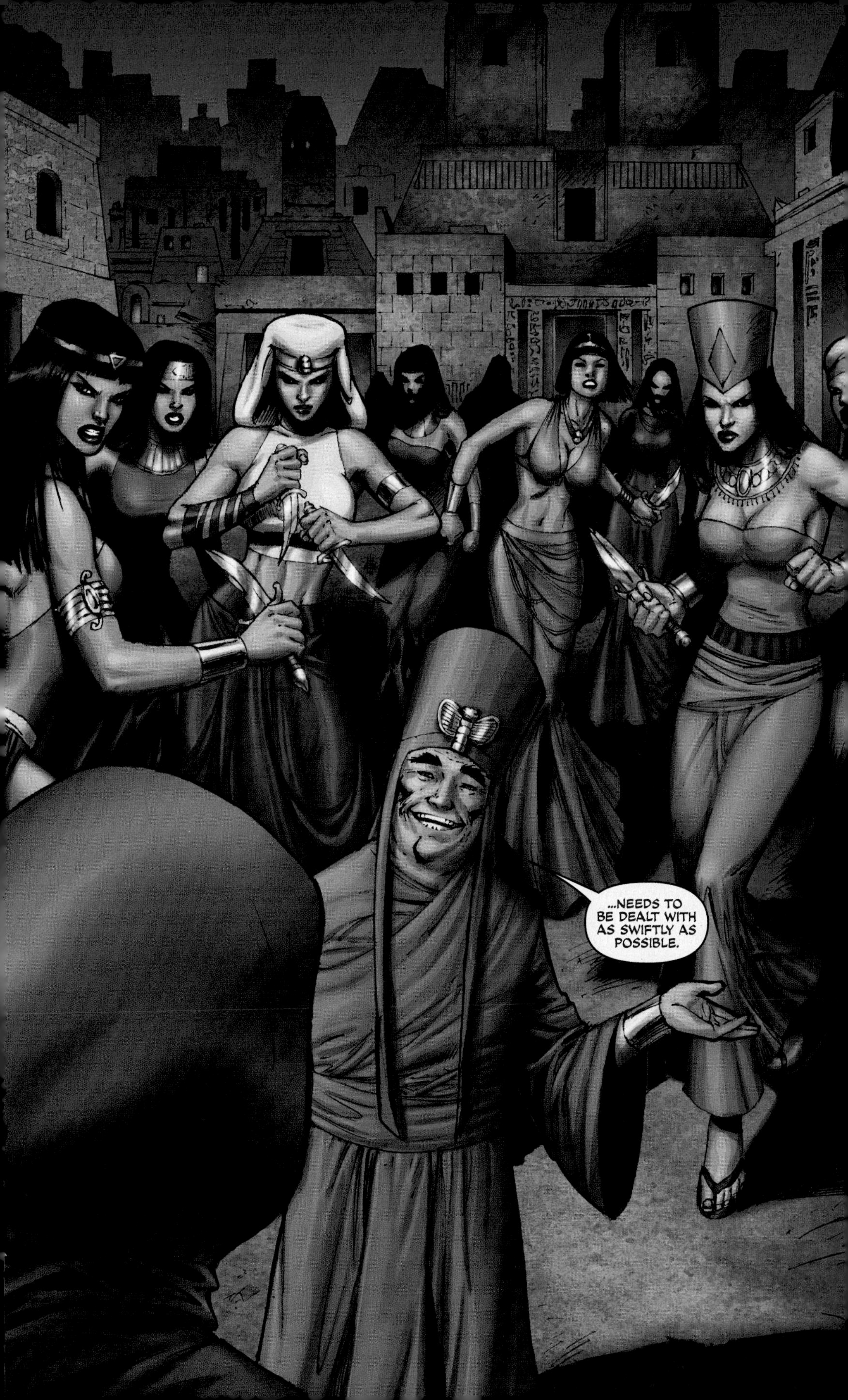
...NEEDS TO BE DEALT WITH AS SWIFTLY AS POSSIBLE.

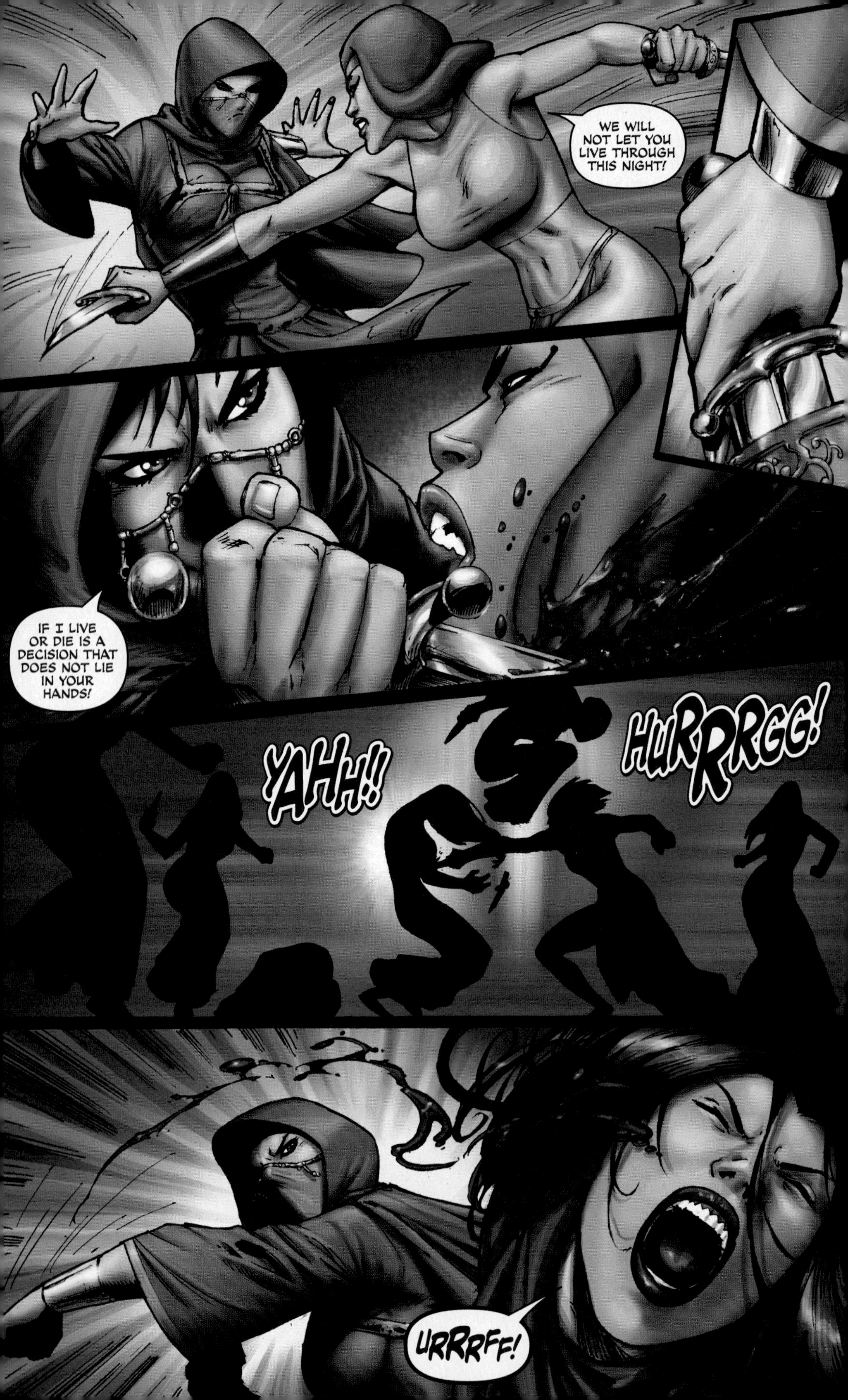
WE WILL NOT LET YOU LIVE THROUGH THIS NIGHT!
IF I LIVE OR DIE IS A DECISION THAT DOES NOT LIE IN YOUR HANDS!
YAHH!!
HURRRGG!
URRRFF!

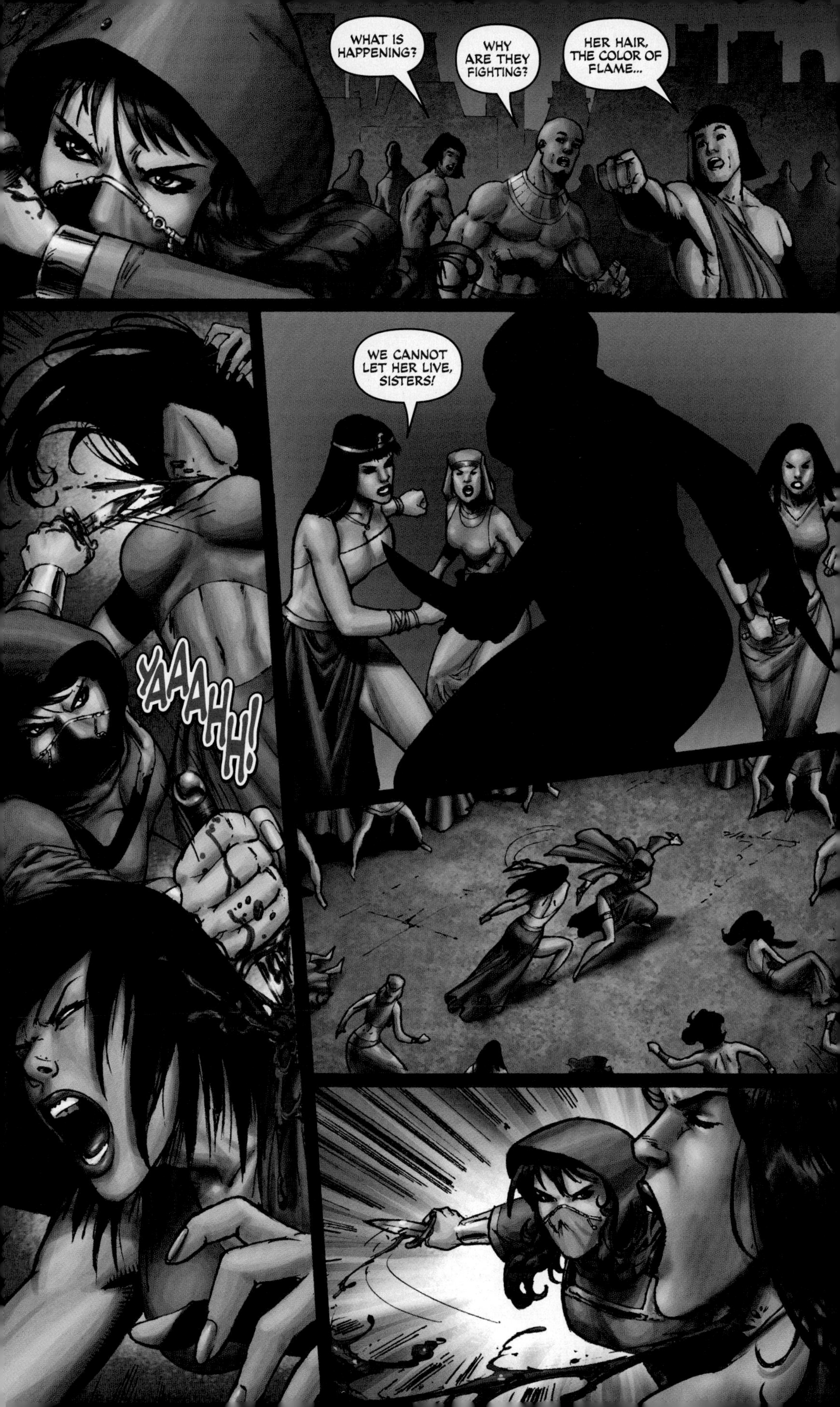
WHAT IS HAPPENING?
WHY ARE THEY FIGHTING?
HER HAIR, THE COLOR OF FLAME...
WE CANNOT LET HER LIVE, SISTERS!
YAAAHH!

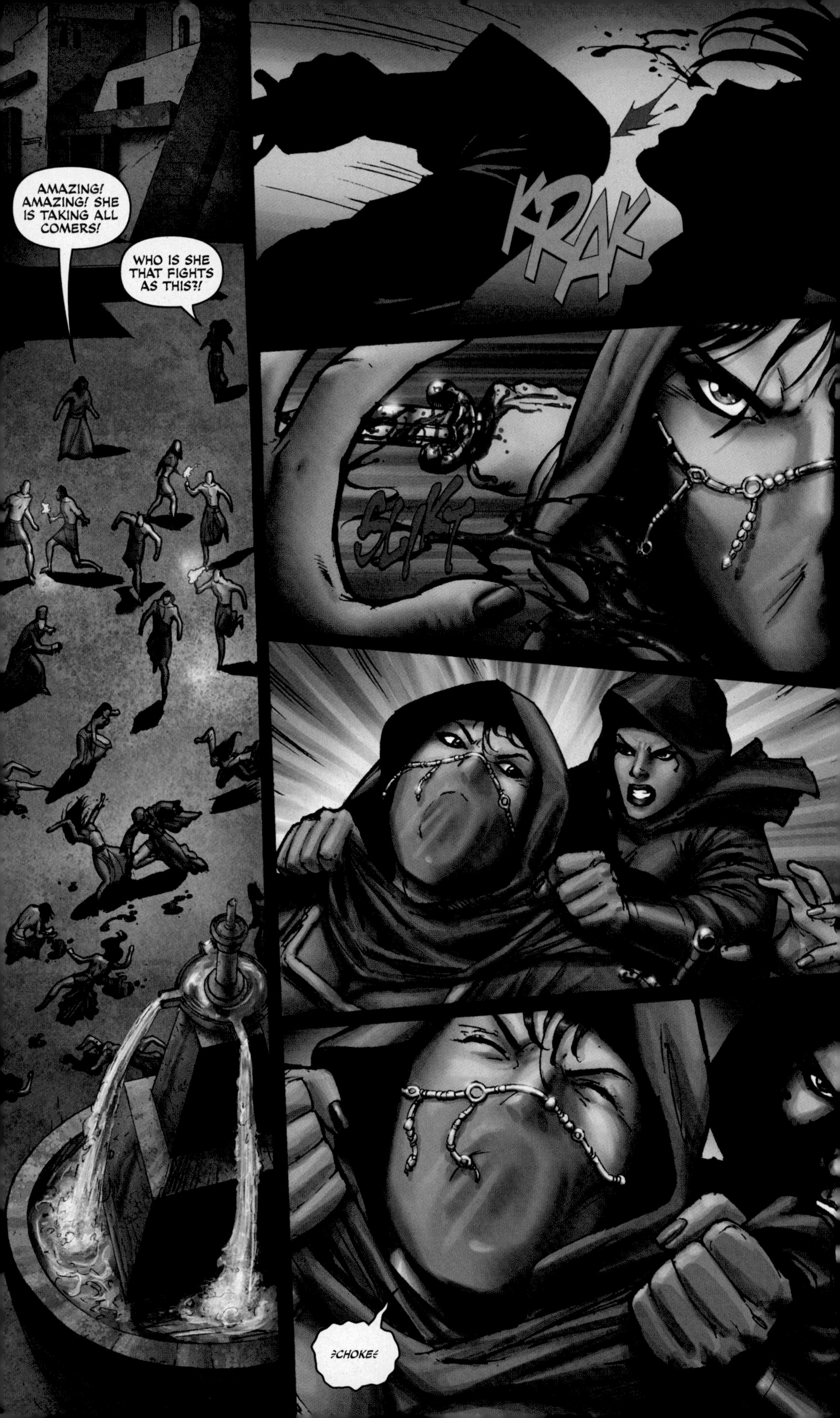

AMAZING! AMAZING! SHE IS TAKING ALL COMERS!
WHO IS SHE THAT FIGHTS AS THIS?!
KRAK
SLIKT
CHOKE

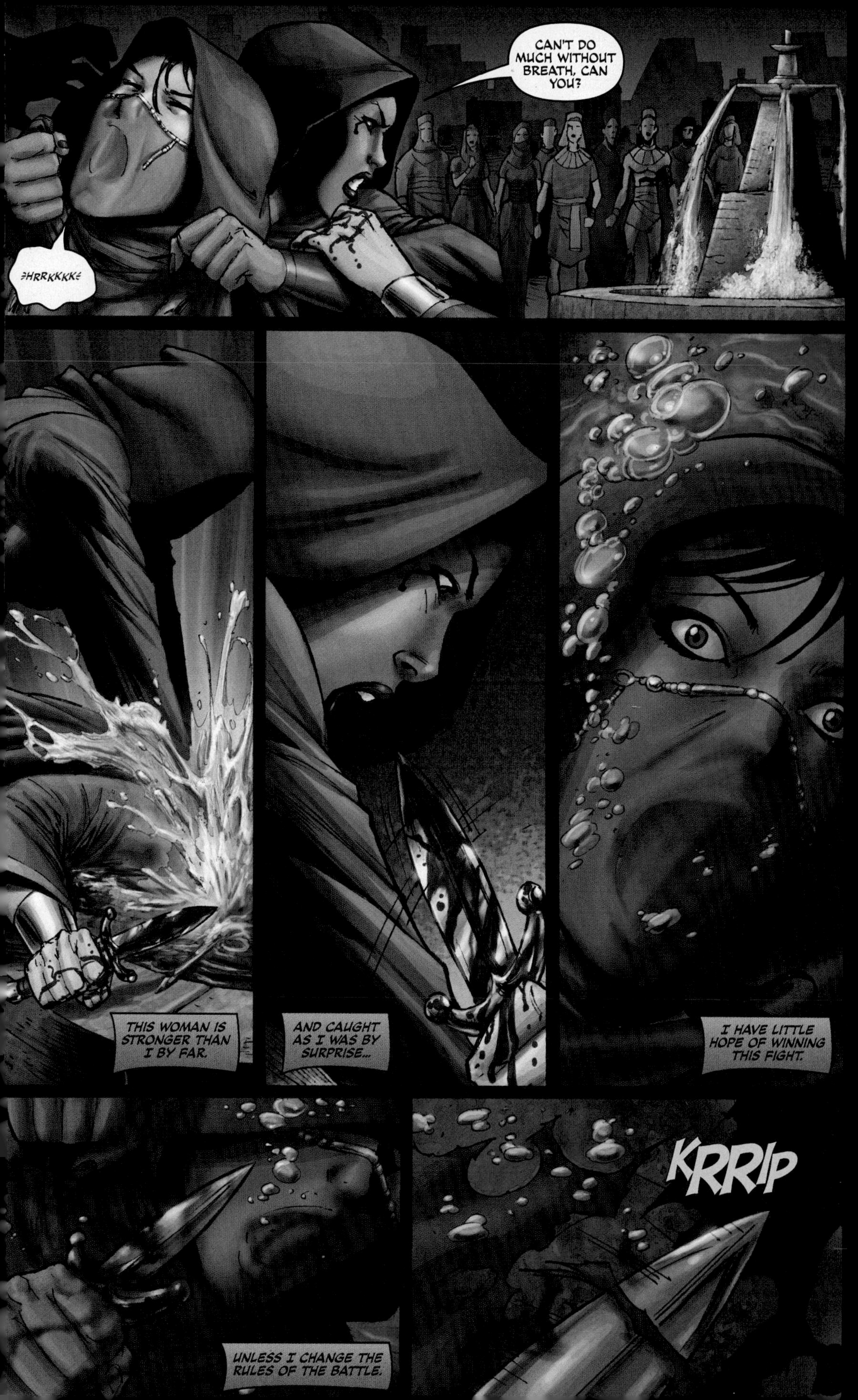

CAN'T DO MUCH WITHOUT BREATH, CAN YOU?
HRRKKKK
THIS WOMAN IS STRONGER THAN I BY FAR.
AND CAUGHT AS I WAS BY SURPRISE...
I HAVE LITTLE HOPE OF WINNING THIS FIGHT.
UNLESS I CHANGE THE RULES OF THE BATTLE.
KRRIP

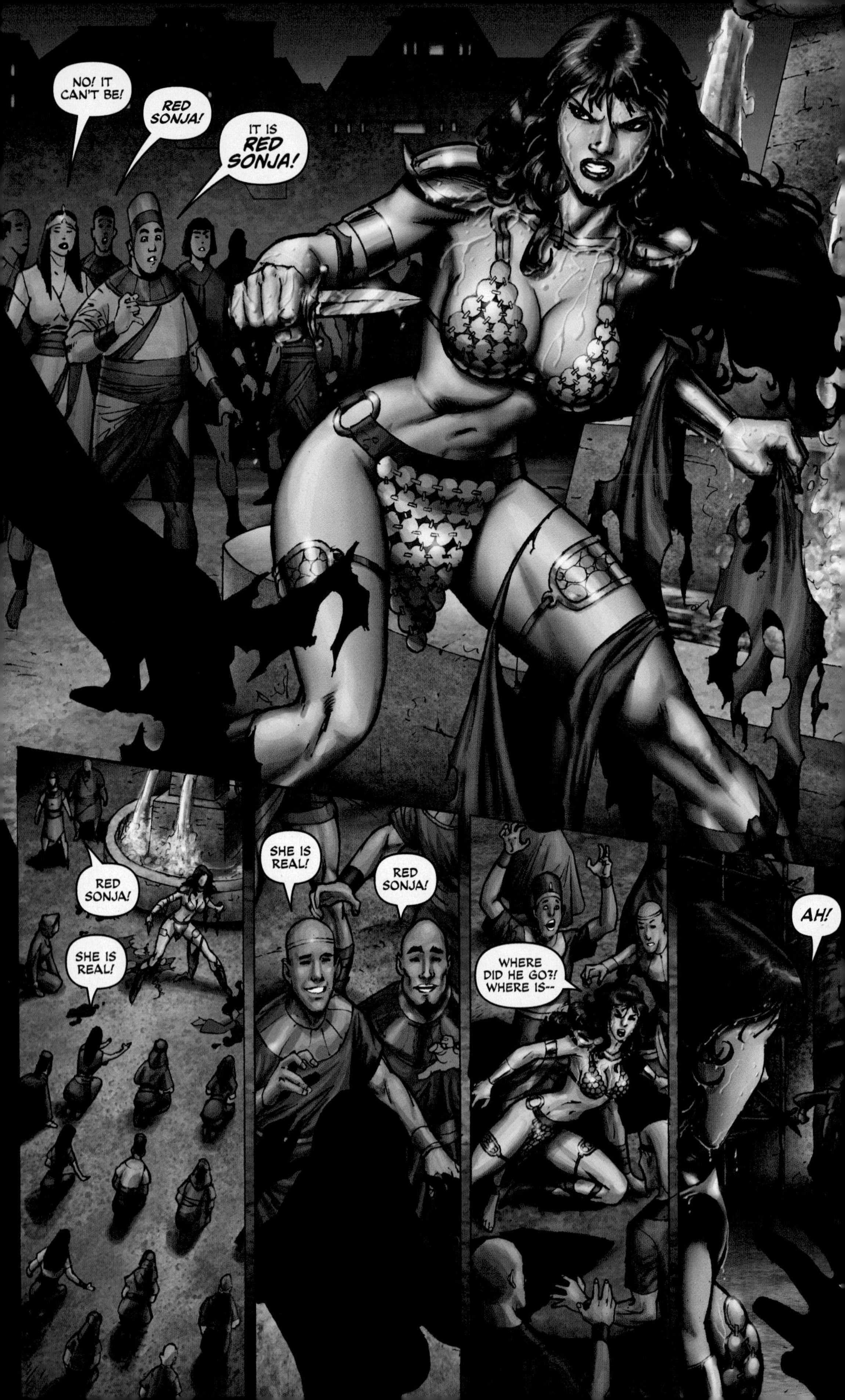
NO! IT CAN'T BE!
RED SONJA!
IT IS RED SONJA!
RED SONJA!
SHE IS REAL!
SHE IS REAL!
RED SONJA!
WHERE DID HE GO?! WHERE IS--
AH!

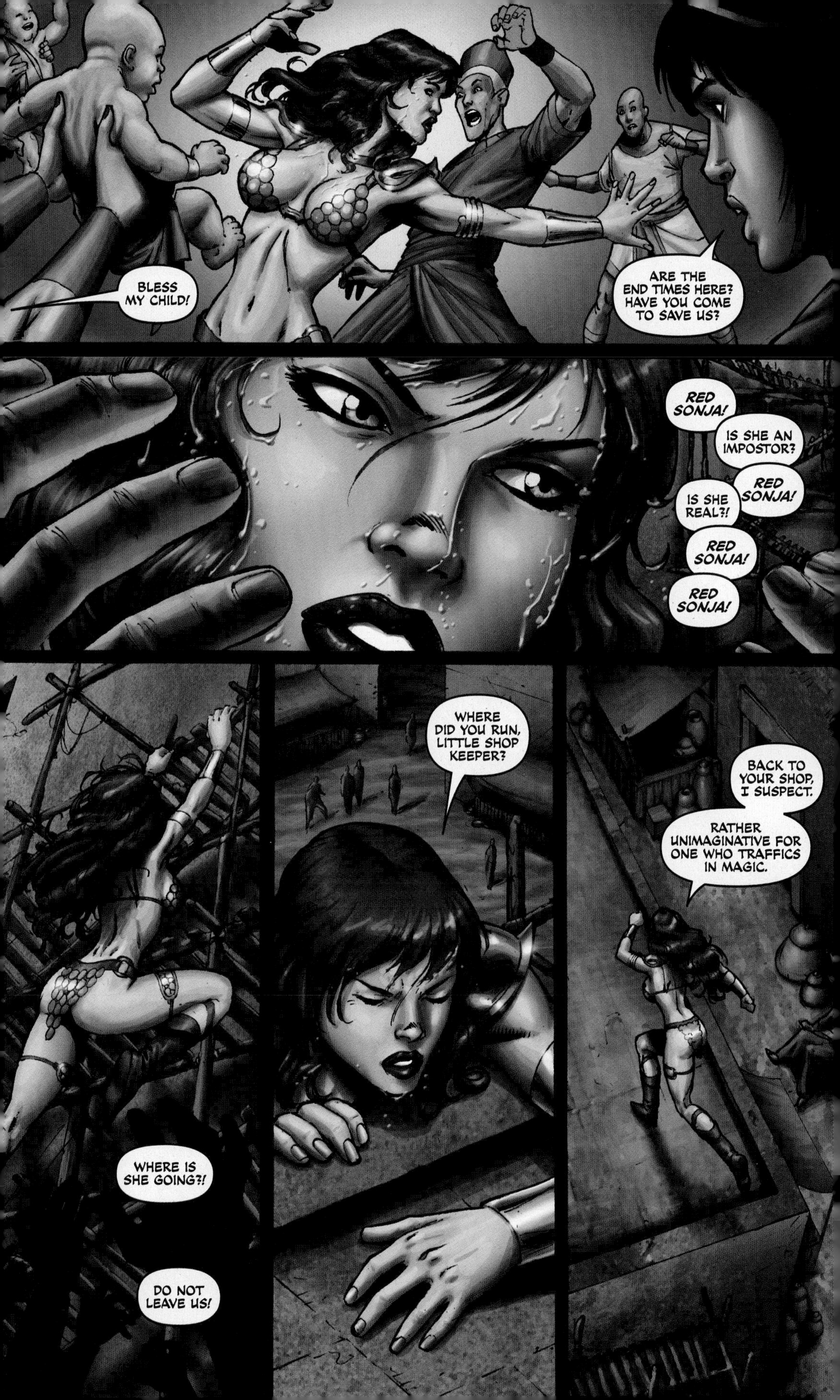
BLESS MY CHILD!
ARE THE END TIMES HERE? HAVE YOU COME TO SAVE US?
RED SONJA!
IS SHE AN IMPOSTOR?
RED SONJA!
IS SHE REAL?!
RED SONJA!
RED SONJA!
WHERE IS SHE GOING?!
DO NOT LEAVE US!
WHERE DID YOU RUN, LITTLE SHOP KEEPER?
BACK TO YOUR SHOP, I SUSPECT.
RATHER UNIMAGINATIVE FOR ONE WHO TRAFFICS IN MAGIC.

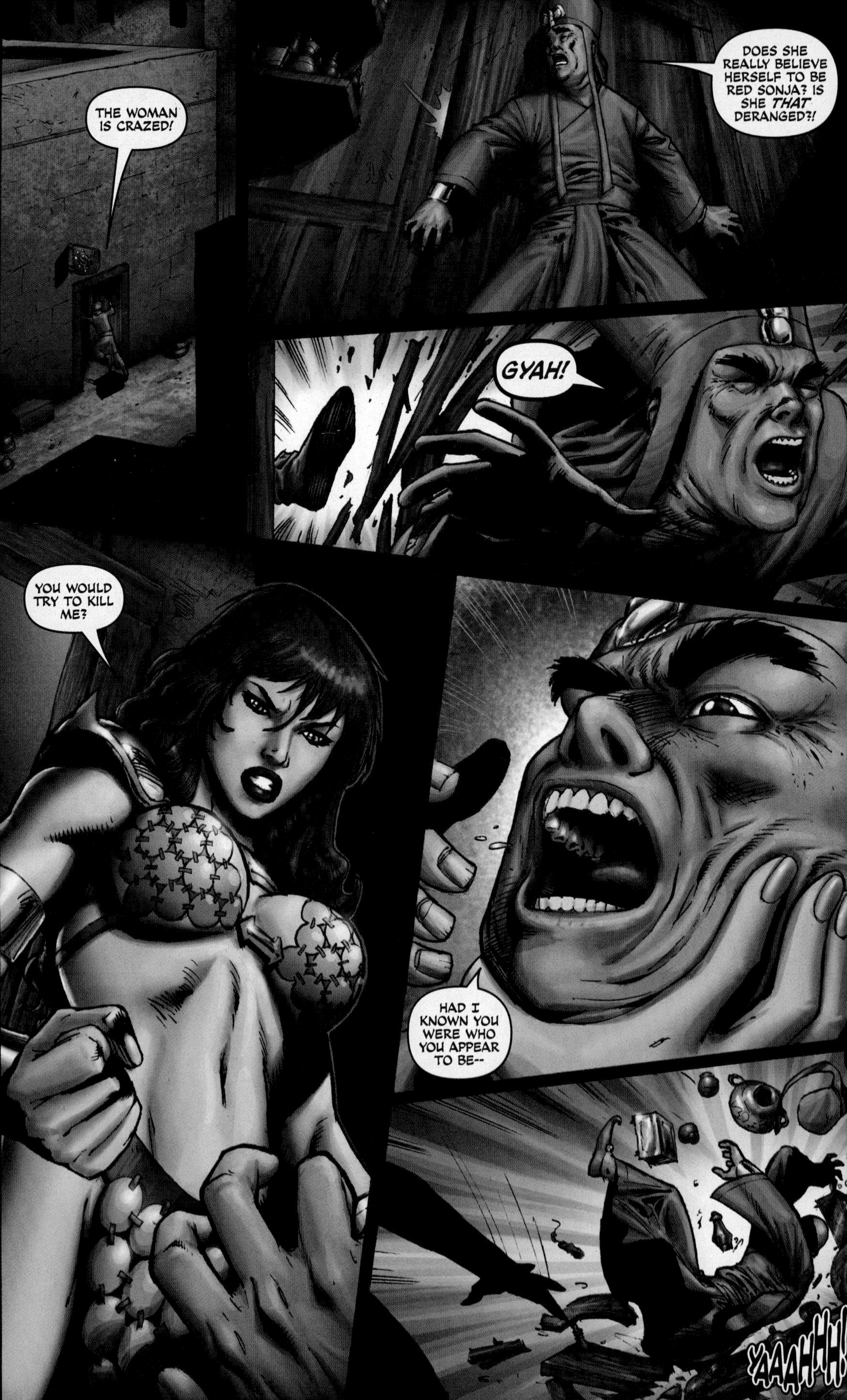
THE WOMAN IS CRAZED!
DOES SHE REALLY BELIEVE HERSELF TO BE RED SONJA? IS SHE *THAT* DERANGED?!
GYAH!
YOU WOULD TRY TO KILL ME?
HAD I KNOWN YOU WERE WHO YOU APPEAR TO BE--
YAAAHHH!

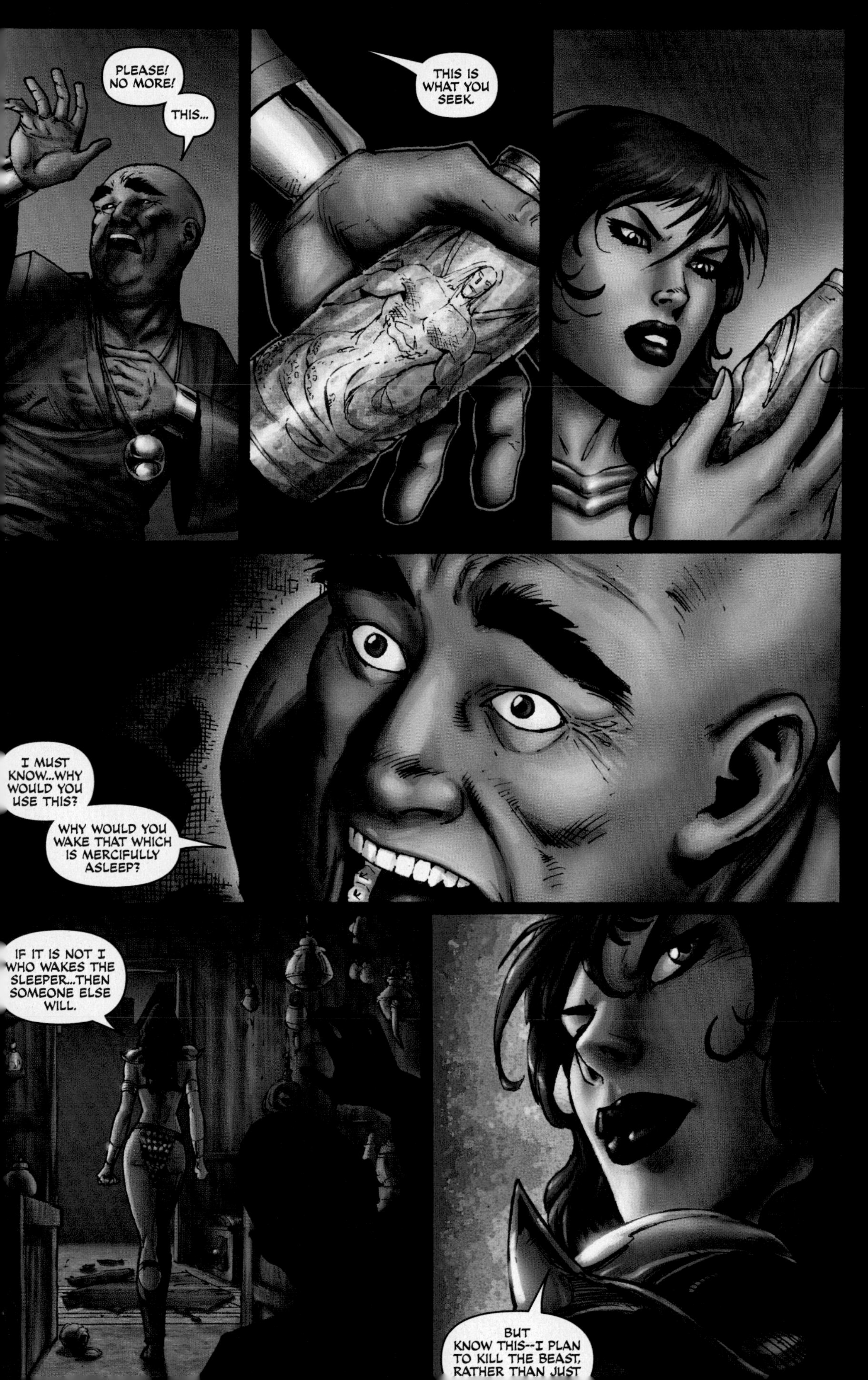
PLEASE! NO MORE!
THIS...
THIS IS WHAT YOU SEEK.
I MUST KNOW...WHY WOULD YOU USE THIS?
WHY WOULD YOU WAKE THAT WHICH IS MERCIFULLY ASLEEP?
IF IT IS NOT I WHO WAKES THE SLEEPER...THEN SOMEONE ELSE WILL.
BUT KNOW THIS--I PLAN TO KILL THE BEAST, RATHER THAN JUST

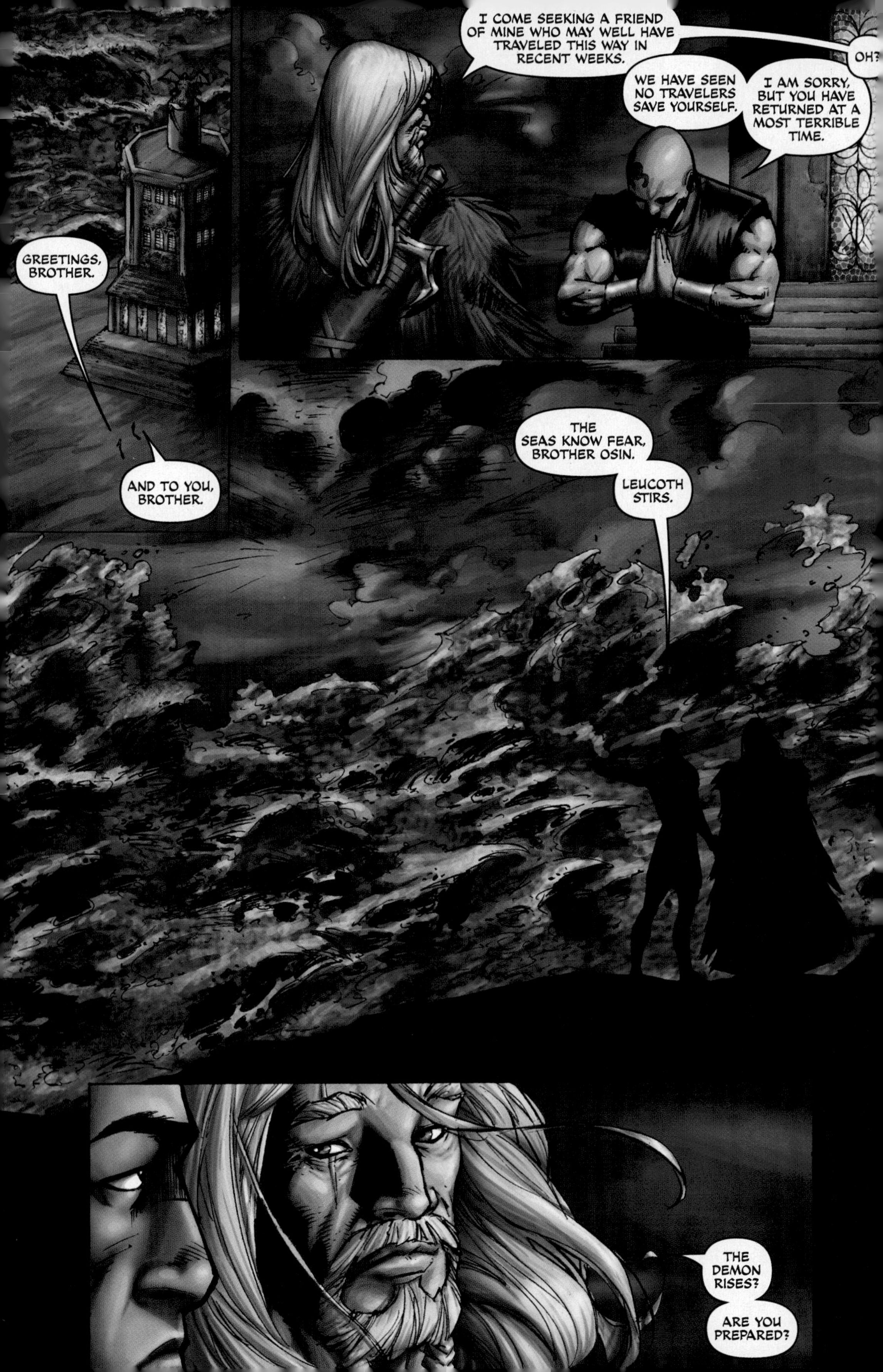
GREETINGS, BROTHER.
AND TO YOU, BROTHER.
I COME SEEKING A FRIEND OF MINE WHO MAY WELL HAVE TRAVELED THIS WAY IN RECENT WEEKS.
WE HAVE SEEN NO TRAVELERS SAVE YOURSELF.
I AM SORRY, BUT YOU HAVE RETURNED AT A MOST TERRIBLE TIME.
OH?
THE SEAS KNOW FEAR, BROTHER OSIN.
LEUCOTH STIRS.
THE DEMON RISES?
ARE YOU PREPARED?

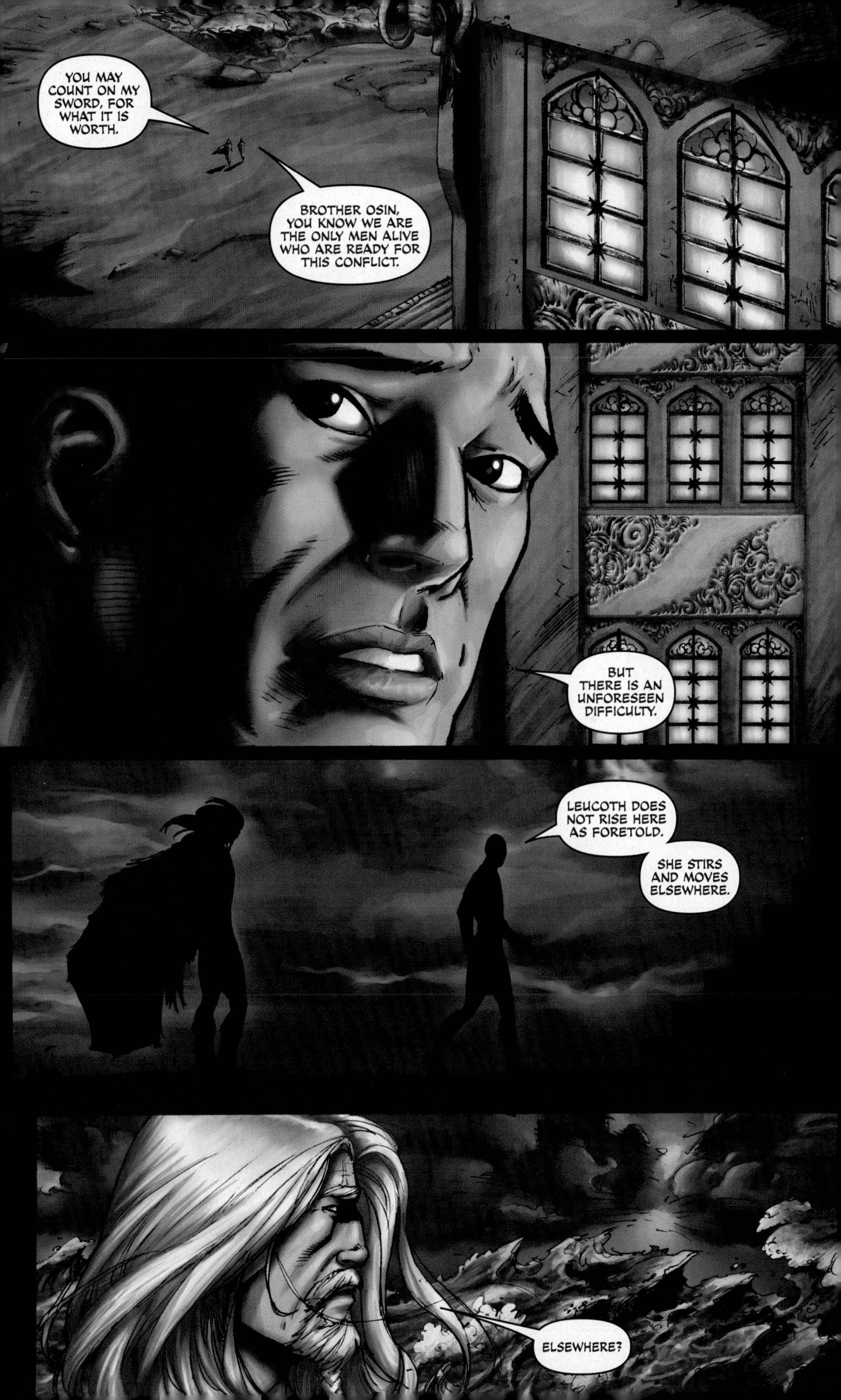
YOU MAY COUNT ON MY SWORD, FOR WHAT IT IS WORTH.
BROTHER OSIN, YOU KNOW WE ARE THE ONLY MEN ALIVE WHO ARE READY FOR THIS CONFLICT.
BUT THERE IS AN UNFORESEEN DIFFICULTY.
LEUCOTH DOES NOT RISE HERE AS FORETOLD.
SHE STIRS AND MOVES ELSEWHERE.
ELSEWHERE?

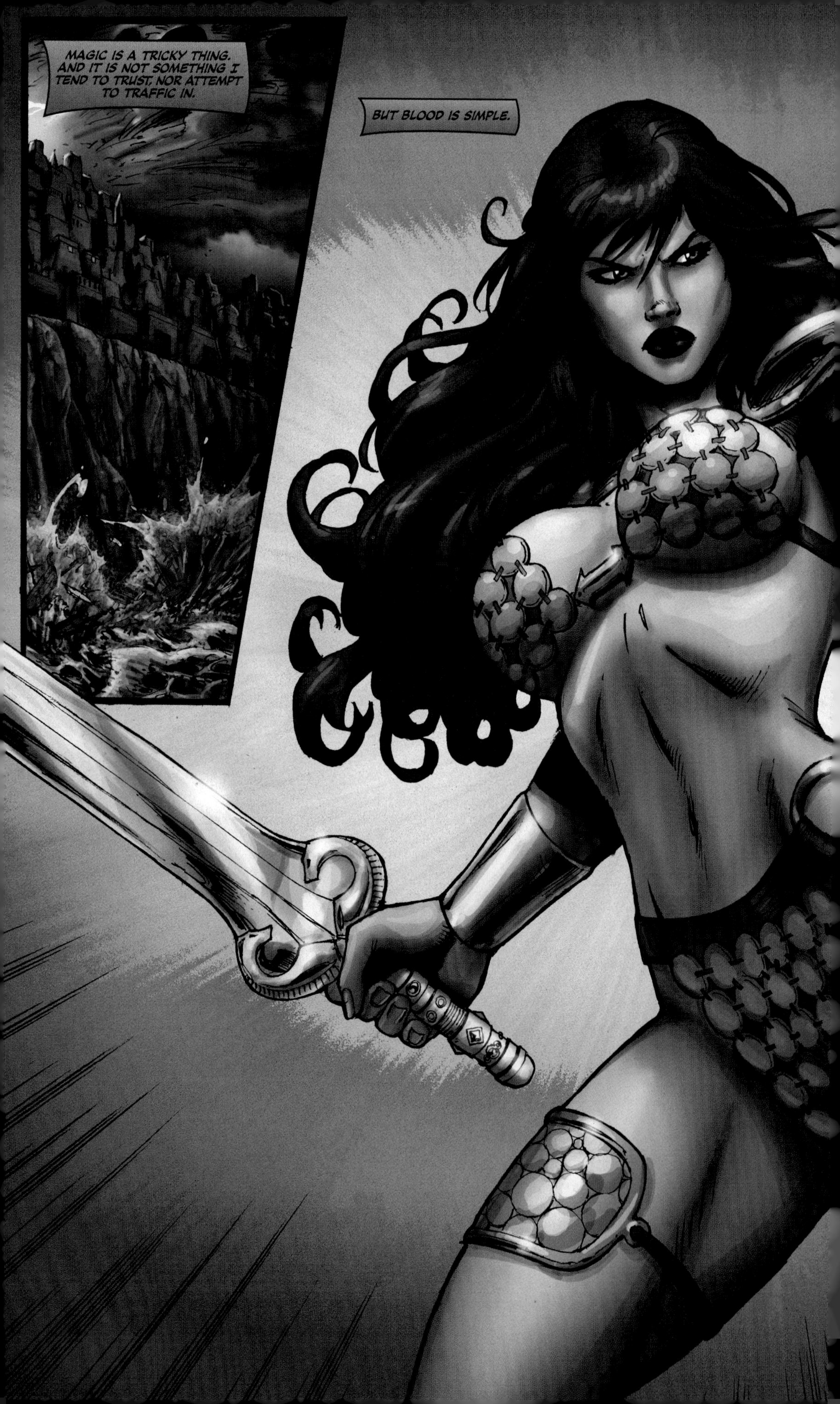

MAGIC IS A TRICKY THING. AND IT IS NOT SOMETHING I TEND TO TRUST, NOR ATTEMPT TO TRAFFIC IN.
BUT BLOOD IS SIMPLE.

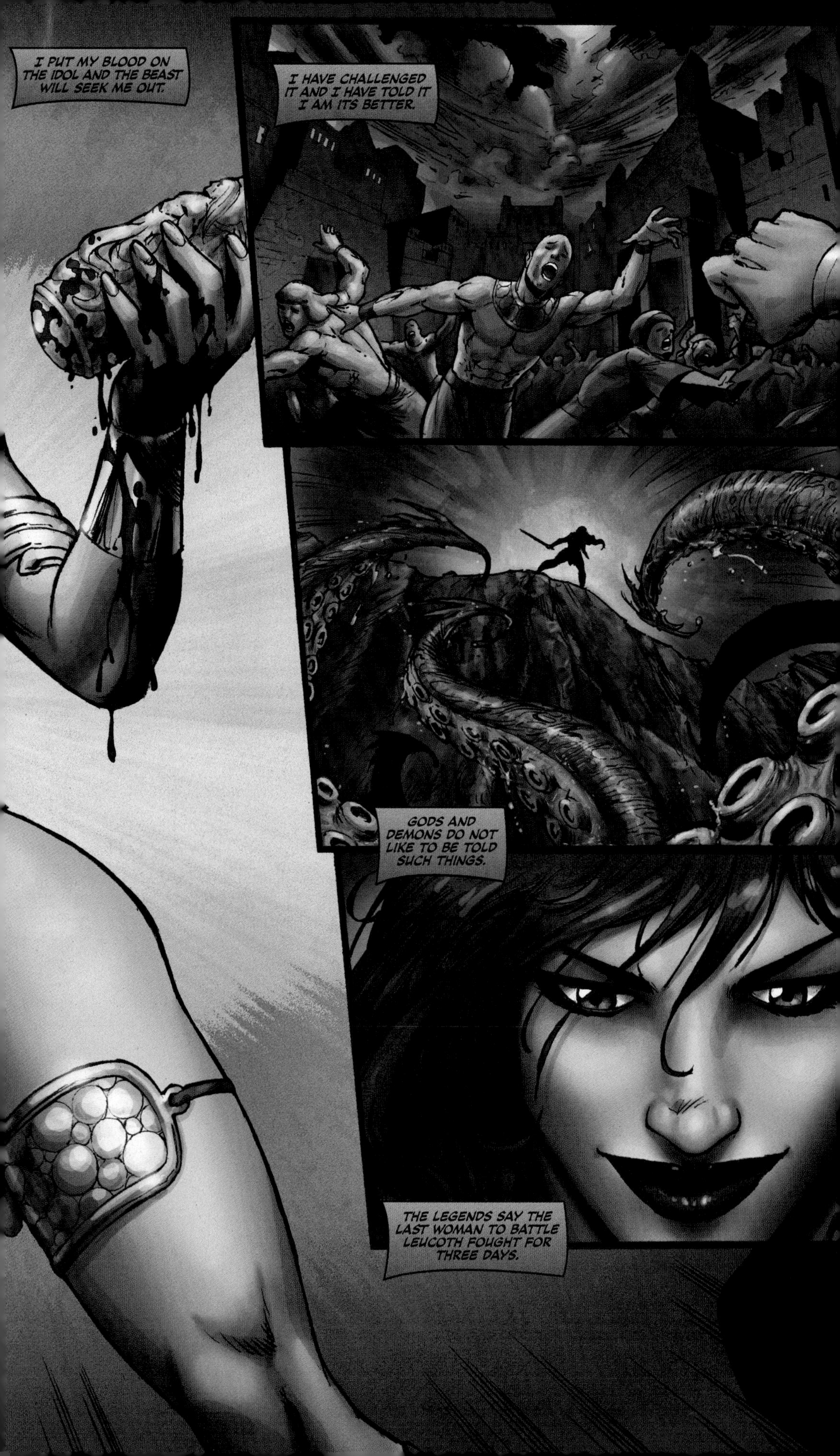
I PUT MY BLOOD ON THE IDOL AND THE BEAST WILL SEEK ME OUT.
I HAVE CHALLENGED IT AND I HAVE TOLD IT I AM ITS BETTER.
GODS AND DEMONS DO NOT LIKE TO BE TOLD SUCH THINGS.
THE LEGENDS SAY THE LAST WOMAN TO BATTLE LEUCOTH FOUGHT FOR THREE DAYS.

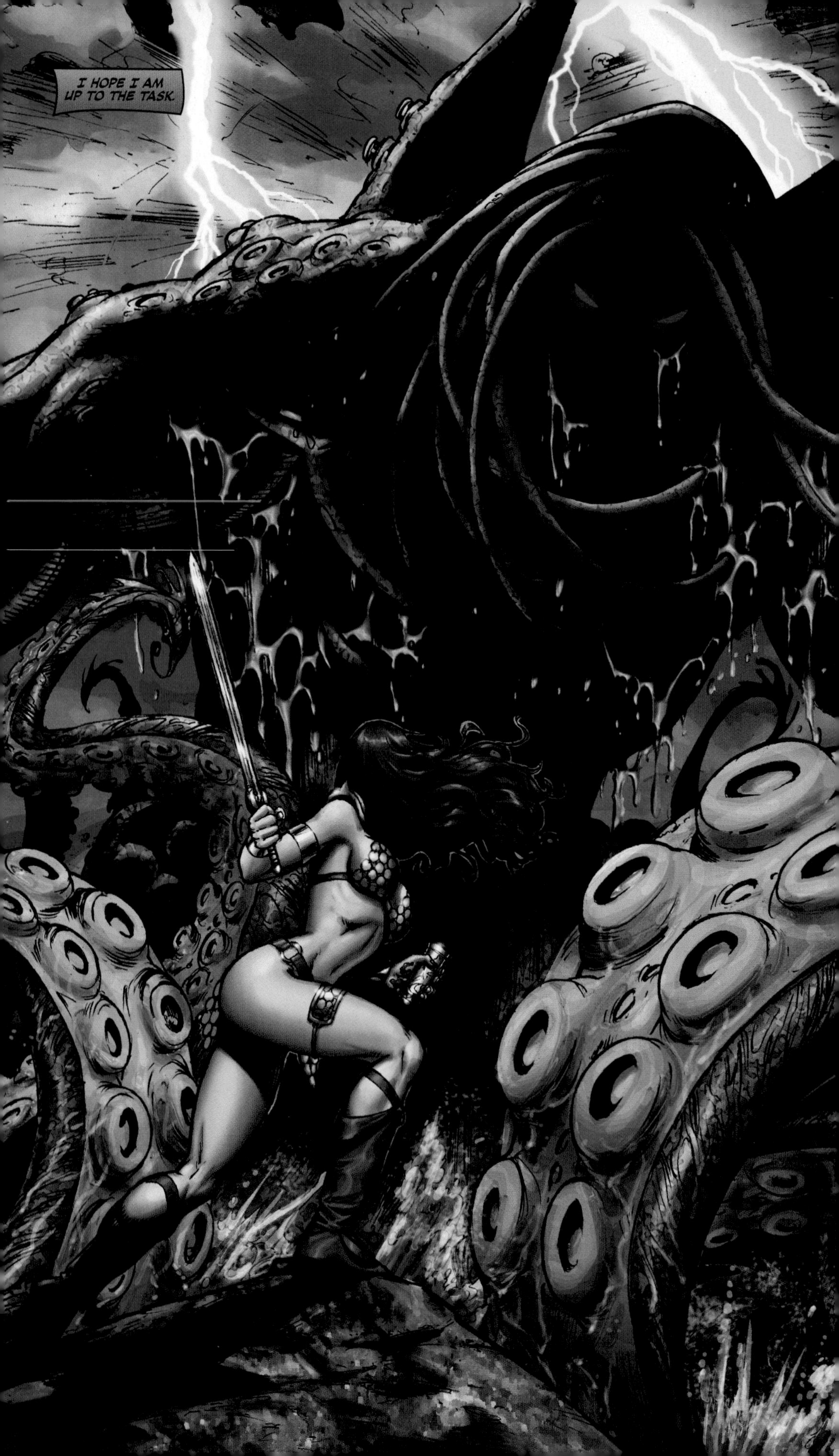
I HOPE I AM UP TO THE TASK.

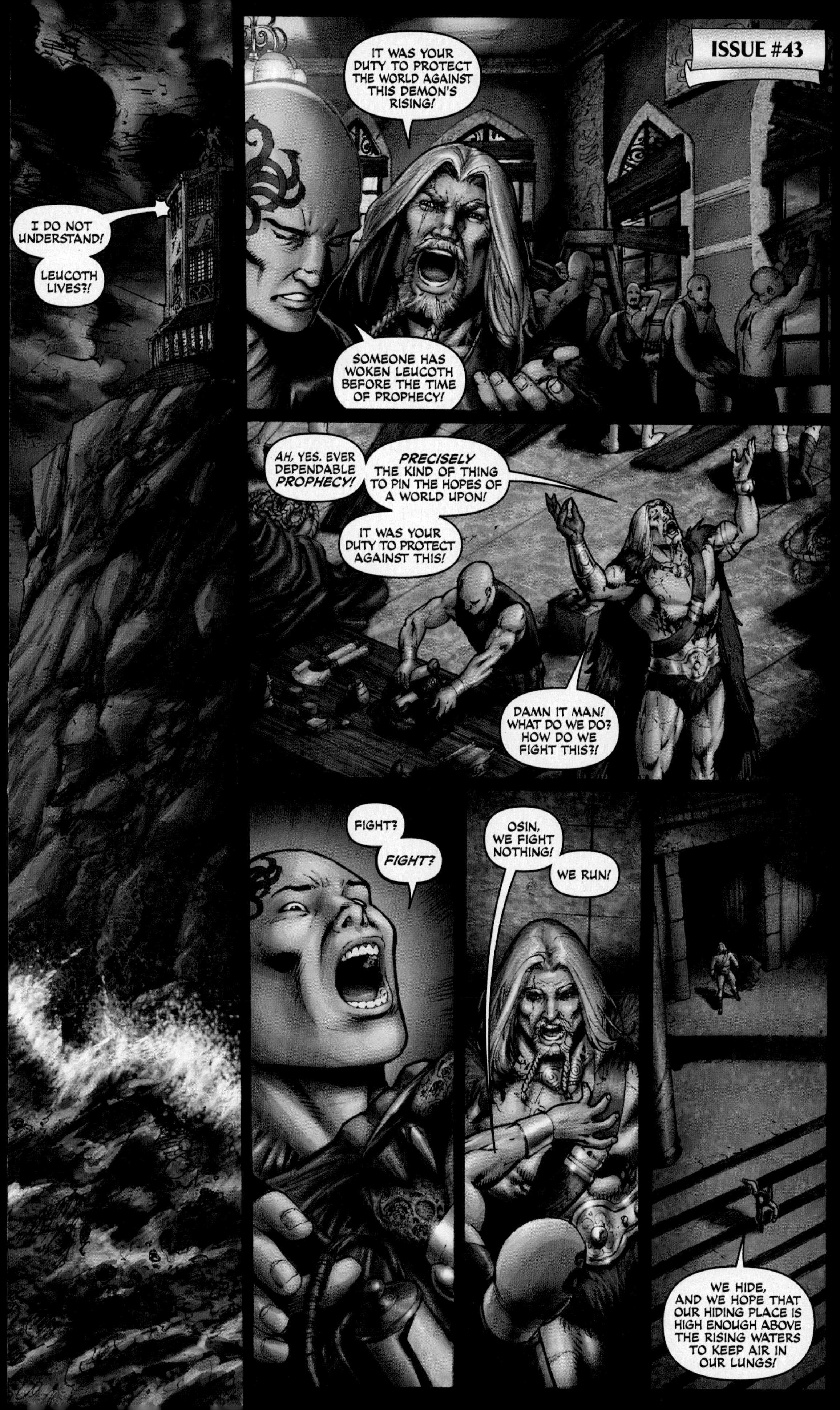
ISSUE #43
I DO NOT UNDERSTAND!
LEUCOTH LIVES?!
IT WAS YOUR DUTY TO PROTECT THE WORLD AGAINST THIS DEMON'S RISING!
SOMEONE HAS WOKEN LEUCOTH BEFORE THE TIME OF PROPHECY!
AH, YES. EVER DEPENDABLE PROPHECY!
PRECISELY THE KIND OF THING TO PIN THE HOPES OF A WORLD UPON!
IT WAS YOUR DUTY TO PROTECT AGAINST THIS!
DAMN IT MAN! WHAT DO WE DO? HOW DO WE FIGHT THIS?!
FIGHT?
FIGHT?
OSIN, WE FIGHT NOTHING!
WE RUN!
WE HIDE, AND WE HOPE THAT OUR HIDING PLACE IS HIGH ENOUGH ABOVE THE RISING WATERS TO KEEP AIR IN OUR LUNGS!

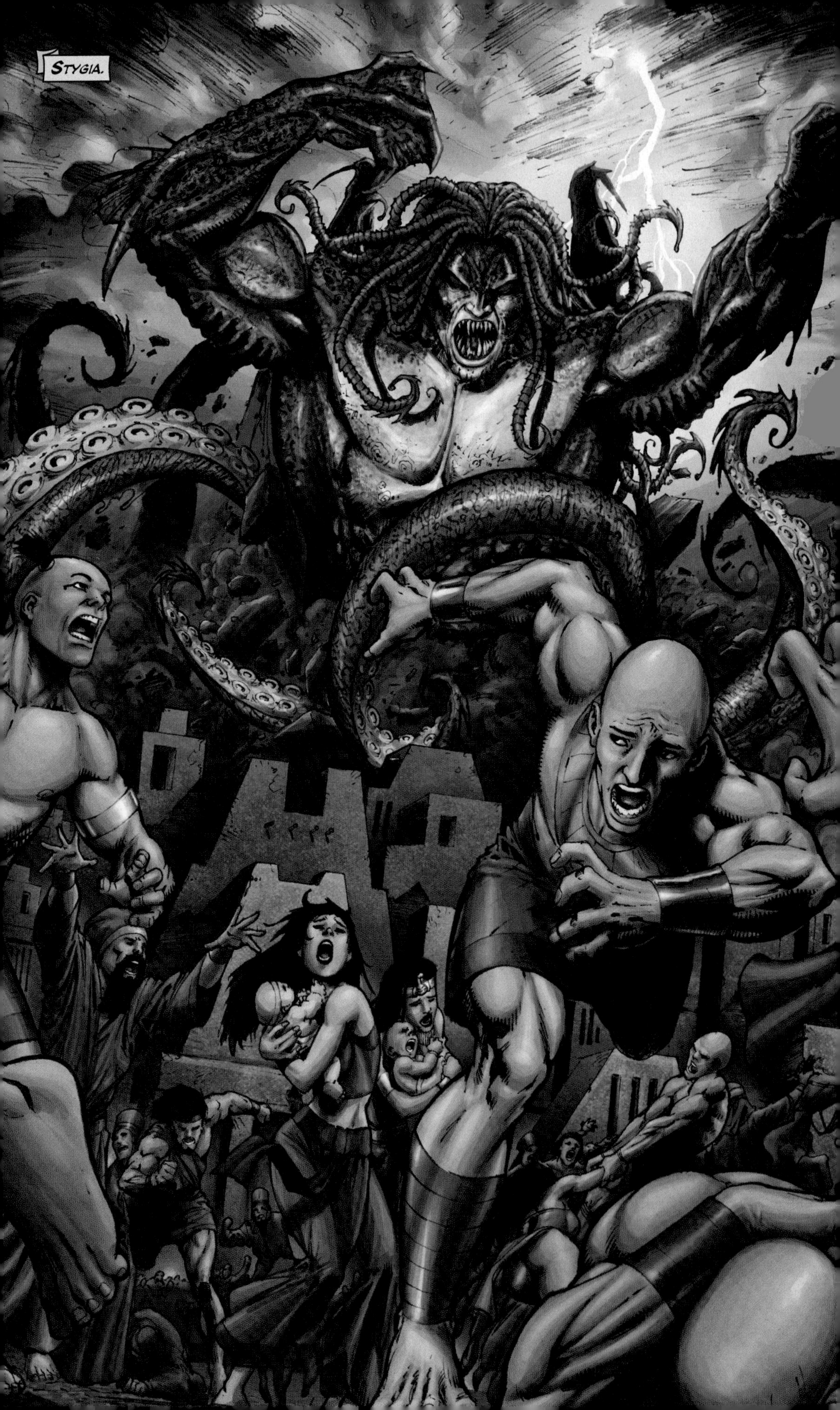
Stygia.

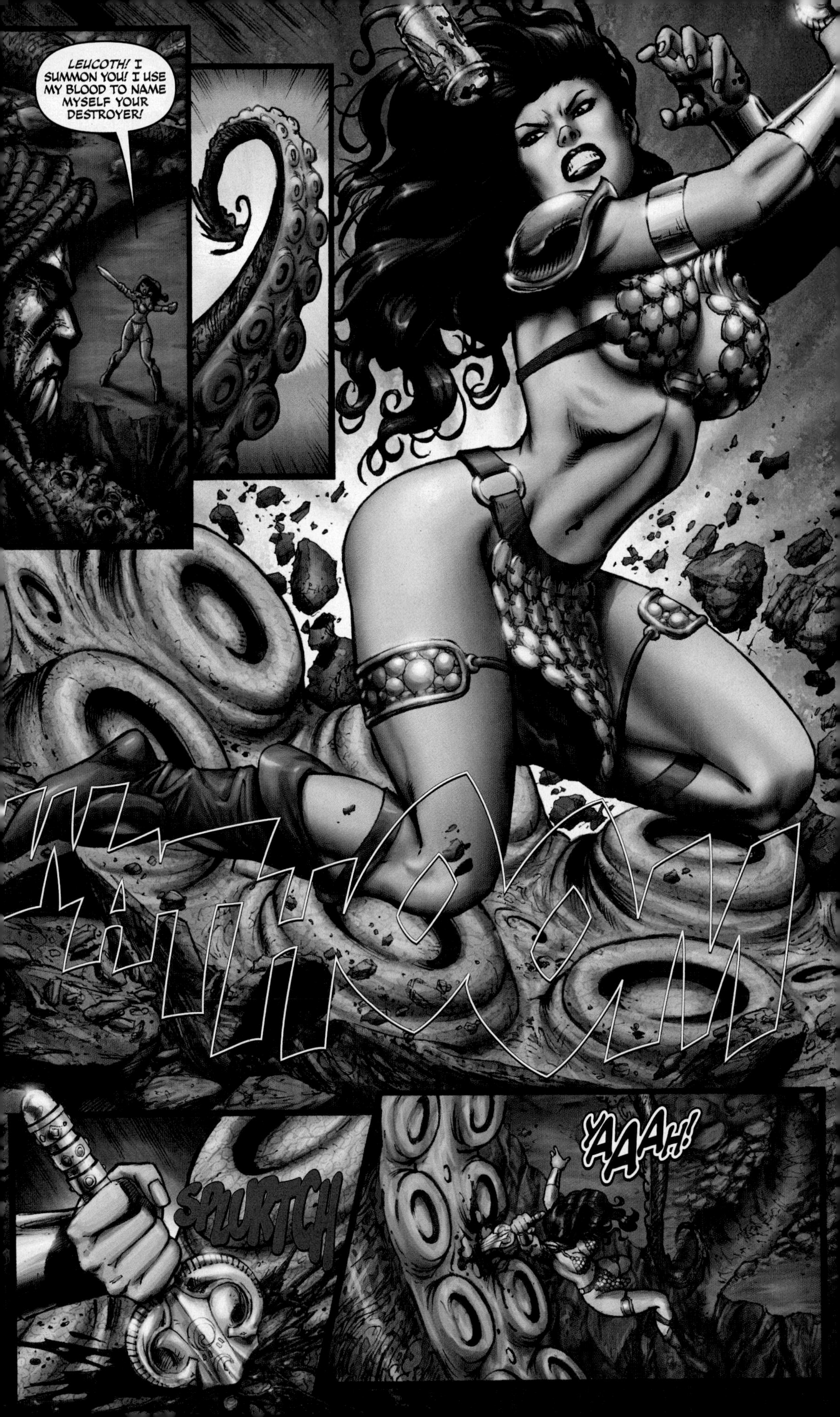
LEUCOTH! I SUMMON YOU! I USE MY BLOOD TO NAME MYSELF YOUR DESTROYER!
WHOOM
SPLURTCH
YAAAH!

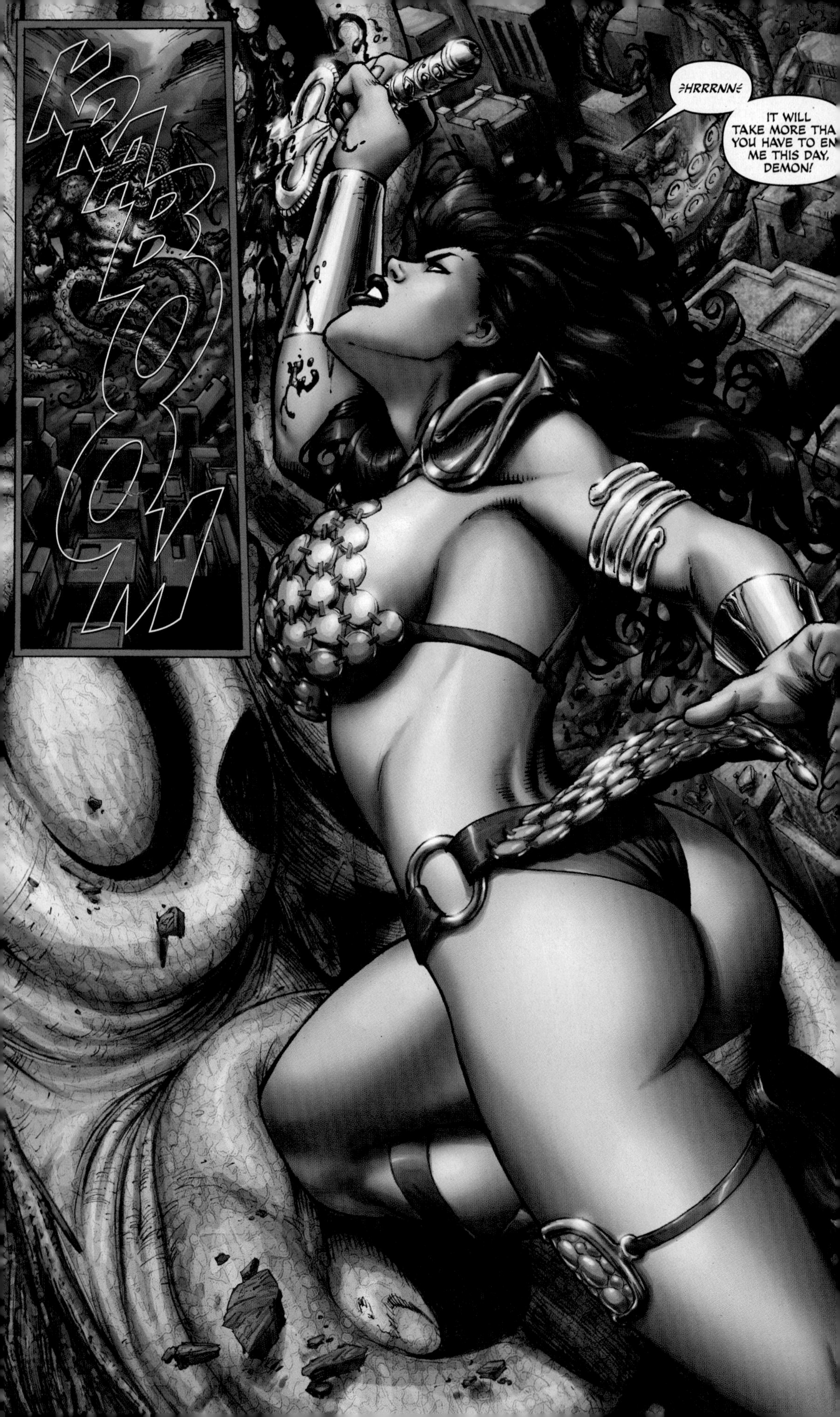
KRAKBOOM
HRRRNN
IT WILL TAKE MORE THA YOU HAVE TO EN ME THIS DAY, DEMON!

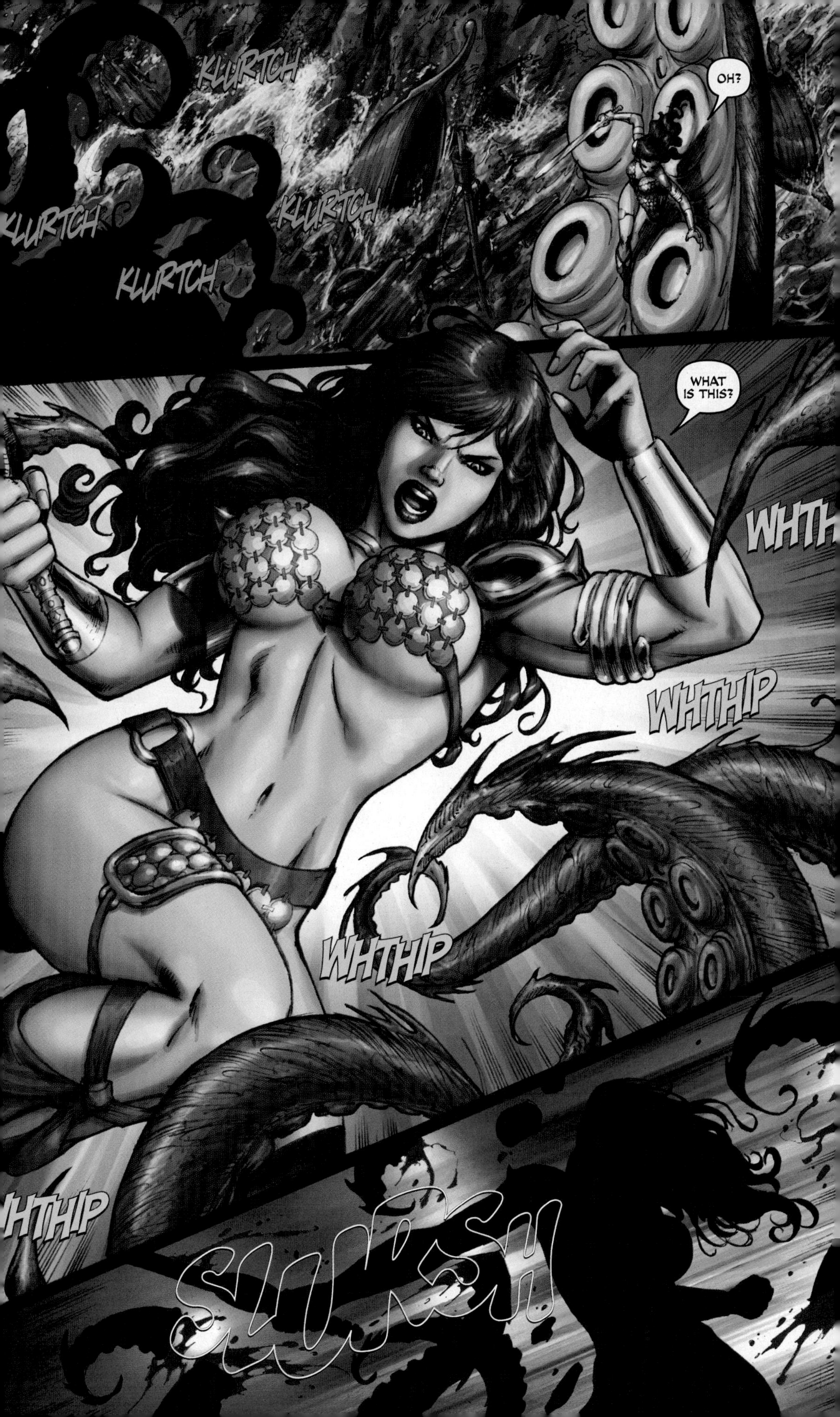
KLURTCH
KLURTCH
KLURTCH
KLURTCH
OH?
WHAT IS THIS?
WHTH
WHTHIP
WHTHIP
HTHIP
SLUSH

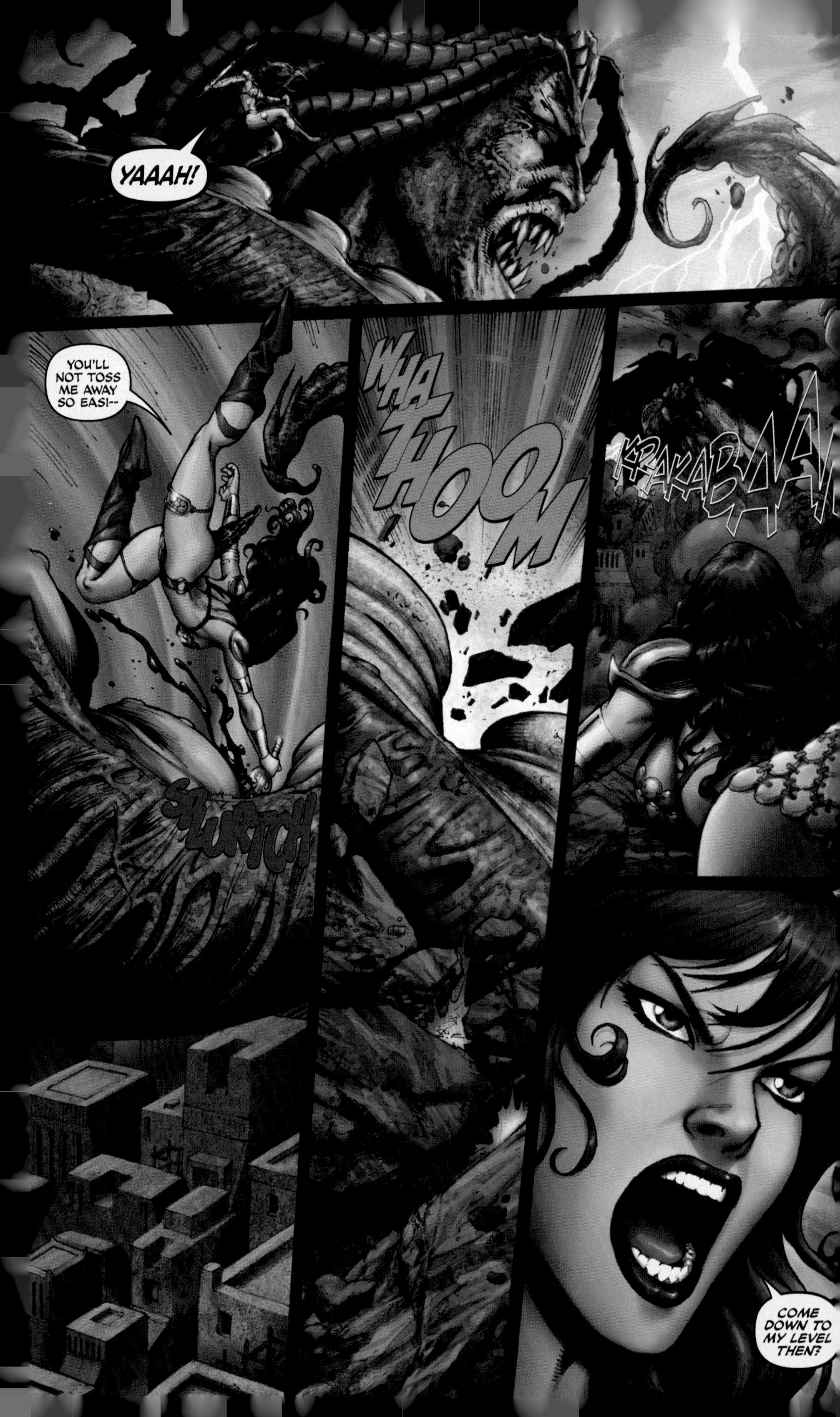
YAAAH!
YOU'LL NOT TOSS ME AWAY SO EASI--
SHLURTCH
WHA THOOM
KRAKABAN
COME DOWN TO MY LEVEL THEN?

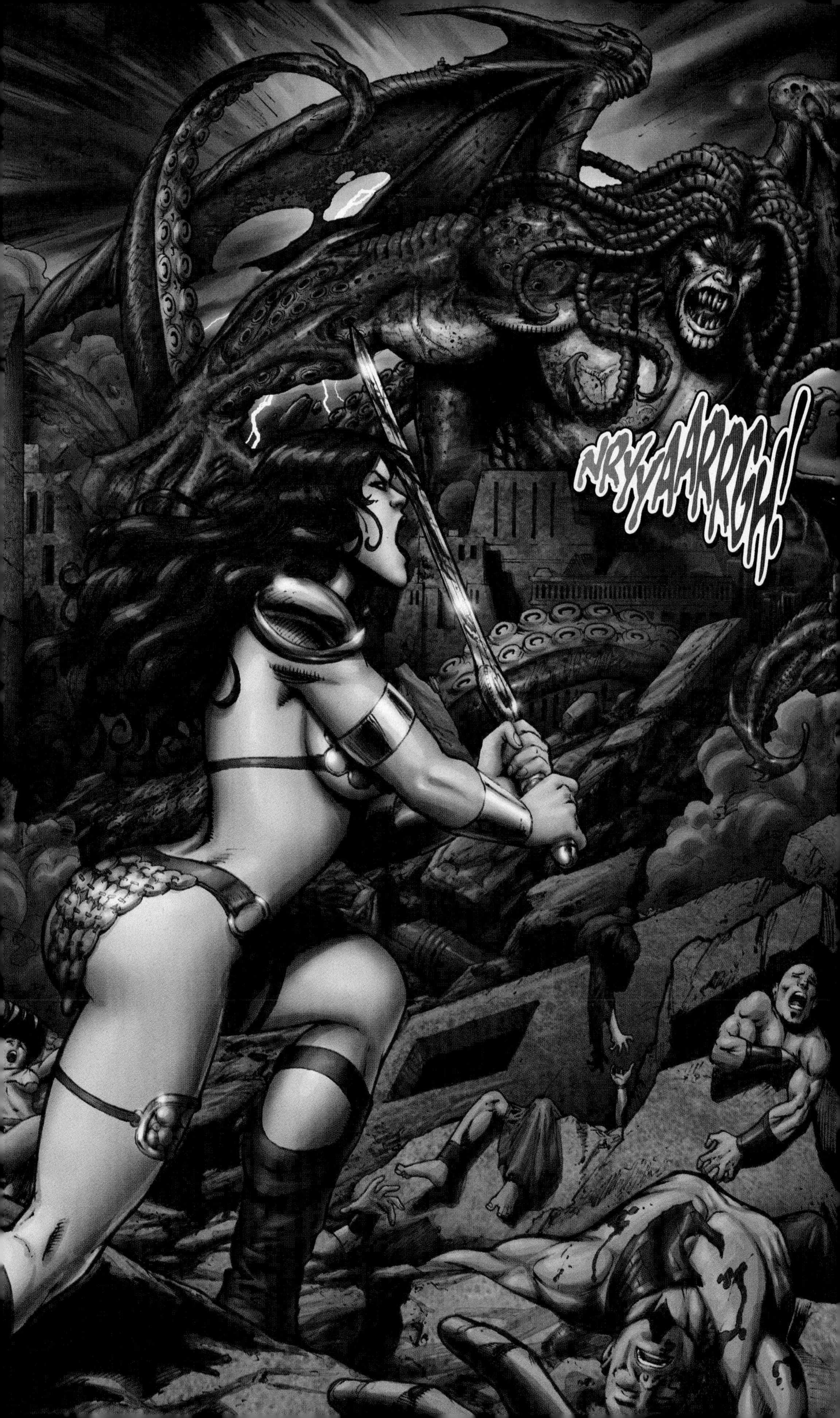
NRYAARRGH!

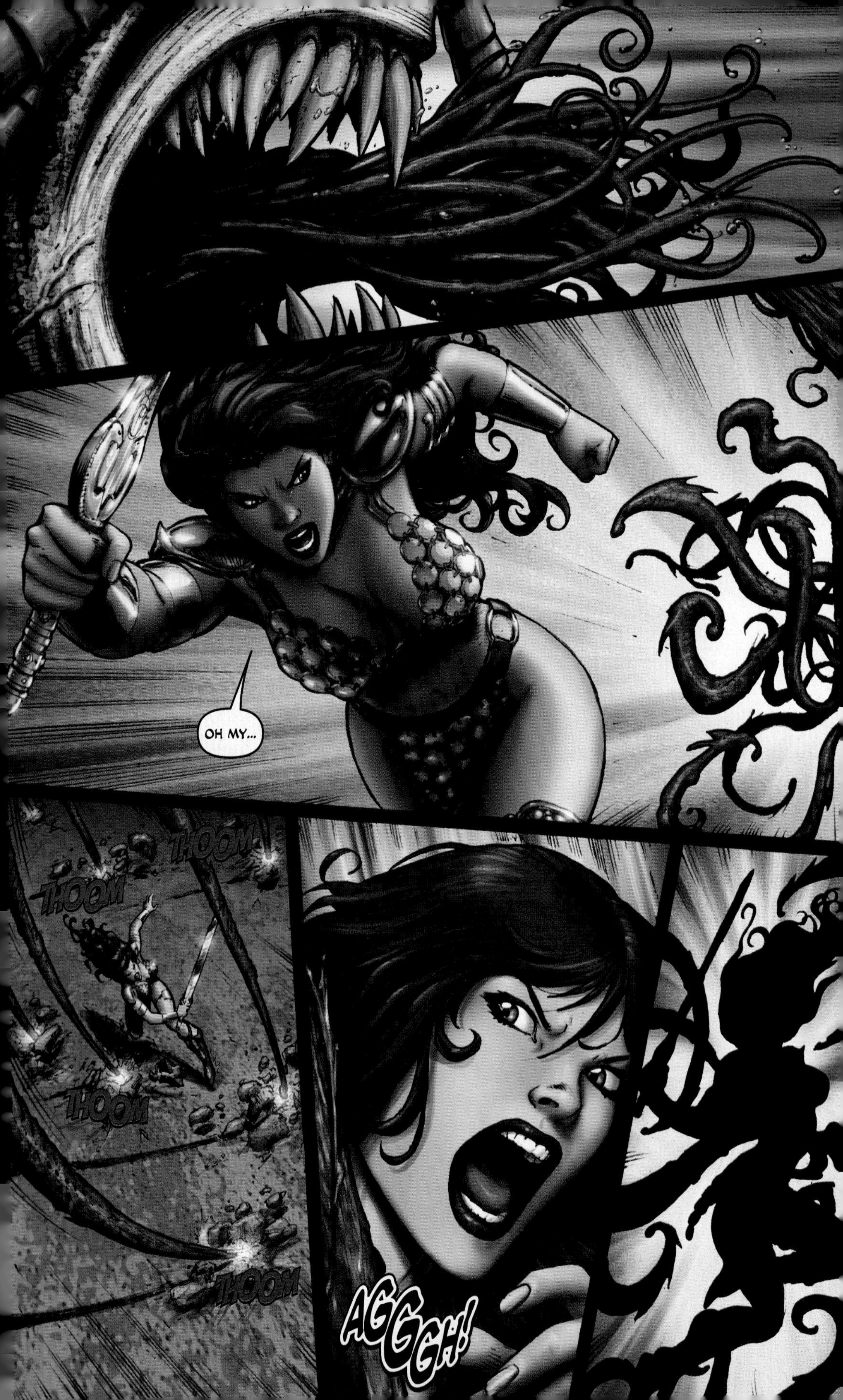
OH MY...
THOOM
THOOM
THOOM
THOOM
AGGGH!

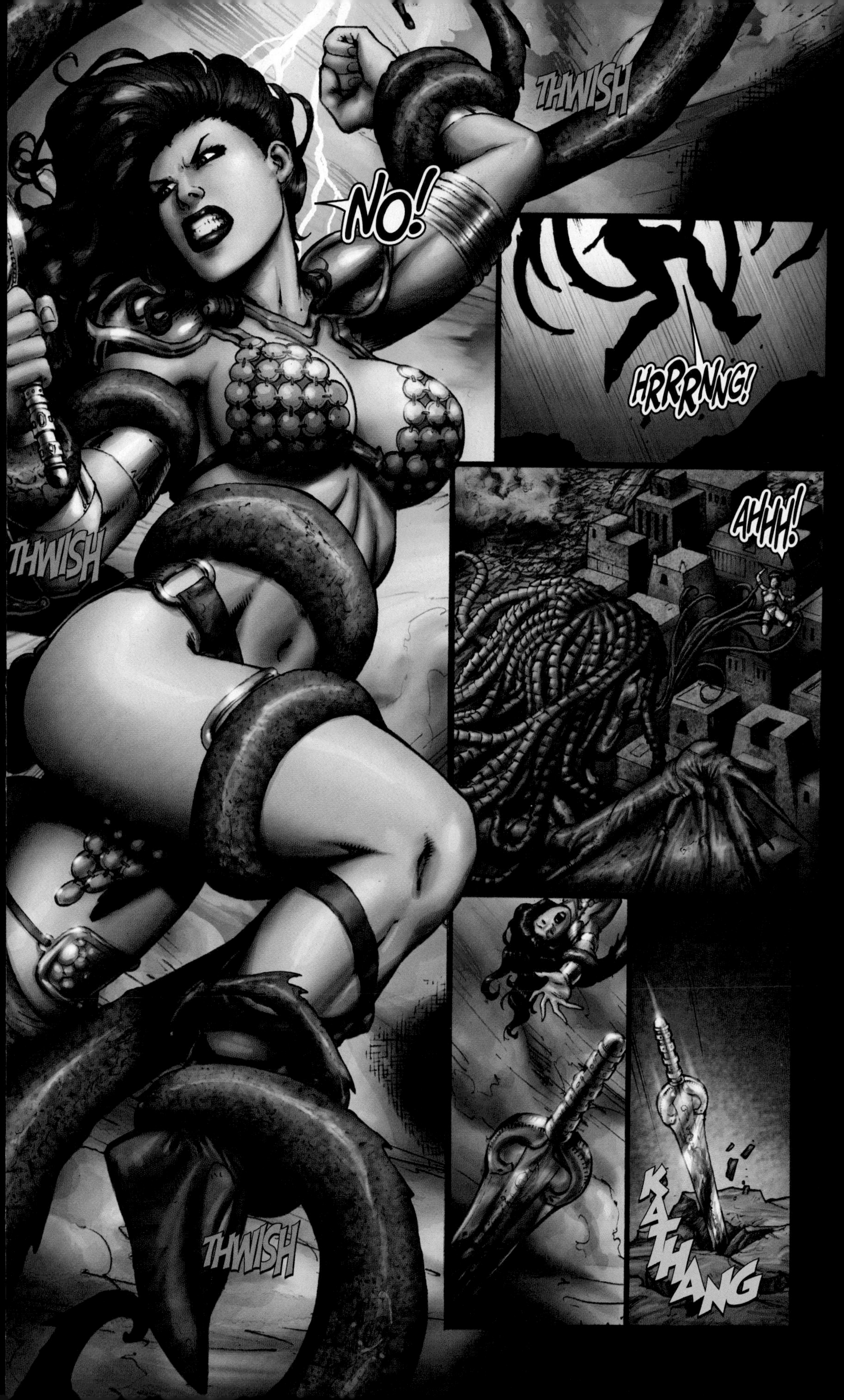
THWISH
NO!
THWISH
HRRRNNG!
AHHH!
THWISH
KATHANG

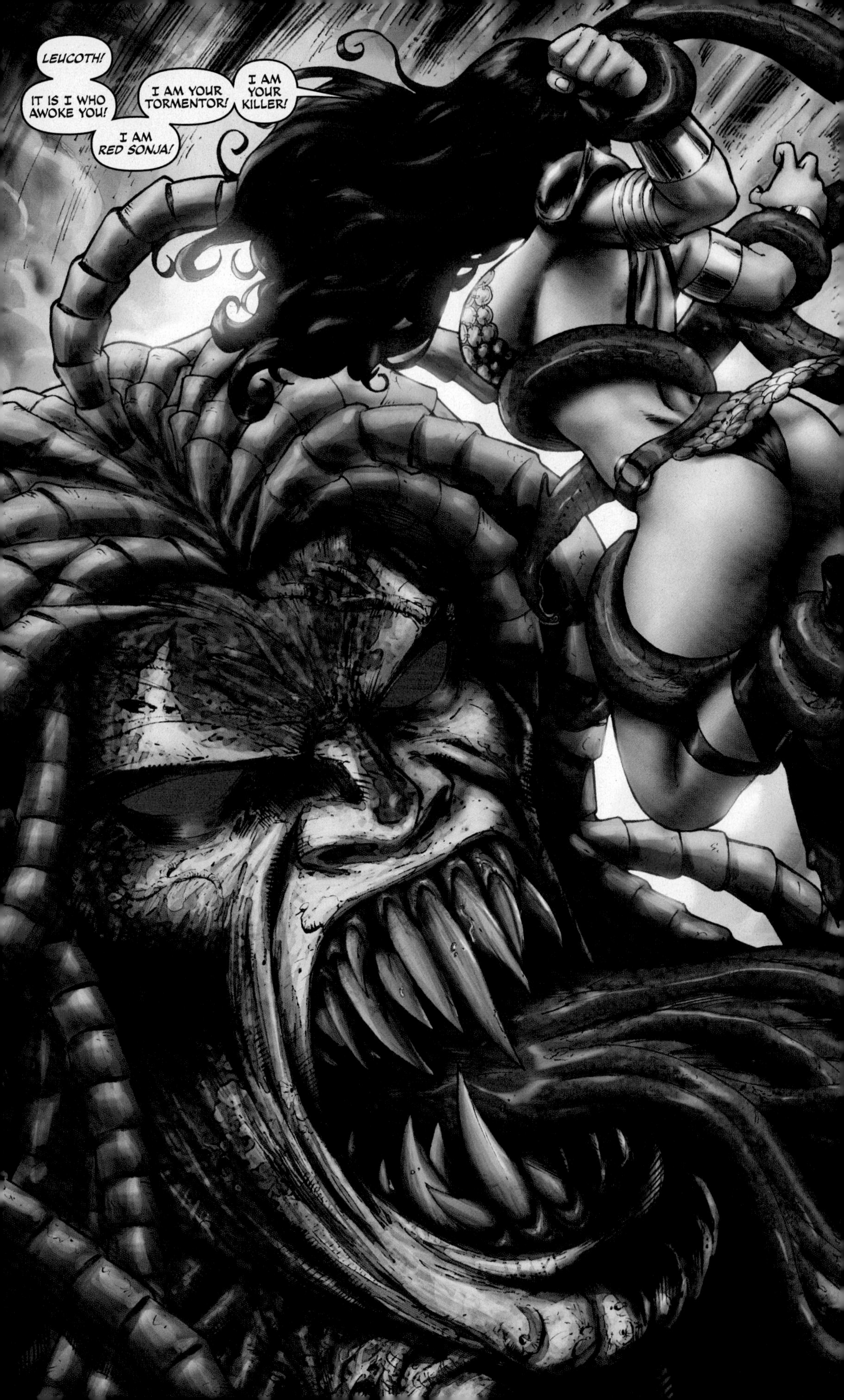
LEUCOTH!
IT IS I WHO AWOKE YOU!
I AM RED SONJA!
I AM YOUR TORMENTOR!
I AM YOUR KILLER!

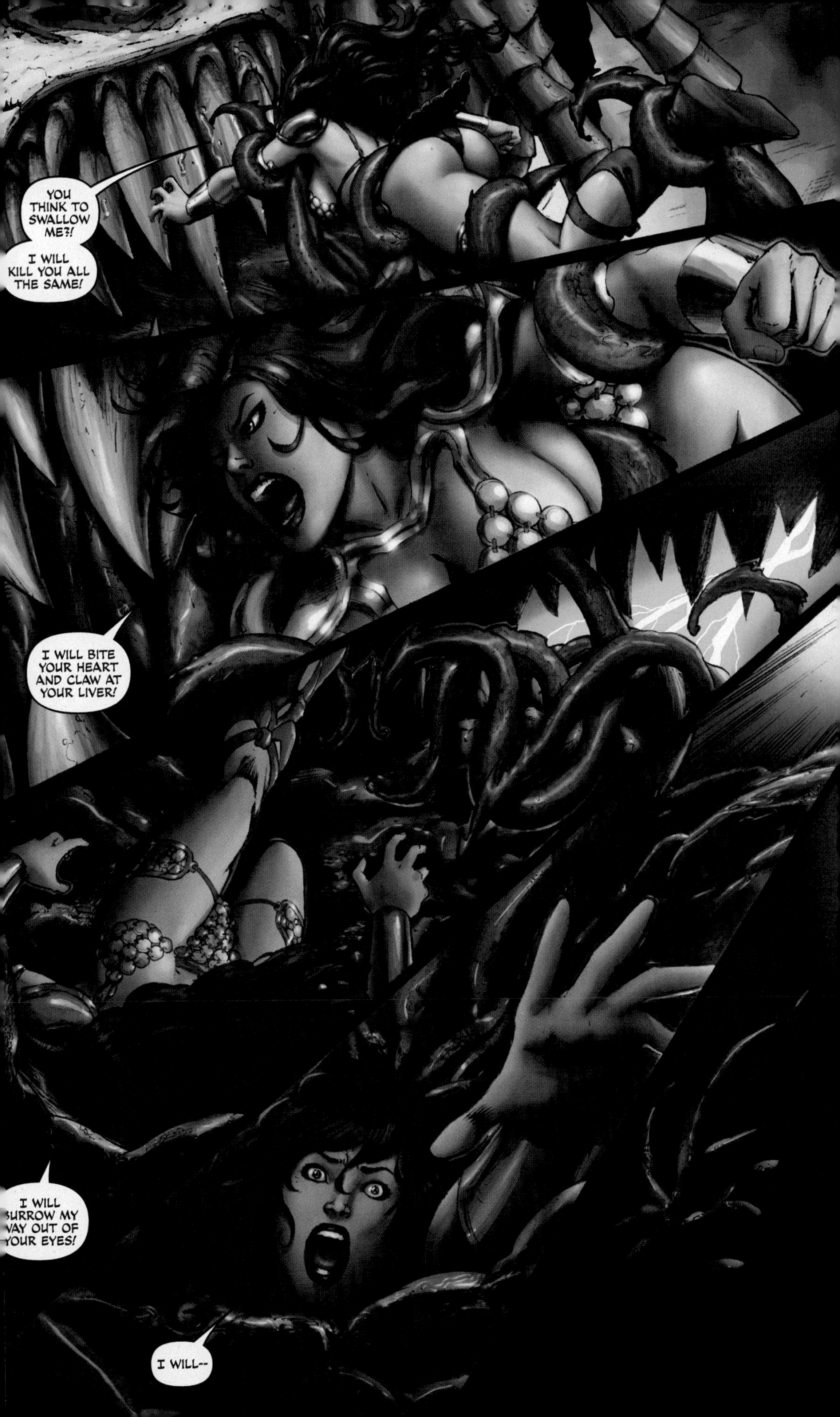
YOU THINK TO SWALLOW ME?!
I WILL KILL YOU ALL THE SAME!
I WILL BITE YOUR HEART AND CLAW AT YOUR LIVER!
I WILL BURROW MY WAY OUT OF YOUR EYES!
I WILL--

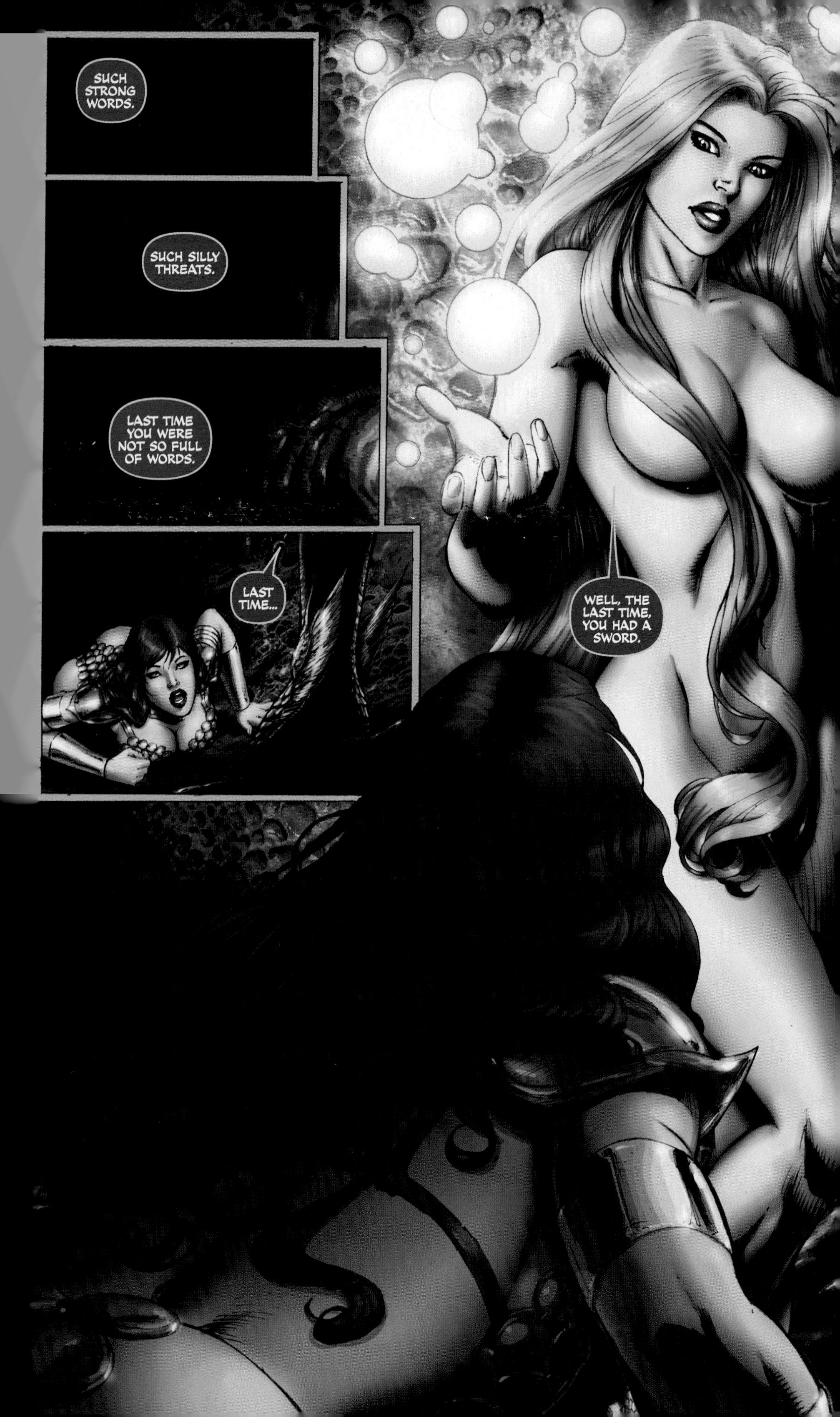
SUCH STRONG WORDS.
SUCH SILLY THREATS.
LAST TIME YOU WERE NOT SO FULL OF WORDS.
LAST TIME...
WELL, THE LAST TIME, YOU HAD A SWORD.

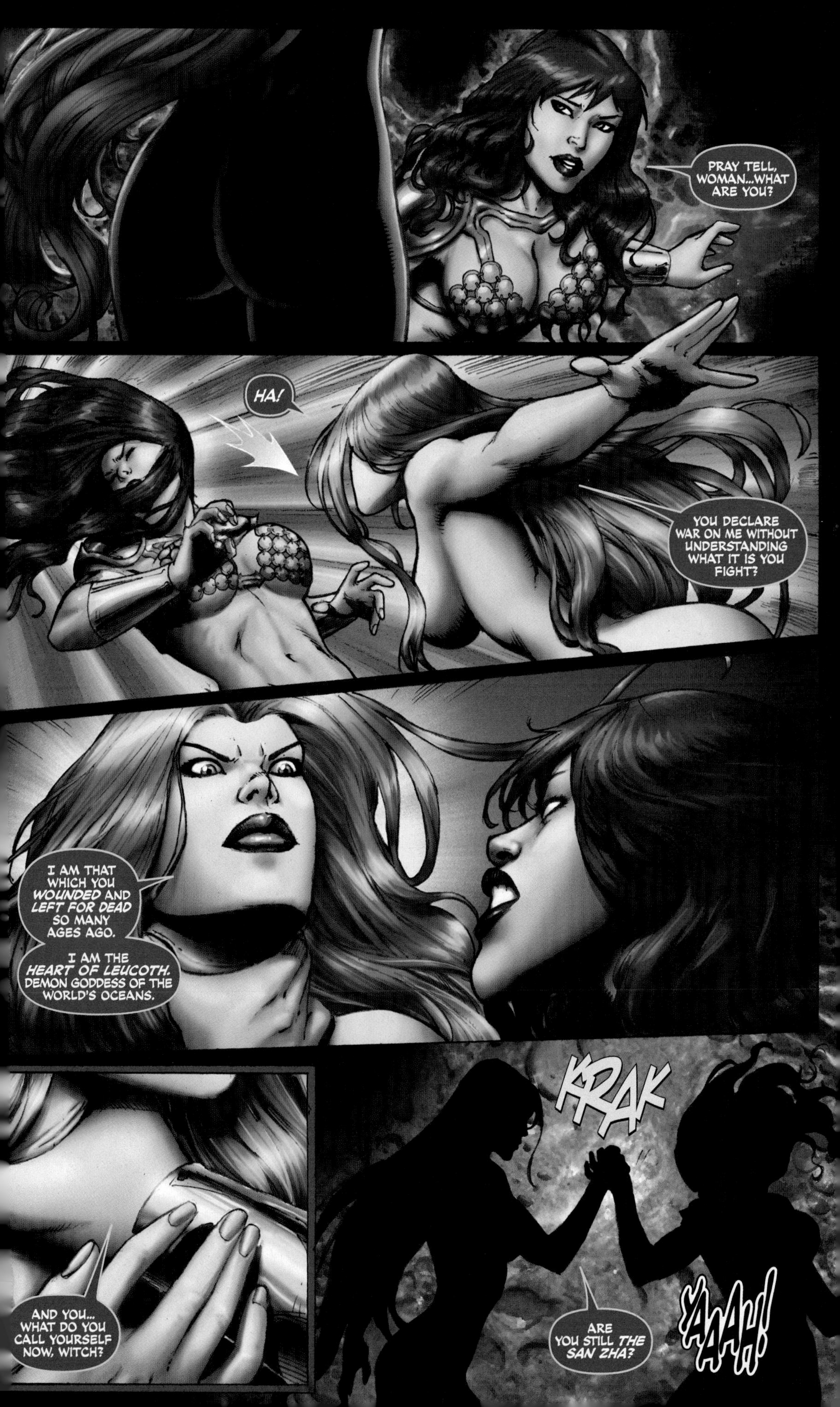
PRAY TELL, WOMAN...WHAT ARE YOU?
HA!
YOU DECLARE WAR ON ME WITHOUT UNDERSTANDING WHAT IT IS YOU FIGHT?
I AM THAT WHICH YOU *WOUNDED* AND *LEFT FOR DEAD* SO MANY AGES AGO.
I AM THE *HEART OF LEUCOTH*. DEMON GODDESS OF THE WORLD'S OCEANS.
KRAK
AND YOU... WHAT DO YOU CALL YOURSELF NOW, WITCH?
ARE YOU STILL *THE SAN ZHA*?
YAAAH!

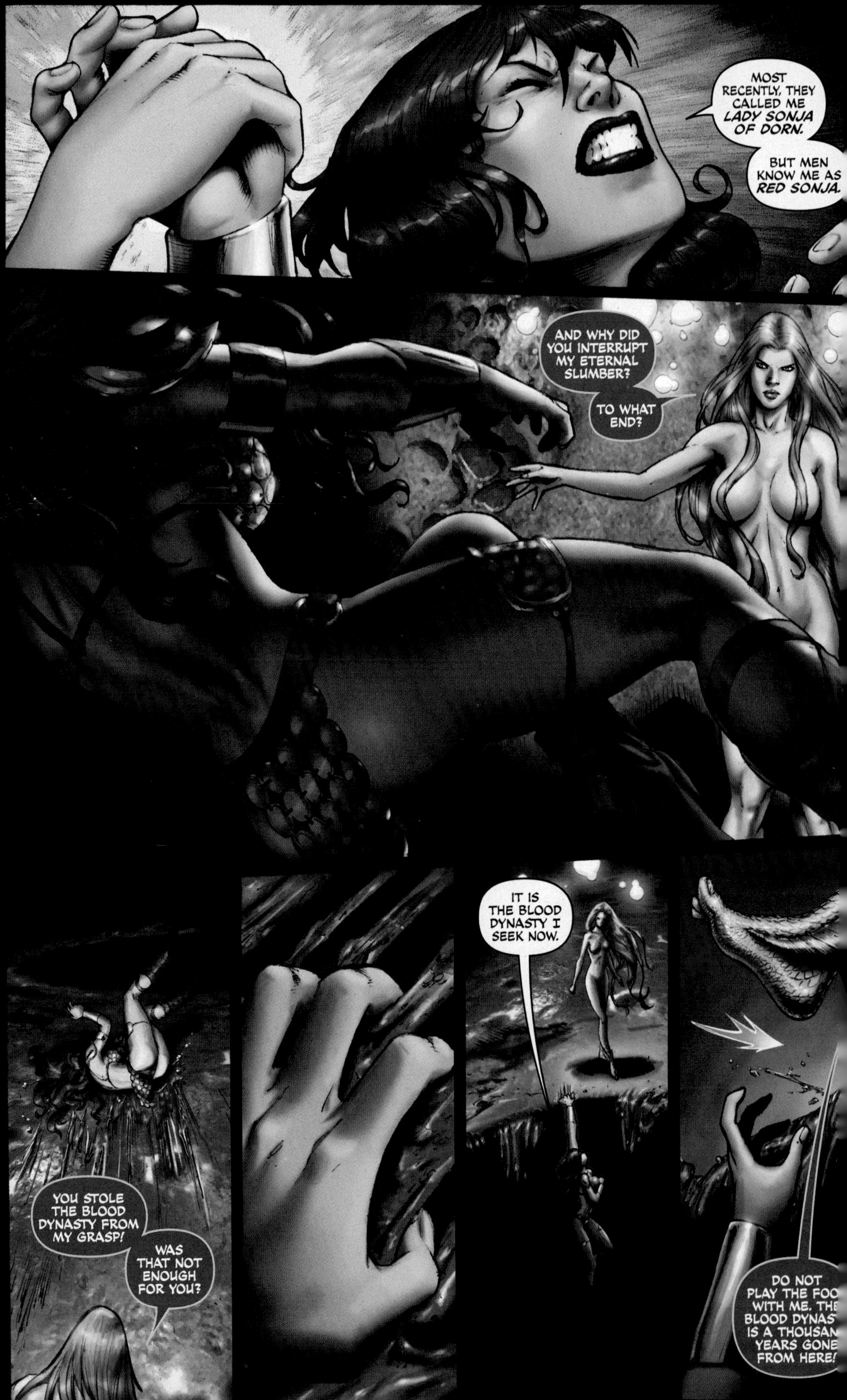
MOST RECENTLY, THEY CALLED ME LADY SONJA OF DORN.
BUT MEN KNOW ME AS RED SONJA.
AND WHY DID YOU INTERRUPT MY ETERNAL SLUMBER?
TO WHAT END?
YOU STOLE THE BLOOD DYNASTY FROM MY GRASP!
WAS THAT NOT ENOUGH FOR YOU?
IT IS THE BLOOD DYNASTY I SEEK NOW.
DO NOT PLAY THE FOO WITH ME. THE BLOOD DYNAS IS A THOUSAN YEARS GONE FROM HERE!

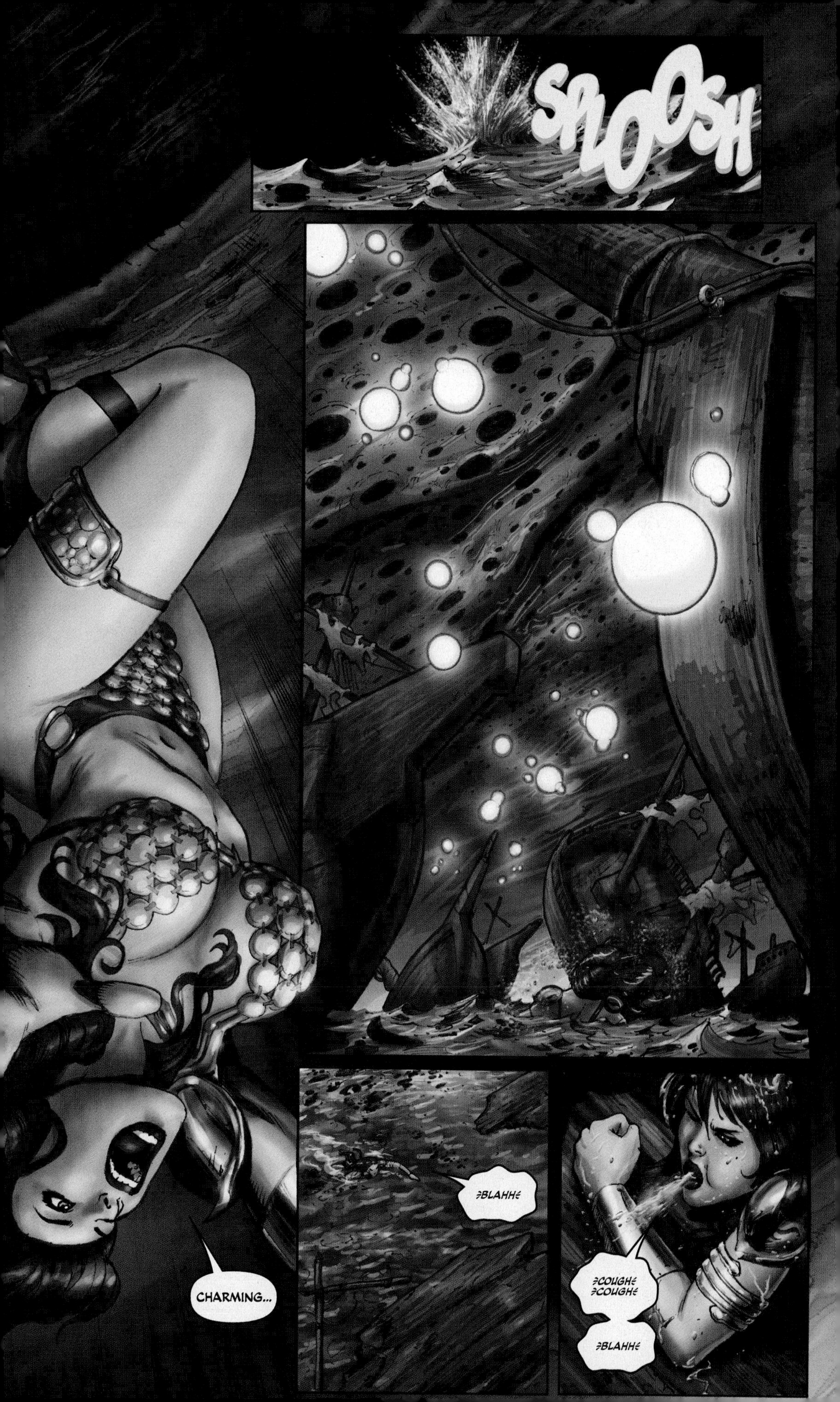
SPLOOSH
CHARMING...
BLAHH
COUGH COUGH
BLAHH

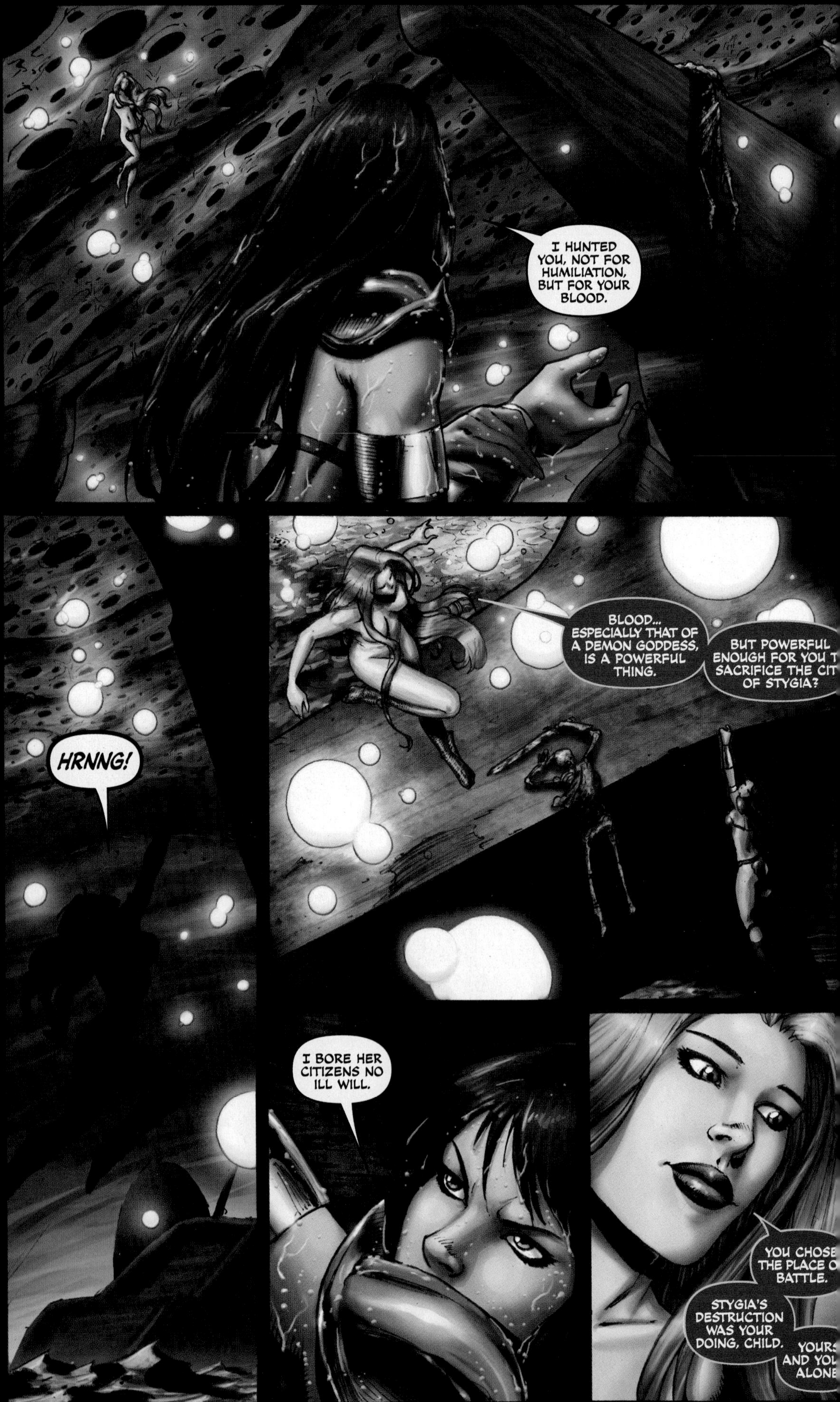

I HUNTED YOU, NOT FOR HUMILIATION, BUT FOR YOUR BLOOD.
HRNNG!
BLOOD... ESPECIALLY THAT OF A DEMON GODDESS, IS A POWERFUL THING.
BUT POWERFUL ENOUGH FOR YOU T SACRIFICE THE CIT OF STYGIA?
I BORE HER CITIZENS NO ILL WILL.
YOU CHOSE THE PLACE O BATTLE.
STYGIA'S DESTRUCTION WAS YOUR DOING, CHILD.
YOURS AND YOU ALONE

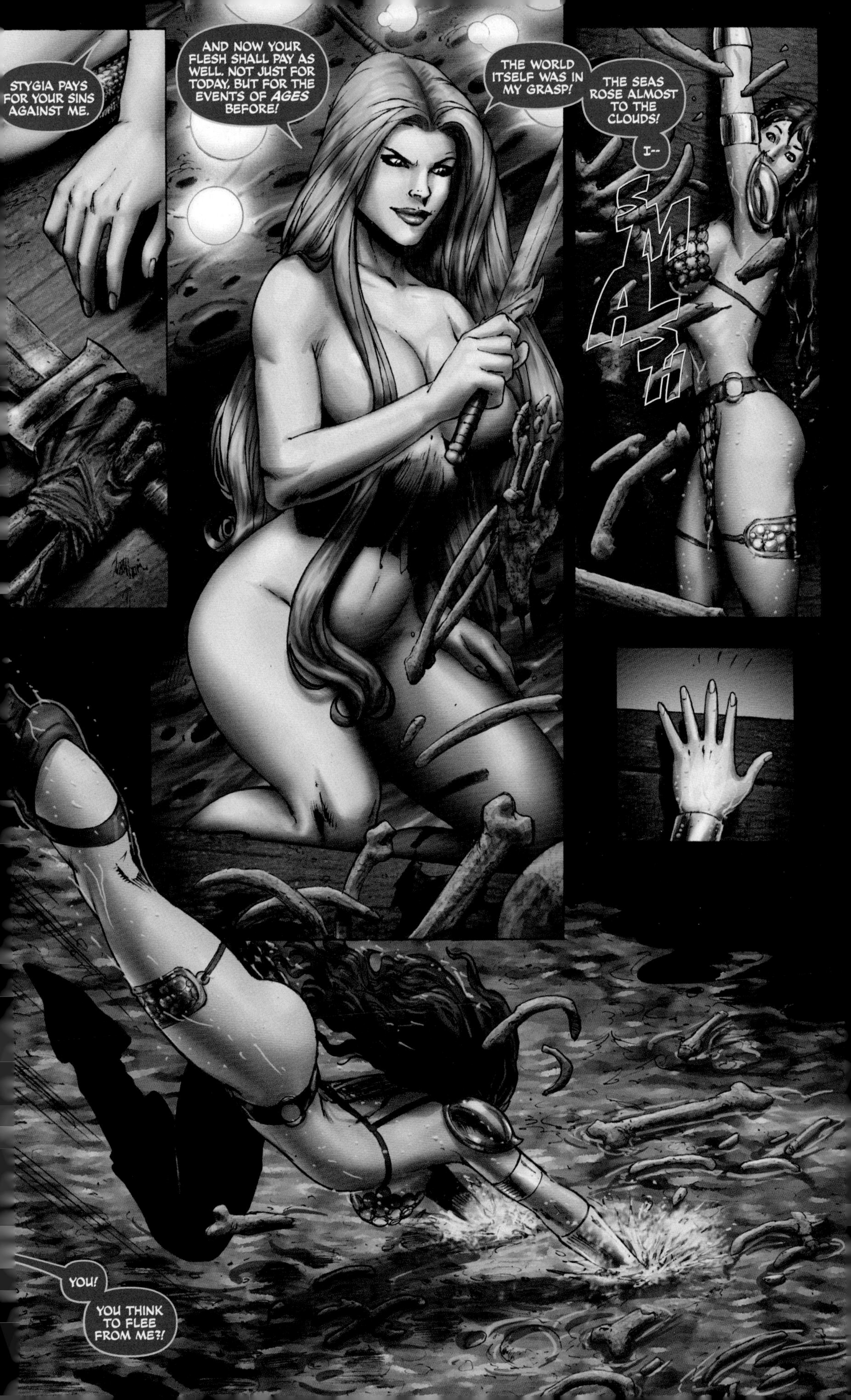
STYGIA PAYS FOR YOUR SINS AGAINST ME.
AND NOW YOUR FLESH SHALL PAY AS WELL. NOT JUST FOR TODAY, BUT FOR THE EVENTS OF AGES BEFORE!
THE WORLD ITSELF WAS IN MY GRASP!
THE SEAS ROSE ALMOST TO THE CLOUDS!
I--
SMASH
YOU!
YOU THINK TO FLEE FROM ME?!

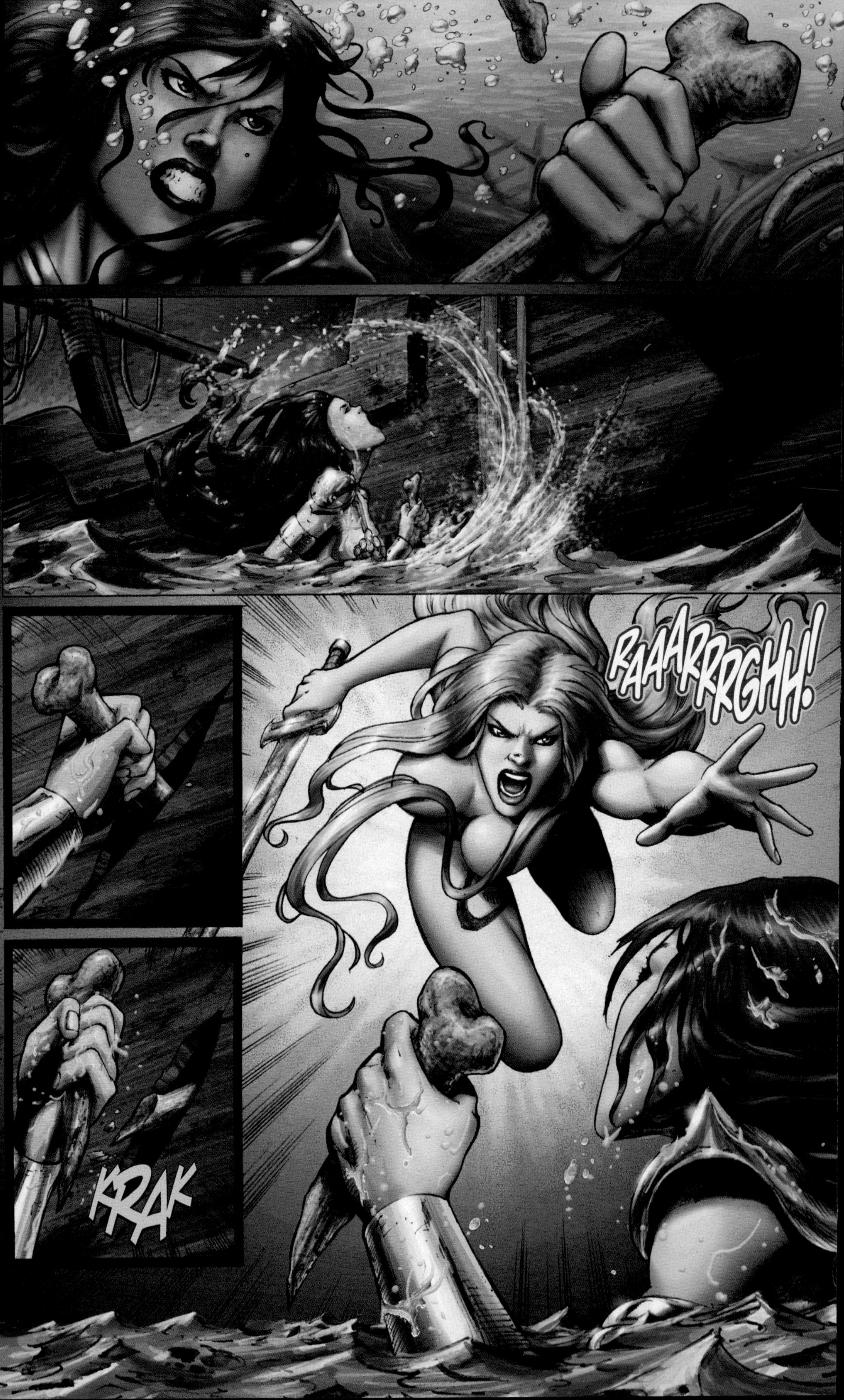
KRAK
RAAARRRGHH!

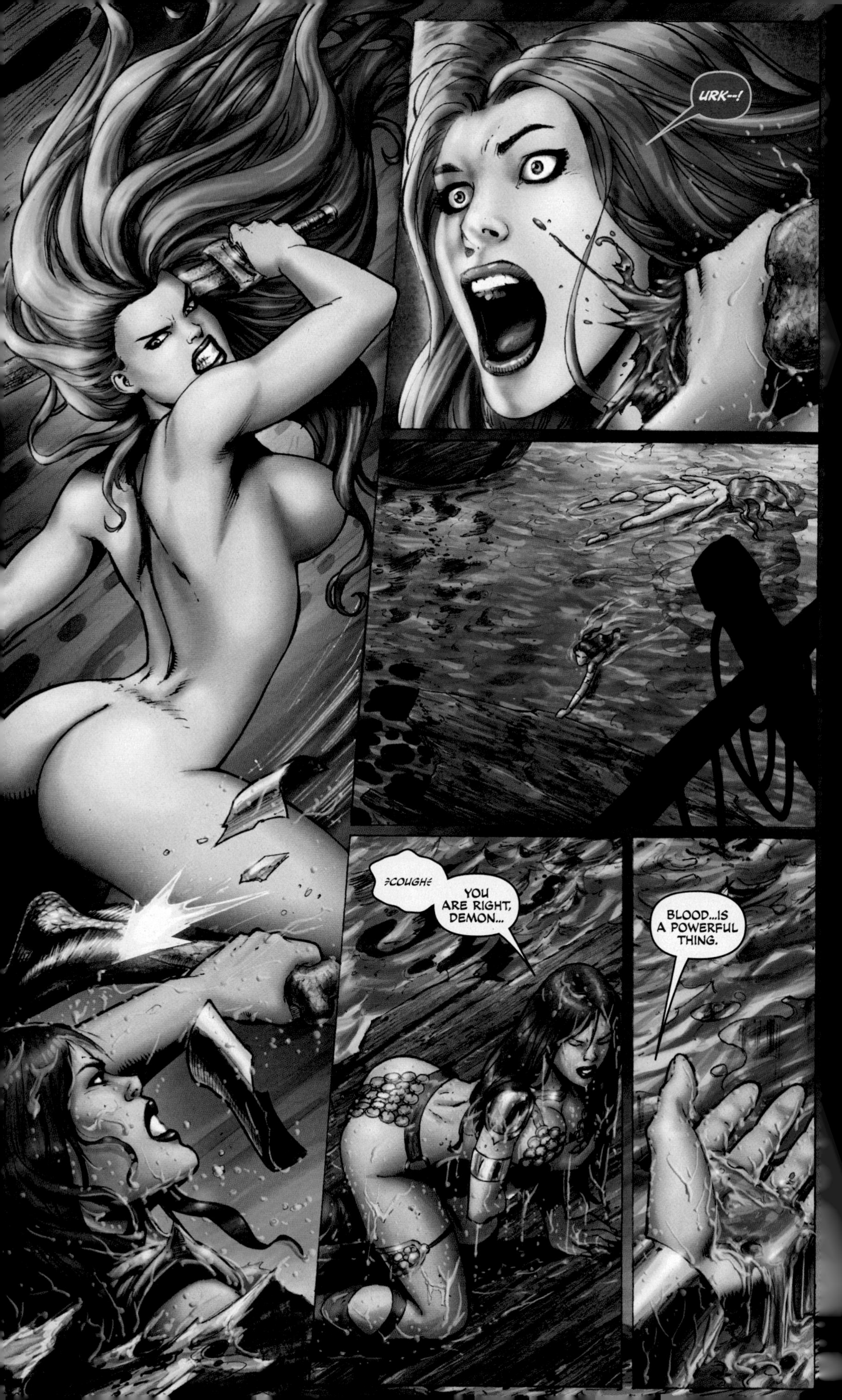
URK--!
≥COUGH≤
YOU ARE RIGHT, DEMON...
BLOOD...IS A POWERFUL THING.

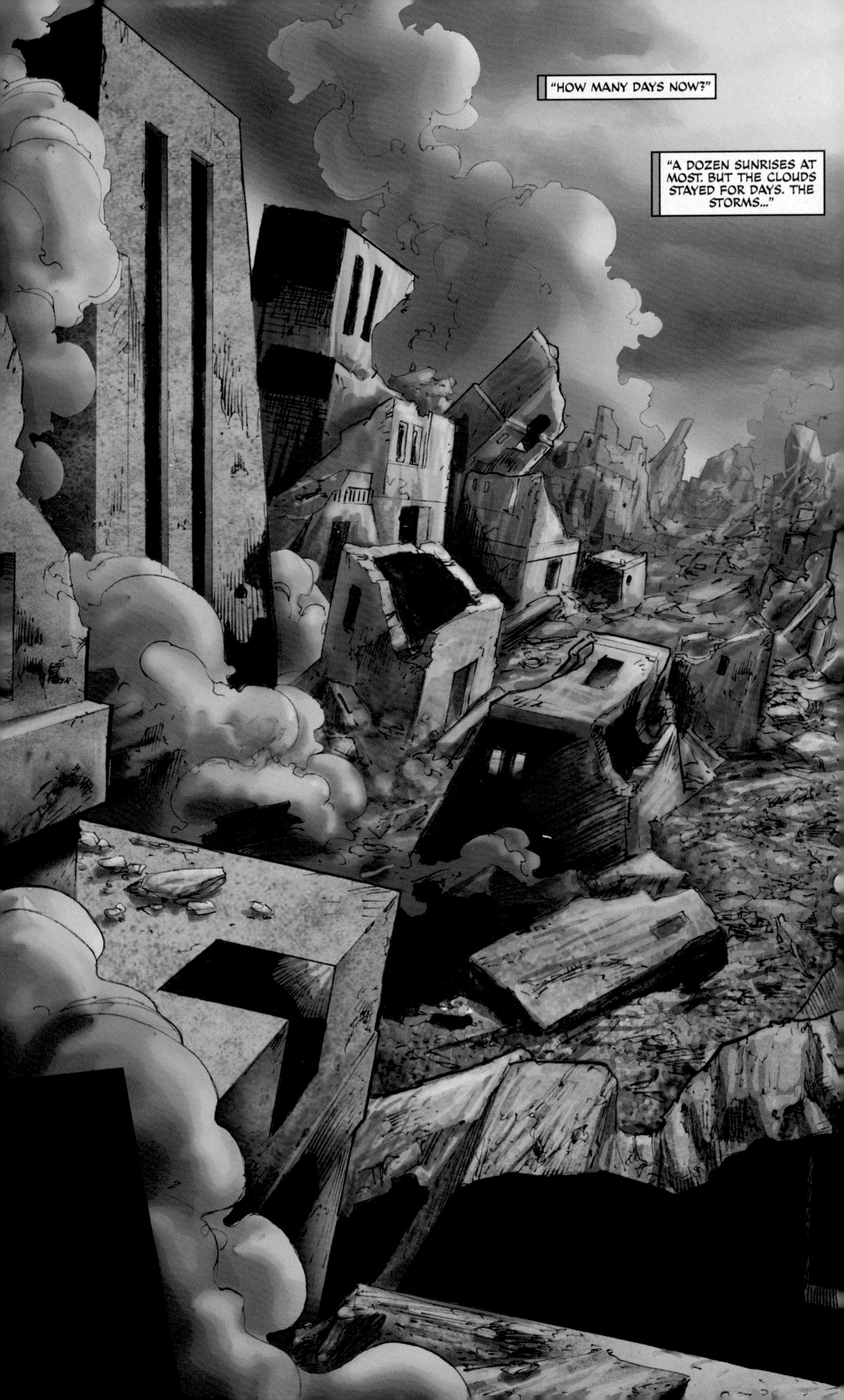
"HOW MANY DAYS NOW?"
"A DOZEN SUNRISES AT MOST. BUT THE CLOUDS STAYED FOR DAYS. THE STORMS..."

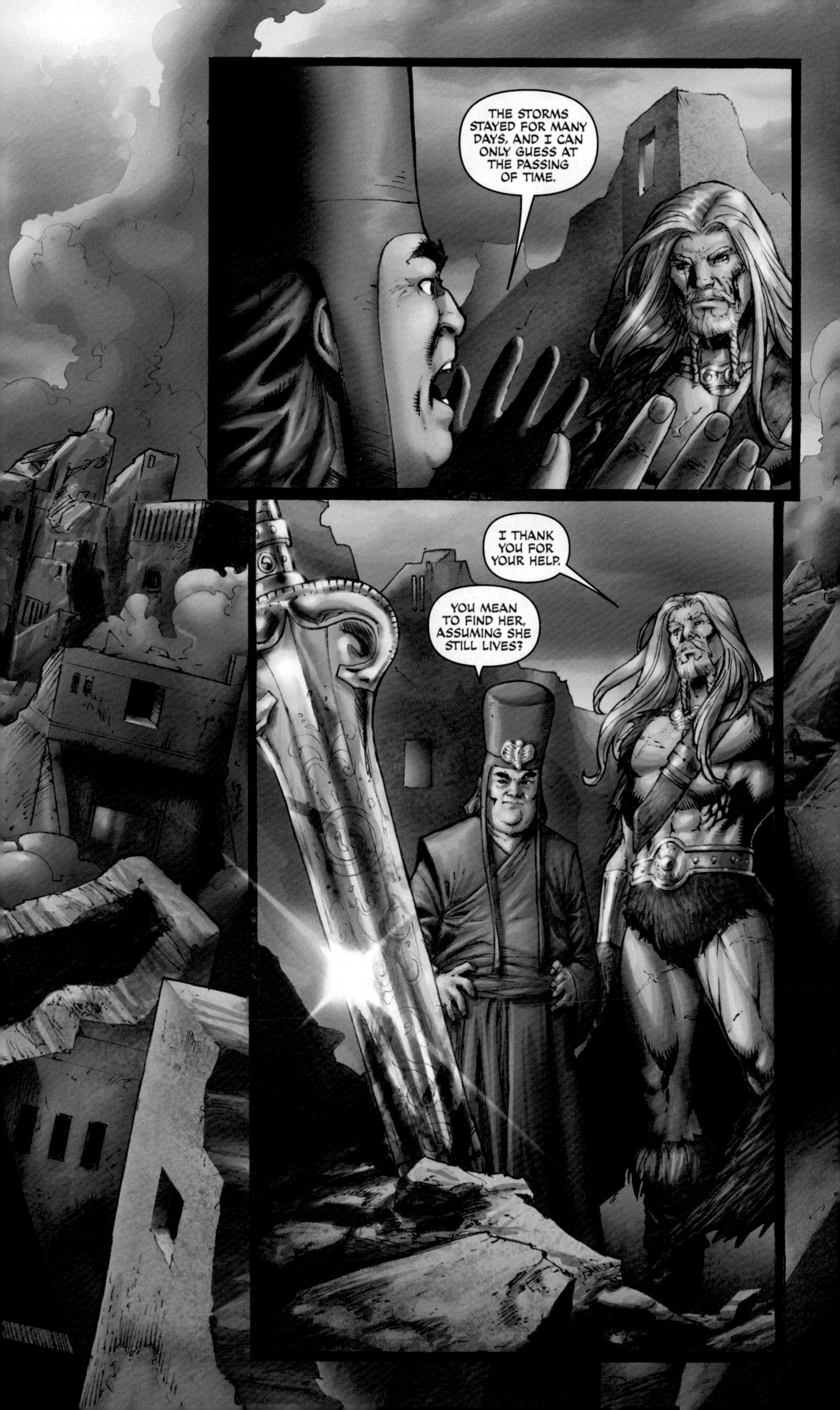

THE STORMS STAYED FOR MANY DAYS, AND I CAN ONLY GUESS AT THE PASSING OF TIME.
I THANK YOU FOR YOUR HELP.
YOU MEAN TO FIND HER, ASSUMING SHE STILL LIVES?

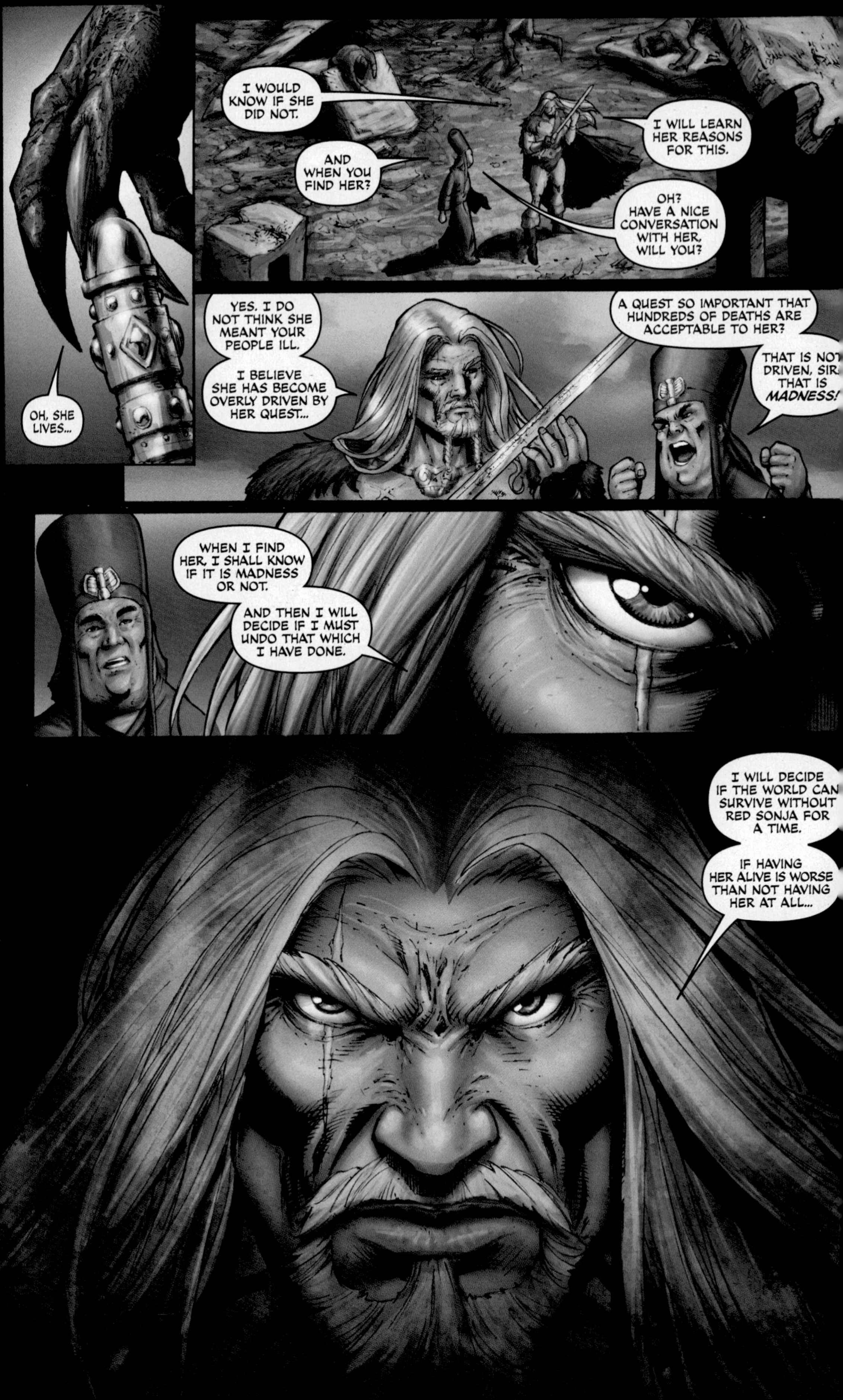
I WOULD KNOW IF SHE DID NOT.
I WILL LEARN HER REASONS FOR THIS.
AND WHEN YOU FIND HER?
OH? HAVE A NICE CONVERSATION WITH HER, WILL YOU?
OH, SHE LIVES...
YES. I DO NOT THINK SHE MEANT YOUR PEOPLE ILL.
I BELIEVE SHE HAS BECOME OVERLY DRIVEN BY HER QUEST...
A QUEST SO IMPORTANT THAT HUNDREDS OF DEATHS ARE ACCEPTABLE TO HER?
THAT IS NOT DRIVEN, SIR. THAT IS MADNESS!
WHEN I FIND HER, I SHALL KNOW IF IT IS MADNESS OR NOT.
AND THEN I WILL DECIDE IF I MUST UNDO THAT WHICH I HAVE DONE.
I WILL DECIDE IF THE WORLD CAN SURVIVE WITHOUT RED SONJA FOR A TIME.
IF HAVING HER ALIVE IS WORSE THAN NOT HAVING HER AT ALL...

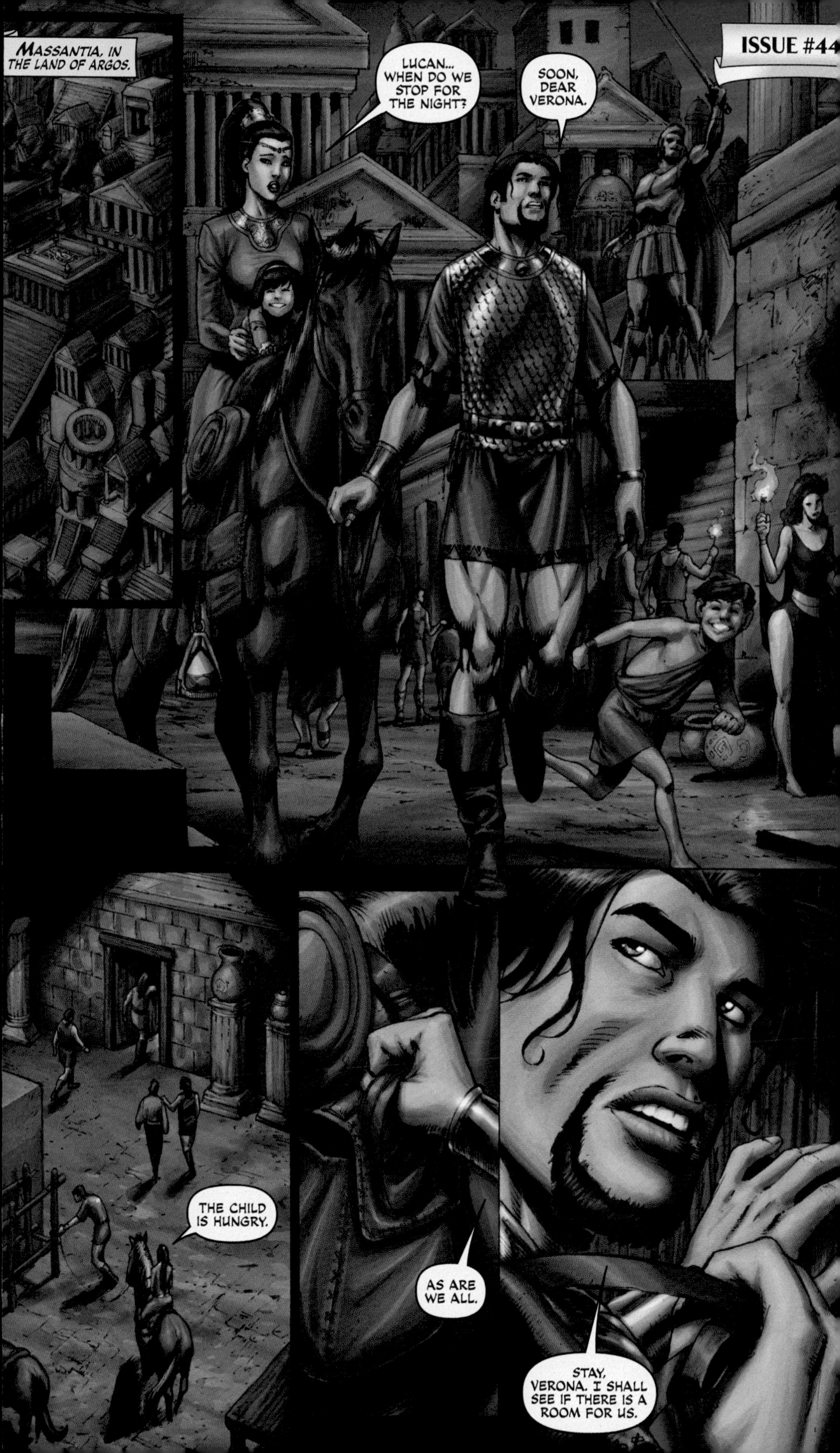
ISSUE #44
MASSANTIA, IN THE LAND OF ARGOS.
LUCAN... WHEN DO WE STOP FOR THE NIGHT?
SOON, DEAR VERONA.
THE CHILD IS HUNGRY.
AS ARE WE ALL.
STAY, VERONA. I SHALL SEE IF THERE IS A ROOM FOR US.

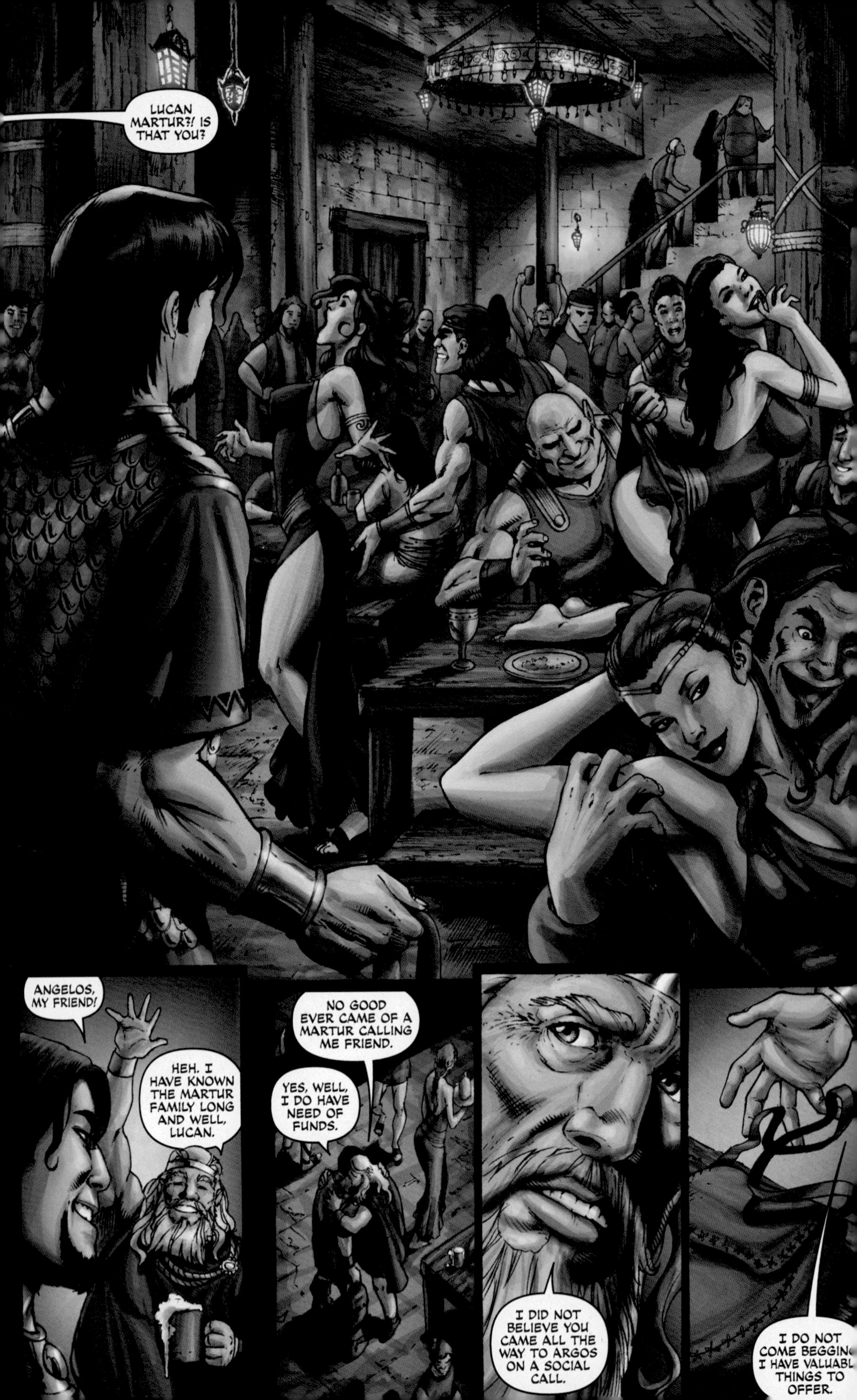
LUCAN MARTUR?! IS THAT YOU?
ANGELOS, MY FRIEND!
HEH. I HAVE KNOWN THE MARTUR FAMILY LONG AND WELL, LUCAN.
NO GOOD EVER CAME OF A MARTUR CALLING ME FRIEND.
YES, WELL, I DO HAVE NEED OF FUNDS.
I DID NOT BELIEVE YOU CAME ALL THE WAY TO ARGOS ON A SOCIAL CALL.
I DO NOT COME BEGGING I HAVE VALUABL THINGS TO OFFER.

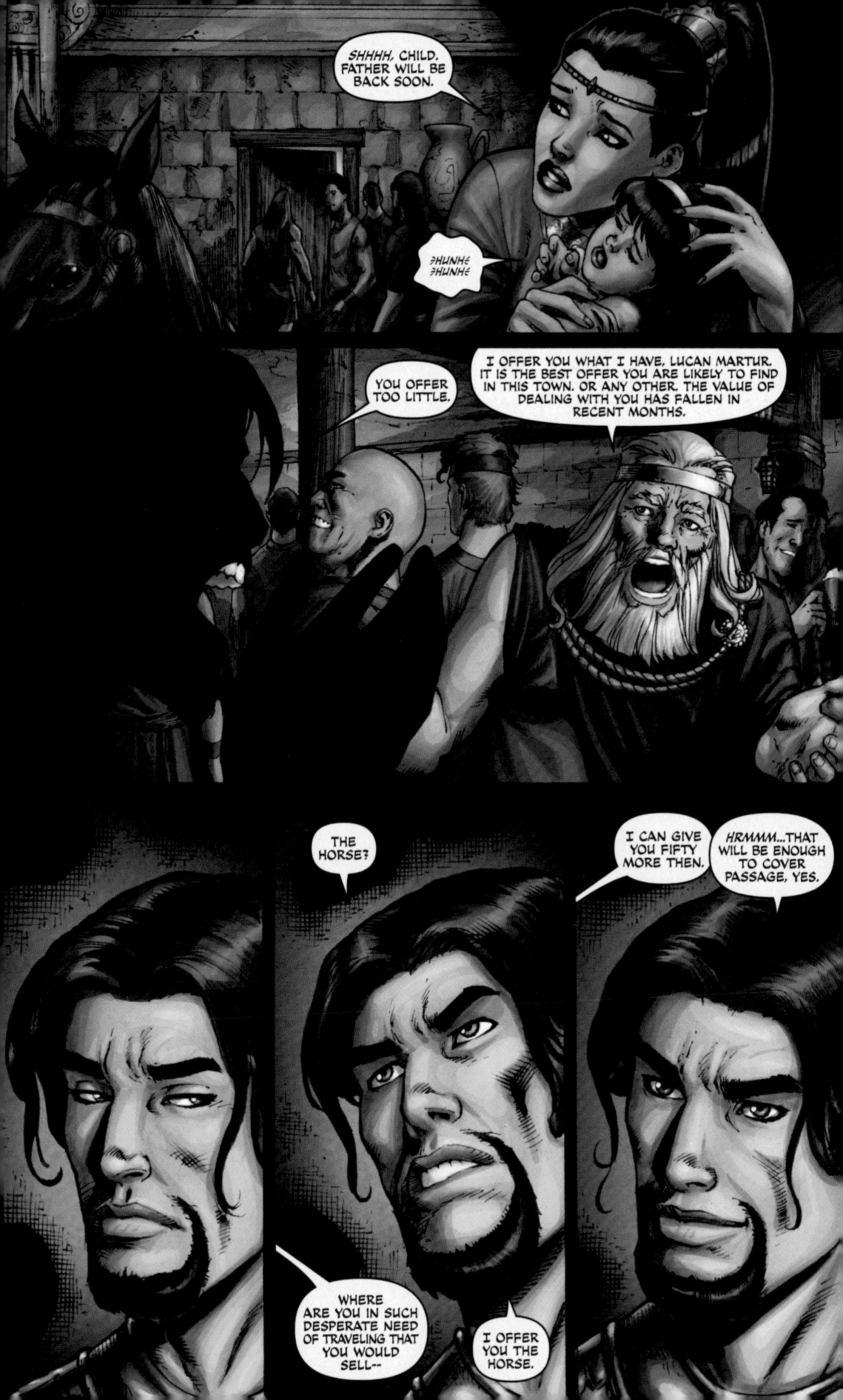
SHHHH, CHILD. FATHER WILL BE BACK SOON.
HUNH HUNH
YOU OFFER TOO LITTLE.
I OFFER YOU WHAT I HAVE, LUCAN MARTUR. IT IS THE BEST OFFER YOU ARE LIKELY TO FIND IN THIS TOWN. OR ANY OTHER. THE VALUE OF DEALING WITH YOU HAS FALLEN IN RECENT MONTHS.
WHERE ARE YOU IN SUCH DESPERATE NEED OF TRAVELING THAT YOU WOULD SELL--
I OFFER YOU THE HORSE.
THE HORSE?
I CAN GIVE YOU FIFTY MORE THEN.
HRMMM...THAT WILL BE ENOUGH TO COVER PASSAGE, YES.

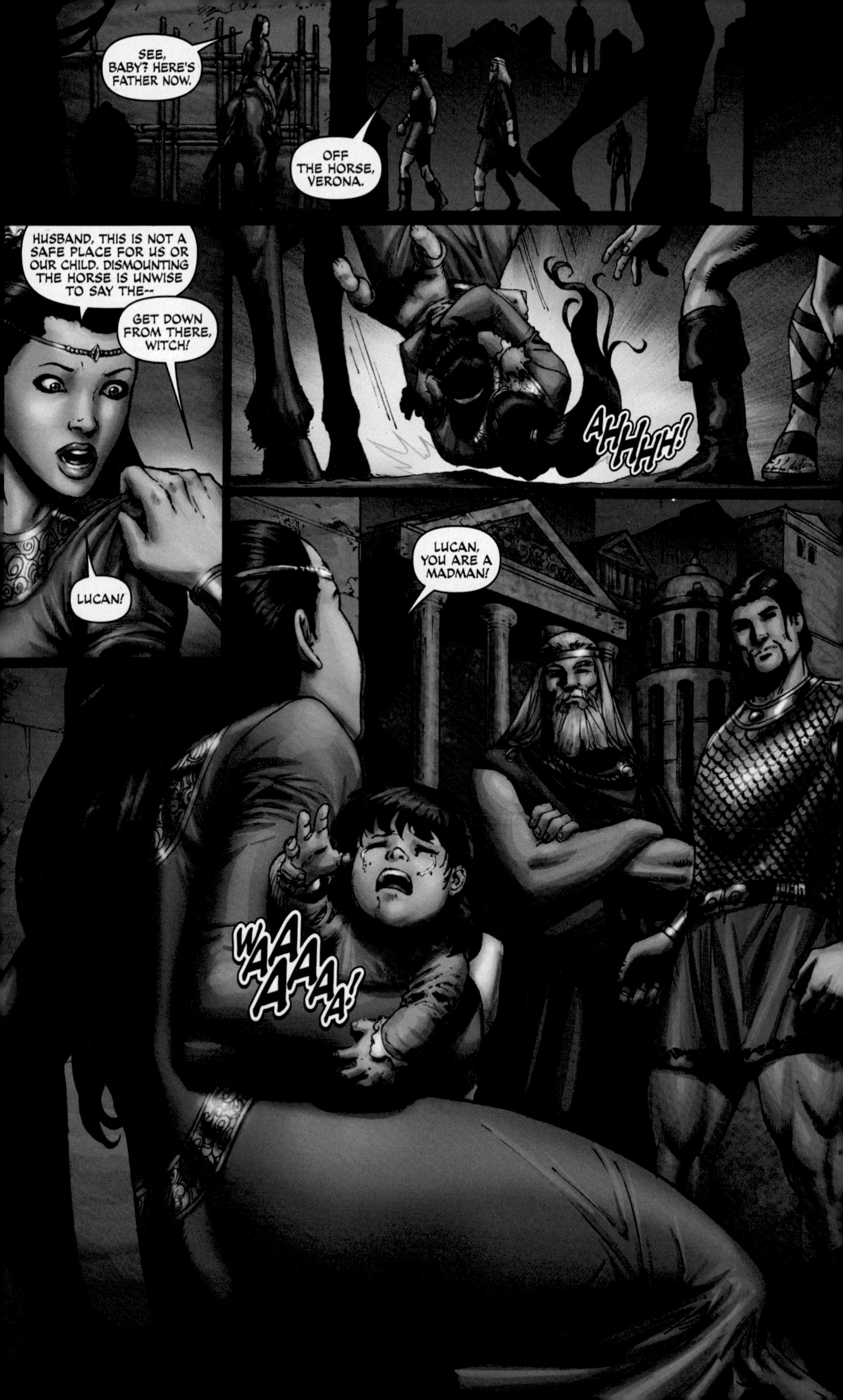
SEE, BABY? HERE'S FATHER NOW.
OFF THE HORSE, VERONA.
HUSBAND, THIS IS NOT A SAFE PLACE FOR US OR OUR CHILD. DISMOUNTING THE HORSE IS UNWISE TO SAY THE--
GET DOWN FROM THERE, WITCH!
AHHHH!
LUCAN!
LUCAN, YOU ARE A MADMAN!
WAAAAAA!

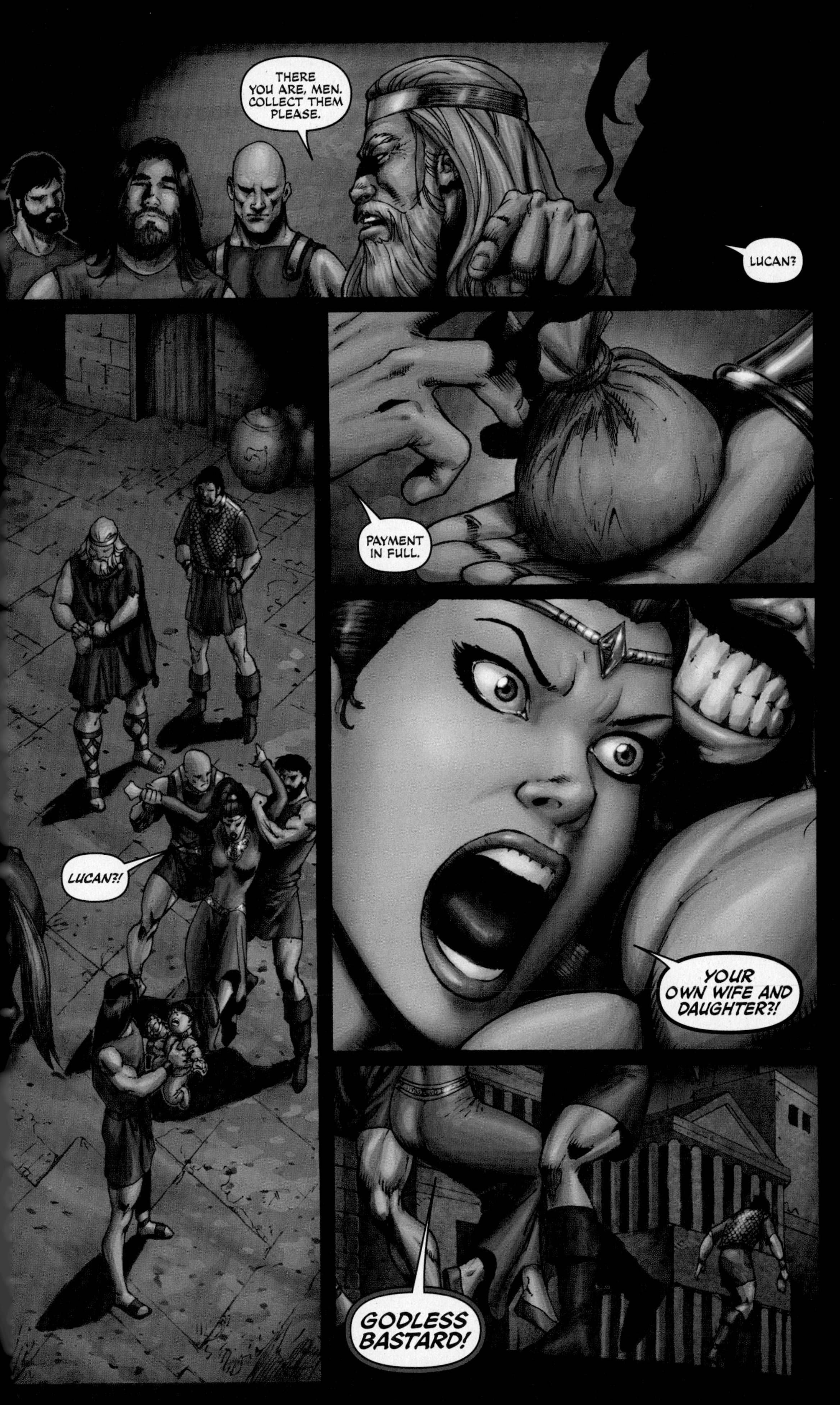
THERE YOU ARE, MEN. COLLECT THEM PLEASE.
LUCAN?
PAYMENT IN FULL.
LUCAN?!
YOUR OWN WIFE AND DAUGHTER?!
GODLESS BASTARD!

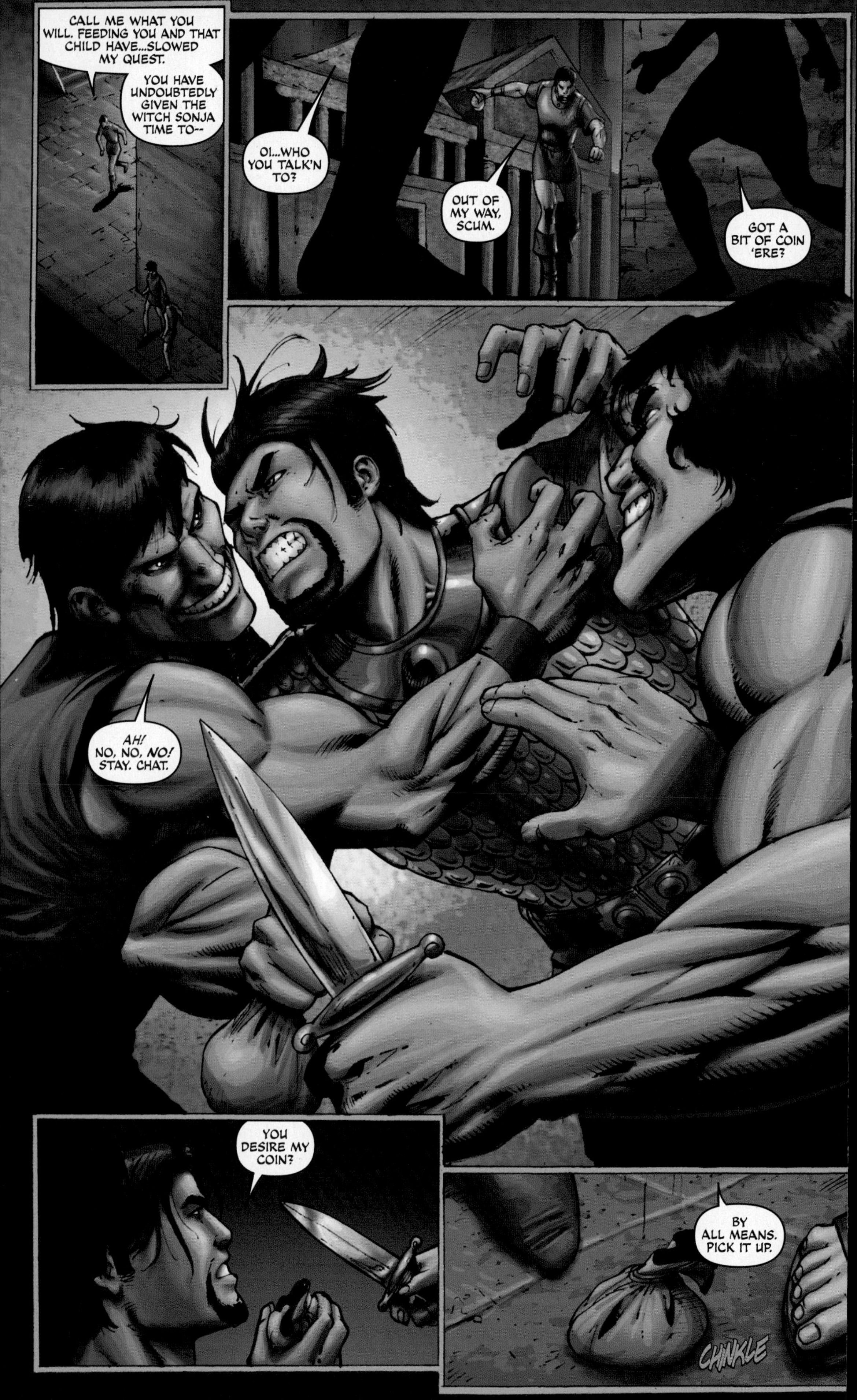
CALL ME WHAT YOU WILL. FEEDING YOU AND THAT CHILD HAVE...SLOWED MY QUEST.
YOU HAVE UNDOUBTEDLY GIVEN THE WITCH SONJA TIME TO--
OI...WHO YOU TALK'N TO?
OUT OF MY WAY, SCUM.
GOT A BIT OF COIN 'ERE?
AH! NO, NO, NO! STAY. CHAT.
YOU DESIRE MY COIN?
BY ALL MEANS. PICK IT UP.
CHINKLE

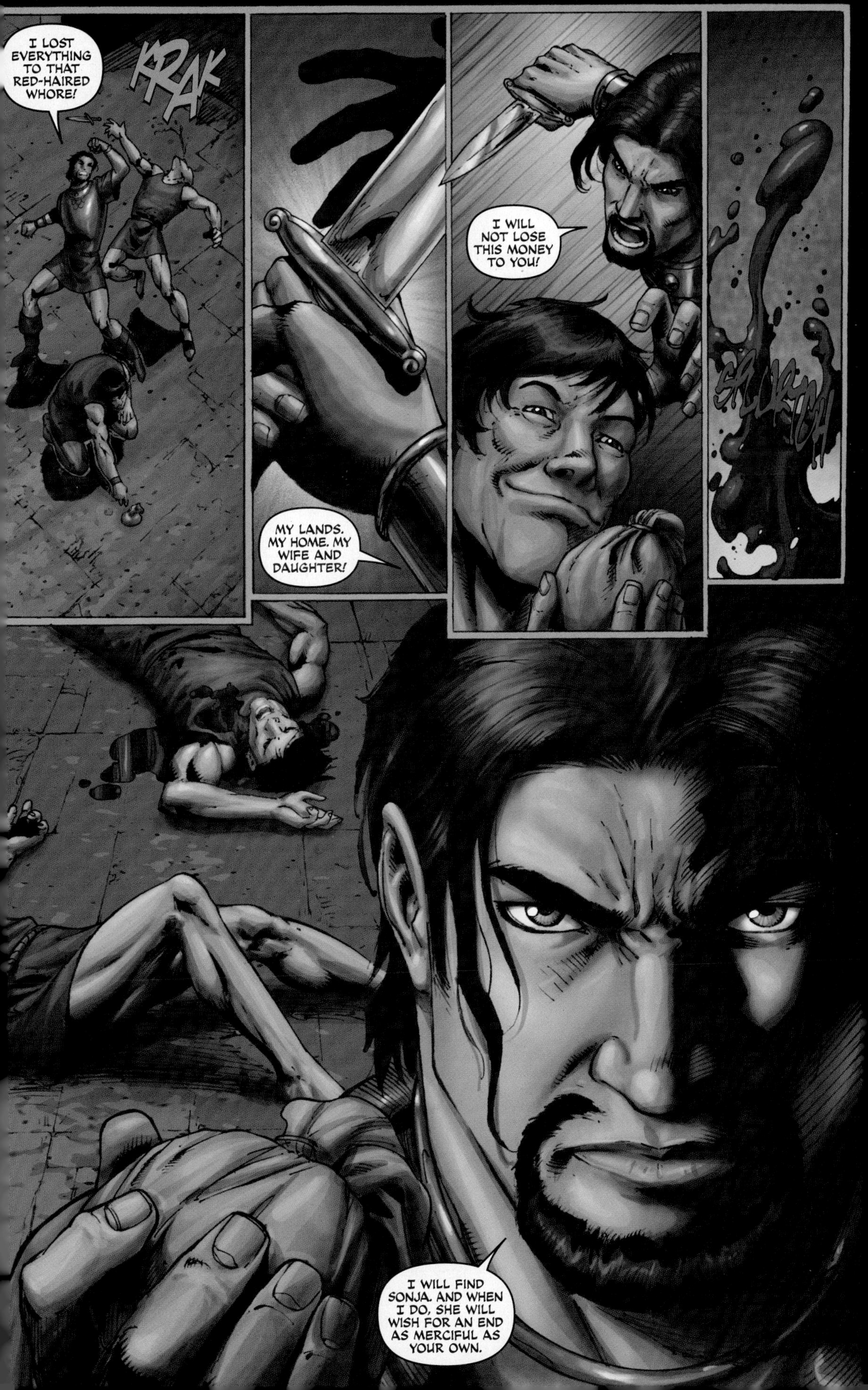
I LOST EVERYTHING TO THAT RED-HAIRED WHORE!
KRAK
MY LANDS. MY HOME. MY WIFE AND DAUGHTER!
I WILL NOT LOSE THIS MONEY TO YOU!
I WILL FIND SONJA. AND WHEN I DO, SHE WILL WISH FOR AN END AS MERCIFUL AS YOUR OWN.

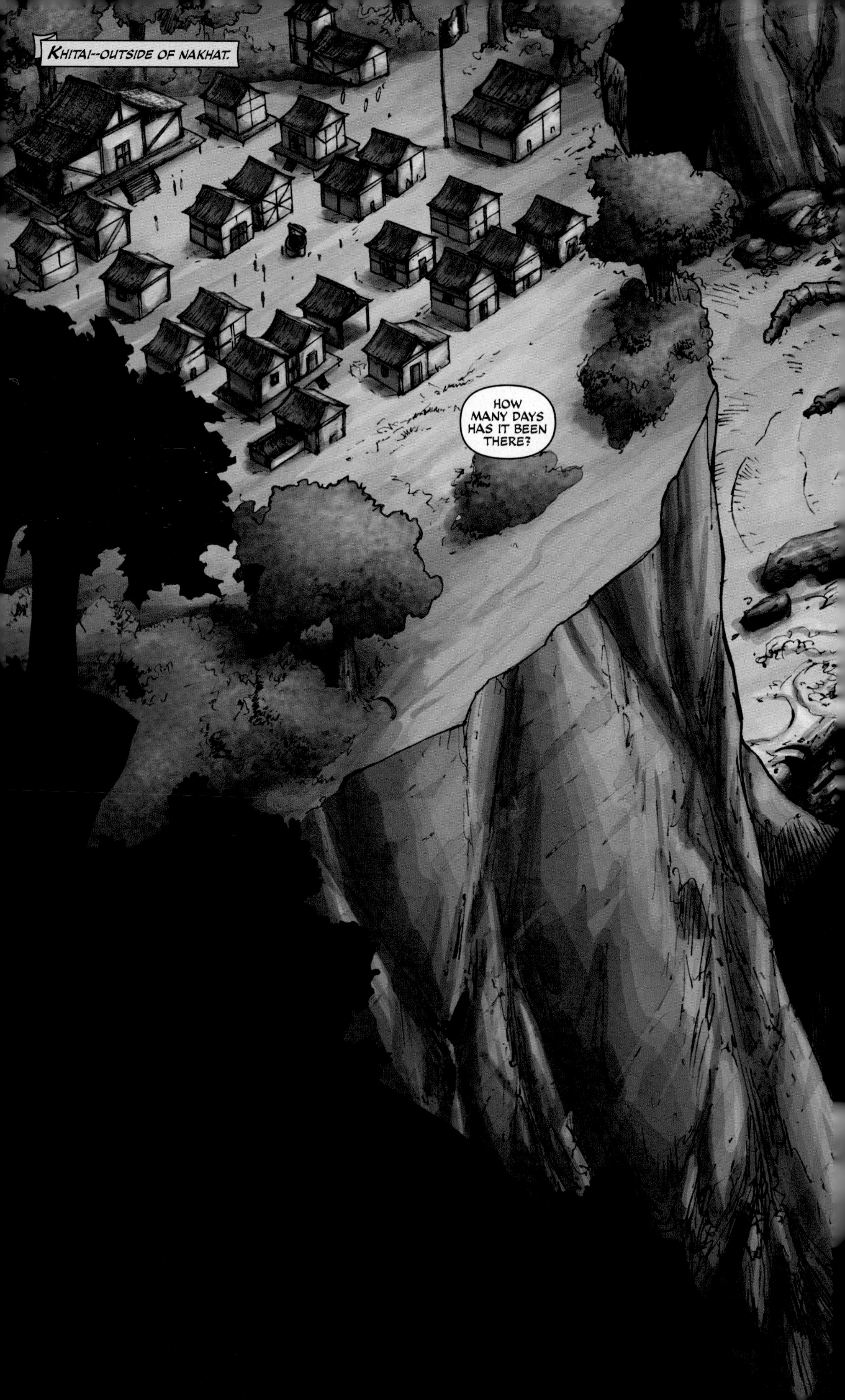
KHITAI--OUTSIDE OF NAKHAT.
HOW MANY DAYS HAS IT BEEN THERE?

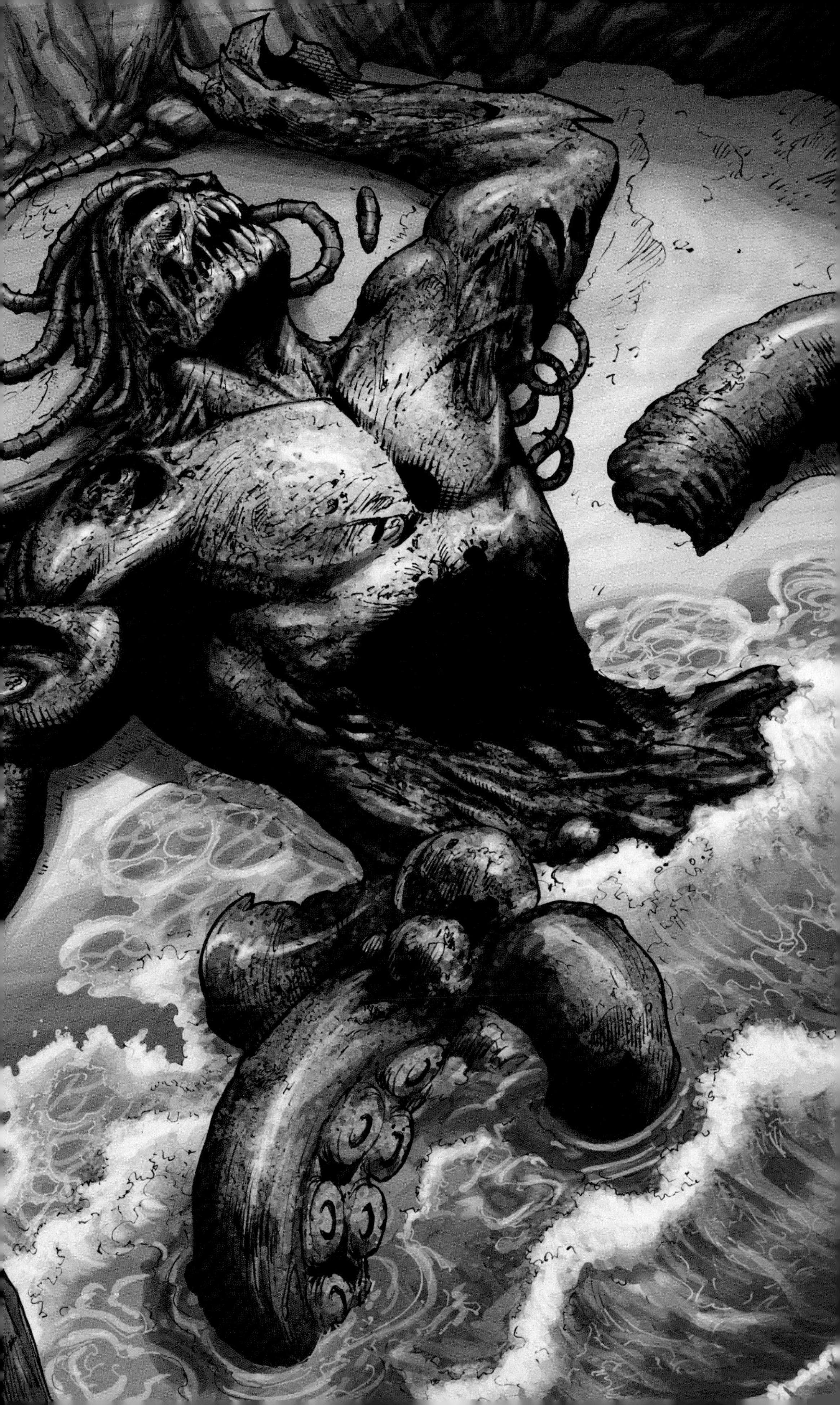

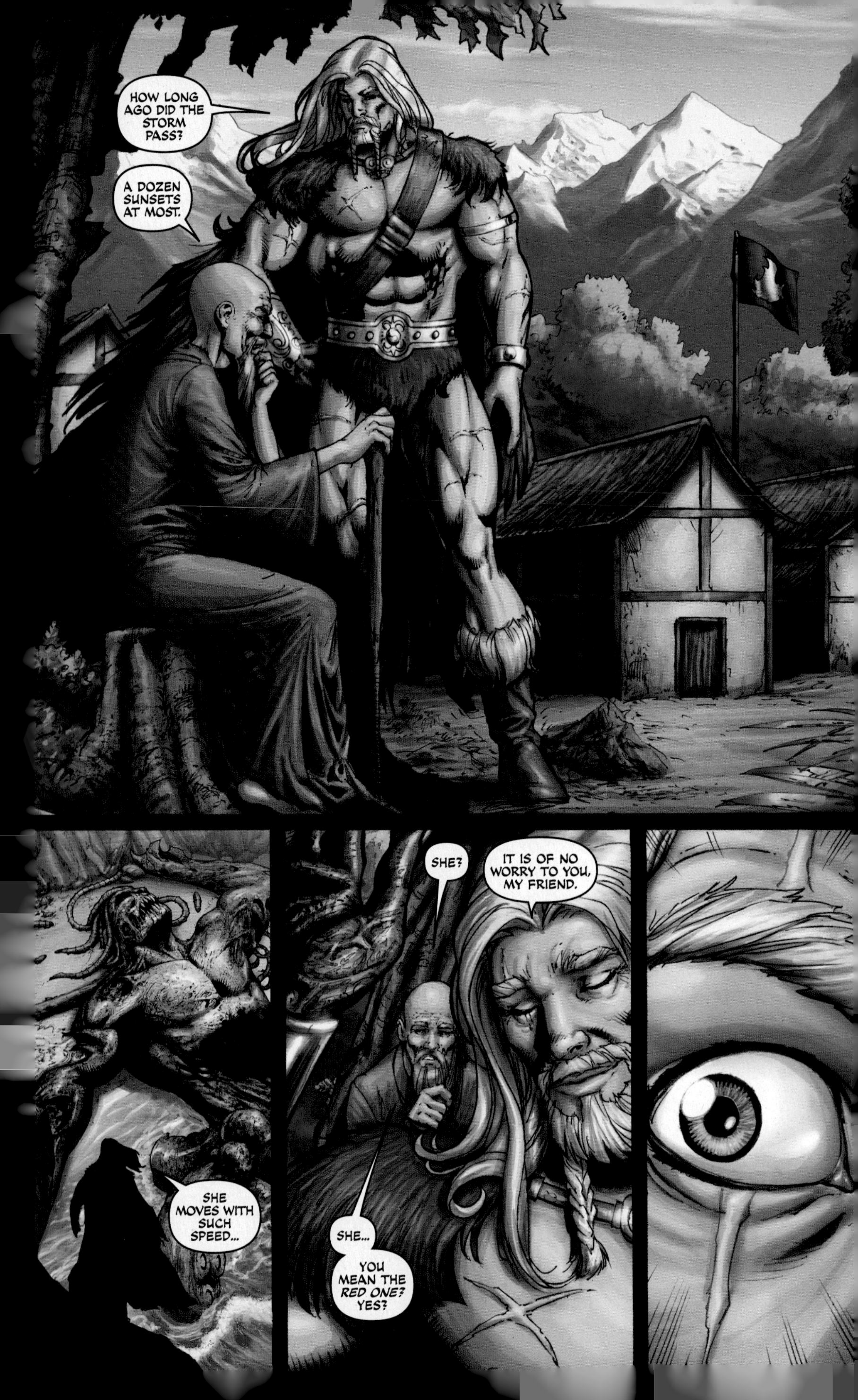
HOW LONG AGO DID THE STORM PASS?
A DOZEN SUNSETS AT MOST.
SHE MOVES WITH SUCH SPEED...
SHE?
IT IS OF NO WORRY TO YOU, MY FRIEND.
SHE...
YOU MEAN THE *RED ONE*? YES?

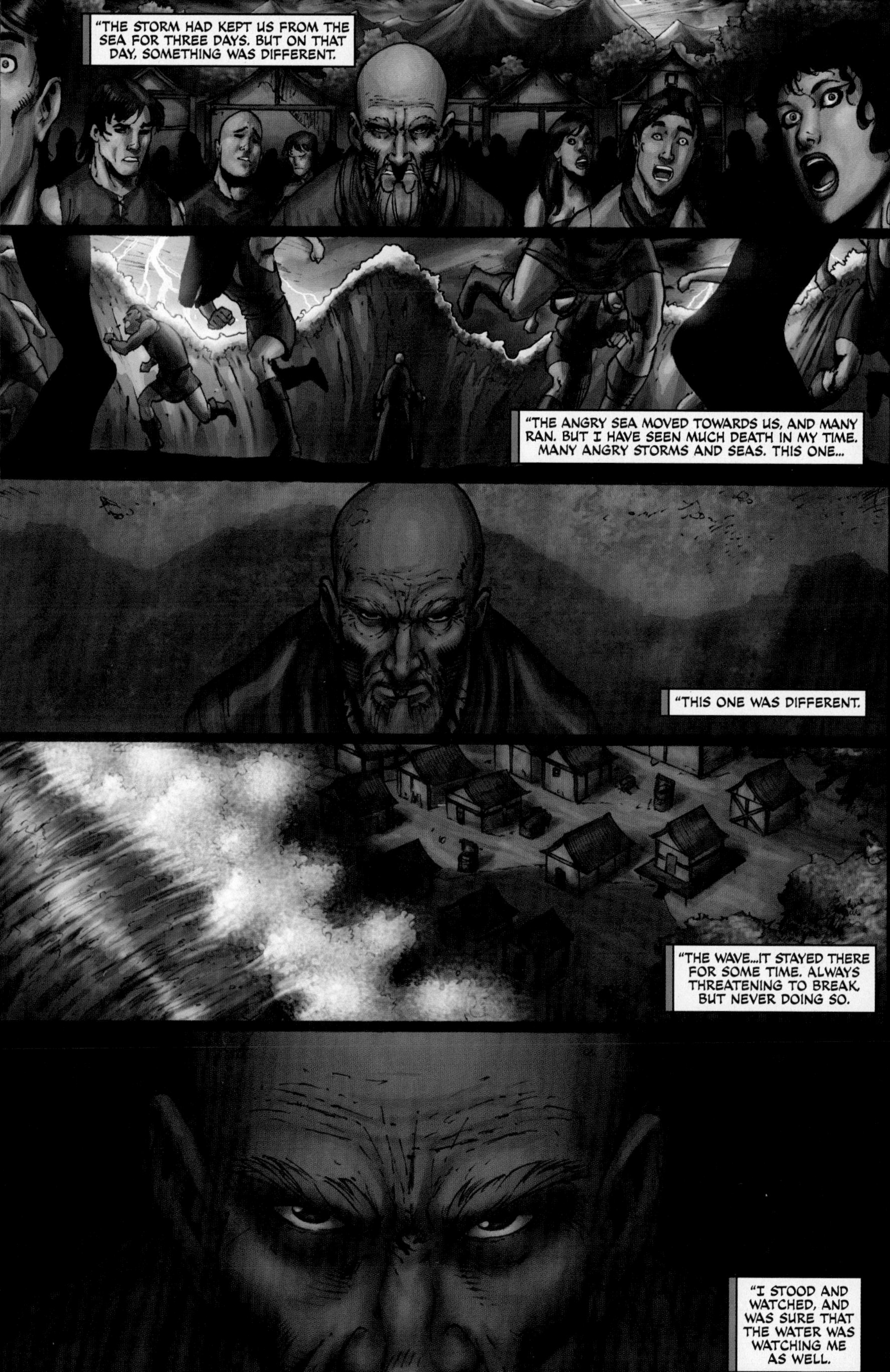
"THE STORM HAD KEPT US FROM THE SEA FOR THREE DAYS. BUT ON THAT DAY, SOMETHING WAS DIFFERENT.
"THE ANGRY SEA MOVED TOWARDS US, AND MANY RAN. BUT I HAVE SEEN MUCH DEATH IN MY TIME. MANY ANGRY STORMS AND SEAS. THIS ONE...
"THIS ONE WAS DIFFERENT.
"THE WAVE...IT STAYED THERE FOR SOME TIME. ALWAYS THREATENING TO BREAK, BUT NEVER DOING SO.
"I STOOD AND WATCHED, AND WAS SURE THAT THE WATER WAS WATCHING ME AS WELL.

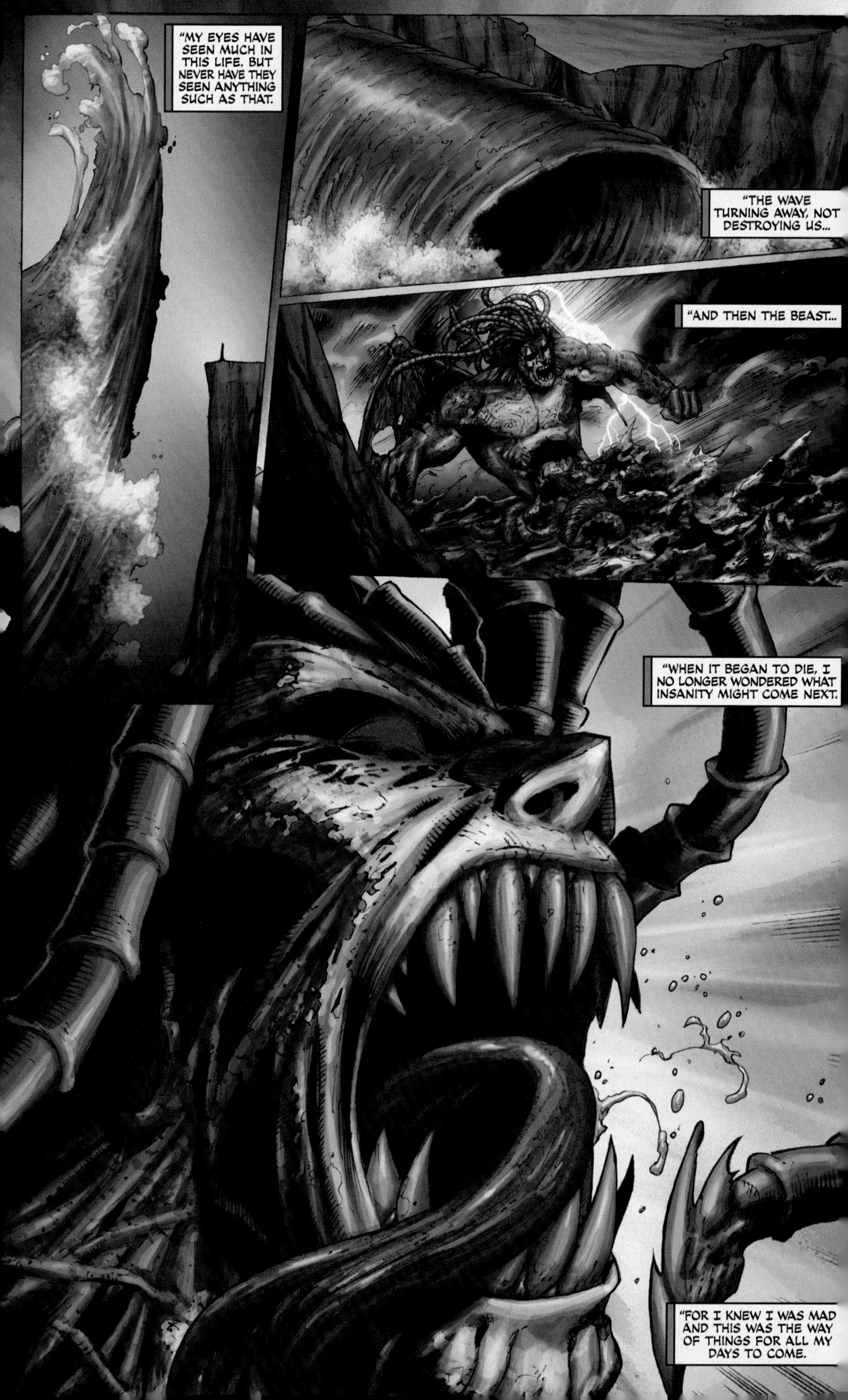
"MY EYES HAVE SEEN MUCH IN THIS LIFE. BUT NEVER HAVE THEY SEEN ANYTHING SUCH AS THAT.
"THE WAVE TURNING AWAY, NOT DESTROYING US...
"AND THEN THE BEAST...
"WHEN IT BEGAN TO DIE, I NO LONGER WONDERED WHAT INSANITY MIGHT COME NEXT.
"FOR I KNEW I WAS MAD AND THIS WAS THE WAY OF THINGS FOR ALL MY DAYS TO COME.

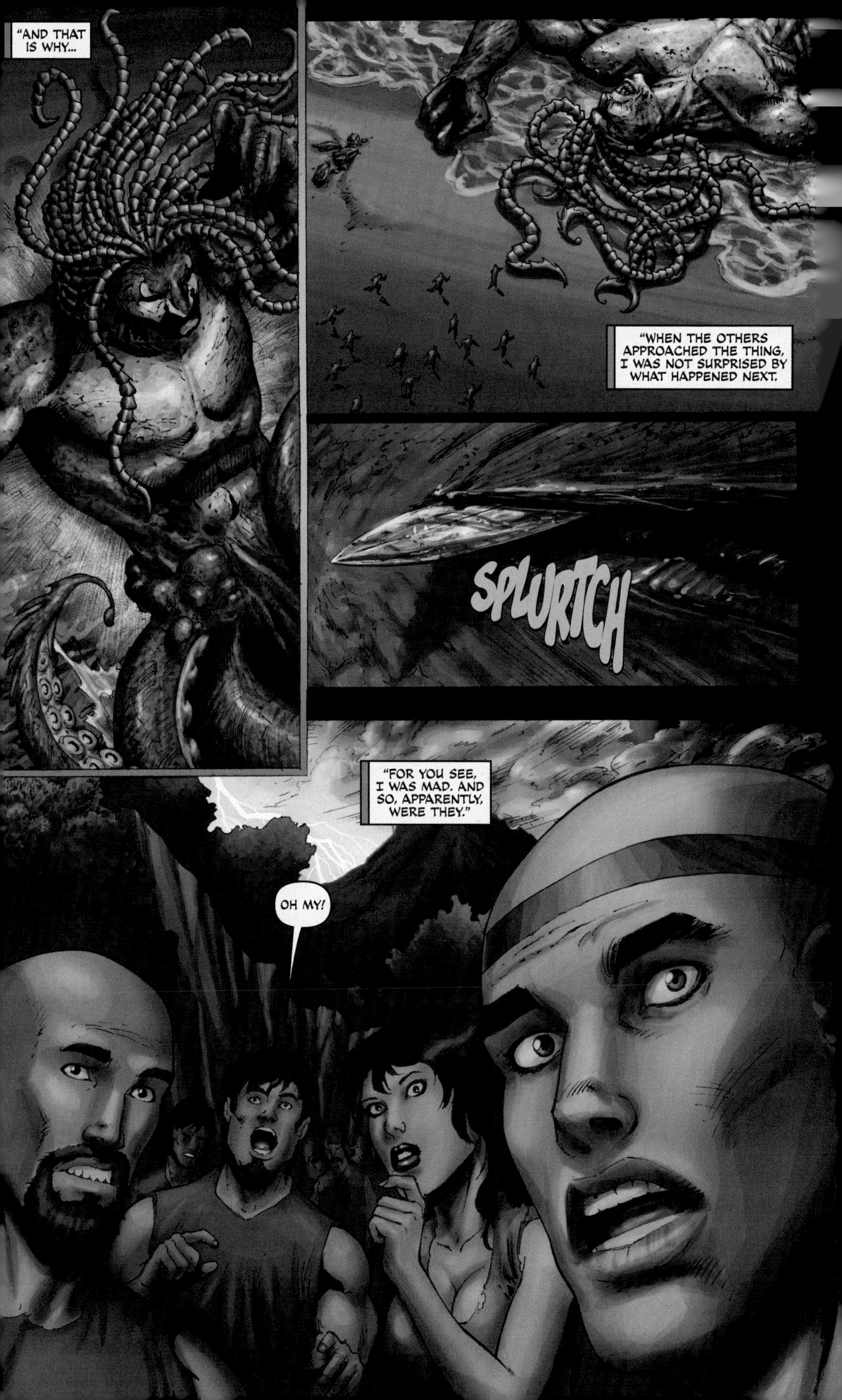

"AND THAT IS WHY...
"WHEN THE OTHERS APPROACHED THE THING, I WAS NOT SURPRISED BY WHAT HAPPENED NEXT.
SPLURTCH
"FOR YOU SEE, I WAS MAD. AND SO, APPARENTLY, WERE THEY."
OH MY!

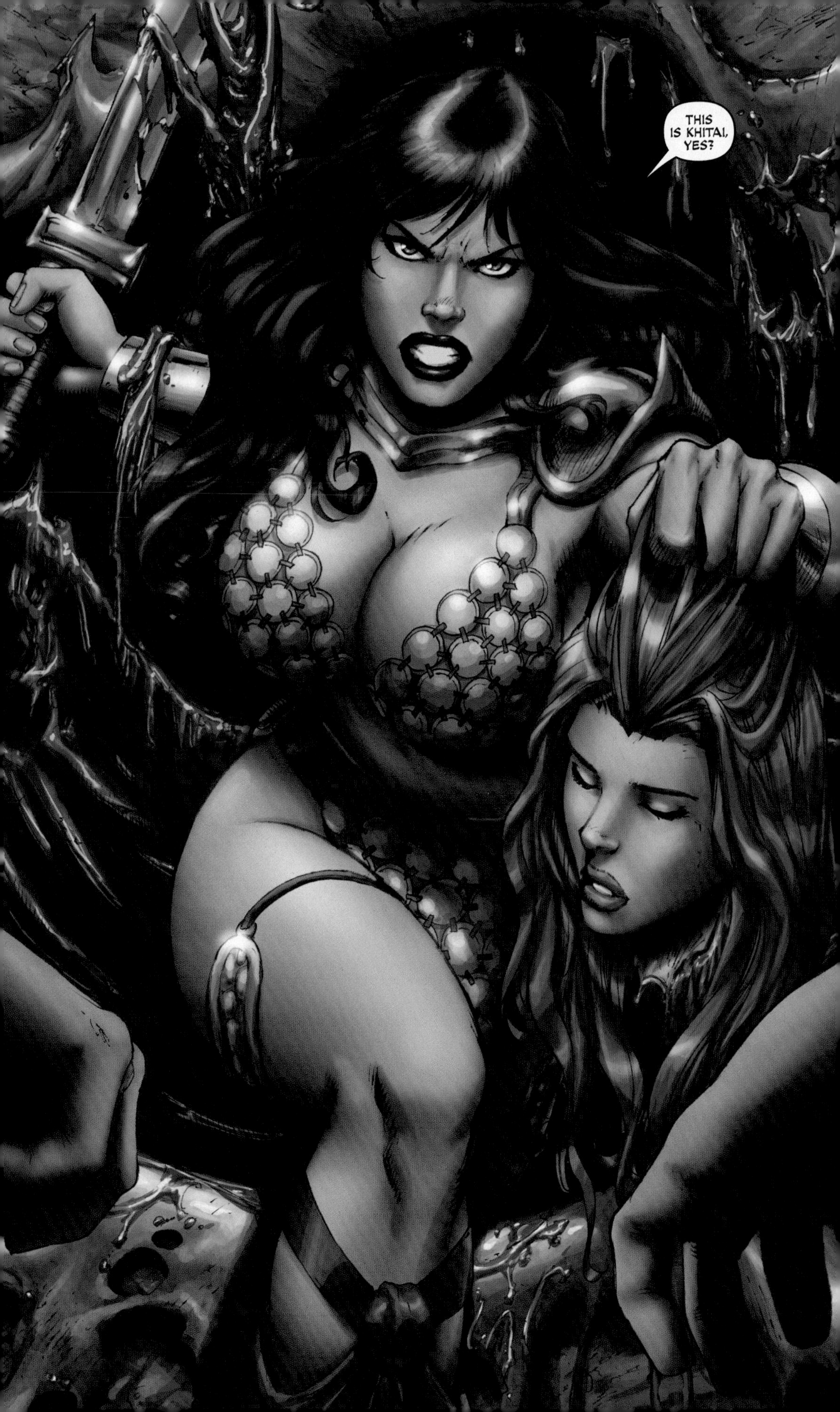
THIS IS KHITAI, YES?

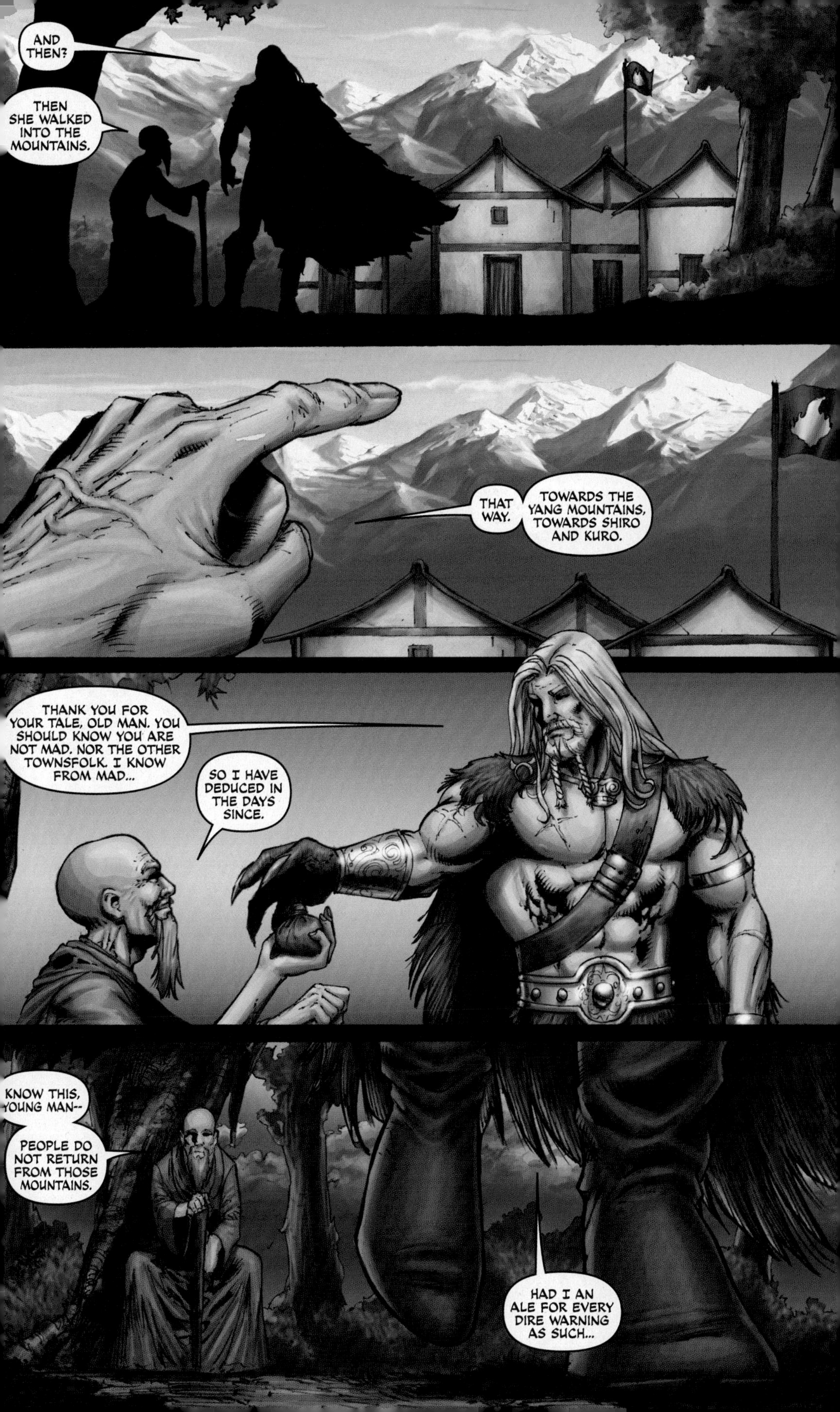
AND THEN?
THEN SHE WALKED INTO THE MOUNTAINS.
THAT WAY.
TOWARDS THE YANG MOUNTAINS, TOWARDS SHIRO AND KURO.
THANK YOU FOR YOUR TALE, OLD MAN. YOU SHOULD KNOW YOU ARE NOT MAD. NOR THE OTHER TOWNSFOLK. I KNOW FROM MAD...
SO I HAVE DEDUCED IN THE DAYS SINCE.
KNOW THIS, YOUNG MAN--
PEOPLE DO NOT RETURN FROM THOSE MOUNTAINS.
HAD I AN ALE FOR EVERY DIRE WARNING AS SUCH...

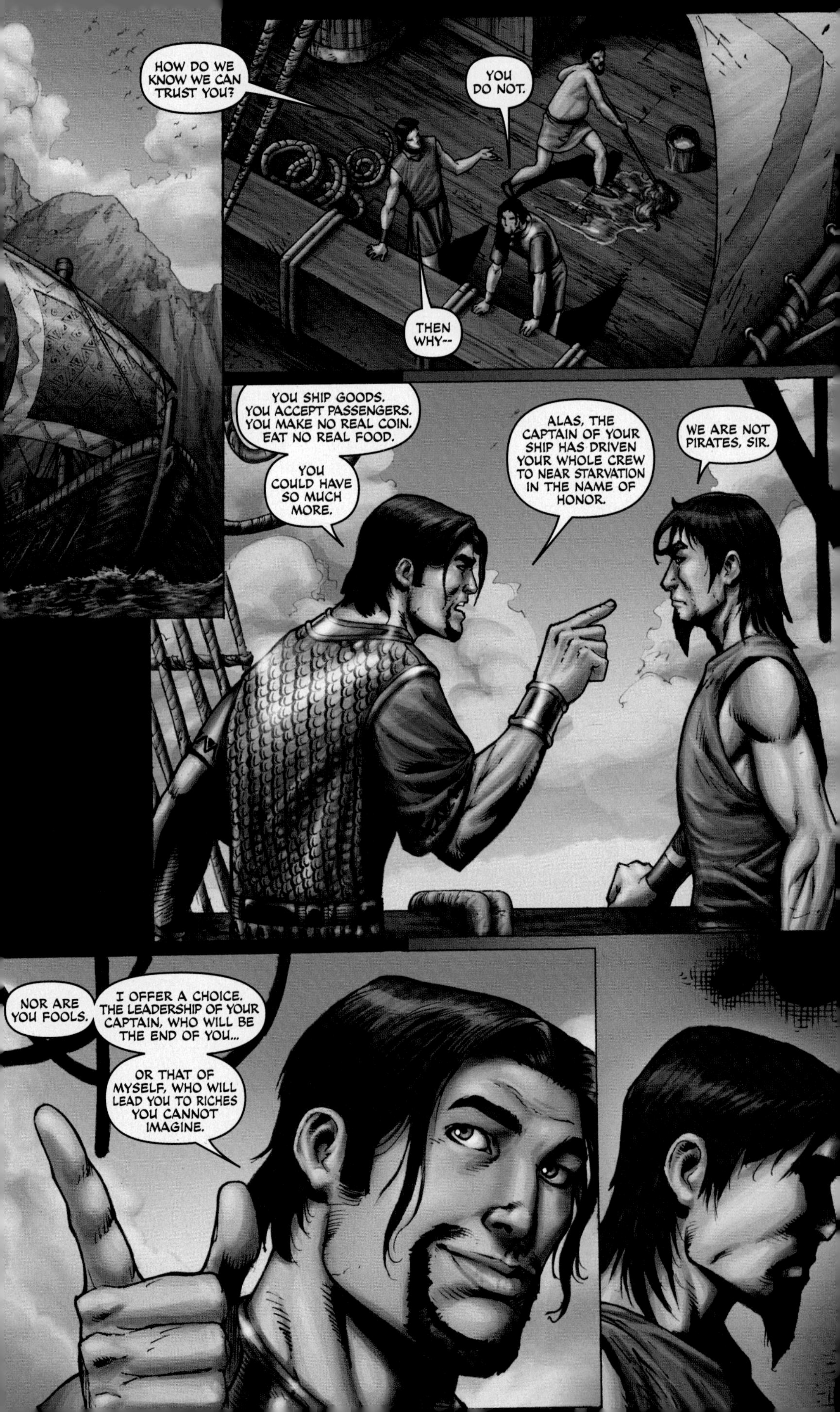
HOW DO WE KNOW WE CAN TRUST YOU?
YOU DO NOT.
THEN WHY--
YOU SHIP GOODS. YOU ACCEPT PASSENGERS. YOU MAKE NO REAL COIN. EAT NO REAL FOOD.
YOU COULD HAVE SO MUCH MORE.
ALAS, THE CAPTAIN OF YOUR SHIP HAS DRIVEN YOUR WHOLE CREW TO NEAR STARVATION IN THE NAME OF HONOR.
WE ARE NOT PIRATES, SIR.
NOR ARE YOU FOOLS.
I OFFER A CHOICE. THE LEADERSHIP OF YOUR CAPTAIN, WHO WILL BE THE END OF YOU...
OR THAT OF MYSELF, WHO WILL LEAD YOU TO RICHES YOU CANNOT IMAGINE.

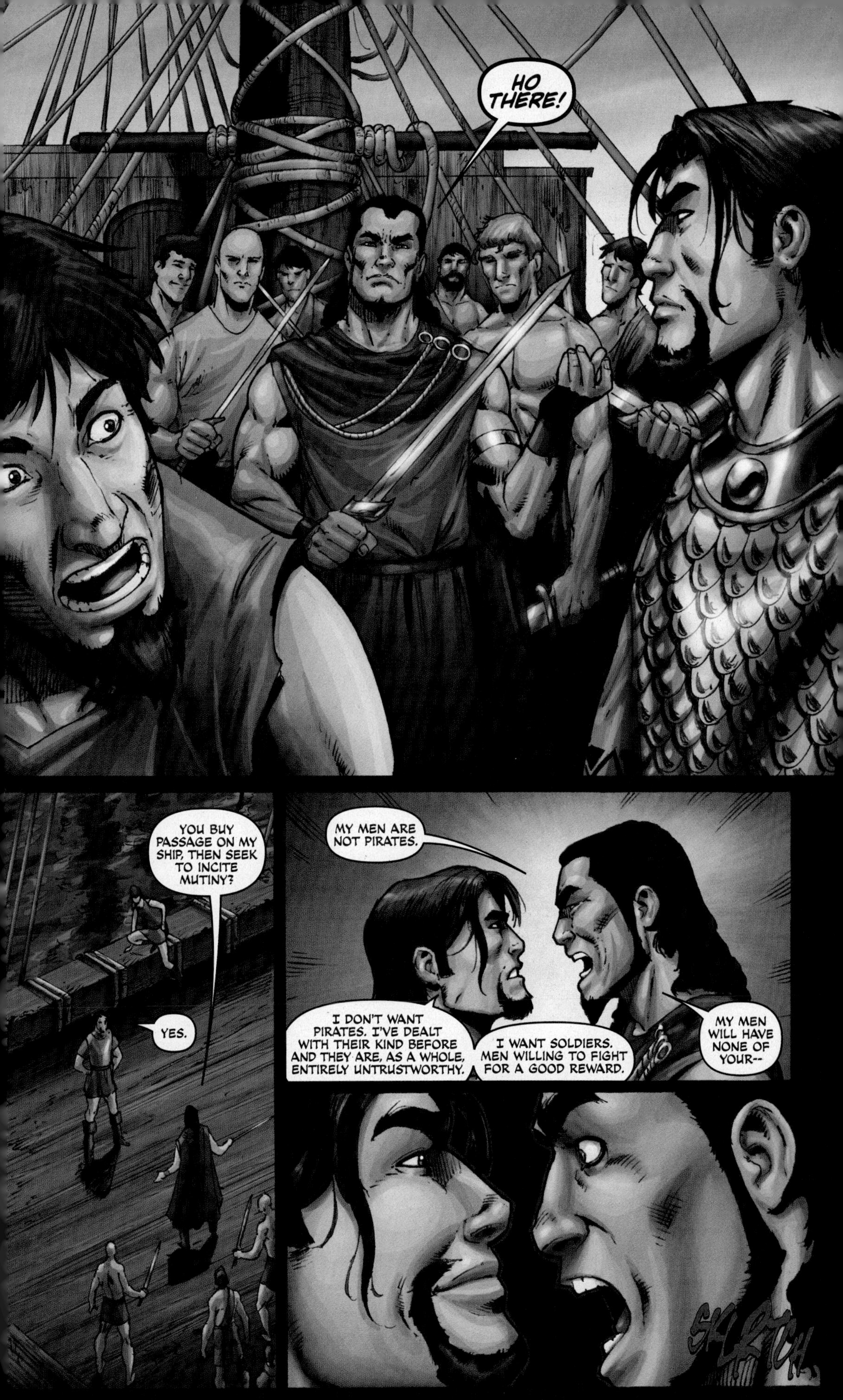
HO THERE!
YOU BUY PASSAGE ON MY SHIP, THEN SEEK TO INCITE MUTINY?
YES.
MY MEN ARE NOT PIRATES.
I DON'T WANT PIRATES. I'VE DEALT WITH THEIR KIND BEFORE AND THEY ARE, AS A WHOLE, ENTIRELY UNTRUSTWORTHY.
I WANT SOLDIERS. MEN WILLING TO FIGHT FOR A GOOD REWARD.
MY MEN WILL HAVE NONE OF YOUR--
SKLRTCH.

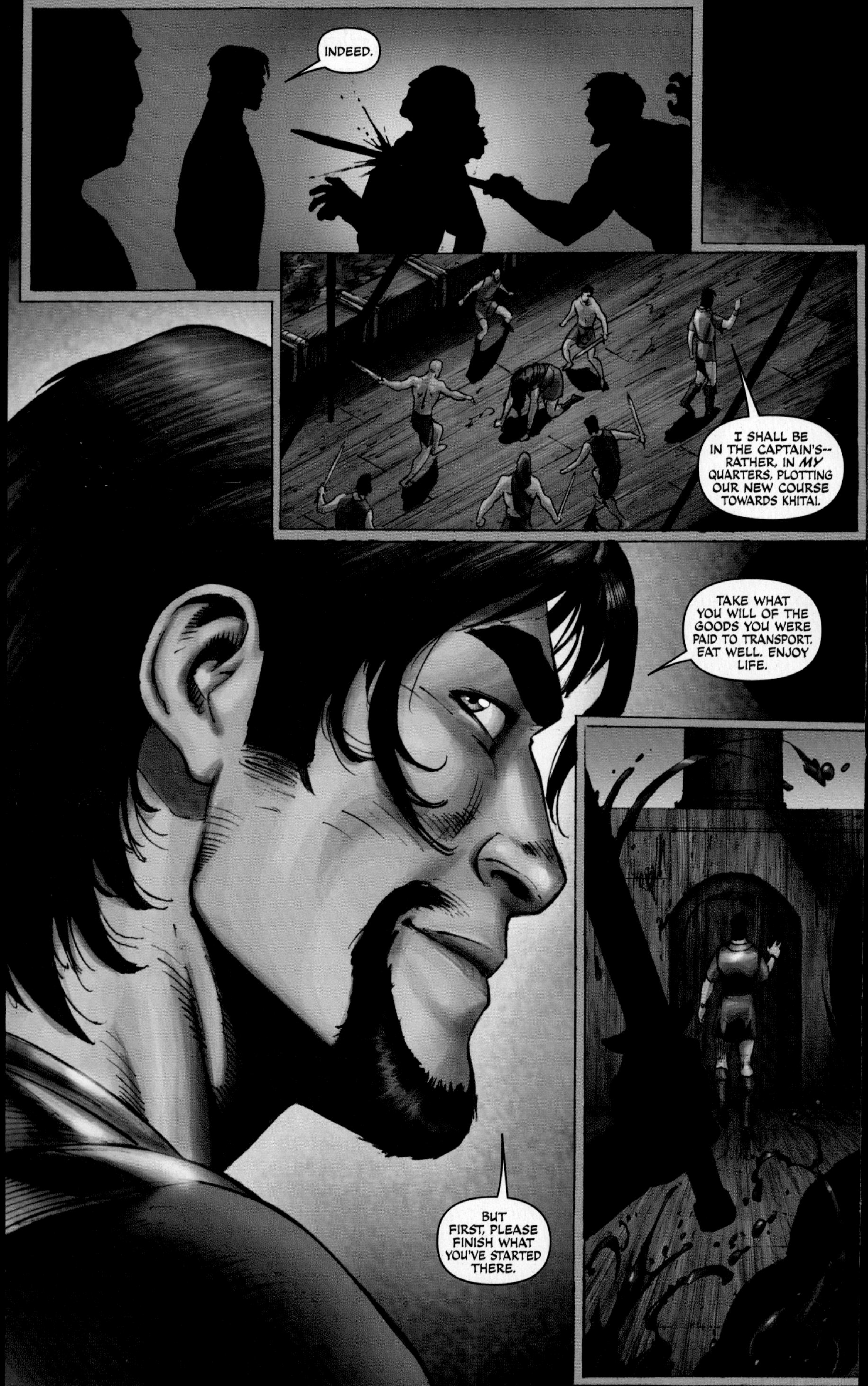
INDEED.
I SHALL BE IN THE CAPTAIN'S-- RATHER, IN *MY* QUARTERS, PLOTTING OUR NEW COURSE TOWARDS KHITAI.
TAKE WHAT YOU WILL OF THE GOODS YOU WERE PAID TO TRANSPORT. EAT WELL. ENJOY LIFE.
BUT FIRST, PLEASE FINISH WHAT YOU'VE STARTED THERE.

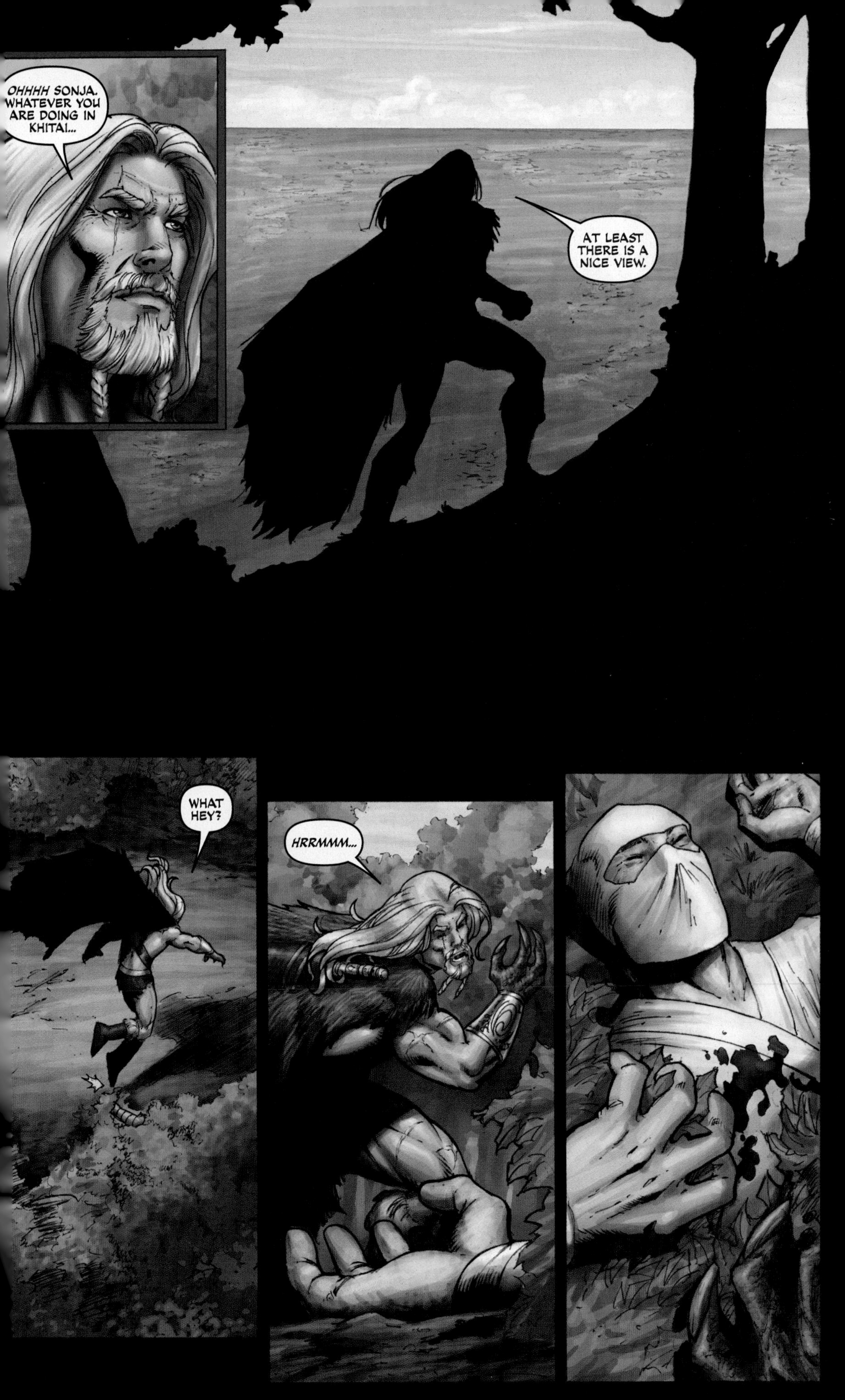
OHHHH SONJA. WHATEVER YOU ARE DOING IN KHITAI...
AT LEAST THERE IS A NICE VIEW.
WHAT HEY?
HRRMMM...

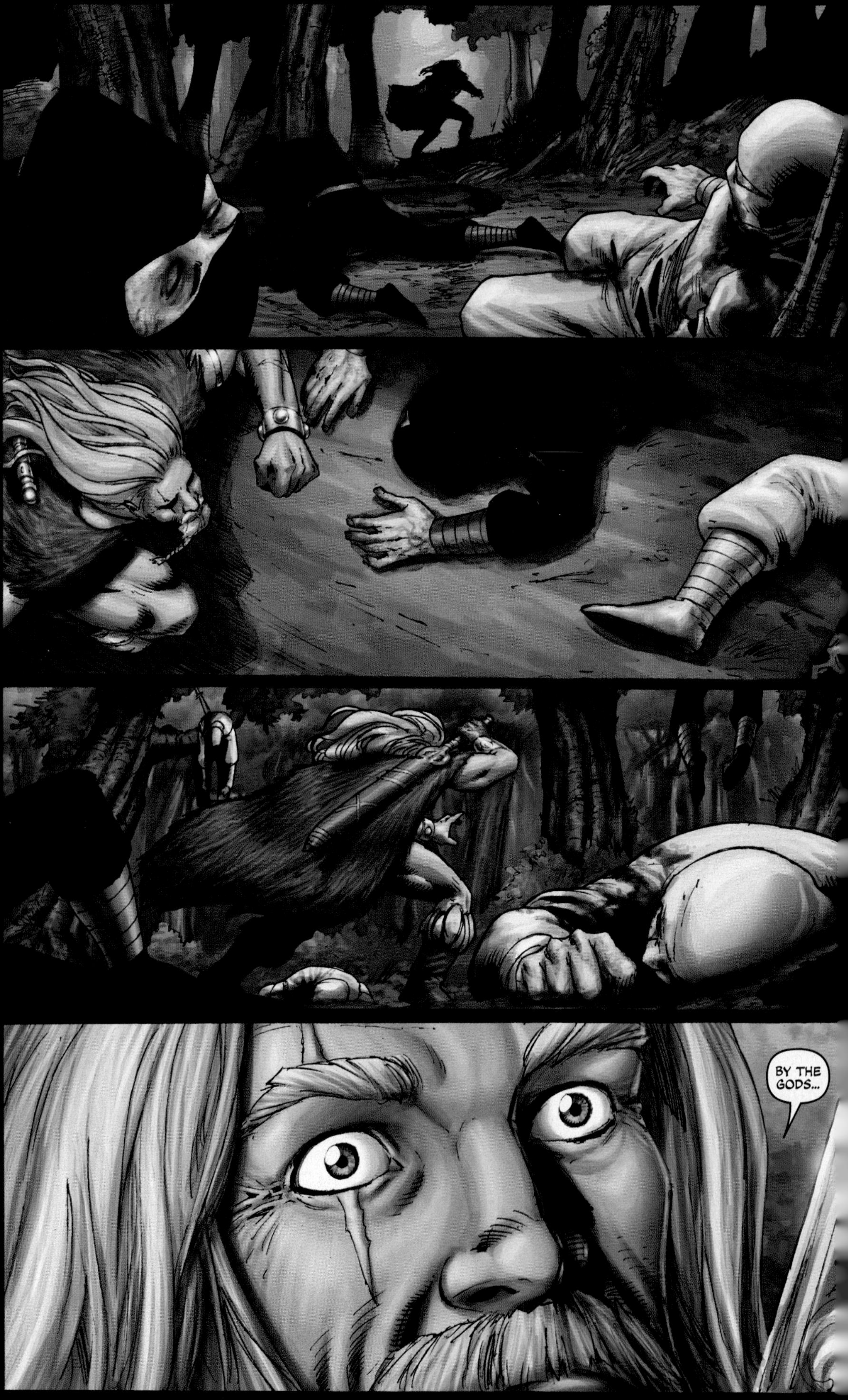
BY THE GODS...

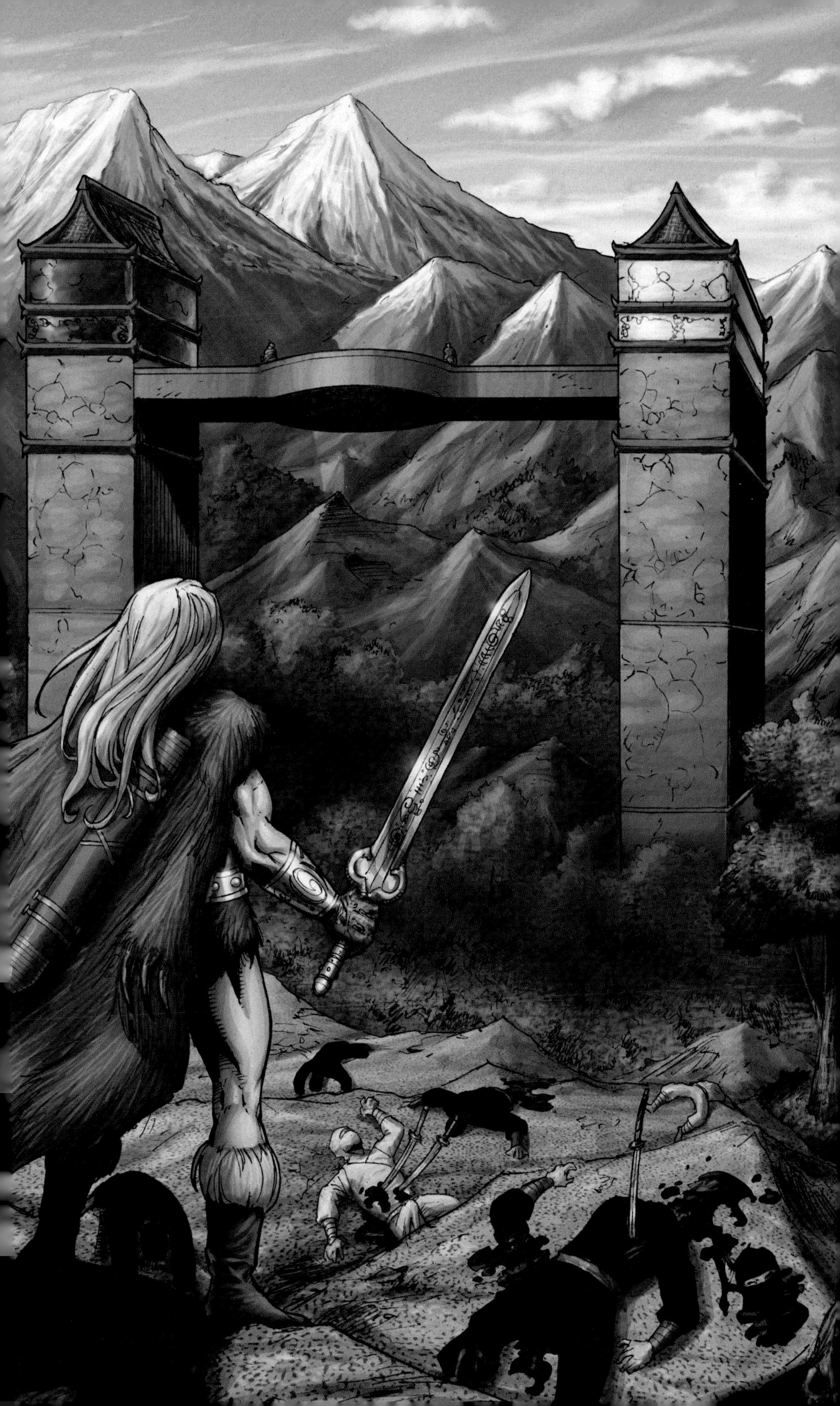

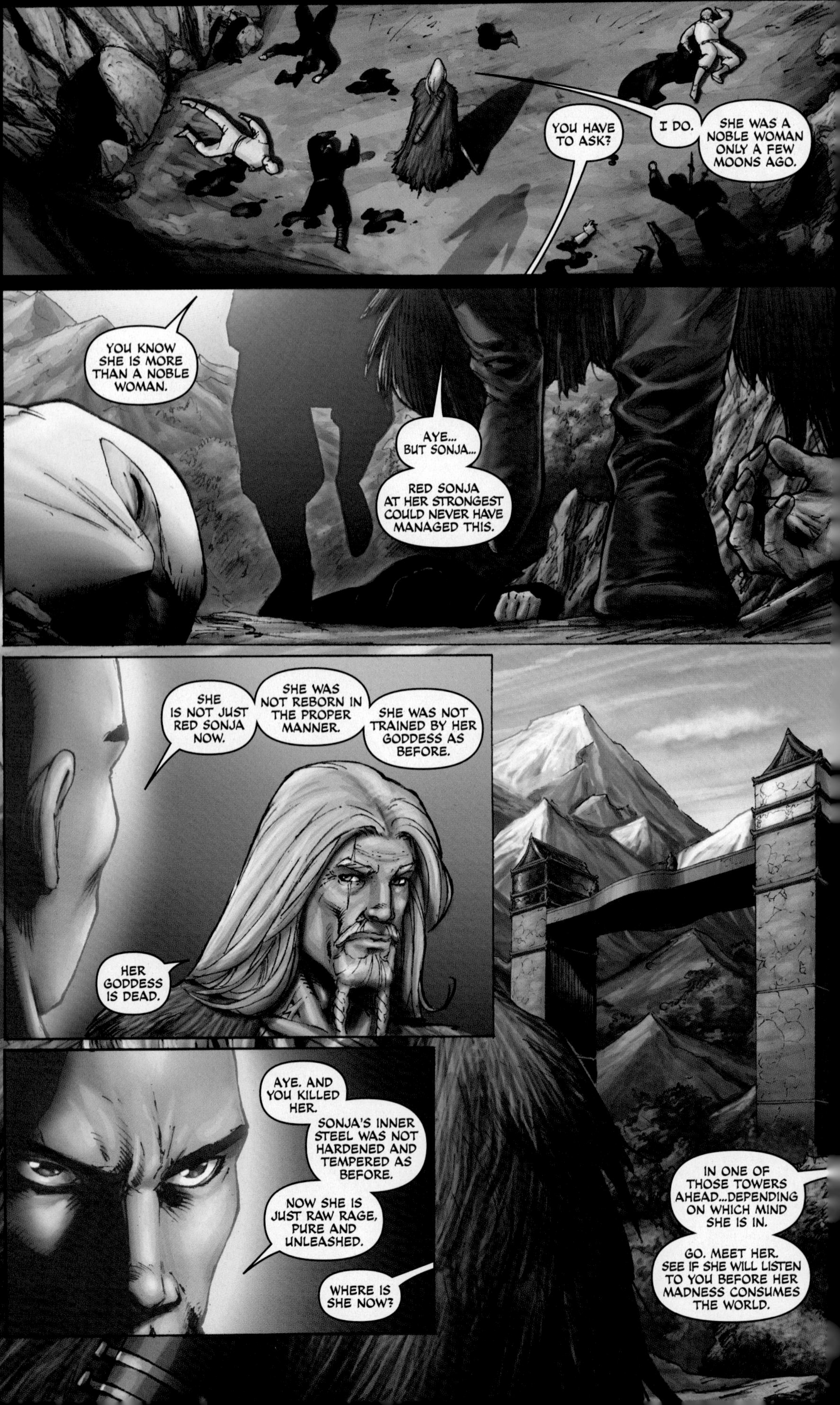

YOU HAVE TO ASK?
I DO.
SHE WAS A NOBLE WOMAN ONLY A FEW MOONS AGO.
YOU KNOW SHE IS MORE THAN A NOBLE WOMAN.
AYE... BUT SONJA...
RED SONJA AT HER STRONGEST COULD NEVER HAVE MANAGED THIS.
SHE IS NOT JUST RED SONJA NOW.
SHE WAS NOT REBORN IN THE PROPER MANNER.
SHE WAS NOT TRAINED BY HER GODDESS AS BEFORE.
HER GODDESS IS DEAD.
AYE. AND YOU KILLED HER.
SONJA'S INNER STEEL WAS NOT HARDENED AND TEMPERED AS BEFORE.
NOW SHE IS JUST RAW RAGE, PURE AND UNLEASHED.
WHERE IS SHE NOW?
IN ONE OF THOSE TOWERS AHEAD...DEPENDING ON WHICH MIND SHE IS IN.
GO. MEET HER. SEE IF SHE WILL LISTEN TO YOU BEFORE HER MADNESS CONSUMES THE WORLD.

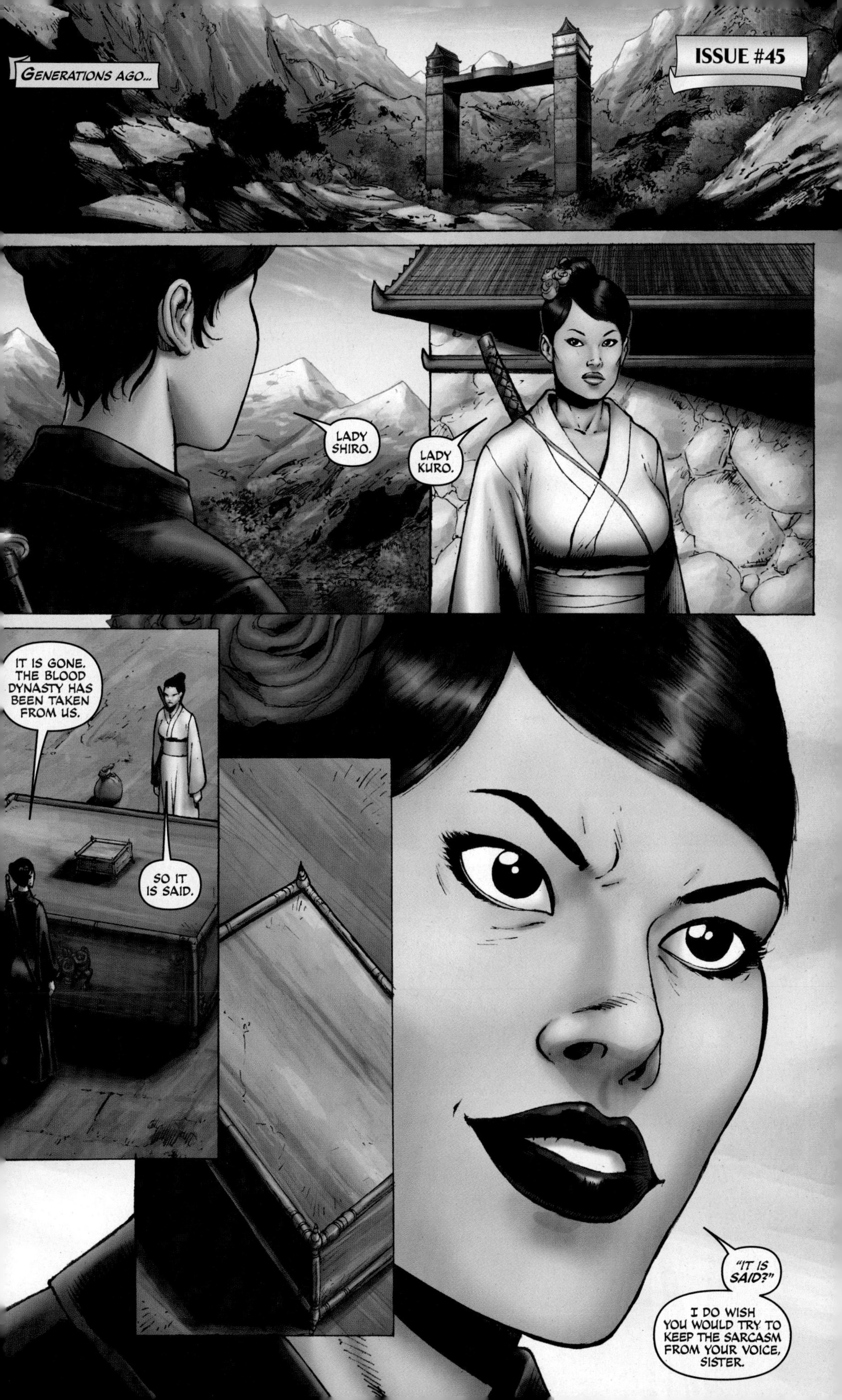
GENERATIONS AGO...
ISSUE #45
LADY SHIRO.
LADY KURO.
IT IS GONE. THE BLOOD DYNASTY HAS BEEN TAKEN FROM US.
SO IT IS SAID.
"IT IS SAID?"
I DO WISH YOU WOULD TRY TO KEEP THE SARCASM FROM YOUR VOICE, SISTER.

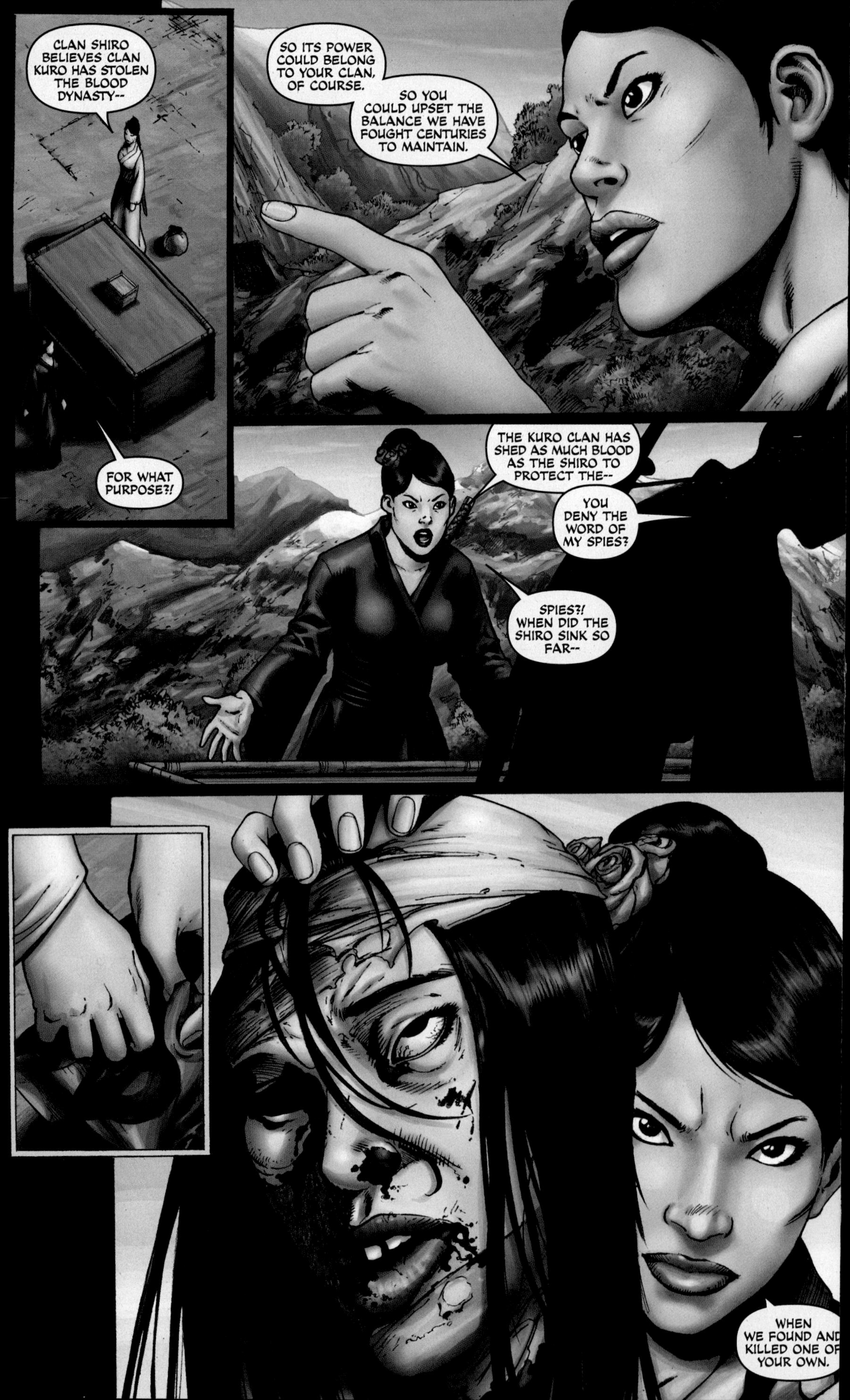
CLAN SHIRO BELIEVES CLAN KURO HAS STOLEN THE BLOOD DYNASTY--
FOR WHAT PURPOSE?!
SO ITS POWER COULD BELONG TO YOUR CLAN, OF COURSE.
SO YOU COULD UPSET THE BALANCE WE HAVE FOUGHT CENTURIES TO MAINTAIN.
THE KURO CLAN HAS SHED AS MUCH BLOOD AS THE SHIRO TO PROTECT THE--
YOU DENY THE WORD OF MY SPIES?
SPIES?! WHEN DID THE SHIRO SINK SO FAR--
WHEN WE FOUND AND KILLED ONE OF YOUR OWN.

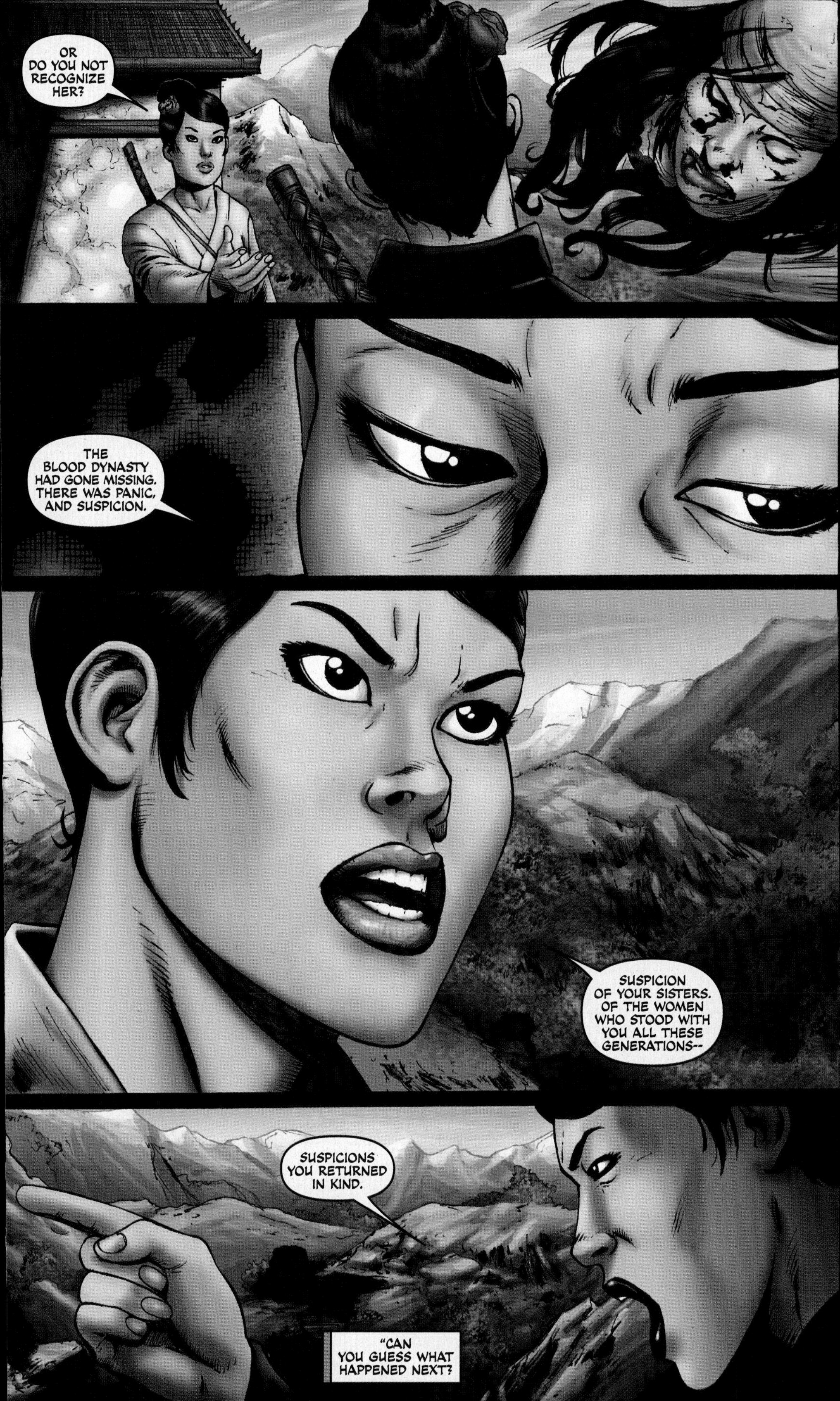
OR DO YOU NOT RECOGNIZE HER?
THE BLOOD DYNASTY HAD GONE MISSING. THERE WAS PANIC, AND SUSPICION.
SUSPICION OF YOUR SISTERS. OF THE WOMEN WHO STOOD WITH YOU ALL THESE GENERATIONS--
SUSPICIONS YOU RETURNED IN KIND.
"CAN YOU GUESS WHAT HAPPENED NEXT?

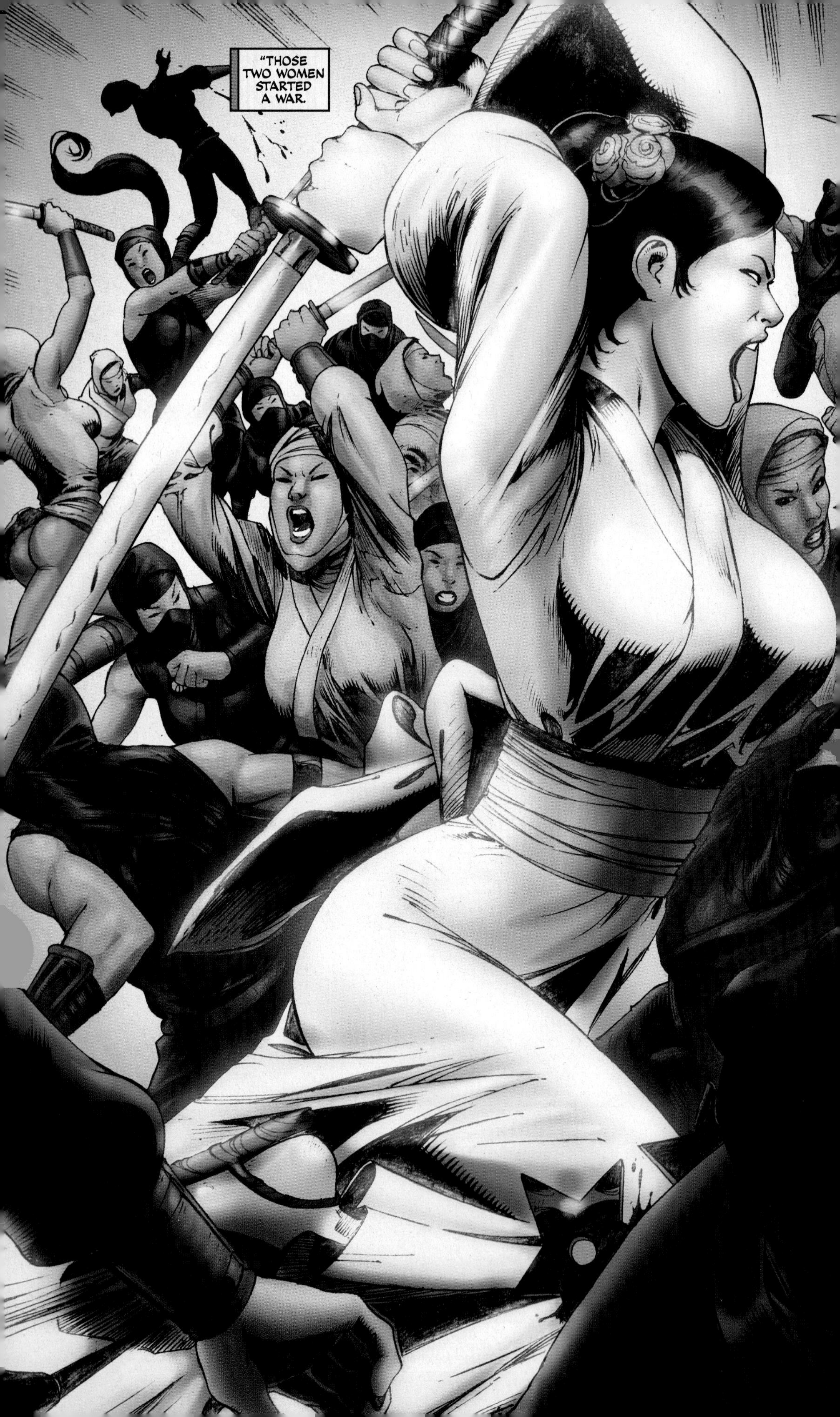
"THOSE TWO WOMEN STARTED A WAR.

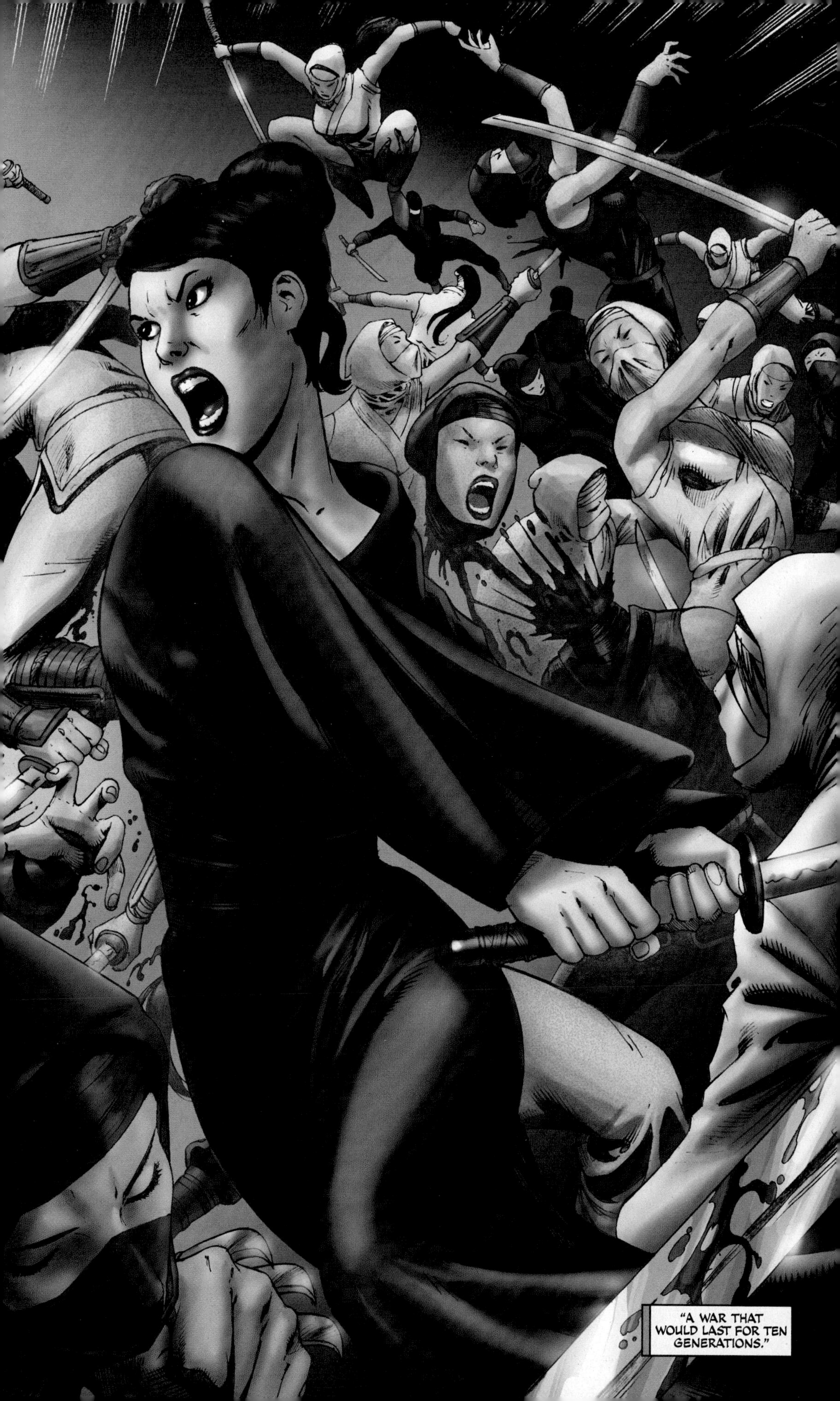
"A WAR THAT WOULD LAST FOR TEN GENERATIONS."

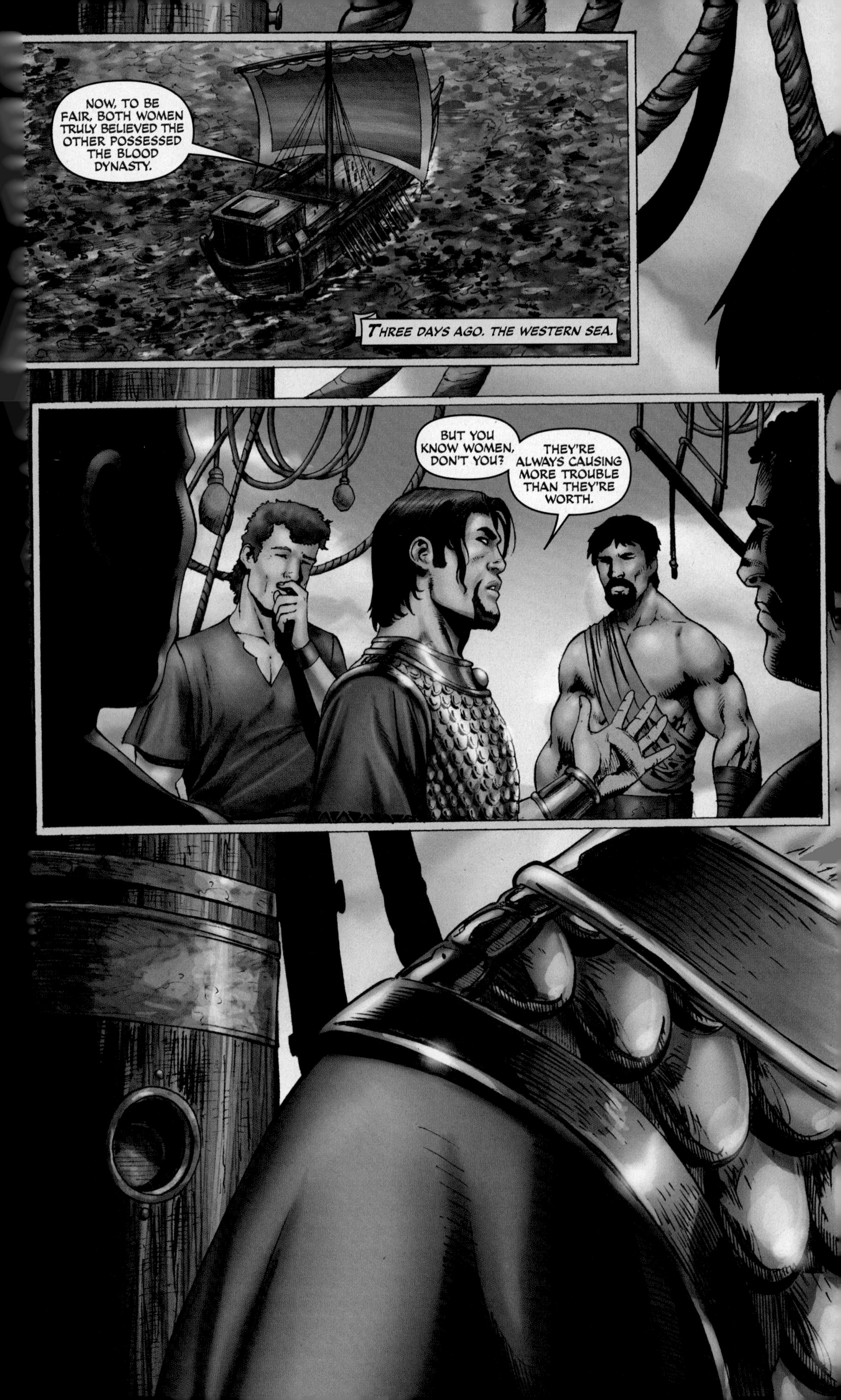

NOW, TO BE FAIR, BOTH WOMEN TRULY BELIEVED THE OTHER POSSESSED THE BLOOD DYNASTY.
THREE DAYS AGO. THE WESTERN SEA.
BUT YOU KNOW WOMEN, DON'T YOU?
THEY'RE ALWAYS CAUSING MORE TROUBLE THAN THEY'RE WORTH.

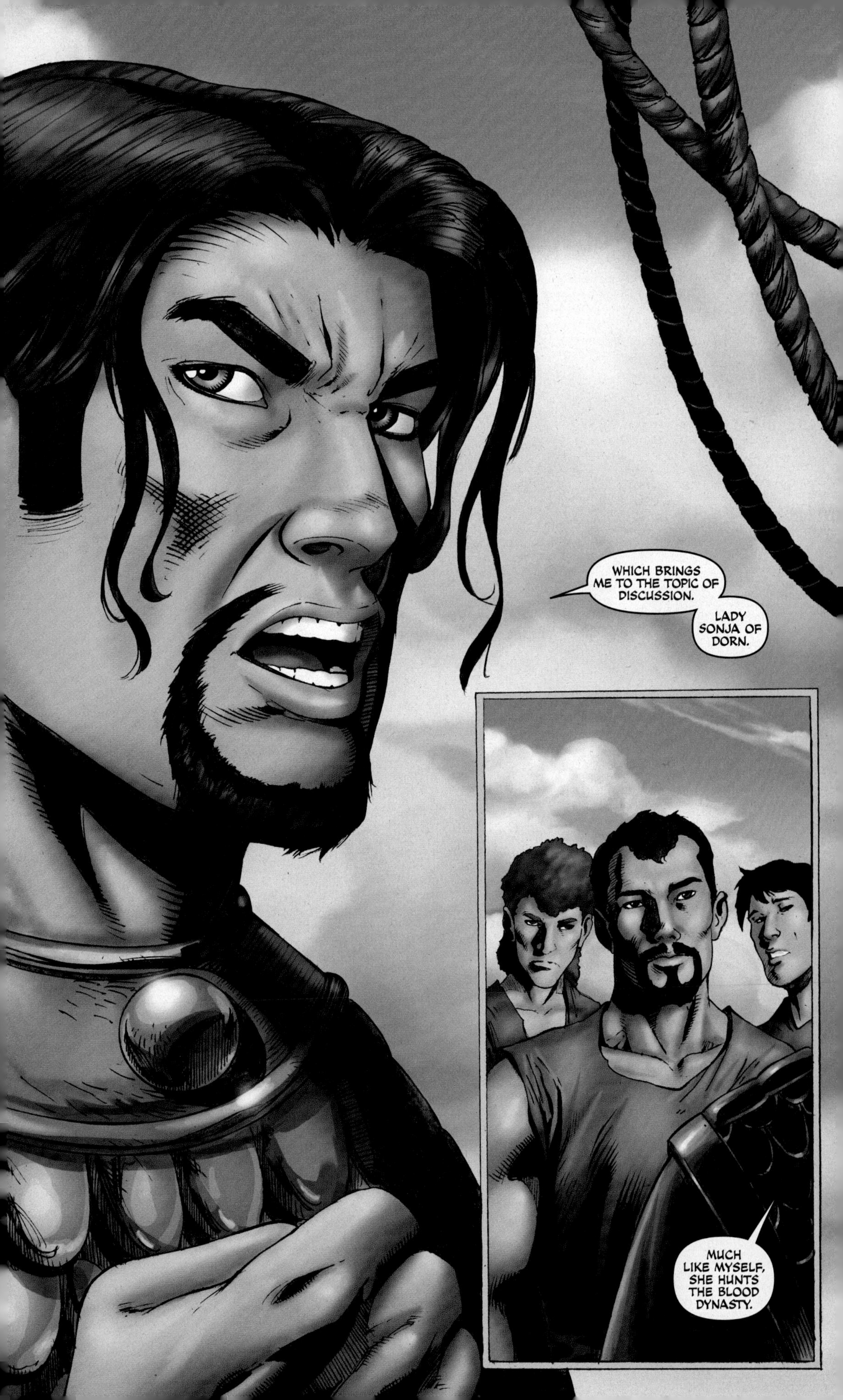
WHICH BRINGS ME TO THE TOPIC OF DISCUSSION.
LADY SONJA OF DORN.
MUCH LIKE MYSELF, SHE HUNTS THE BLOOD DYNASTY.

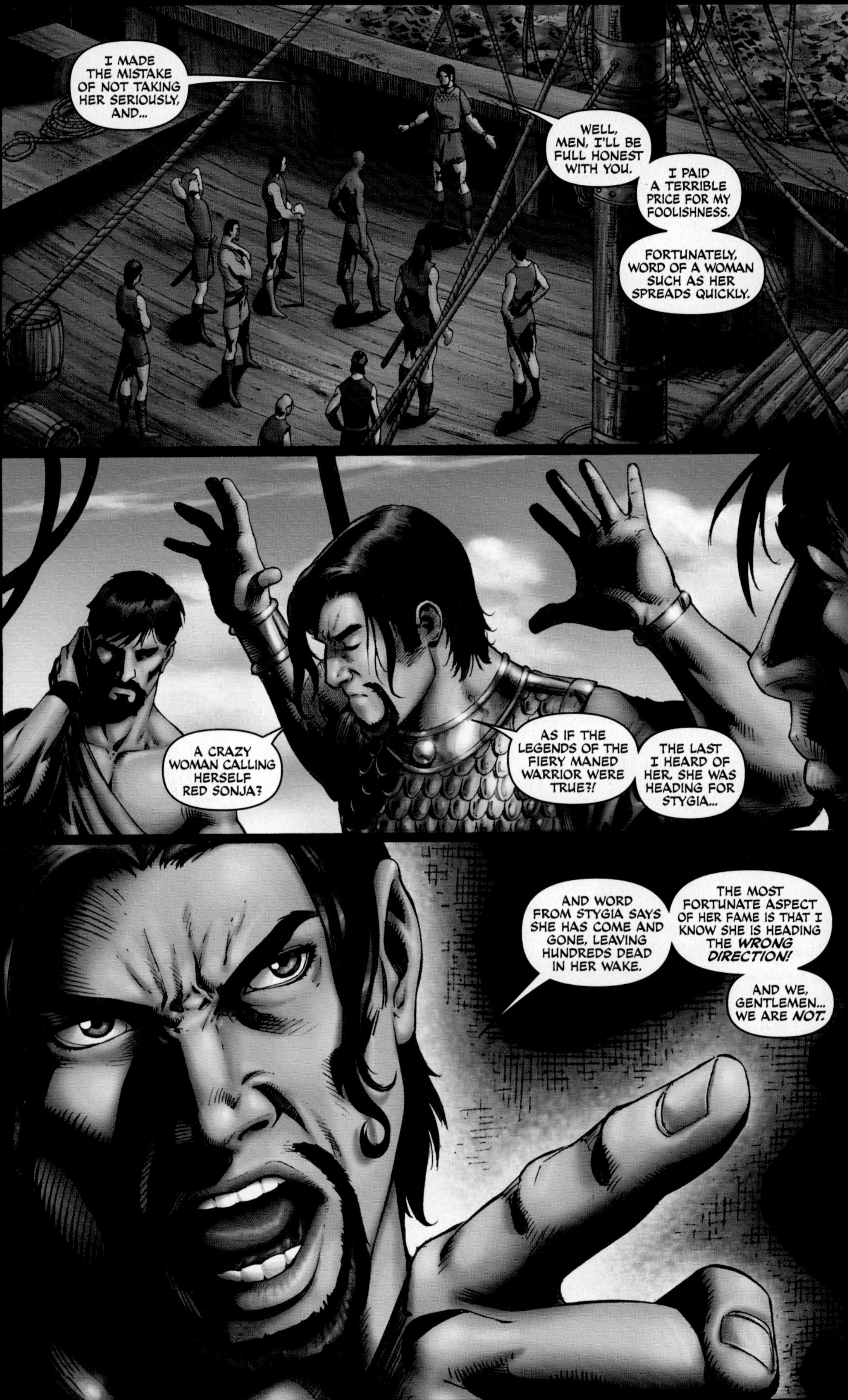
I MADE THE MISTAKE OF NOT TAKING HER SERIOUSLY, AND...
WELL, MEN, I'LL BE FULL HONEST WITH YOU.
I PAID A TERRIBLE PRICE FOR MY FOOLISHNESS.
FORTUNATELY, WORD OF A WOMAN SUCH AS HER SPREADS QUICKLY.
A CRAZY WOMAN CALLING HERSELF RED SONJA?
AS IF THE LEGENDS OF THE FIERY MANED WARRIOR WERE TRUE?!
THE LAST I HEARD OF HER, SHE WAS HEADING FOR STYGIA...
AND WORD FROM STYGIA SAYS SHE HAS COME AND GONE, LEAVING HUNDREDS DEAD IN HER WAKE.
THE MOST FORTUNATE ASPECT OF HER FAME IS THAT I KNOW SHE IS HEADING THE *WRONG DIRECTION!*
AND WE, GENTLEMEN... WE ARE *NOT.*

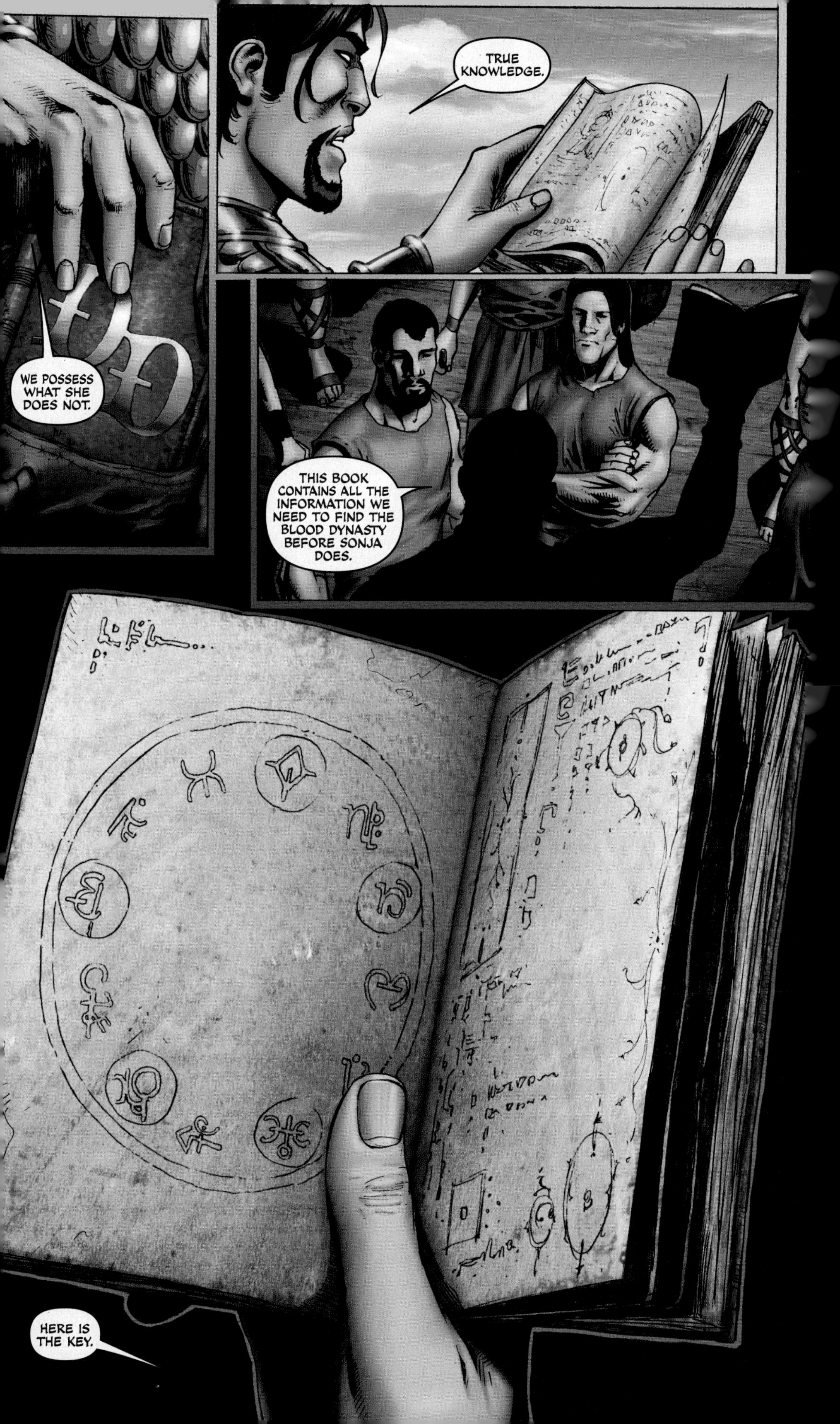
TRUE KNOWLEDGE.
WE POSSESS WHAT SHE DOES NOT.
THIS BOOK CONTAINS ALL THE INFORMATION WE NEED TO FIND THE BLOOD DYNASTY BEFORE SONJA DOES.
HERE IS THE KEY.

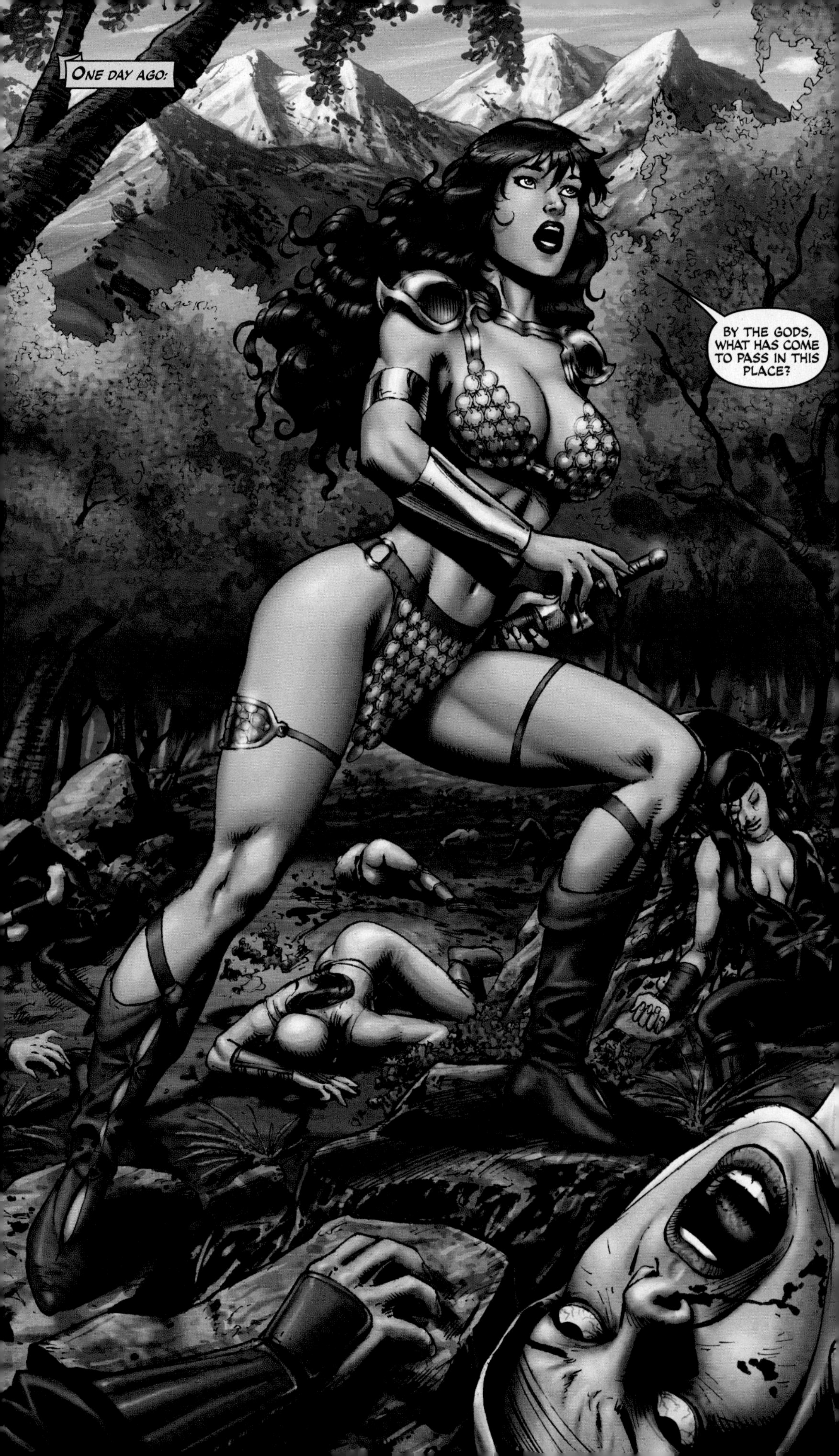
ONE DAY AGO:
BY THE GODS, WHAT HAS COME TO PASS IN THIS PLACE?

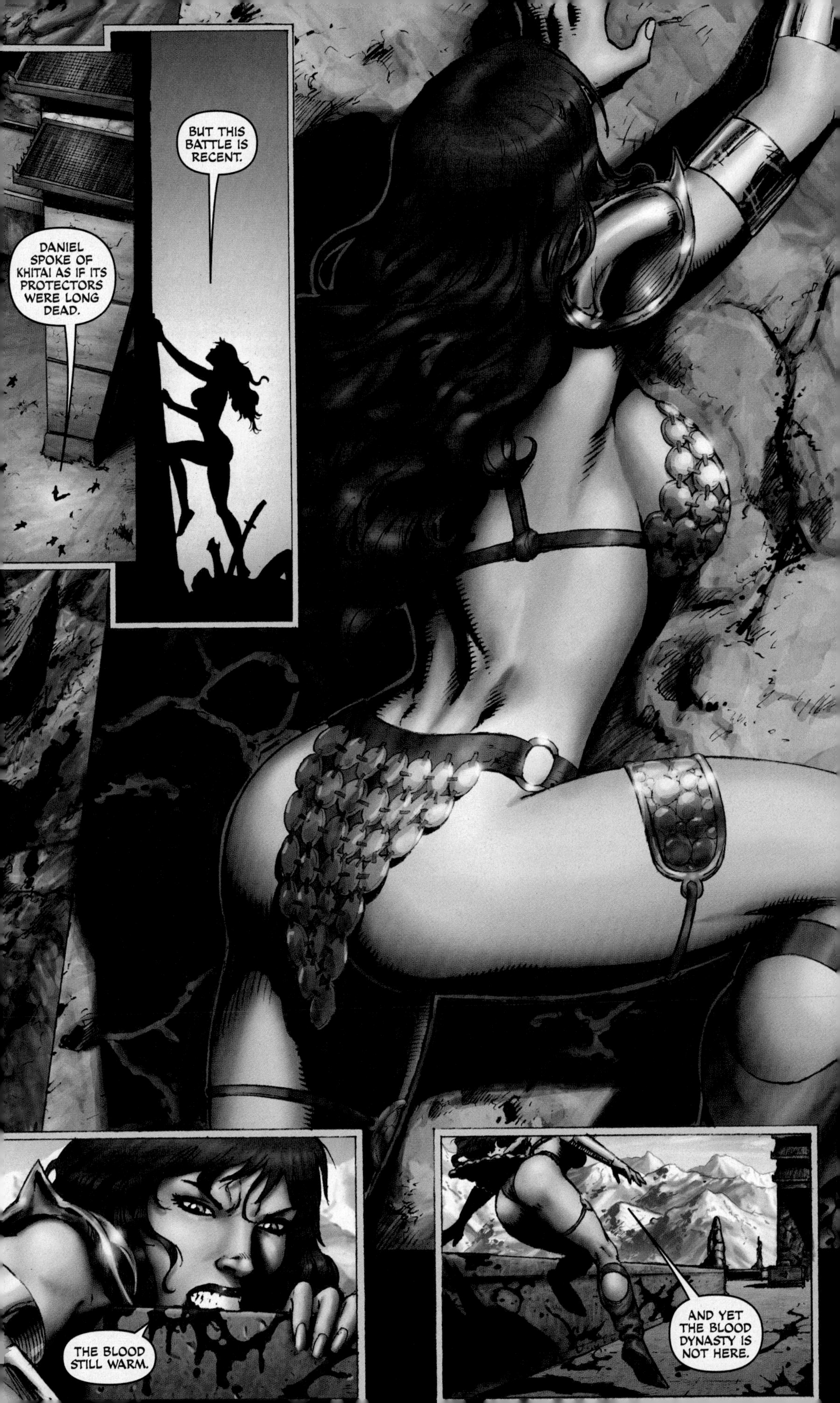
DANIEL SPOKE OF KHITAI AS IF ITS PROTECTORS WERE LONG DEAD.
BUT THIS BATTLE IS RECENT.
THE BLOOD STILL WARM.
AND YET THE BLOOD DYNASTY IS NOT HERE.

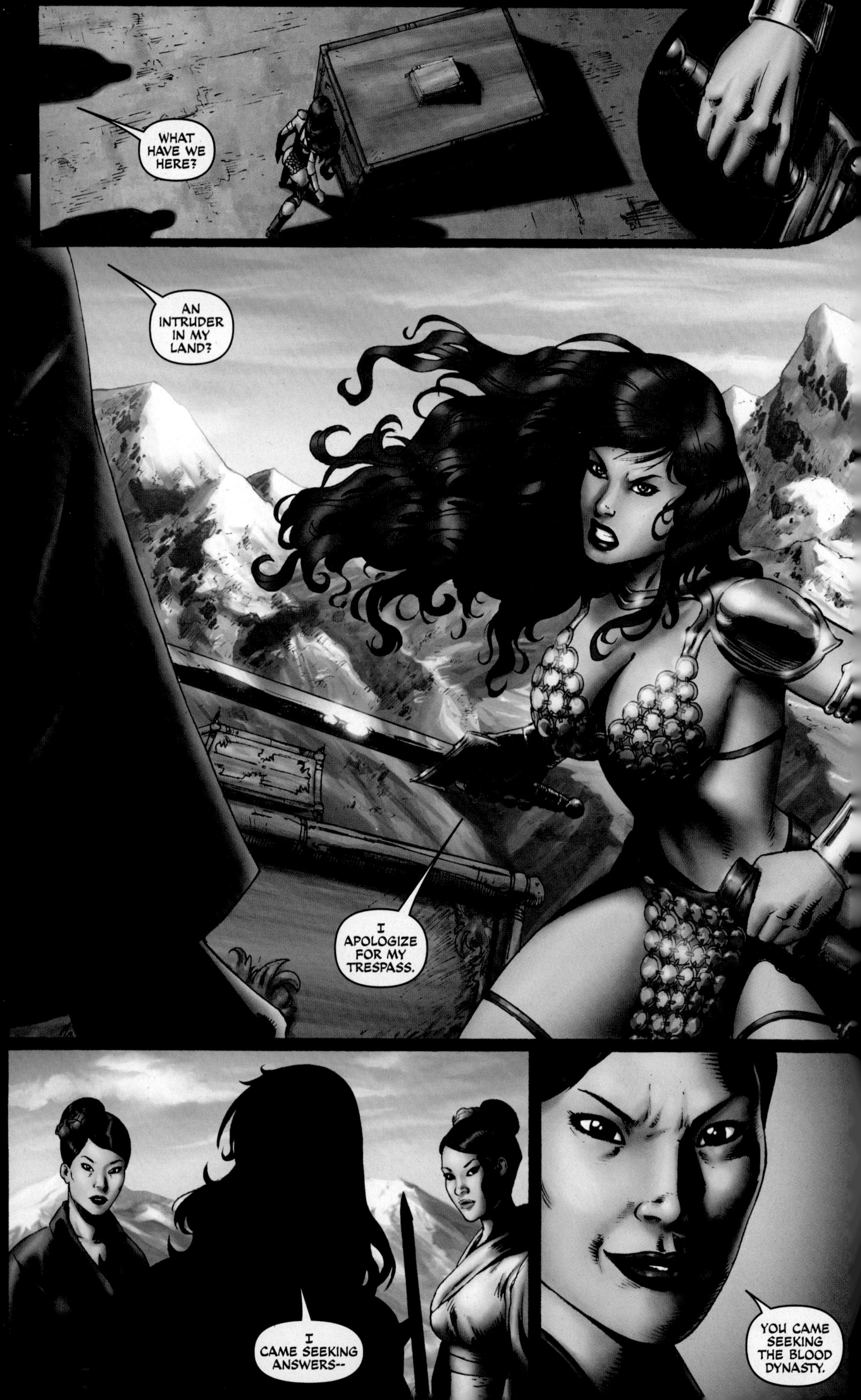
WHAT HAVE WE HERE?
AN INTRUDER IN MY LAND?
I APOLOGIZE FOR MY TRESPASS.
I CAME SEEKING ANSWERS--
YOU CAME SEEKING THE BLOOD DYNASTY.

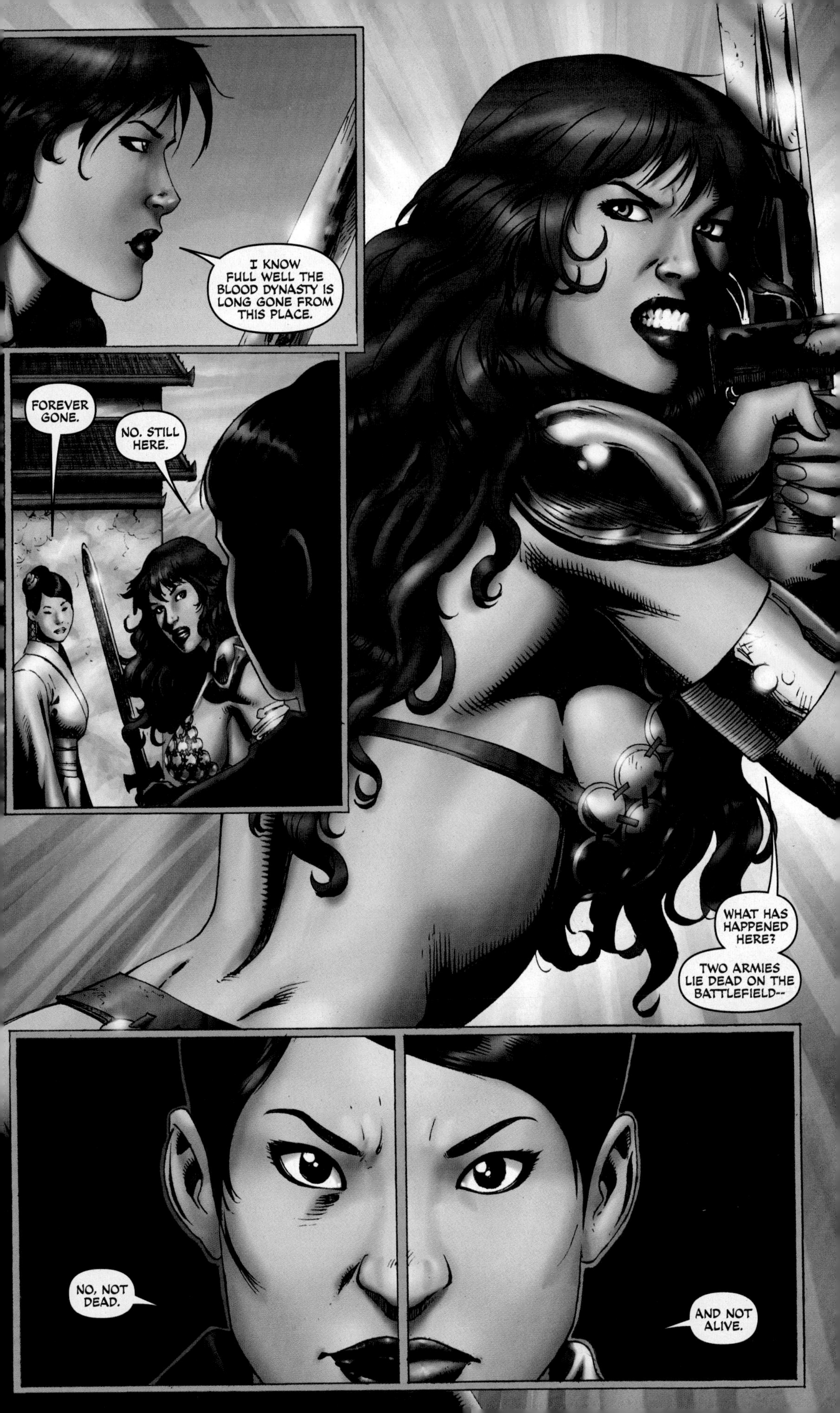
I KNOW FULL WELL THE BLOOD DYNASTY IS LONG GONE FROM THIS PLACE.
FOREVER GONE.
NO. STILL HERE.
WHAT HAS HAPPENED HERE?
TWO ARMIES LIE DEAD ON THE BATTLEFIELD--
NO, NOT DEAD.
AND NOT ALIVE.

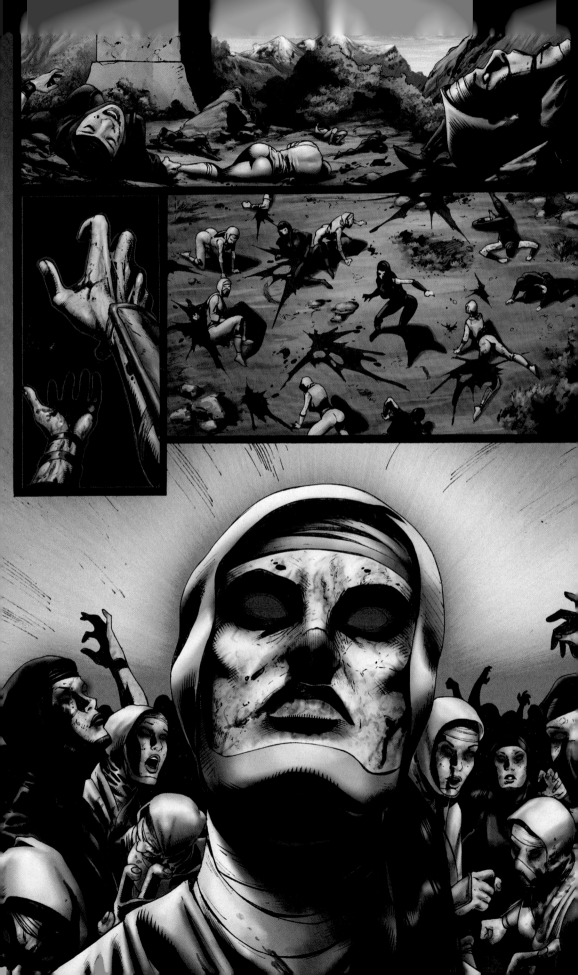

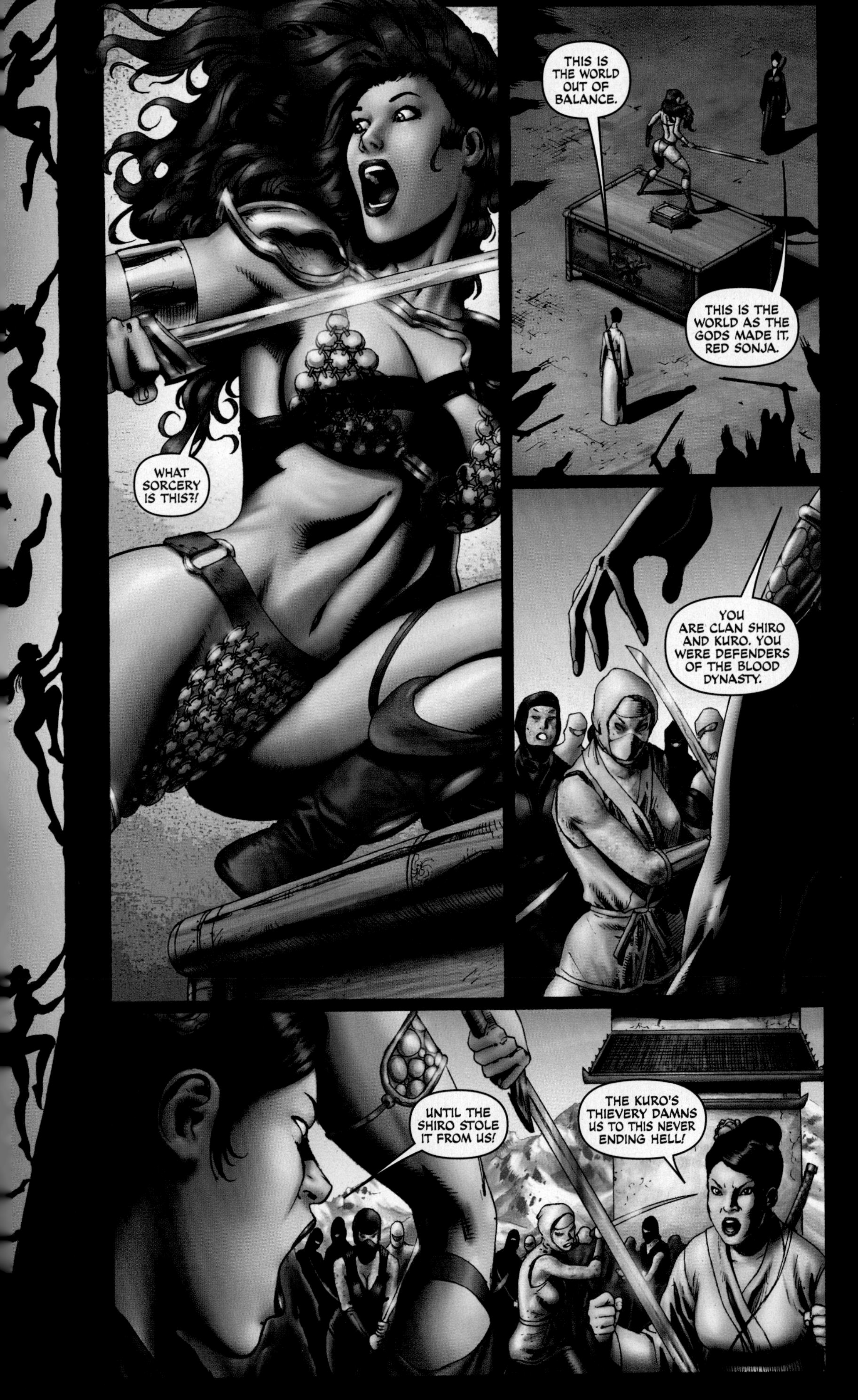
WHAT SORCERY IS THIS?!
THIS IS THE WORLD OUT OF BALANCE.
THIS IS THE WORLD AS THE GODS MADE IT, RED SONJA.
YOU ARE CLAN SHIRO AND KURO. YOU WERE DEFENDERS OF THE BLOOD DYNASTY.
UNTIL THE SHIRO STOLE IT FROM US!
THE KURO'S THIEVERY DAMNS US TO THIS NEVER ENDING HELL!

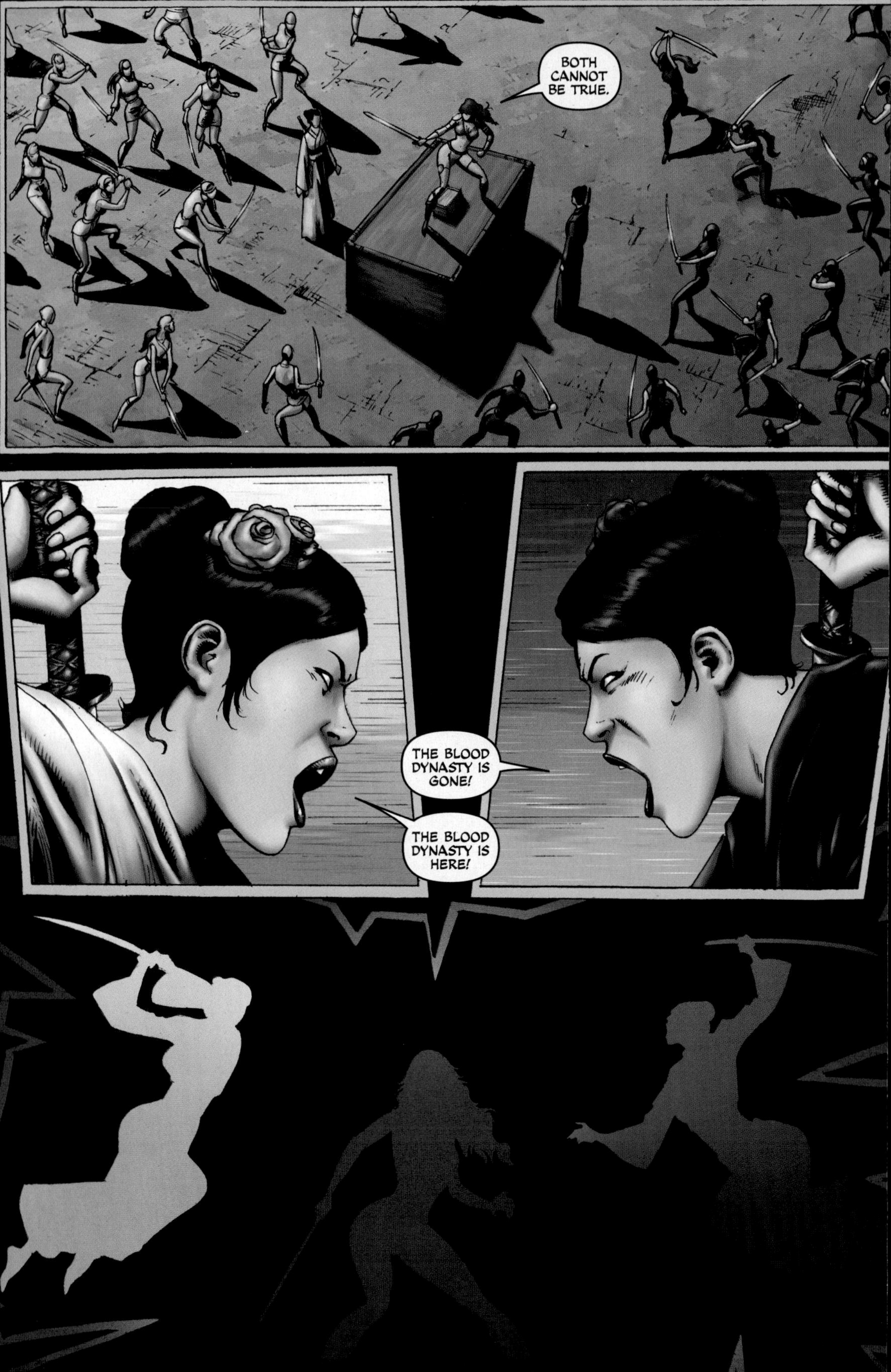

BOTH CANNOT BE TRUE.
THE BLOOD DYNASTY IS GONE!
THE BLOOD DYNASTY IS HERE!

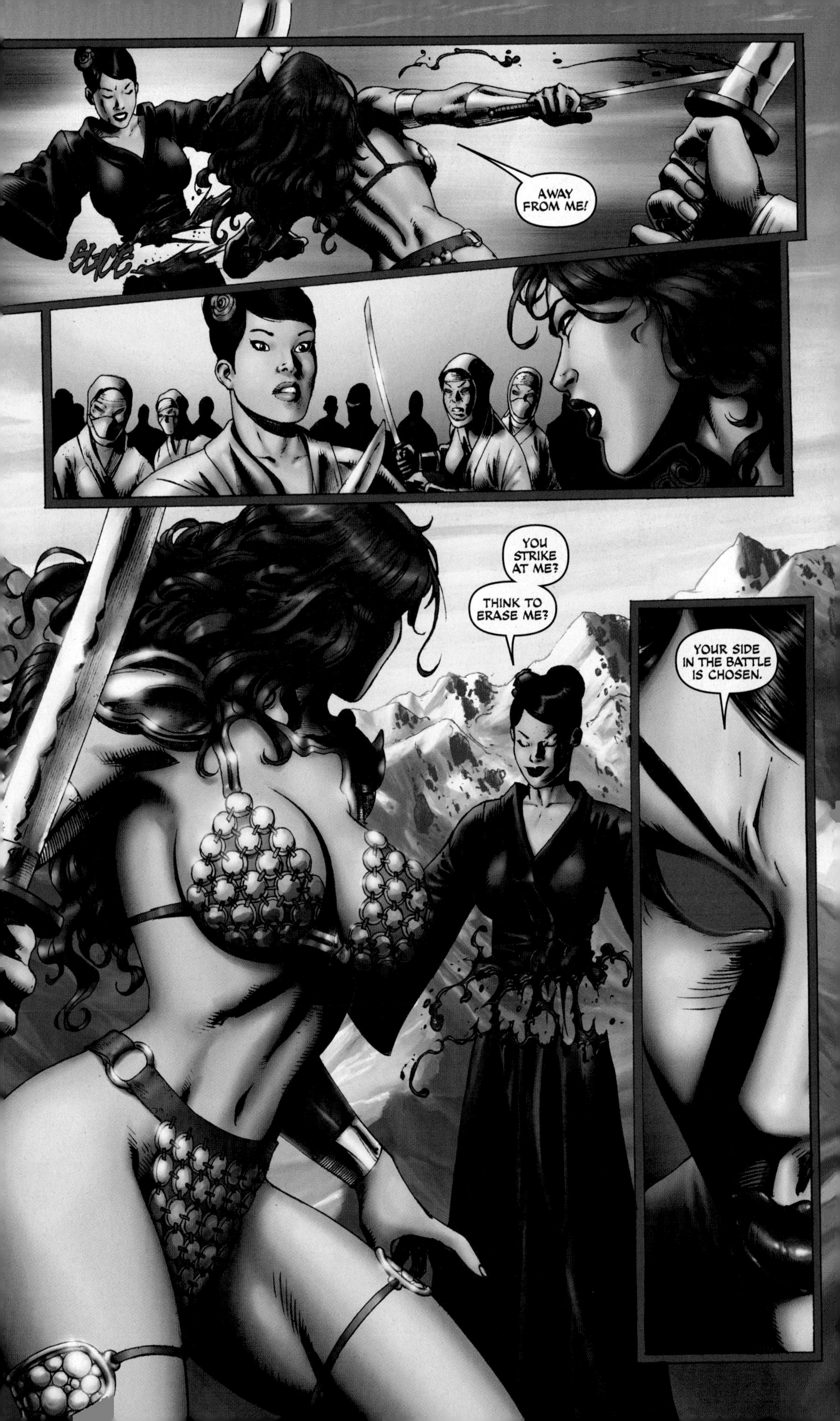
AWAY FROM ME!
SLICE
YOU STRIKE AT ME?
THINK TO ERASE ME?
YOUR SIDE IN THE BATTLE IS CHOSEN.

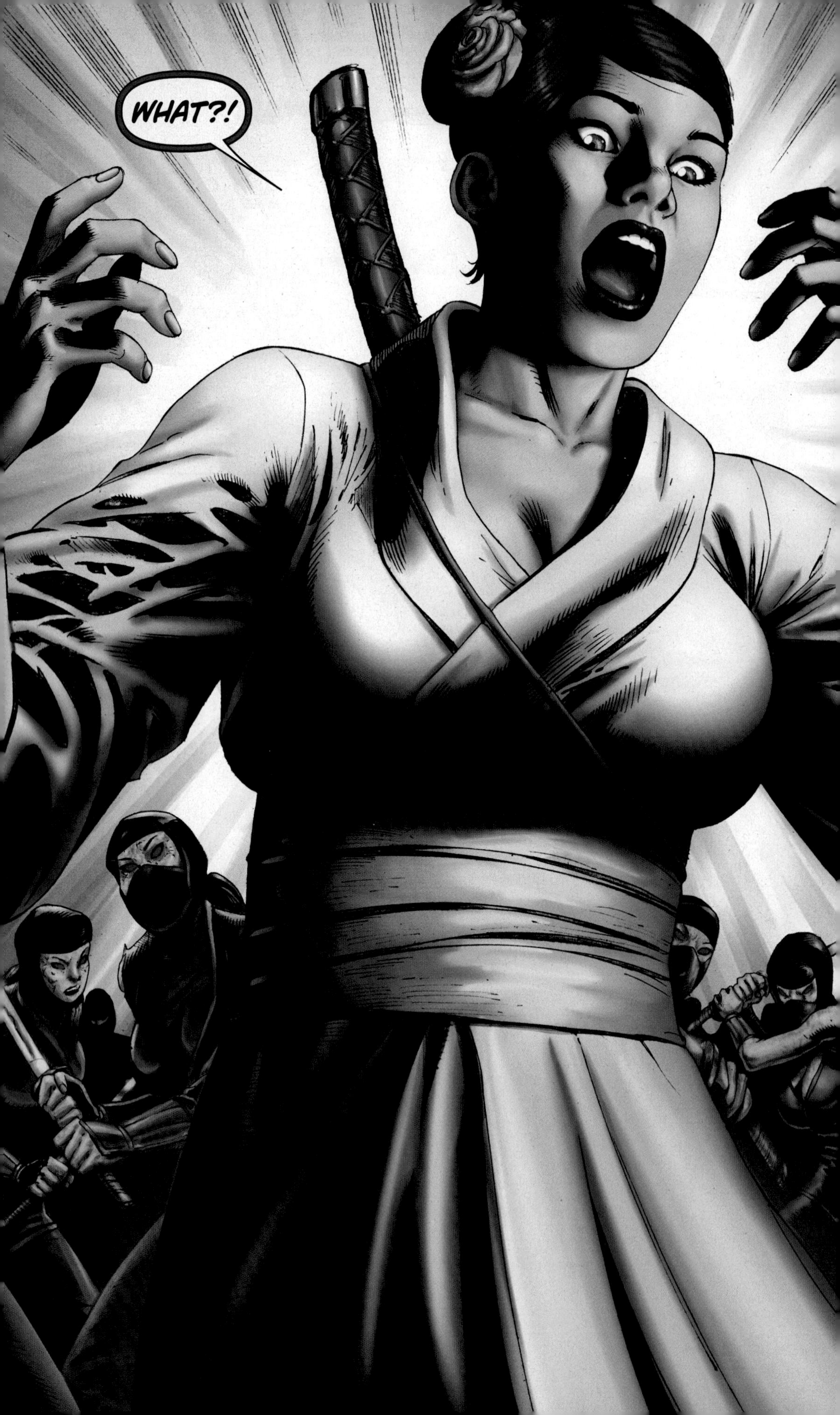
WHAT?!

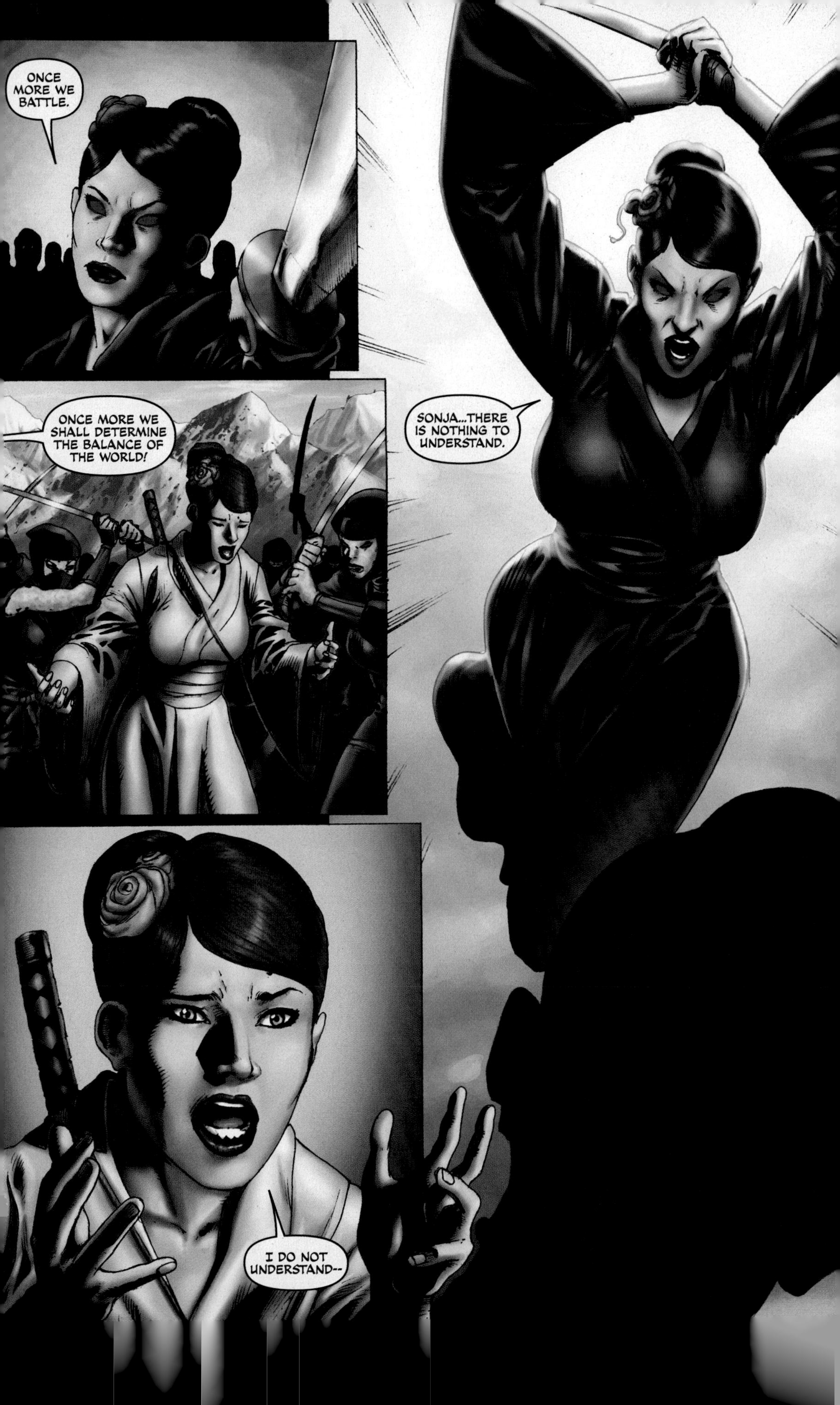
ONCE MORE WE BATTLE.
ONCE MORE WE SHALL DETERMINE THE BALANCE OF THE WORLD!
I DO NOT UNDERSTAND--
SONJA...THERE IS NOTHING TO UNDERSTAND.

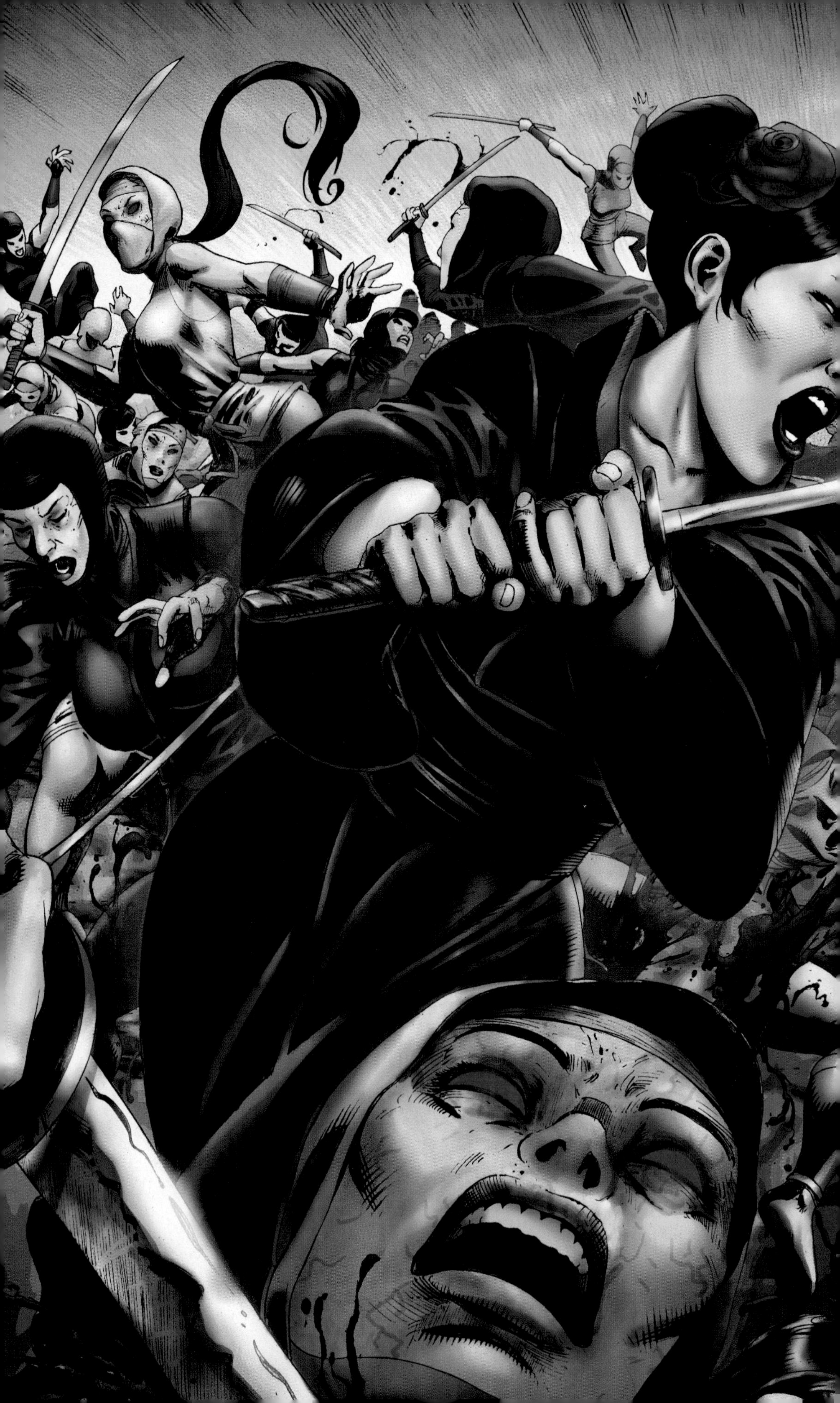

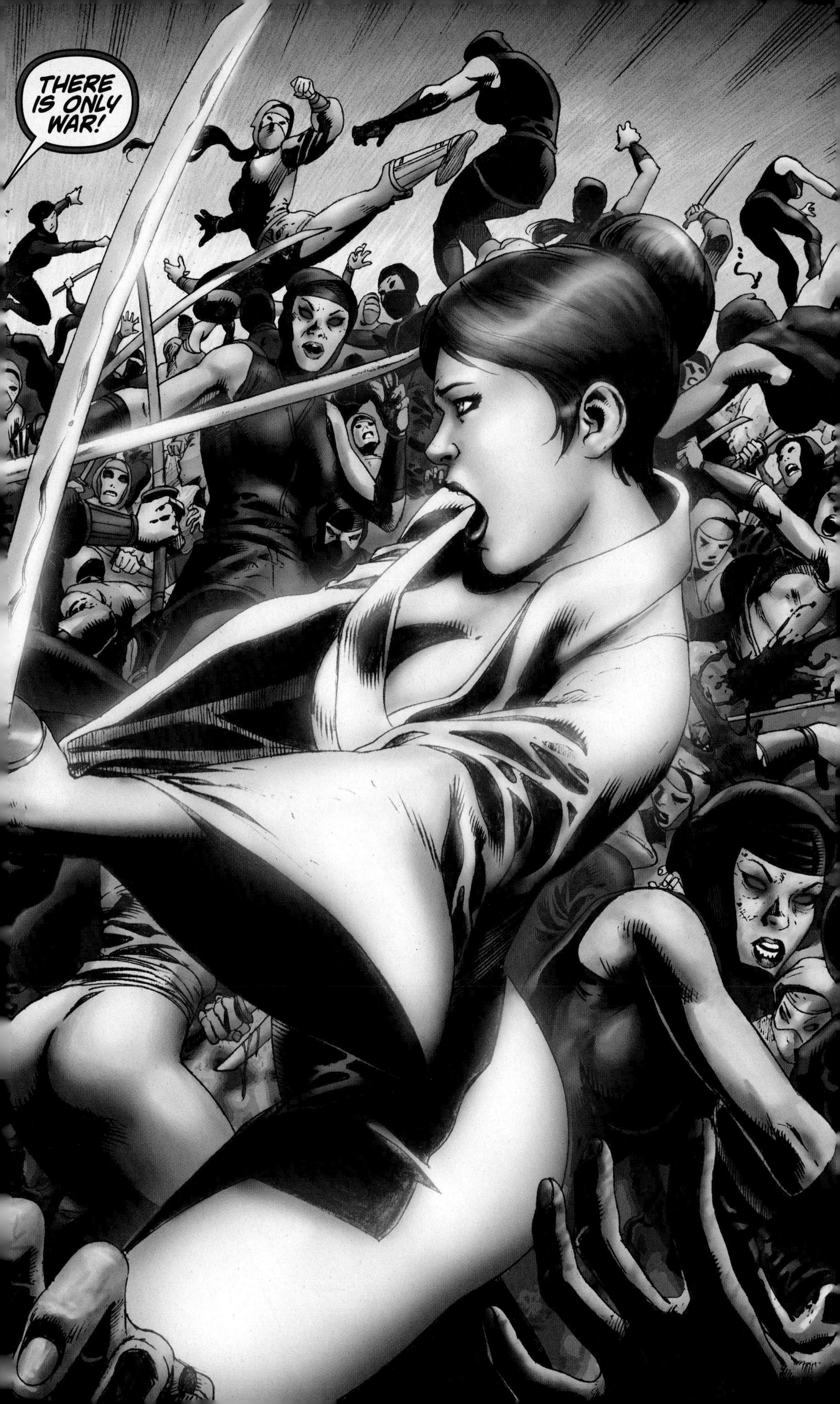
THERE IS ONLY WAR!

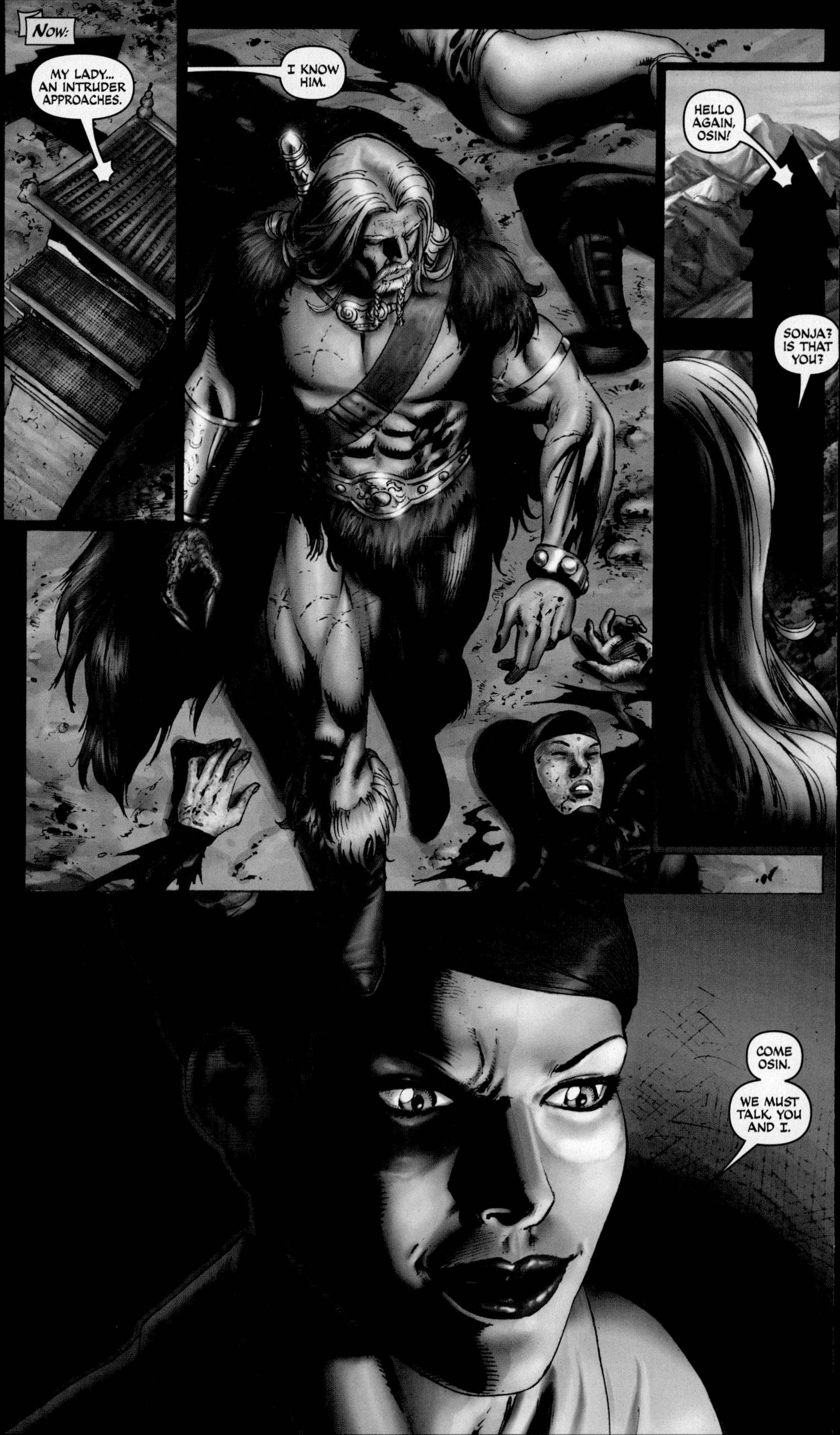
Now:
MY LADY... AN INTRUDER APPROACHES.
I KNOW HIM.
HELLO AGAIN, OSIN!
SONJA? IS THAT YOU?
COME OSIN.
WE MUST TALK, YOU AND I.

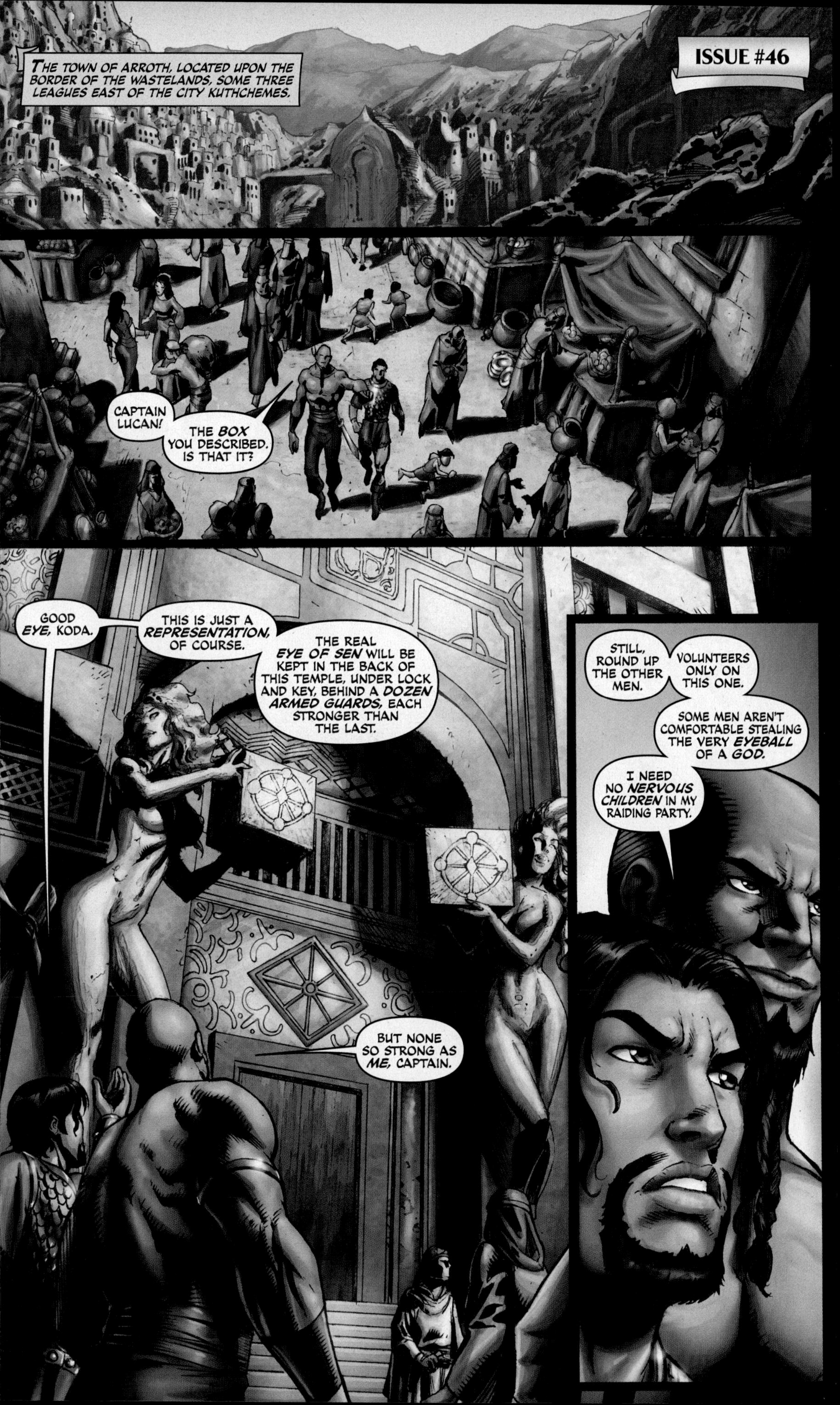

ISSUE #46
THE TOWN OF ARROTH, LOCATED UPON THE BORDER OF THE WASTELANDS, SOME THREE LEAGUES EAST OF THE CITY KUTHCHEMES.
CAPTAIN LUCAN!
THE BOX YOU DESCRIBED. IS THAT IT?
GOOD EYE, KODA.
THIS IS JUST A REPRESENTATION, OF COURSE.
THE REAL EYE OF SEN WILL BE KEPT IN THE BACK OF THIS TEMPLE, UNDER LOCK AND KEY, BEHIND A DOZEN ARMED GUARDS, EACH STRONGER THAN THE LAST.
BUT NONE SO STRONG AS ME, CAPTAIN.
STILL, ROUND UP THE OTHER MEN.
VOLUNTEERS ONLY ON THIS ONE.
SOME MEN AREN'T COMFORTABLE STEALING THE VERY EYEBALL OF A GOD.
I NEED NO NERVOUS CHILDREN IN MY RAIDING PARTY.

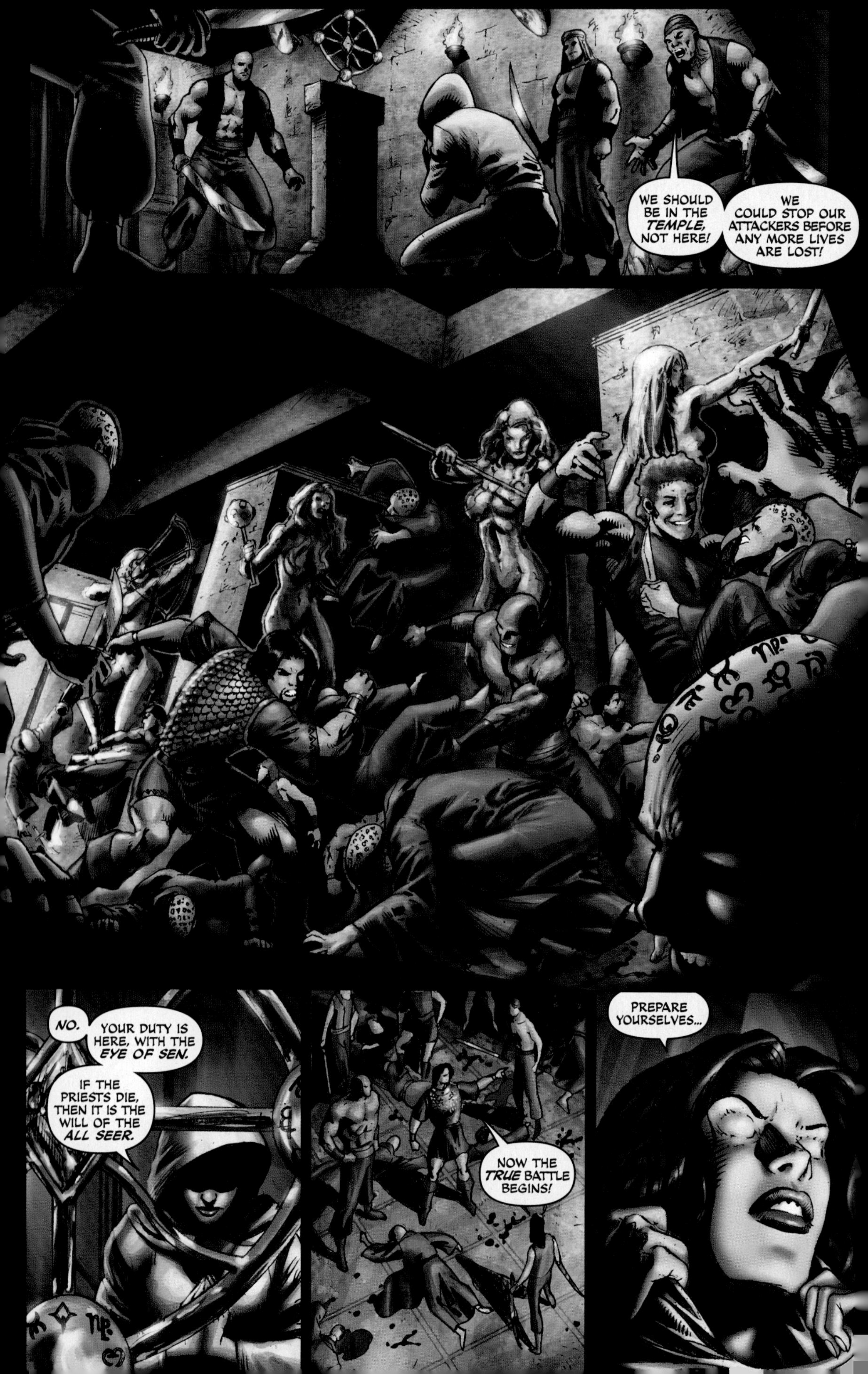
WE SHOULD BE IN THE *TEMPLE,* NOT HERE!
WE COULD STOP OUR ATTACKERS BEFORE ANY MORE LIVES ARE LOST!
NO.
YOUR DUTY IS HERE, WITH THE *EYE OF SEN.*
IF THE PRIESTS DIE, THEN IT IS THE WILL OF THE *ALL SEER.*
NOW THE *TRUE* BATTLE BEGINS!
PREPARE YOURSELVES...

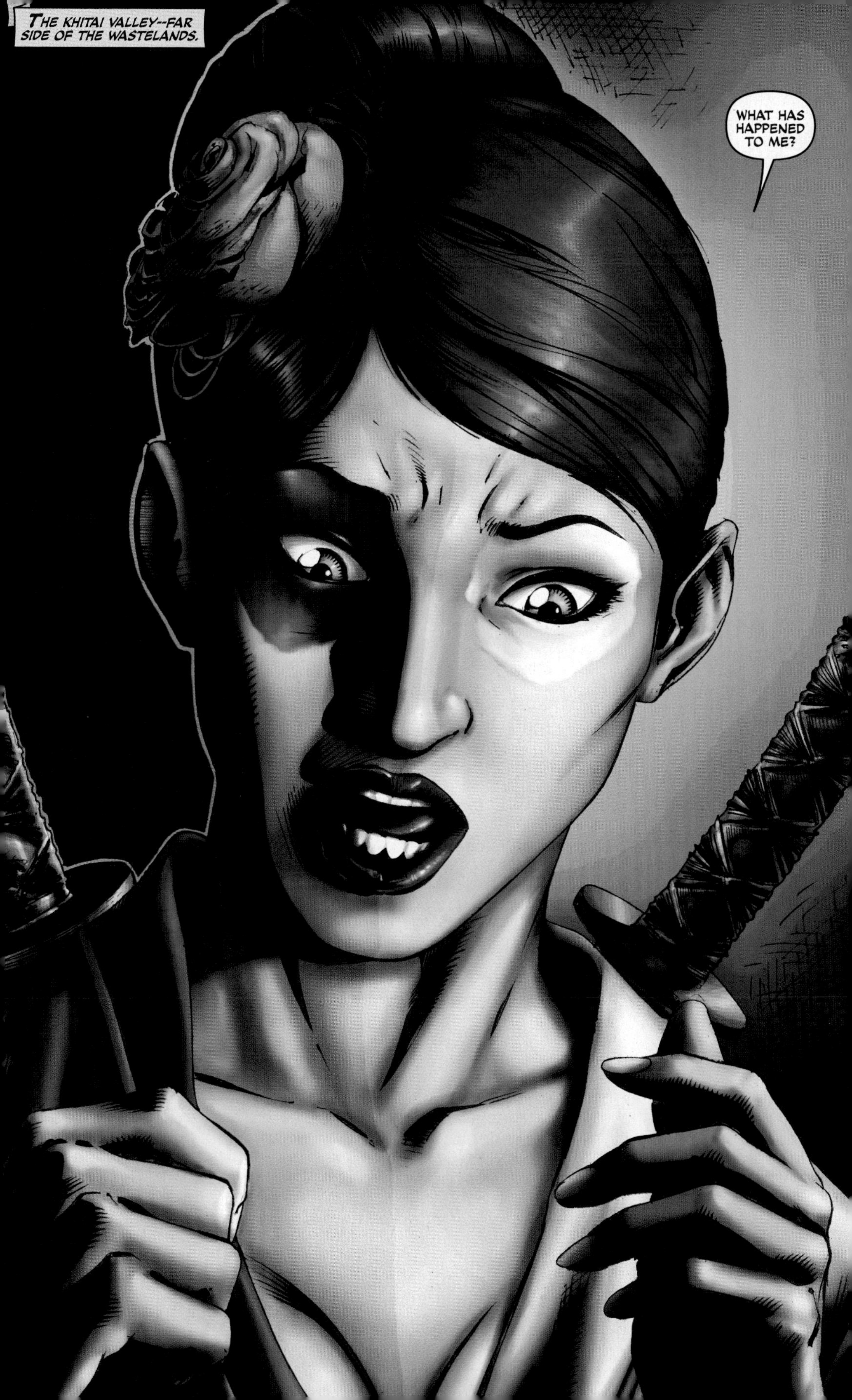
THE KHITAI VALLEY--FAR SIDE OF THE WASTELANDS.
WHAT HAS HAPPENED TO ME?

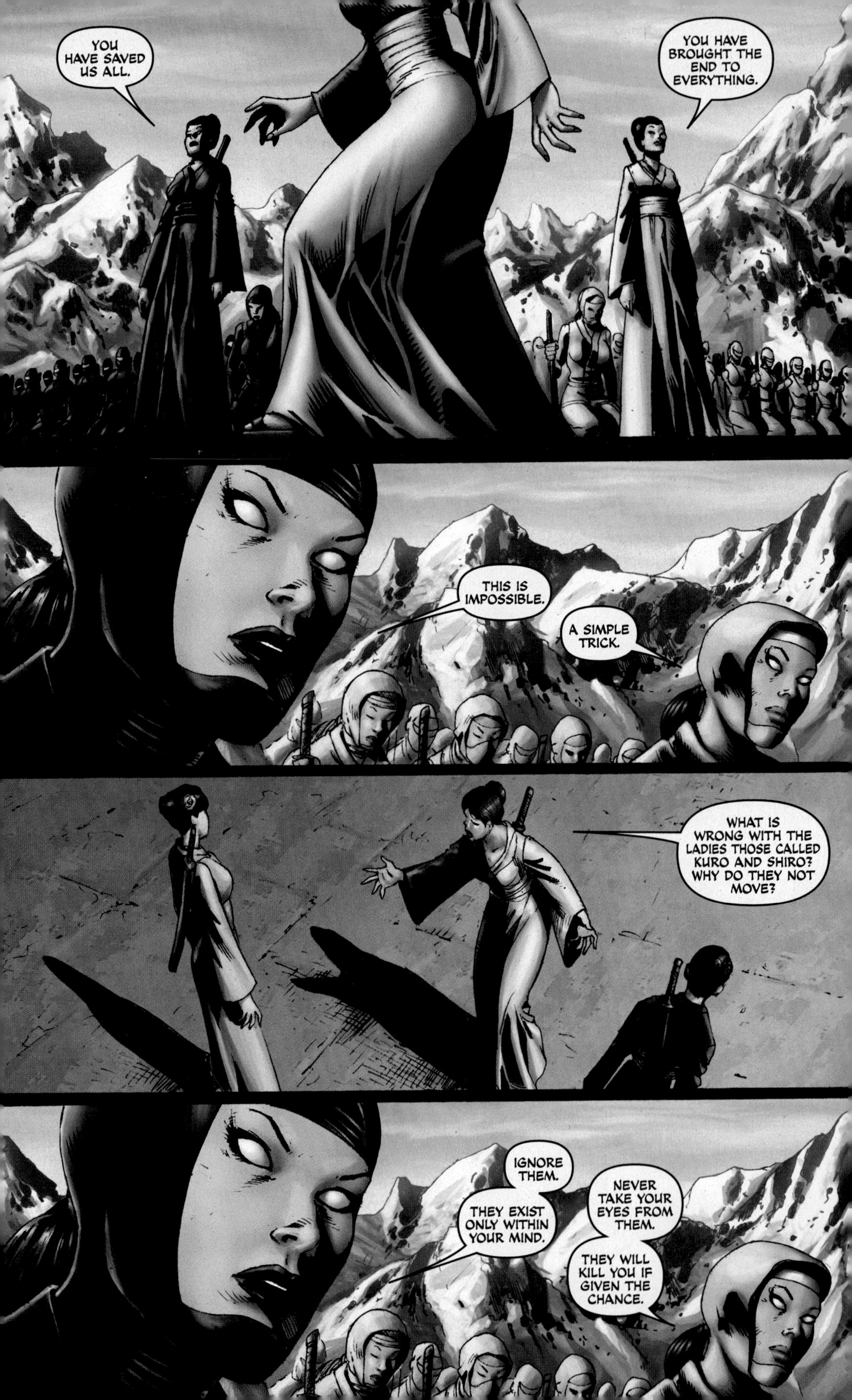
YOU HAVE SAVED US ALL.
YOU HAVE BROUGHT THE END TO EVERYTHING.
THIS IS IMPOSSIBLE.
A SIMPLE TRICK.
WHAT IS WRONG WITH THE LADIES THOSE CALLED KURO AND SHIRO? WHY DO THEY NOT MOVE?
IGNORE THEM.
THEY EXIST ONLY WITHIN YOUR MIND.
NEVER TAKE YOUR EYES FROM THEM.
THEY WILL KILL YOU IF GIVEN THE CHANCE.

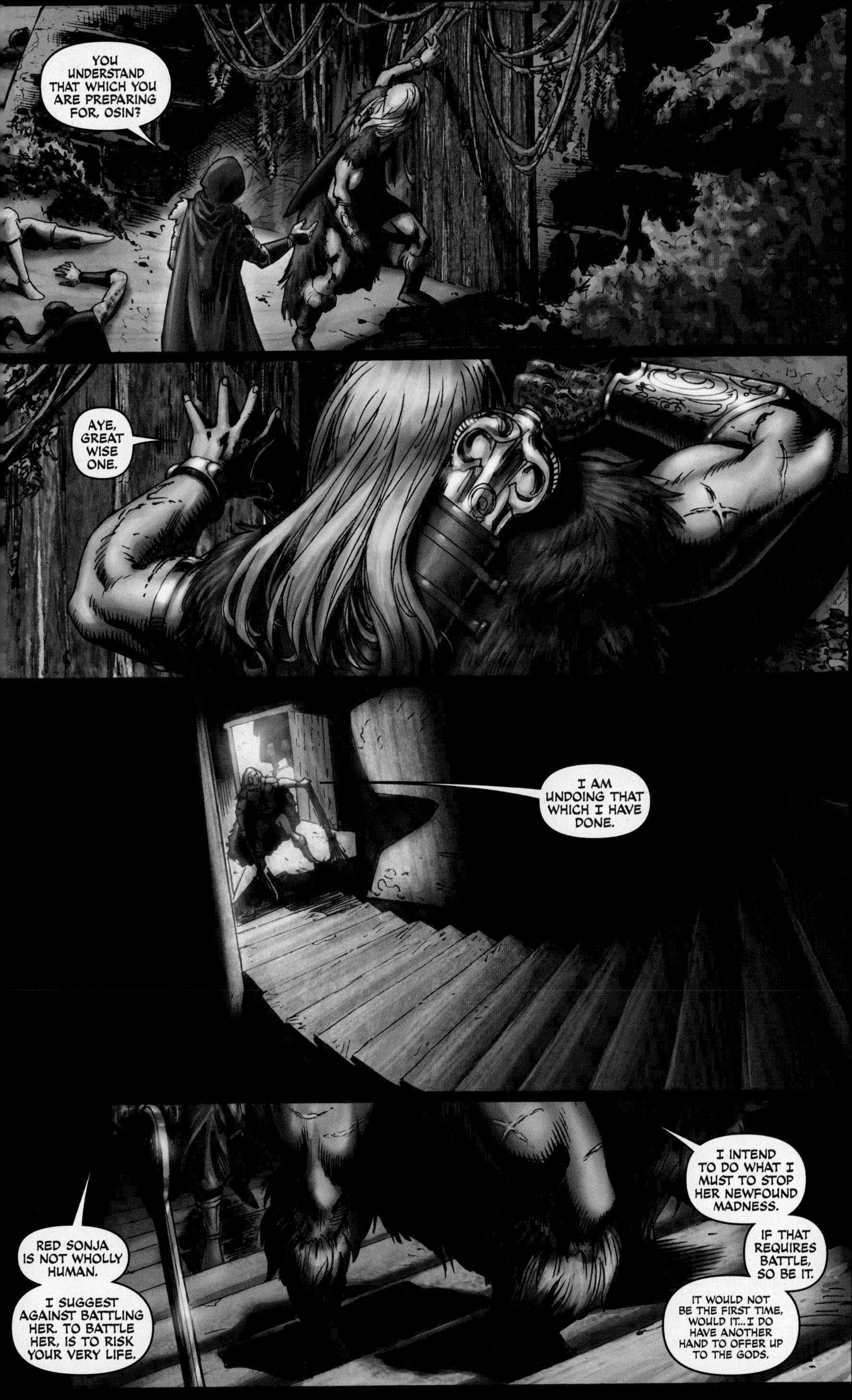
YOU UNDERSTAND THAT WHICH YOU ARE PREPARING FOR, OSIN?
AYE, GREAT WISE ONE.
I AM UNDOING THAT WHICH I HAVE DONE.
RED SONJA IS NOT WHOLLY HUMAN.
I SUGGEST AGAINST BATTLING HER. TO BATTLE HER, IS TO RISK YOUR VERY LIFE.
I INTEND TO DO WHAT I MUST TO STOP HER NEWFOUND MADNESS.
IF THAT REQUIRES BATTLE, SO BE IT.
IT WOULD NOT BE THE FIRST TIME, WOULD IT...I DO HAVE ANOTHER HAND TO OFFER UP TO THE GODS.

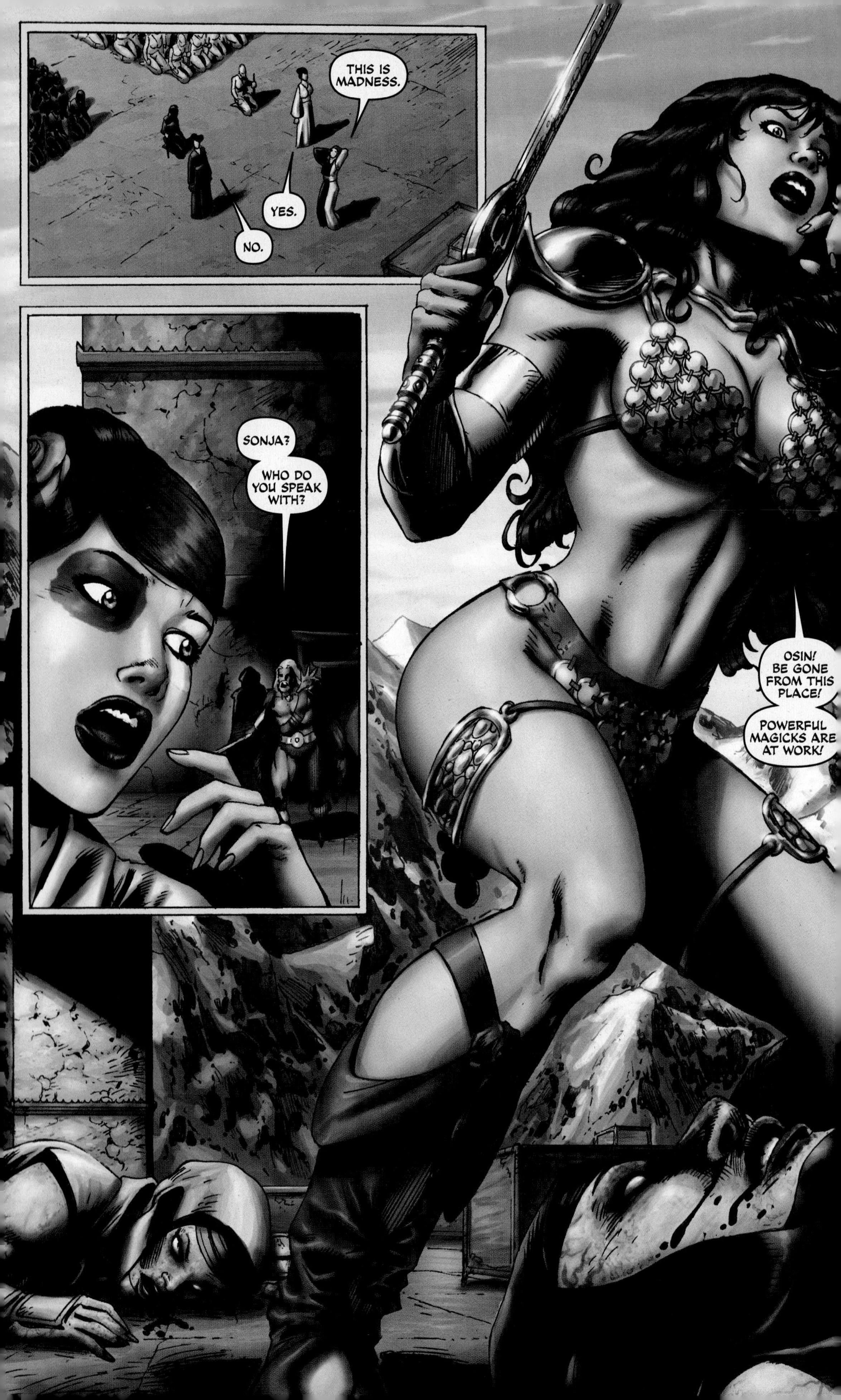

THIS IS MADNESS.
YES.
NO.
SONJA?
WHO DO YOU SPEAK WITH?
OSIN! BE GONE FROM THIS PLACE!
POWERFUL MAGICKS ARE AT WORK!

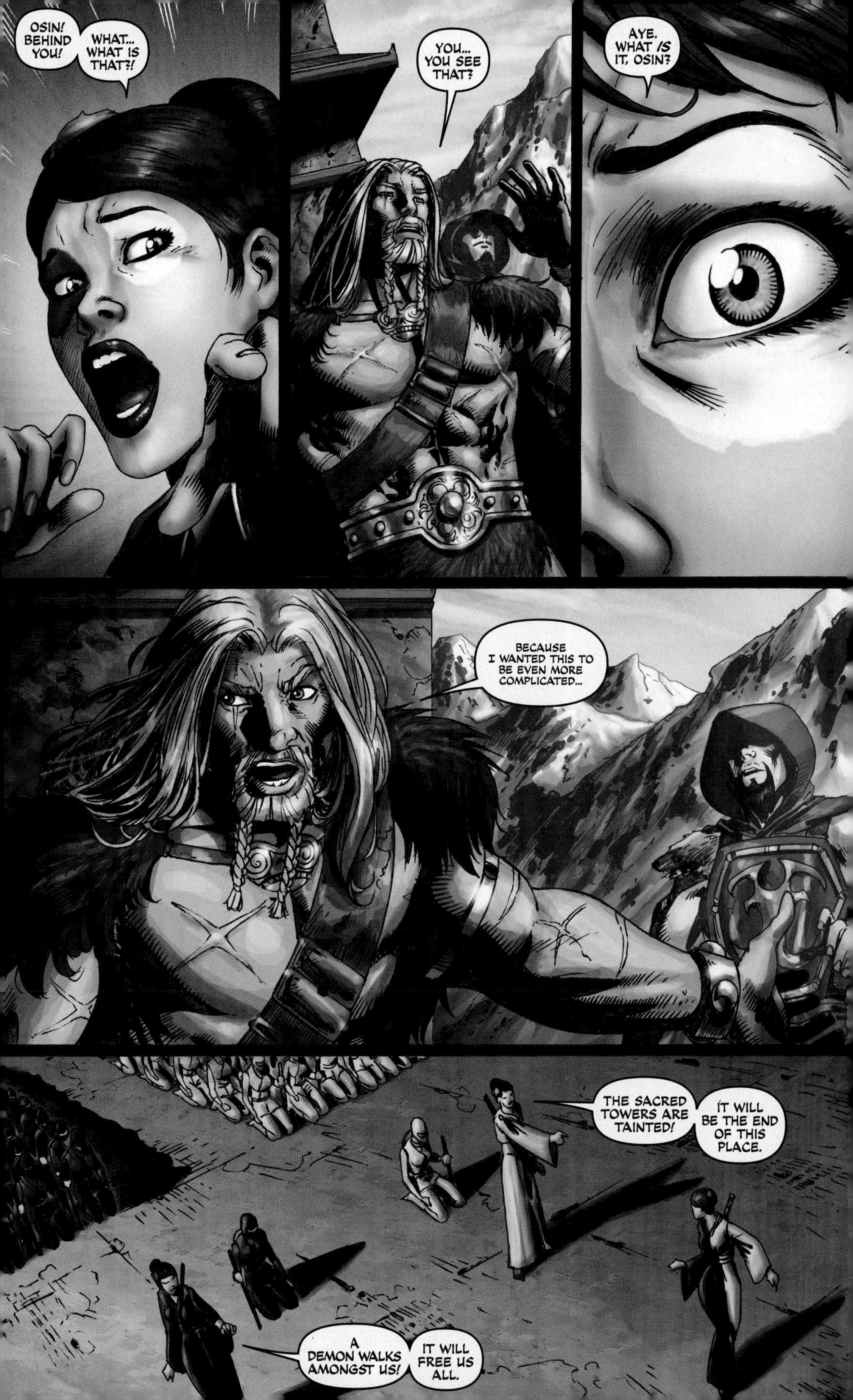
OSIN! BEHIND YOU!
WHAT... WHAT IS THAT?!
YOU... YOU SEE THAT?
AYE. WHAT IS IT, OSIN?
BECAUSE I WANTED THIS TO BE EVEN MORE COMPLICATED...
THE SACRED TOWERS ARE TAINTED!
IT WILL BE THE END OF THIS PLACE.
A DEMON WALKS AMONGST US!
IT WILL FREE US ALL.

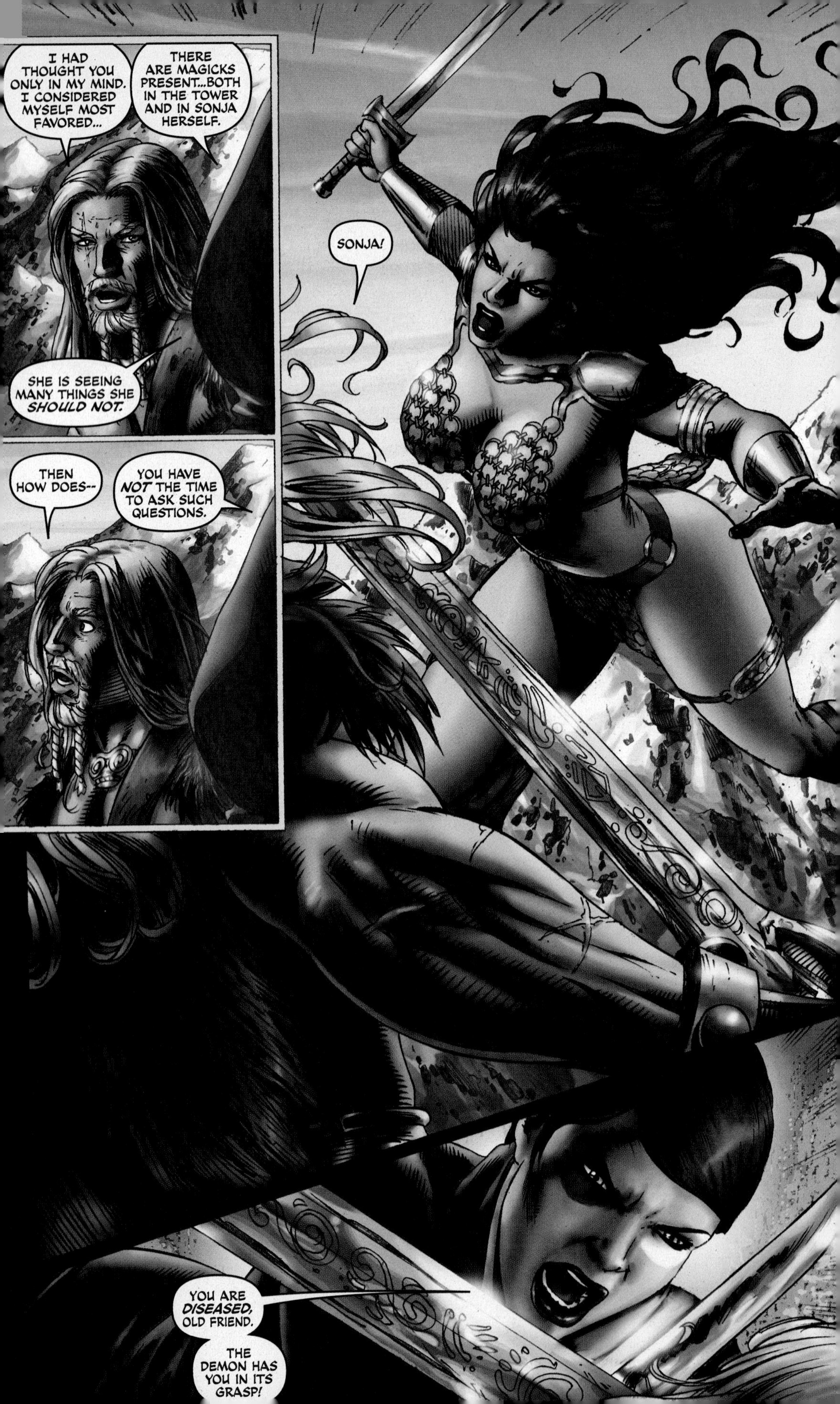
I HAD THOUGHT YOU ONLY IN MY MIND. I CONSIDERED MYSELF MOST FAVORED...
THERE ARE MAGICKS PRESENT...BOTH IN THE TOWER AND IN SONJA HERSELF.
SHE IS SEEING MANY THINGS SHE *SHOULD NOT.*
THEN HOW DOES--
YOU HAVE *NOT* THE TIME TO ASK SUCH QUESTIONS.
SONJA!
YOU ARE *DISEASED,* OLD FRIEND.
THE DEMON HAS YOU IN ITS GRASP!

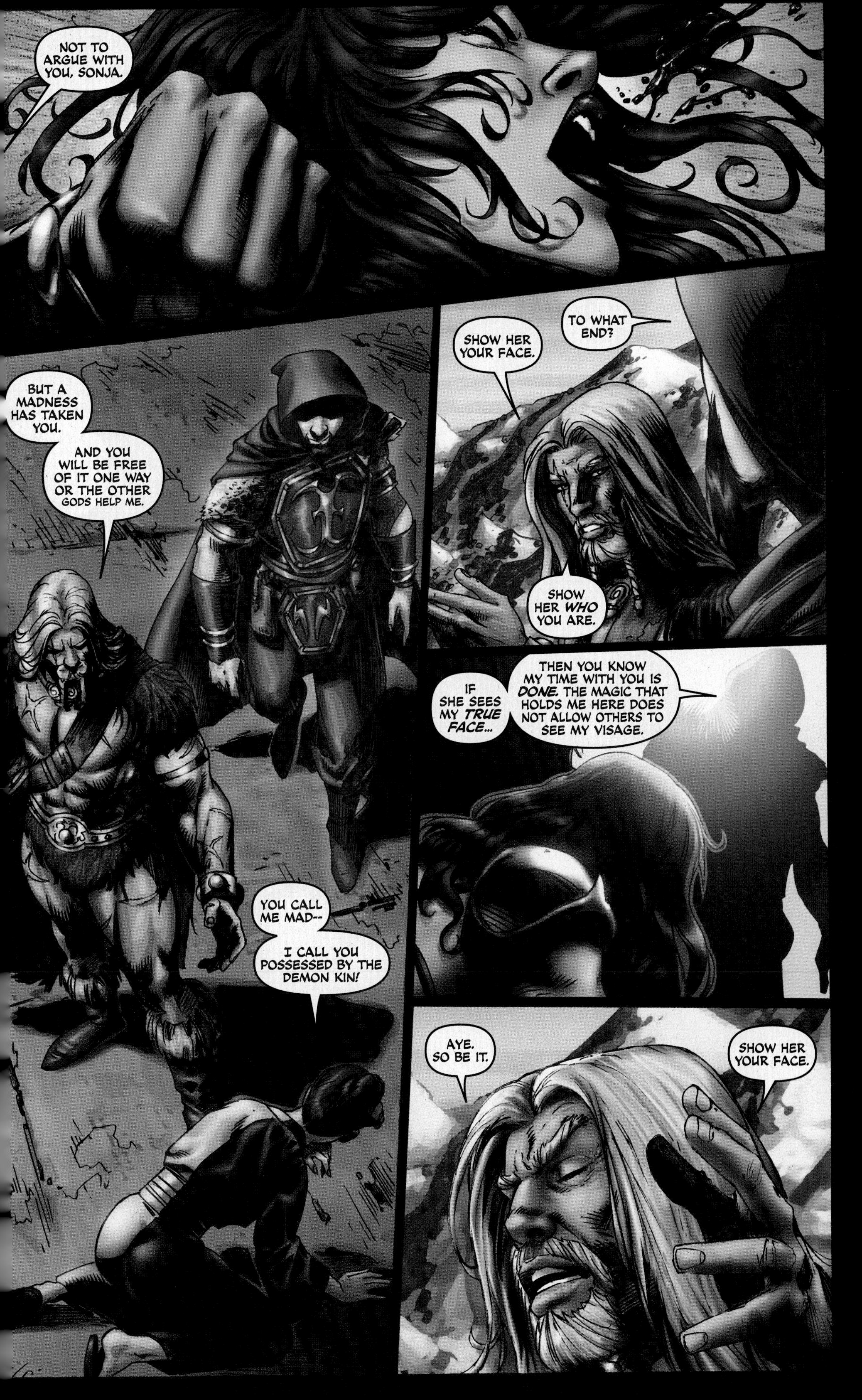
NOT TO ARGUE WITH YOU, SONJA.
BUT A MADNESS HAS TAKEN YOU.
AND YOU WILL BE FREE OF IT ONE WAY OR THE OTHER GODS HELP ME.
YOU CALL ME MAD--
I CALL YOU POSSESSED BY THE DEMON KIN!
SHOW HER YOUR FACE.
TO WHAT END?
SHOW HER *WHO* YOU ARE.
IF SHE SEES MY *TRUE FACE*...
THEN YOU KNOW MY TIME WITH YOU IS *DONE.* THE MAGIC THAT HOLDS ME HERE DOES NOT ALLOW OTHERS TO SEE MY VISAGE.
AYE. SO BE IT.
SHOW HER YOUR FACE.

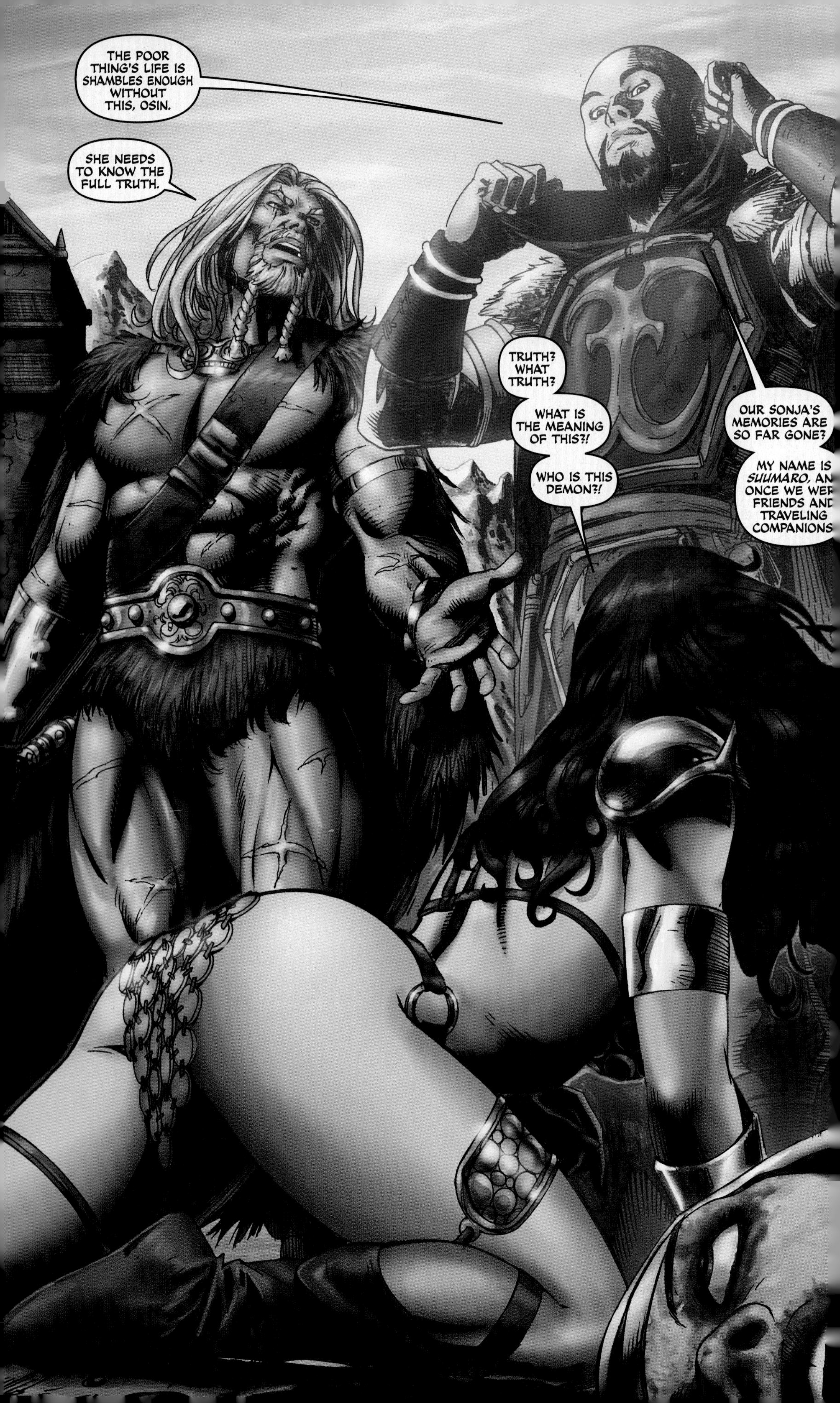
THE POOR THING'S LIFE IS SHAMBLES ENOUGH WITHOUT THIS, OSIN.
SHE NEEDS TO KNOW THE FULL TRUTH.
TRUTH? WHAT TRUTH?
WHAT IS THE MEANING OF THIS?!
WHO IS THIS DEMON?!
OUR SONJA'S MEMORIES ARE SO FAR GONE?
MY NAME IS *SUUMARO*, AN ONCE WE WER FRIENDS AN TRAVELING COMPANIONS

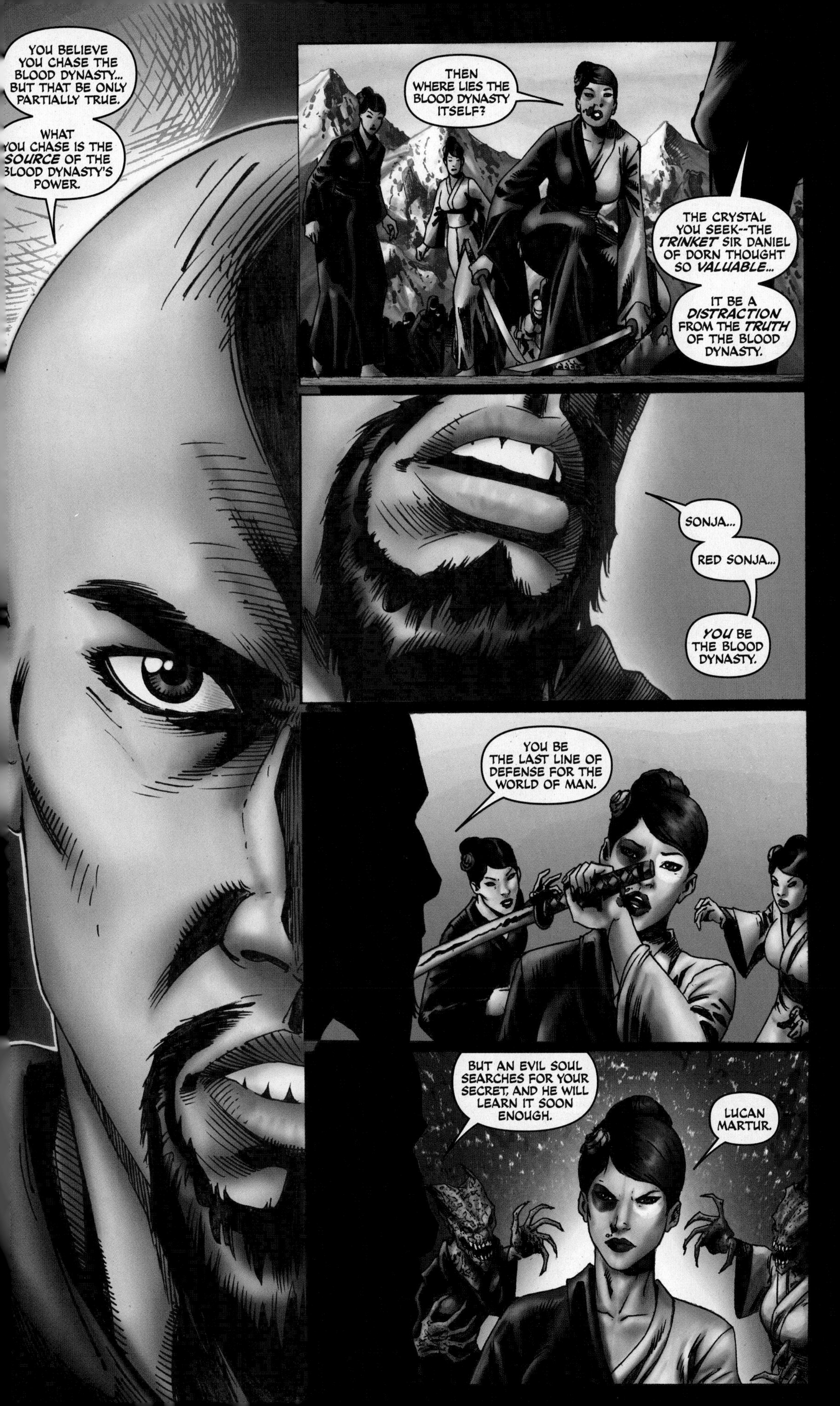
YOU BELIEVE YOU CHASE THE BLOOD DYNASTY... BUT THAT BE ONLY PARTIALLY TRUE.
WHAT YOU CHASE IS THE *SOURCE* OF THE BLOOD DYNASTY'S POWER.
THEN WHERE LIES THE BLOOD DYNASTY ITSELF?
THE CRYSTAL YOU SEEK--THE *TRINKET* SIR DANIEL OF DORN THOUGHT SO *VALUABLE*...
IT BE A *DISTRACTION* FROM THE *TRUTH* OF THE BLOOD DYNASTY.
SONJA...
RED SONJA...
YOU BE THE BLOOD DYNASTY.
YOU BE THE LAST LINE OF DEFENSE FOR THE WORLD OF MAN.
BUT AN EVIL SOUL SEARCHES FOR YOUR SECRET, AND HE WILL LEARN IT SOON ENOUGH.
LUCAN MARTUR.

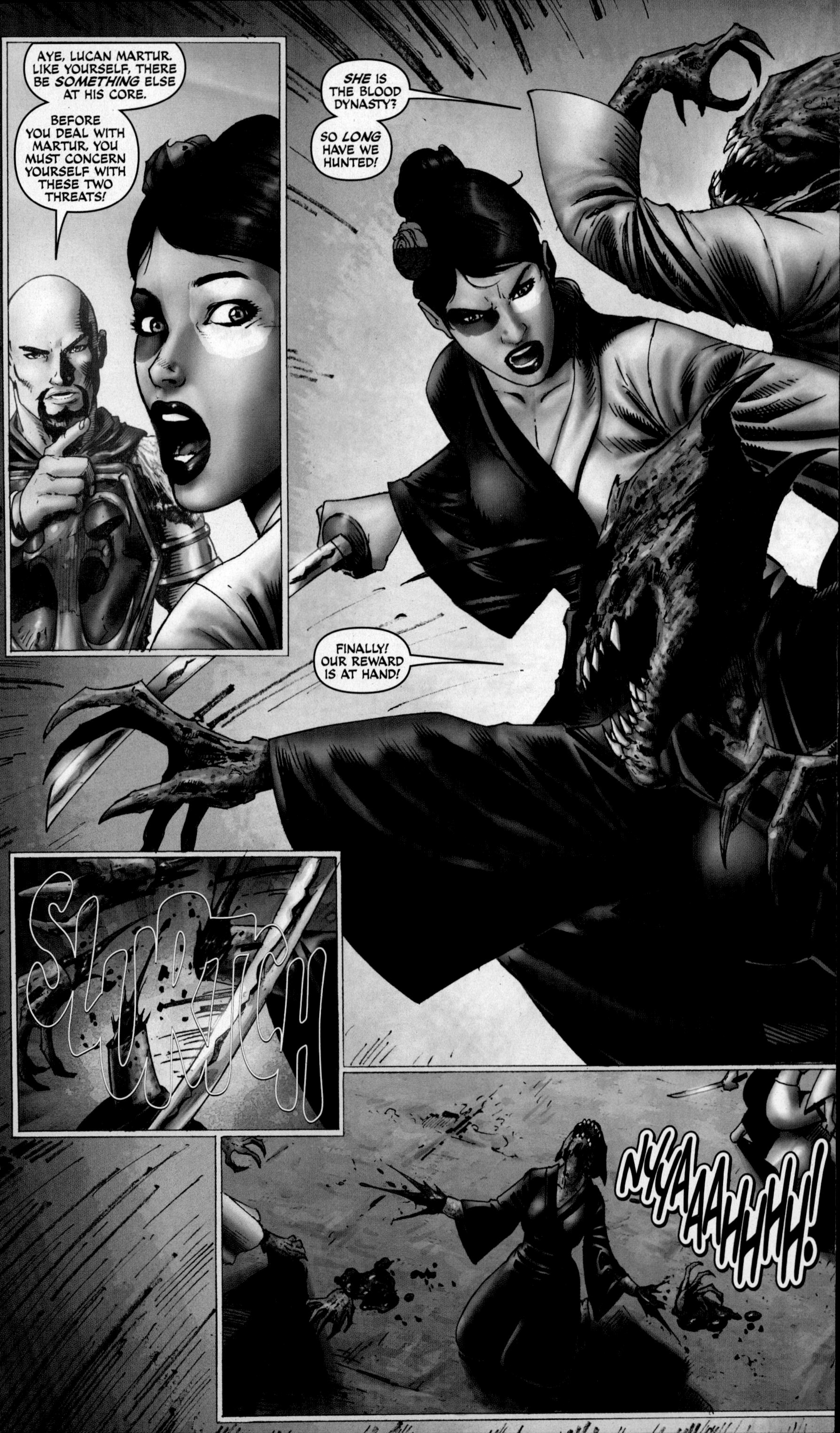

AYE, LUCAN MARTUR. LIKE YOURSELF, THERE BE SOMETHING ELSE AT HIS CORE.
BEFORE YOU DEAL WITH MARTUR, YOU MUST CONCERN YOURSELF WITH THESE TWO THREATS!
SHE IS THE BLOOD DYNASTY?
SO LONG HAVE WE HUNTED!
FINALLY! OUR REWARD IS AT HAND!
SLURTCH
NYYAAAHHHH!

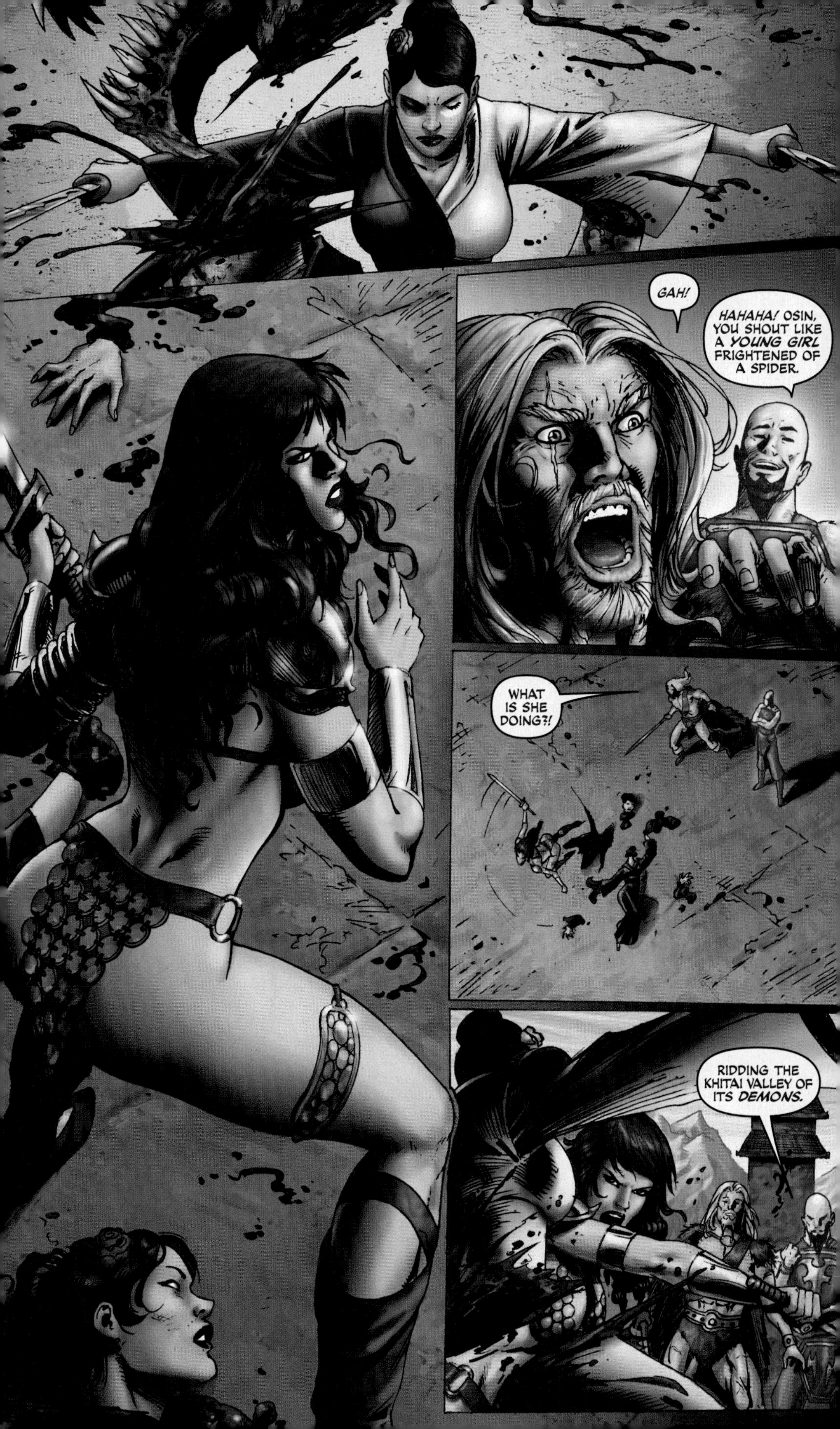
GAH!
HAHAHA! OSIN, YOU SHOUT LIKE A YOUNG GIRL FRIGHTENED OF A SPIDER.
WHAT IS SHE DOING?!
RIDDING THE KHITAI VALLEY OF ITS DEMONS.

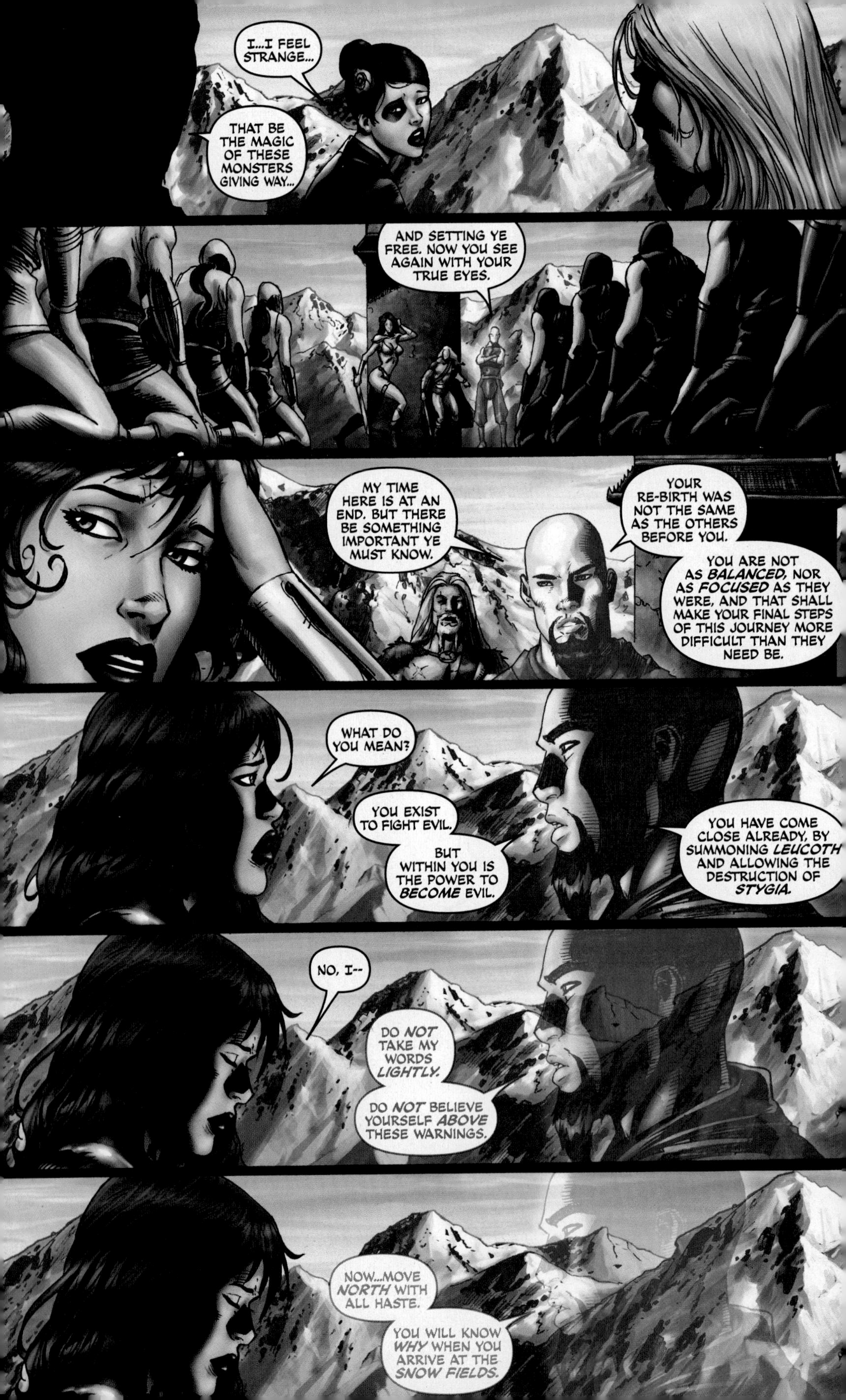

I...I FEEL STRANGE...
THAT BE THE MAGIC OF THESE MONSTERS GIVING WAY...
AND SETTING YE FREE. NOW YOU SEE AGAIN WITH YOUR TRUE EYES.
MY TIME HERE IS AT AN END. BUT THERE BE SOMETHING IMPORTANT YE MUST KNOW.
YOUR RE-BIRTH WAS NOT THE SAME AS THE OTHERS BEFORE YOU.
YOU ARE NOT AS BALANCED, NOR AS FOCUSED AS THEY WERE, AND THAT SHALL MAKE YOUR FINAL STEPS OF THIS JOURNEY MORE DIFFICULT THAN THEY NEED BE.
WHAT DO YOU MEAN?
YOU EXIST TO FIGHT EVIL.
BUT WITHIN YOU IS THE POWER TO BECOME EVIL.
YOU HAVE COME CLOSE ALREADY, BY SUMMONING LEUCOTH AND ALLOWING THE DESTRUCTION OF STYGIA.
NO, I--
DO NOT TAKE MY WORDS LIGHTLY.
DO NOT BELIEVE YOURSELF ABOVE THESE WARNINGS.
NOW...MOVE NORTH WITH ALL HASTE.
YOU WILL KNOW WHY WHEN YOU ARRIVE AT THE SNOW FIELDS.

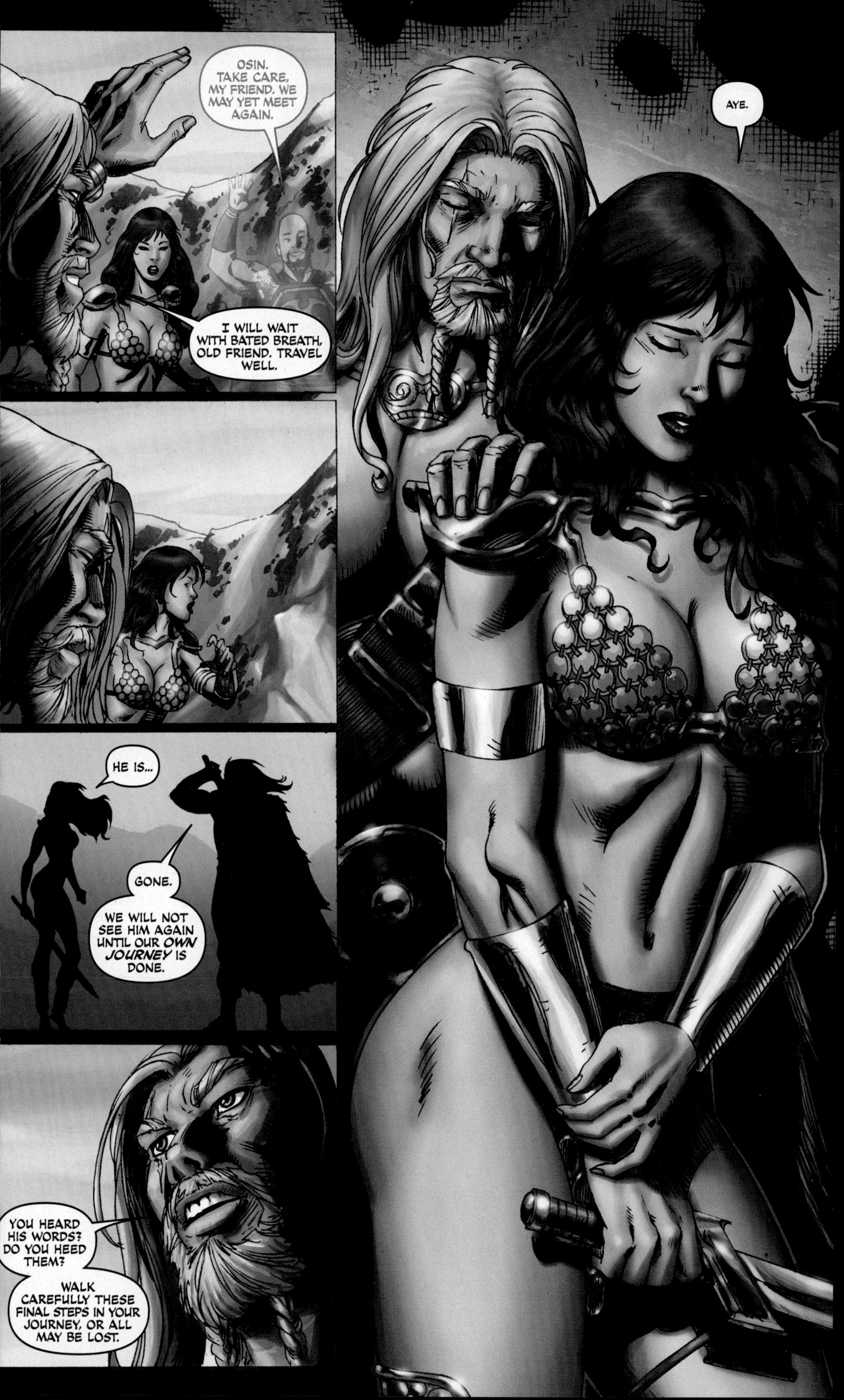
OSIN. TAKE CARE, MY FRIEND. WE MAY YET MEET AGAIN.
I WILL WAIT WITH BATED BREATH, OLD FRIEND. TRAVEL WELL.
HE IS...
GONE.
WE WILL NOT SEE HIM AGAIN UNTIL OUR *OWN JOURNEY* IS DONE.
YOU HEARD HIS WORDS? DO YOU HEED THEM?
WALK CAREFULLY THESE FINAL STEPS IN YOUR JOURNEY, OR ALL MAY BE LOST.
AYE.

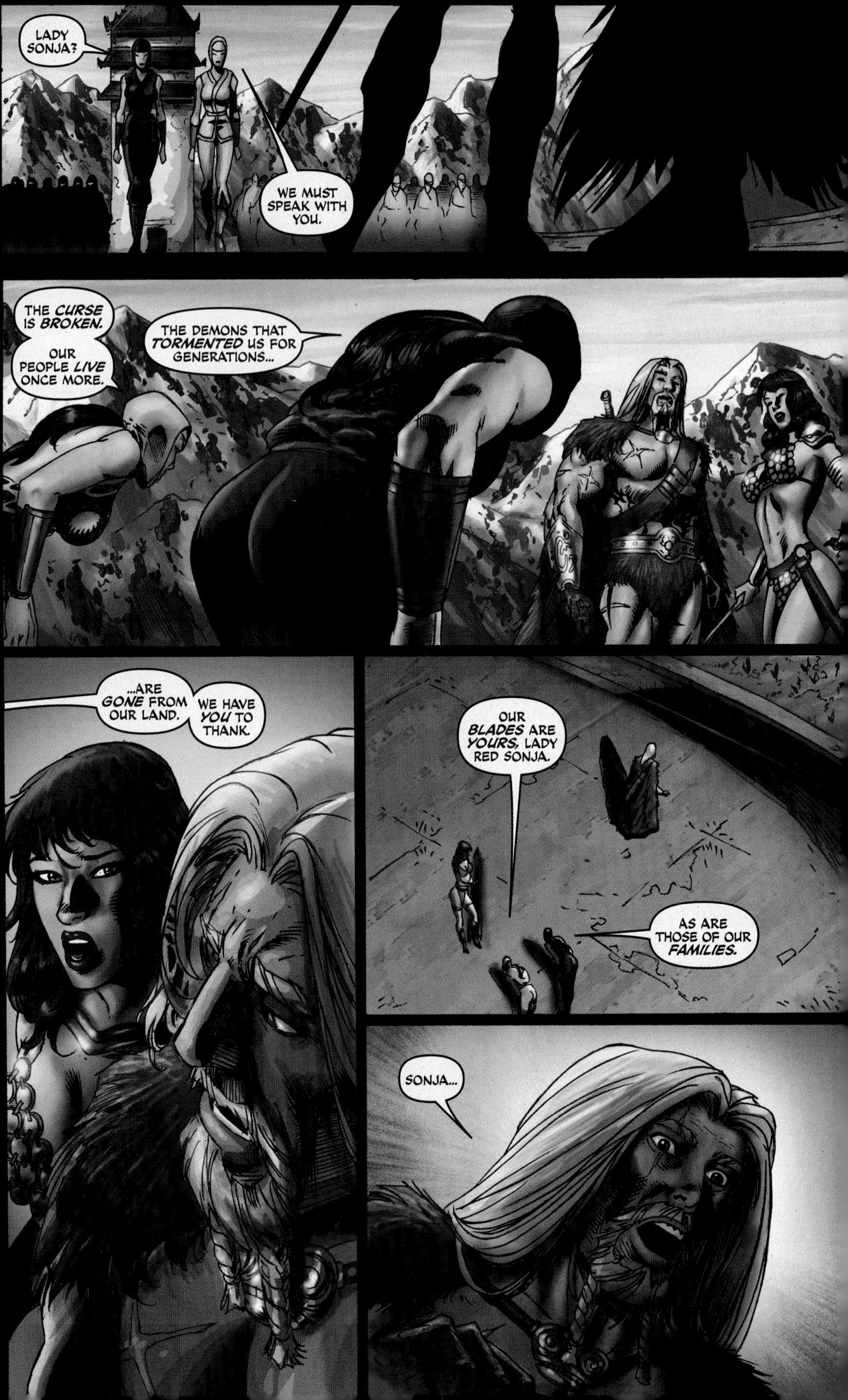

LADY SONJA?
WE MUST SPEAK WITH YOU.
THE CURSE IS BROKEN.
OUR PEOPLE LIVE ONCE MORE.
THE DEMONS THAT TORMENTED US FOR GENERATIONS...
...ARE GONE FROM OUR LAND.
WE HAVE YOU TO THANK.
OUR BLADES ARE YOURS, LADY RED SONJA.
AS ARE THOSE OF OUR FAMILIES.
SONJA...

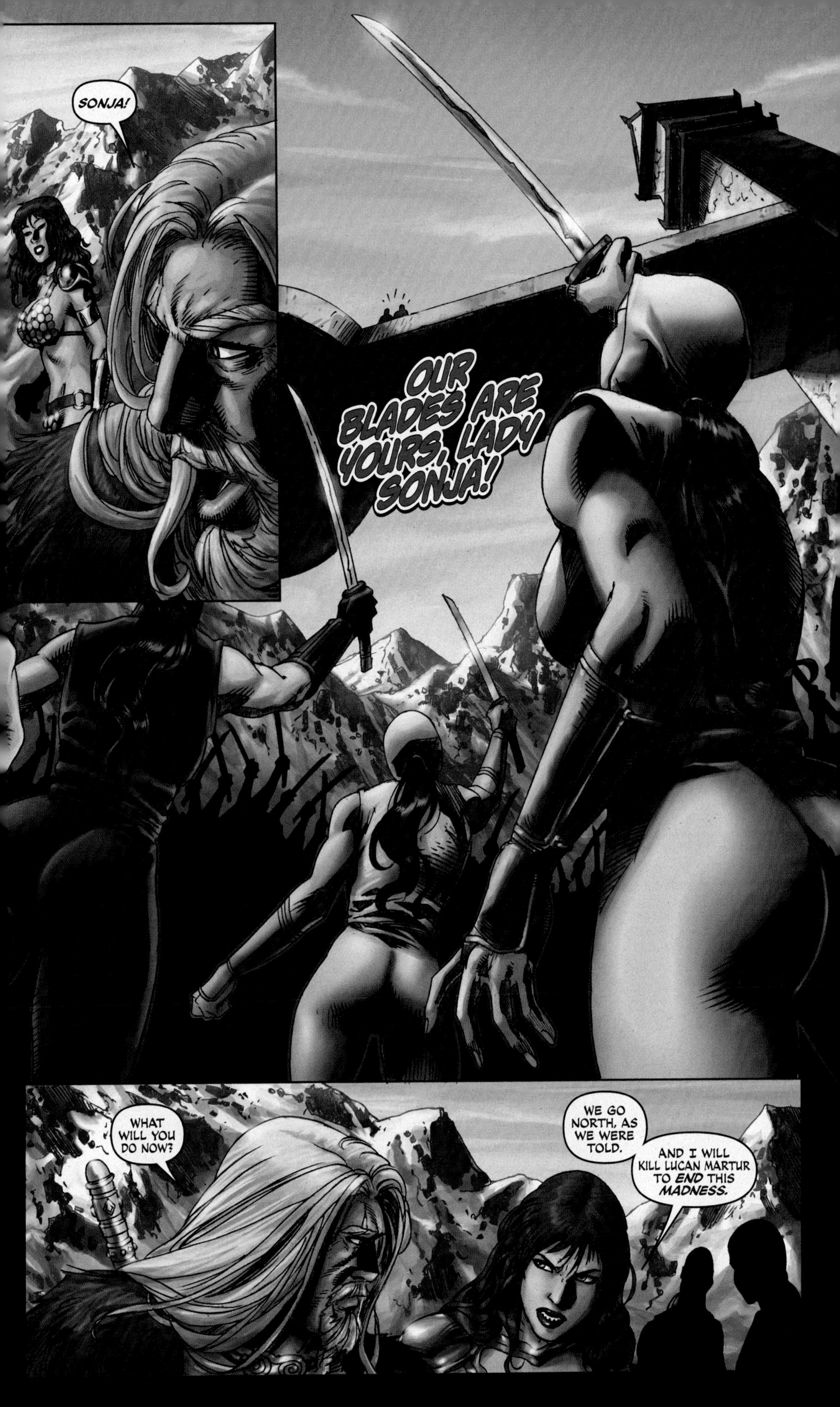
SONJA!
OUR BLADES ARE YOURS, LADY SONJA!
WHAT WILL YOU DO NOW?
WE GO NORTH, AS WE WERE TOLD.
AND I WILL KILL LUCAN MARTUR TO END THIS MADNESS.

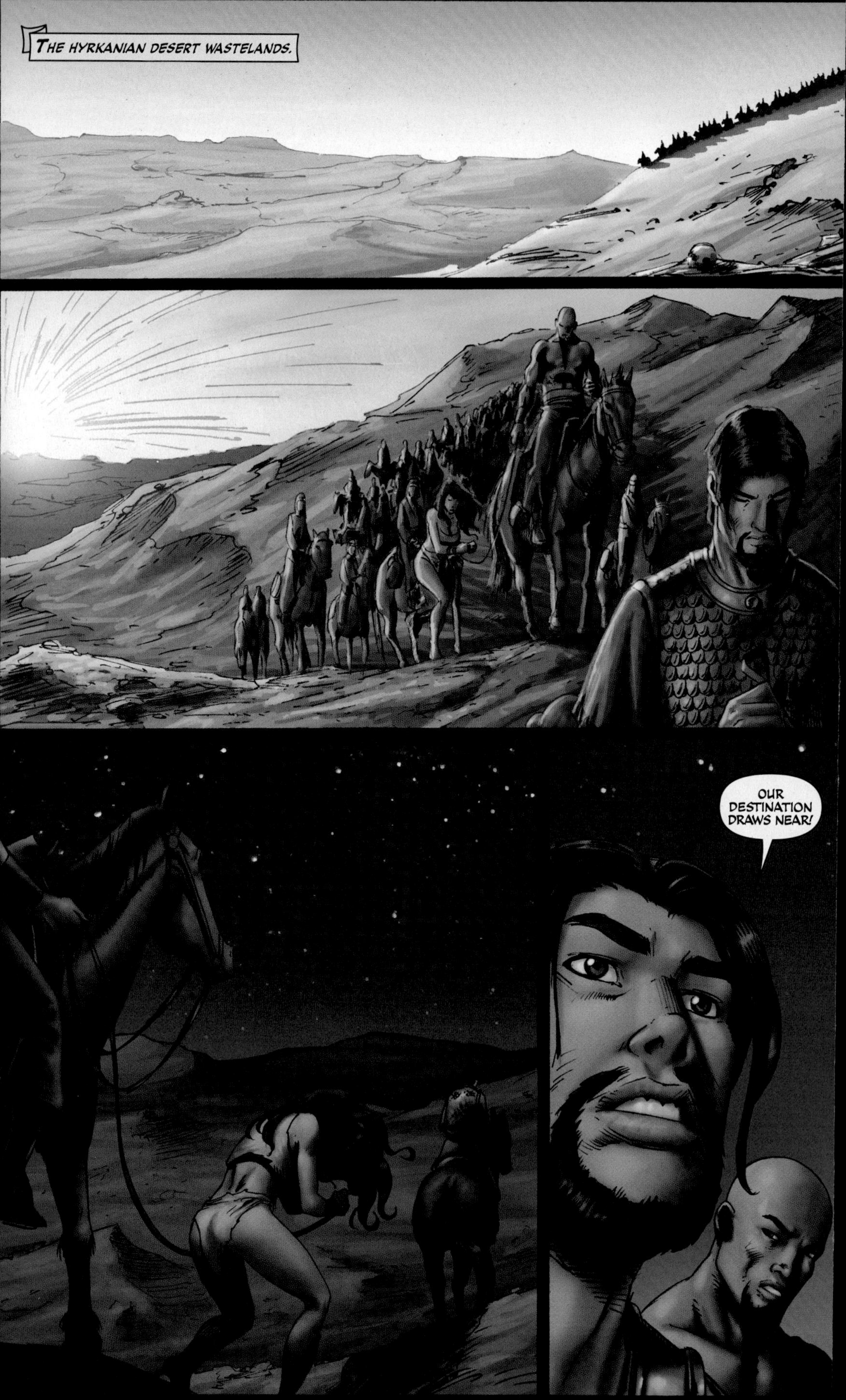
THE HYRKANIAN DESERT WASTELANDS.
OUR DESTINATION DRAWS NEAR!

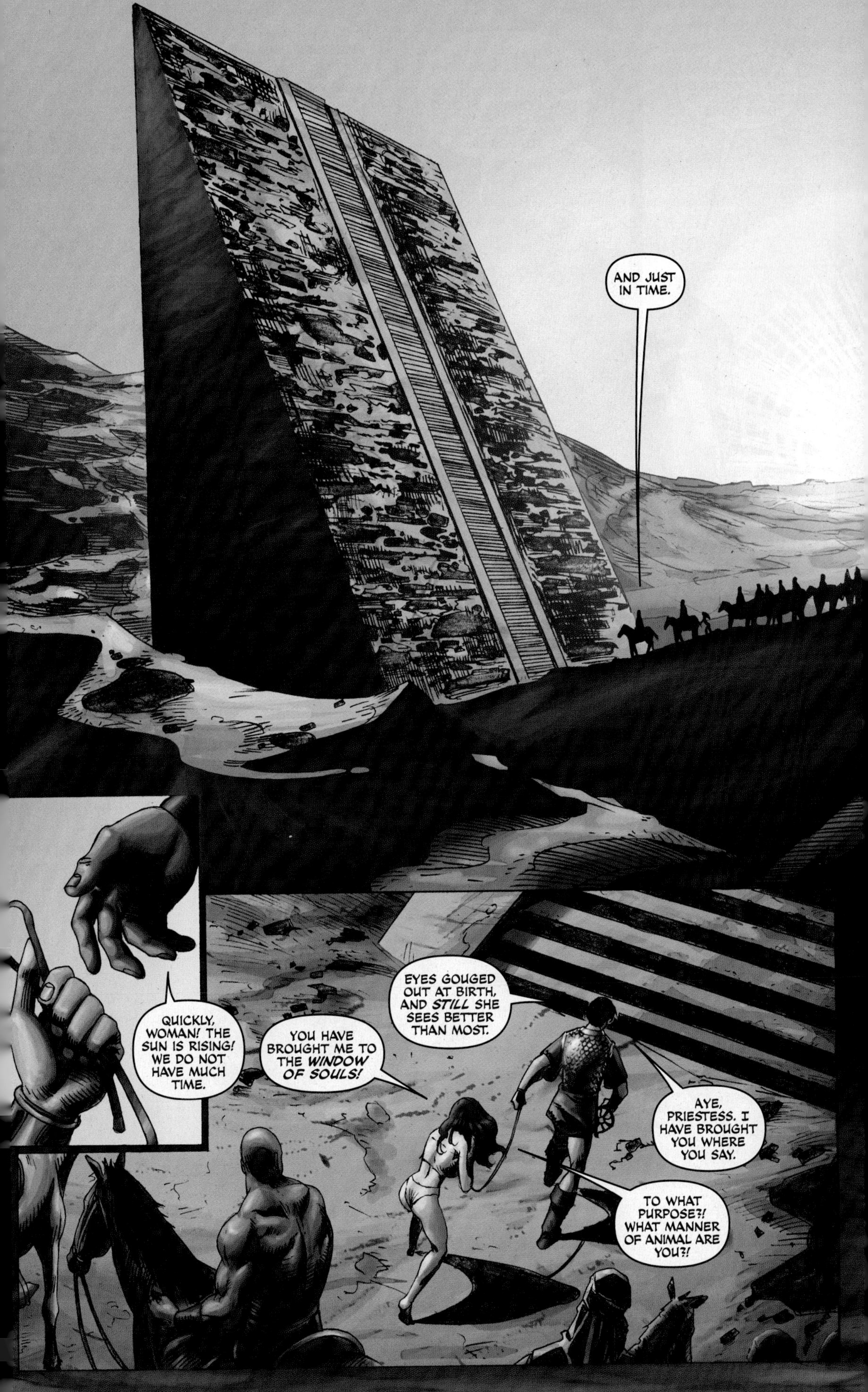
AND JUST IN TIME.
QUICKLY, WOMAN! THE SUN IS RISING! WE DO NOT HAVE MUCH TIME.
EYES GOUGED OUT AT BIRTH, AND *STILL* SHE SEES BETTER THAN MOST.
YOU HAVE BROUGHT ME TO THE *WINDOW OF SOULS!*
AYE, PRIESTESS. I HAVE BROUGHT YOU WHERE YOU SAY.
TO WHAT PURPOSE?! WHAT MANNER OF ANIMAL ARE YOU?!

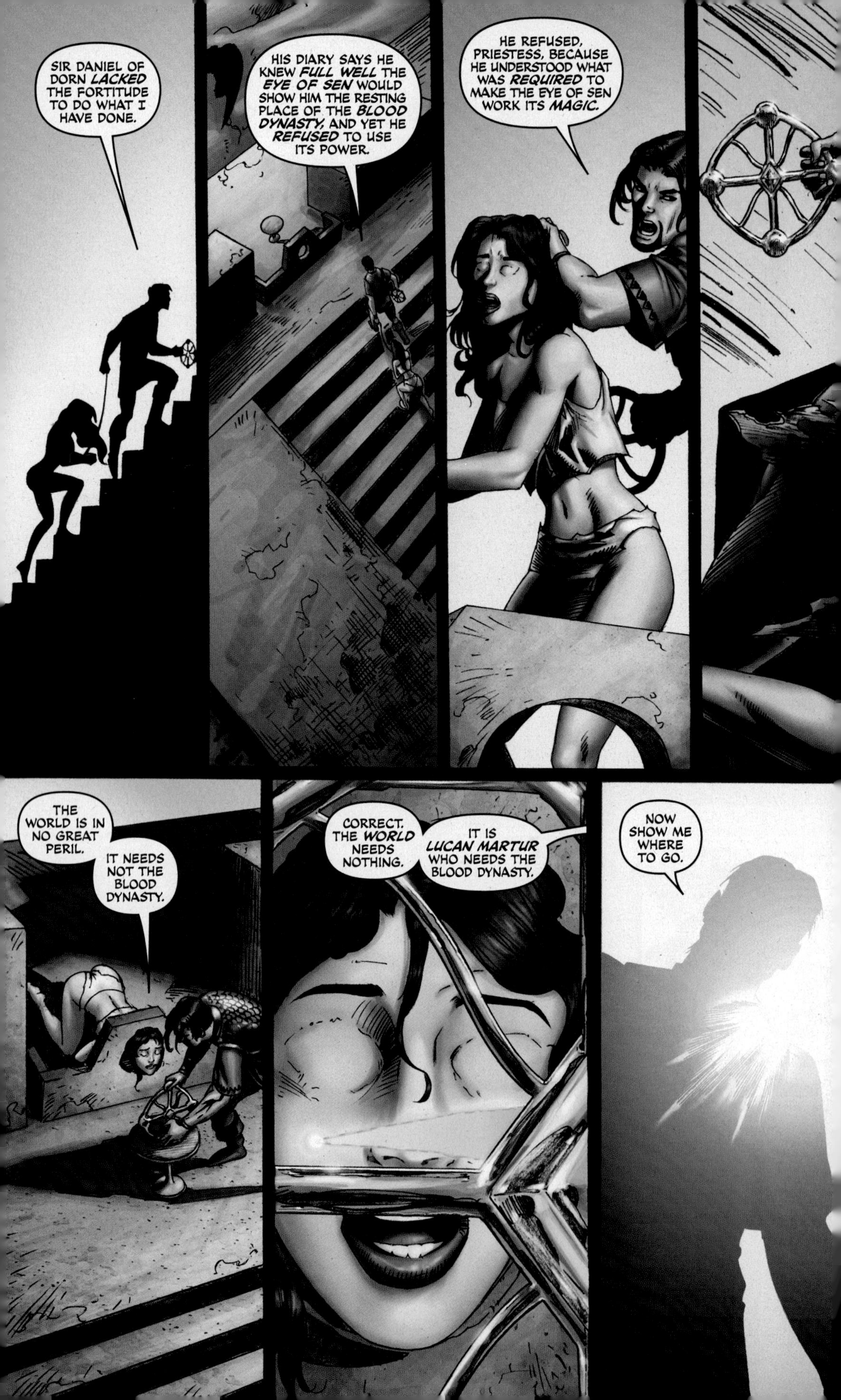
SIR DANIEL OF DORN *LACKED* THE FORTITUDE TO DO WHAT I HAVE DONE.
HIS DIARY SAYS HE KNEW *FULL WELL* THE *EYE OF SEN* WOULD SHOW HIM THE RESTING PLACE OF THE *BLOOD DYNASTY,* AND YET HE *REFUSED* TO USE ITS POWER.
HE REFUSED, PRIESTESS, BECAUSE HE UNDERSTOOD WHAT WAS *REQUIRED* TO MAKE THE EYE OF SEN WORK ITS *MAGIC.*
THE WORLD IS IN NO GREAT PERIL.
IT NEEDS NOT THE BLOOD DYNASTY.
CORRECT. THE *WORLD* NEEDS NOTHING.
IT IS *LUCAN MARTUR* WHO NEEDS THE BLOOD DYNASTY.
NOW SHOW ME WHERE TO GO.

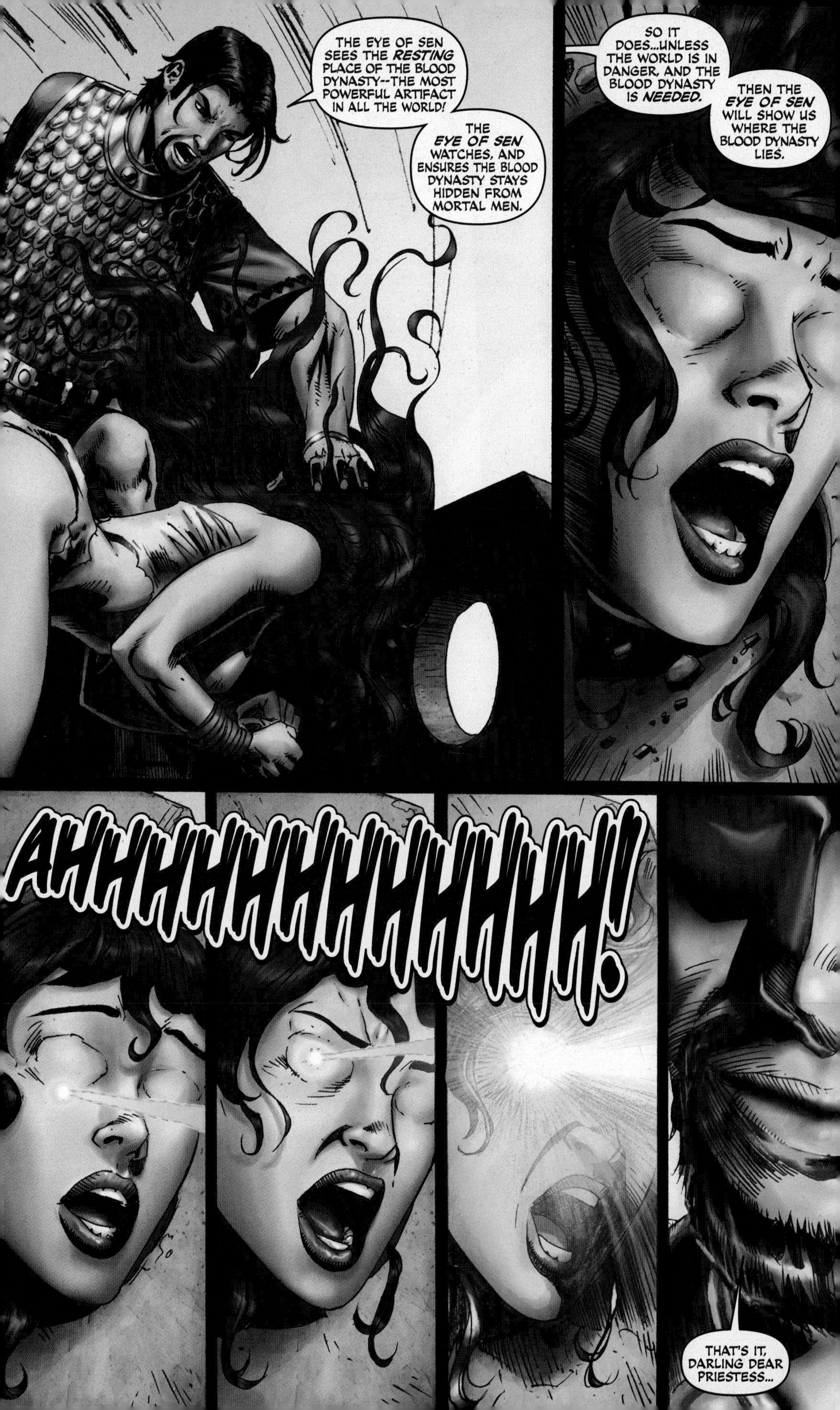

THE EYE OF SEN SEES THE *RESTING* PLACE OF THE BLOOD DYNASTY--THE MOST POWERFUL ARTIFACT IN ALL THE WORLD!
THE *EYE OF SEN* WATCHES, AND ENSURES THE BLOOD DYNASTY STAYS HIDDEN FROM MORTAL MEN.
SO IT DOES...UNLESS THE WORLD IS IN DANGER, AND THE BLOOD DYNASTY IS *NEEDED.*
THEN THE *EYE OF SEN* WILL SHOW US WHERE THE BLOOD DYNASTY LIES.
AHHHHHHHHHHHHHHHH!
THAT'S IT, DARLING DEAR PRIESTESS...

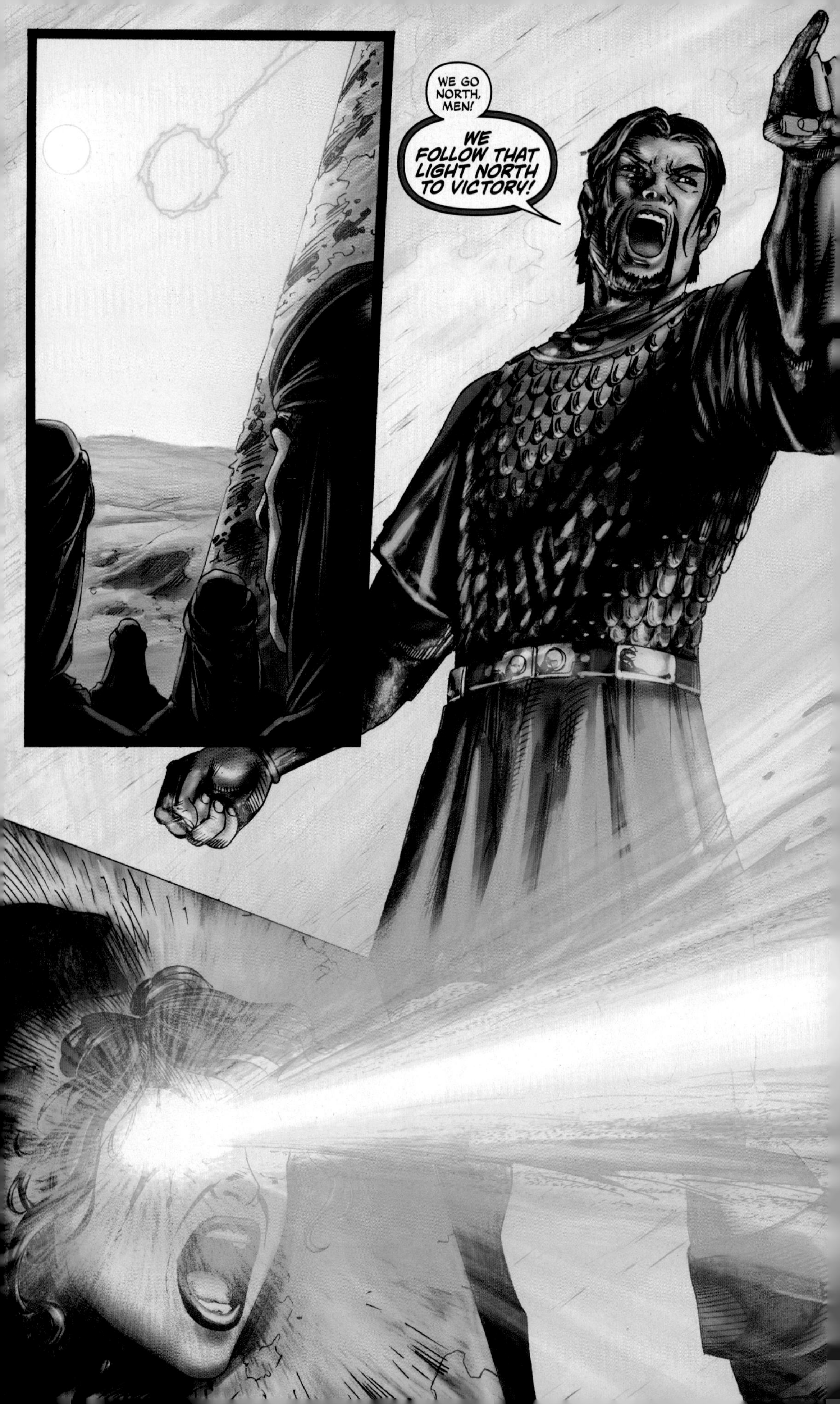
WE GO NORTH, MEN!
WE FOLLOW THAT LIGHT NORTH TO VICTORY!

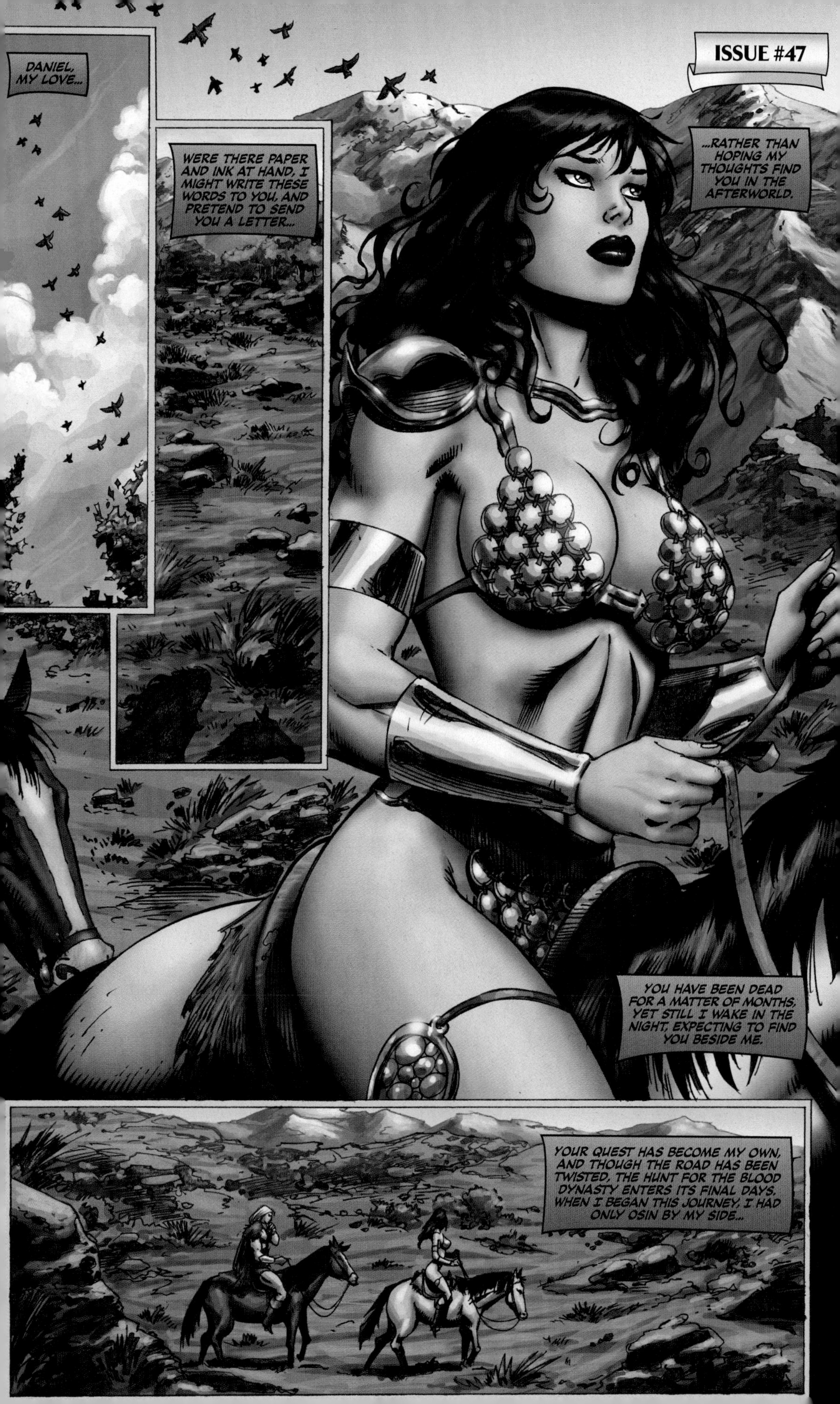
ISSUE #47
DANIEL, MY LOVE...
WERE THERE PAPER AND INK AT HAND, I MIGHT WRITE THESE WORDS TO YOU, AND PRETEND TO SEND YOU A LETTER...
...RATHER THAN HOPING MY THOUGHTS FIND YOU IN THE AFTERWORLD.
YOU HAVE BEEN DEAD FOR A MATTER OF MONTHS; YET STILL I WAKE IN THE NIGHT, EXPECTING TO FIND YOU BESIDE ME.
YOUR QUEST HAS BECOME MY OWN, AND THOUGH THE ROAD HAS BEEN TWISTED, THE HUNT FOR THE BLOOD DYNASTY ENTERS ITS FINAL DAYS. WHEN I BEGAN THIS JOURNEY, I HAD ONLY OSIN BY MY SIDE...

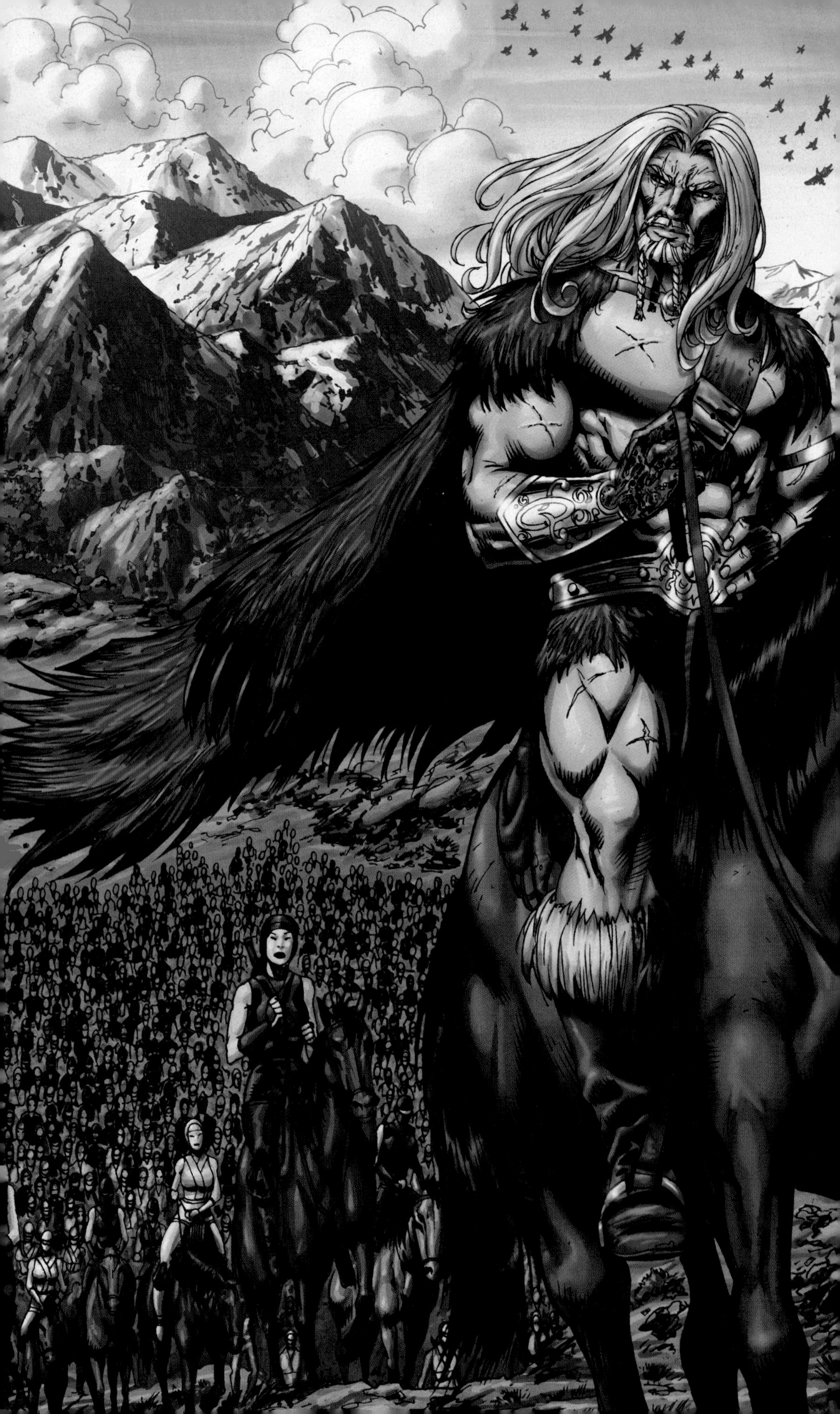

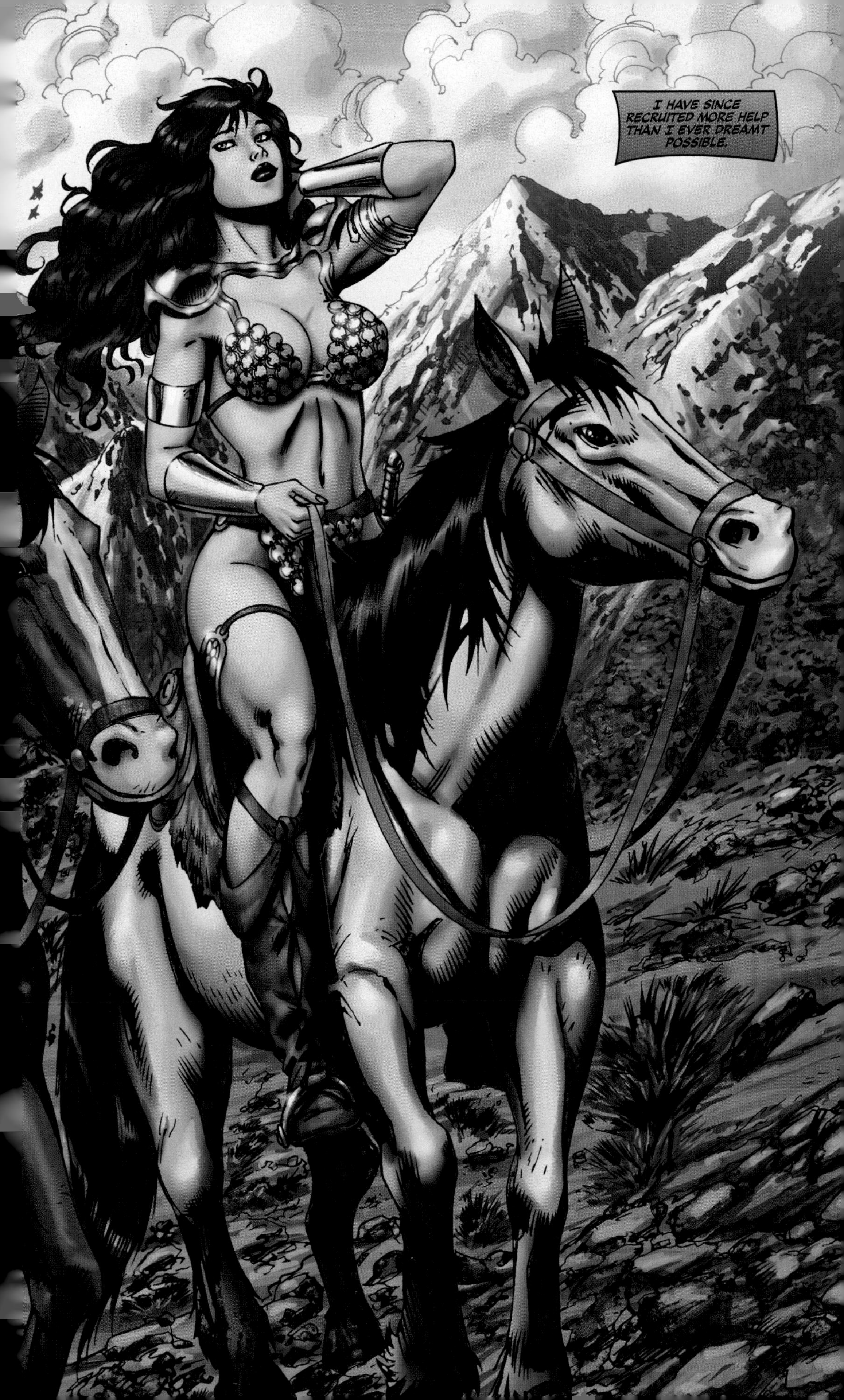
I HAVE SINCE RECRUITED MORE HELP THAN I EVER DREAMT POSSIBLE.

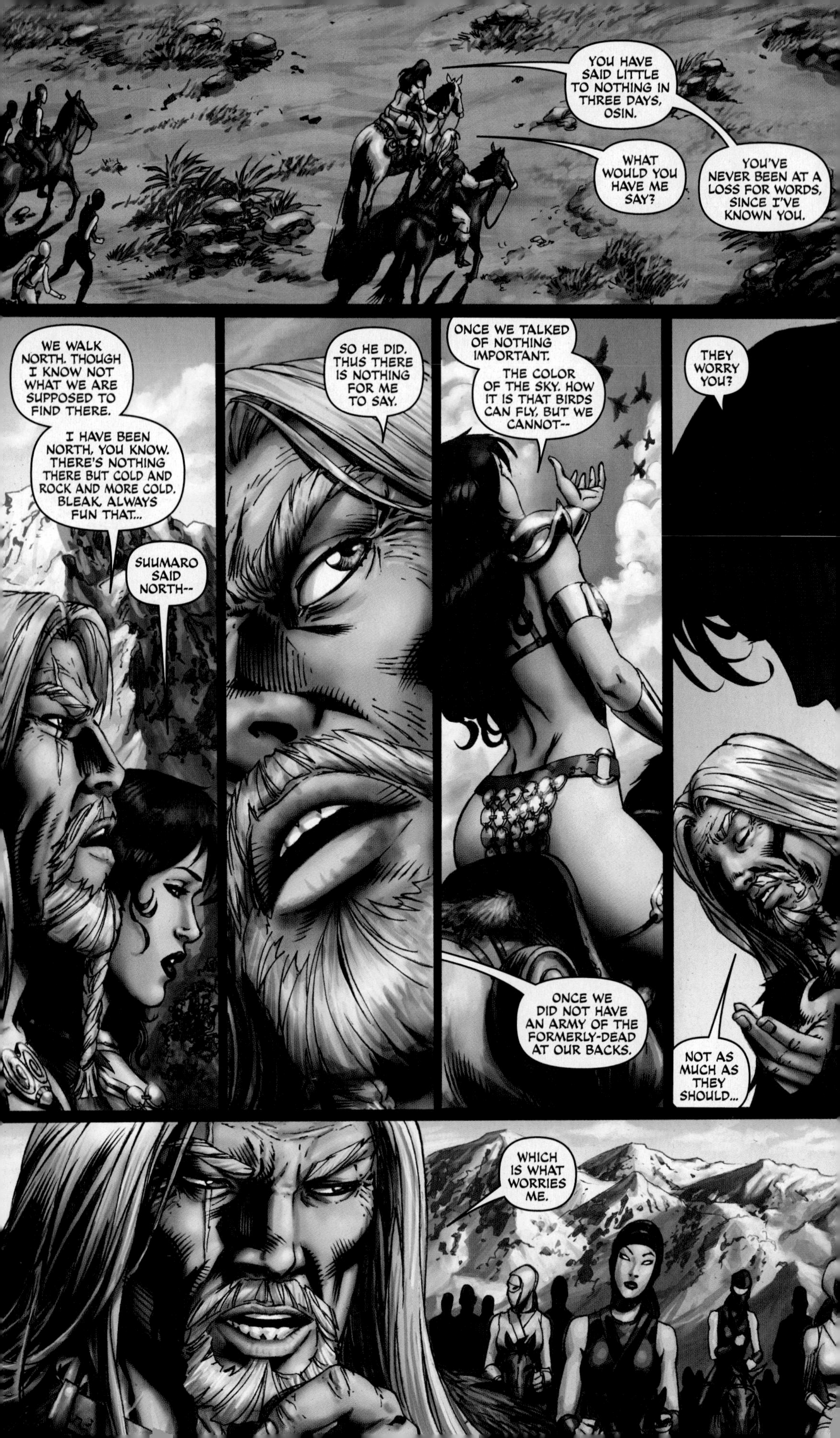
YOU HAVE SAID LITTLE TO NOTHING IN THREE DAYS, OSIN.
YOU'VE NEVER BEEN AT A LOSS FOR WORDS, SINCE I'VE KNOWN YOU.
WHAT WOULD YOU HAVE ME SAY?
WE WALK NORTH. THOUGH I KNOW NOT WHAT WE ARE SUPPOSED TO FIND THERE.
I HAVE BEEN NORTH, YOU KNOW. THERE'S NOTHING THERE BUT COLD AND ROCK AND MORE COLD. BLEAK, ALWAYS FUN THAT...
SUUMARO SAID NORTH--
SO HE DID. THUS THERE IS NOTHING FOR ME TO SAY.
ONCE WE TALKED OF NOTHING IMPORTANT.
THE COLOR OF THE SKY. HOW IT IS THAT BIRDS CAN FLY, BUT WE CANNOT--
ONCE WE DID NOT HAVE AN ARMY OF THE FORMERLY-DEAD AT OUR BACKS.
THEY WORRY YOU?
NOT AS MUCH AS THEY SHOULD...
WHICH IS WHAT WORRIES ME.

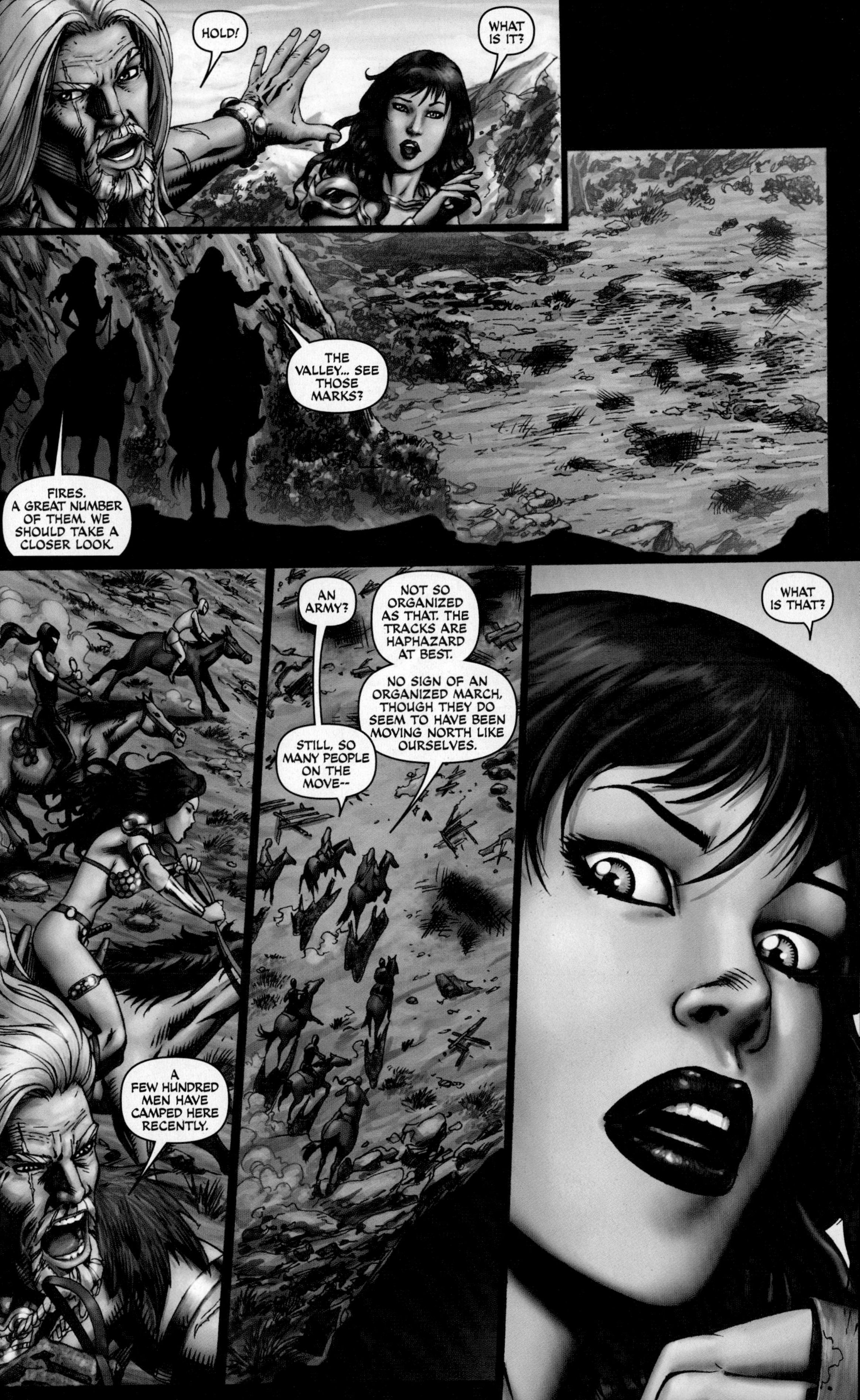
HOLD!
WHAT IS IT?
THE VALLEY... SEE THOSE MARKS?
FIRES. A GREAT NUMBER OF THEM. WE SHOULD TAKE A CLOSER LOOK.
A FEW HUNDRED MEN HAVE CAMPED HERE RECENTLY.
AN ARMY?
NOT SO ORGANIZED AS THAT. THE TRACKS ARE HAPHAZARD AT BEST.
NO SIGN OF AN ORGANIZED MARCH, THOUGH THEY DO SEEM TO HAVE BEEN MOVING NORTH LIKE OURSELVES.
STILL, SO MANY PEOPLE ON THE MOVE--
WHAT IS THAT?

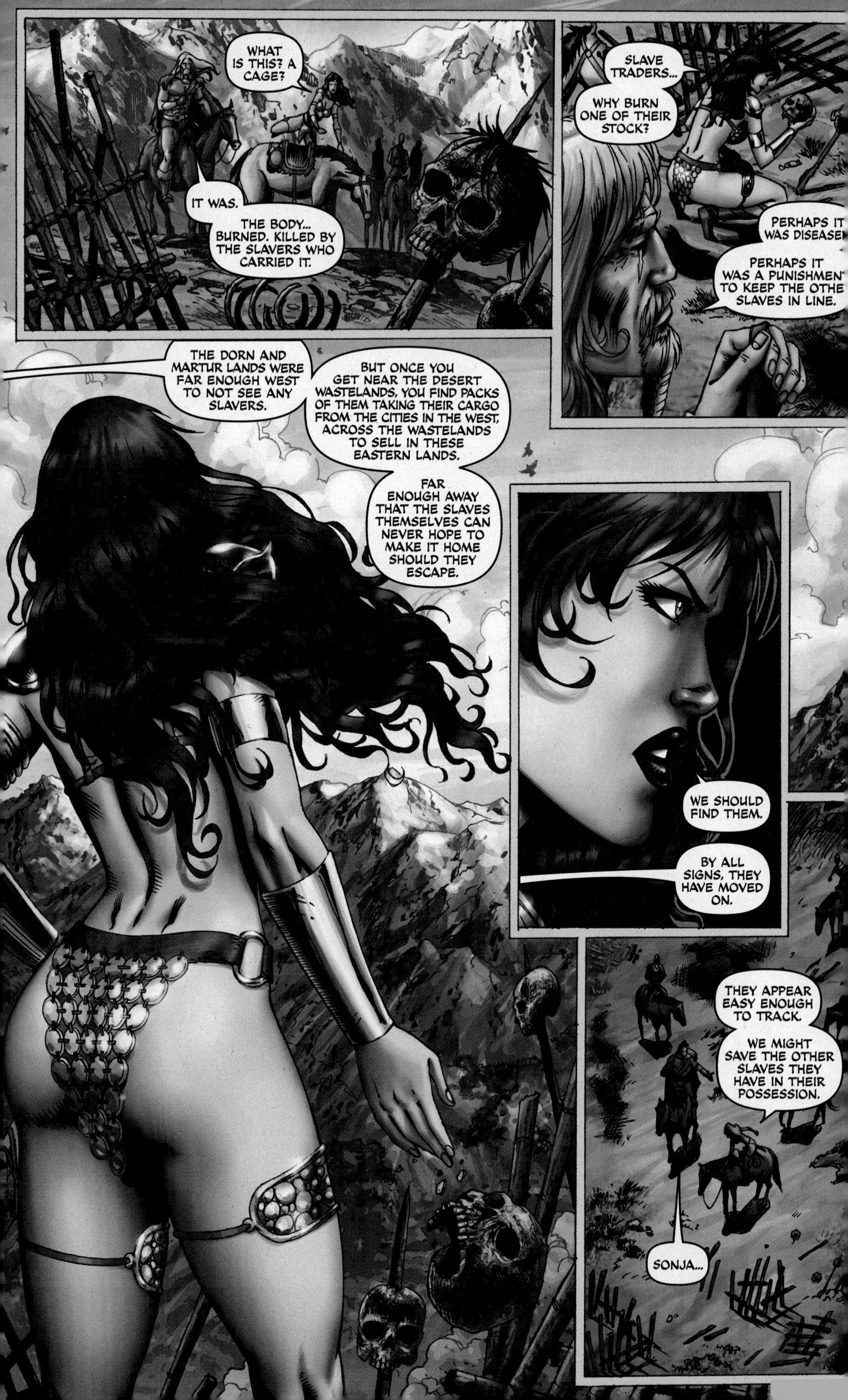
WHAT IS THIS? A CAGE?
IT WAS.
THE BODY... BURNED. KILLED BY THE SLAVERS WHO CARRIED IT.
SLAVE TRADERS...
WHY BURN ONE OF THEIR STOCK?
PERHAPS IT WAS DISEASE
PERHAPS IT WAS A PUNISHMEN TO KEEP THE OTHE SLAVES IN LINE.
THE DORN AND MARTUR LANDS WERE FAR ENOUGH WEST TO NOT SEE ANY SLAVERS.
BUT ONCE YOU GET NEAR THE DESERT WASTELANDS, YOU FIND PACKS OF THEM TAKING THEIR CARGO FROM THE CITIES IN THE WEST, ACROSS THE WASTELANDS TO SELL IN THESE EASTERN LANDS.
FAR ENOUGH AWAY THAT THE SLAVES THEMSELVES CAN NEVER HOPE TO MAKE IT HOME SHOULD THEY ESCAPE.
WE SHOULD FIND THEM.
BY ALL SIGNS, THEY HAVE MOVED ON.
THEY APPEAR EASY ENOUGH TO TRACK.
WE MIGHT SAVE THE OTHER SLAVES THEY HAVE IN THEIR POSSESSION.
SONJA...

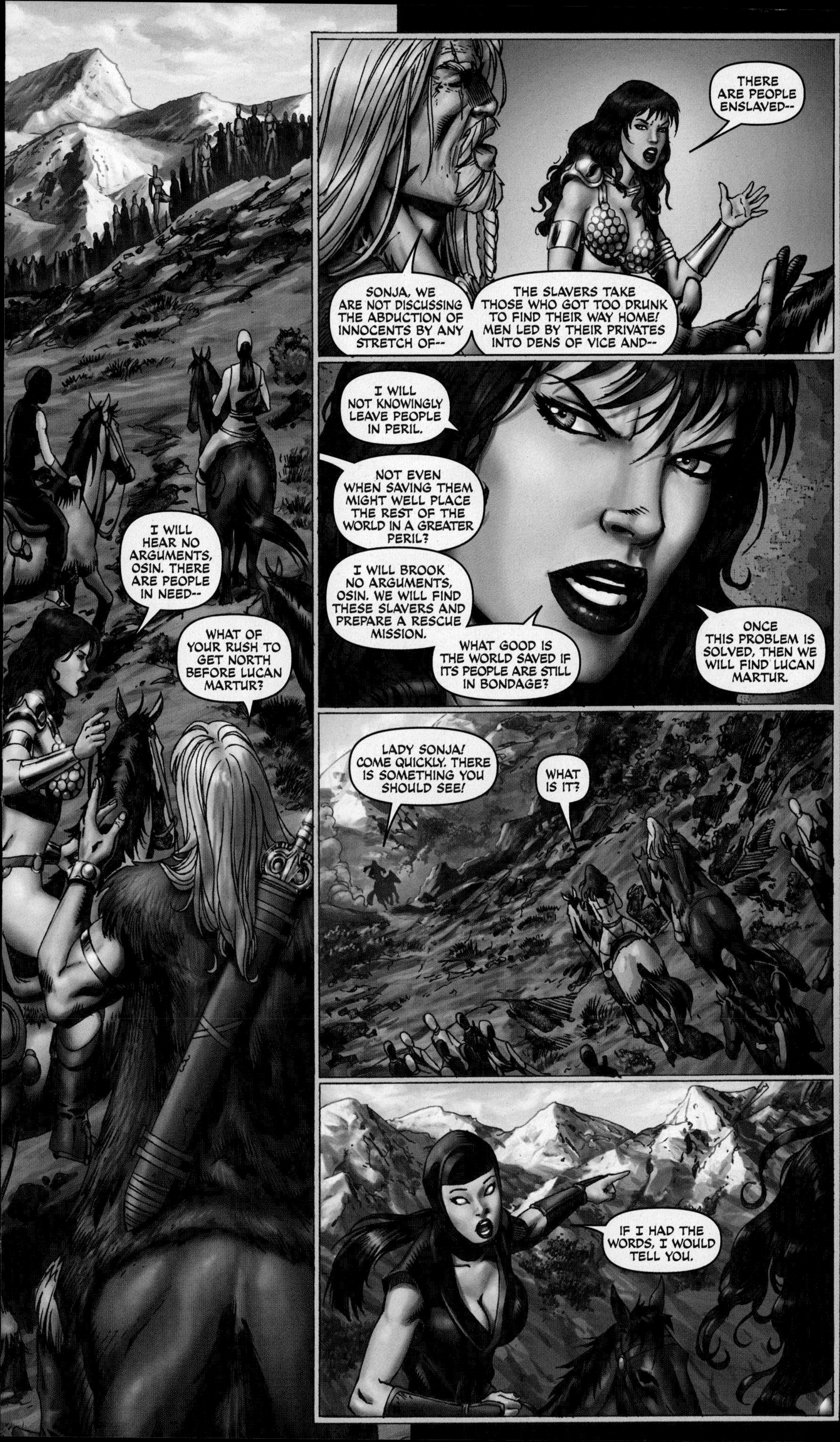
I WILL HEAR NO ARGUMENTS, OSIN. THERE ARE PEOPLE IN NEED--
WHAT OF YOUR RUSH TO GET NORTH BEFORE LUCAN MARTUR?
THERE ARE PEOPLE ENSLAVED--
SONJA, WE ARE NOT DISCUSSING THE ABDUCTION OF INNOCENTS BY ANY STRETCH OF--
THE SLAVERS TAKE THOSE WHO GOT TOO DRUNK TO FIND THEIR WAY HOME! MEN LED BY THEIR PRIVATES INTO DENS OF VICE AND--
I WILL NOT KNOWINGLY LEAVE PEOPLE IN PERIL.
NOT EVEN WHEN SAVING THEM MIGHT WELL PLACE THE REST OF THE WORLD IN A GREATER PERIL?
I WILL BROOK NO ARGUMENTS, OSIN. WE WILL FIND THESE SLAVERS AND PREPARE A RESCUE MISSION.
WHAT GOOD IS THE WORLD SAVED IF ITS PEOPLE ARE STILL IN BONDAGE?
ONCE THIS PROBLEM IS SOLVED, THEN WE WILL FIND LUCAN MARTUR.
LADY SONJA! COME QUICKLY. THERE IS SOMETHING YOU SHOULD SEE!
WHAT IS IT?
IF I HAD THE WORDS, I WOULD TELL YOU.

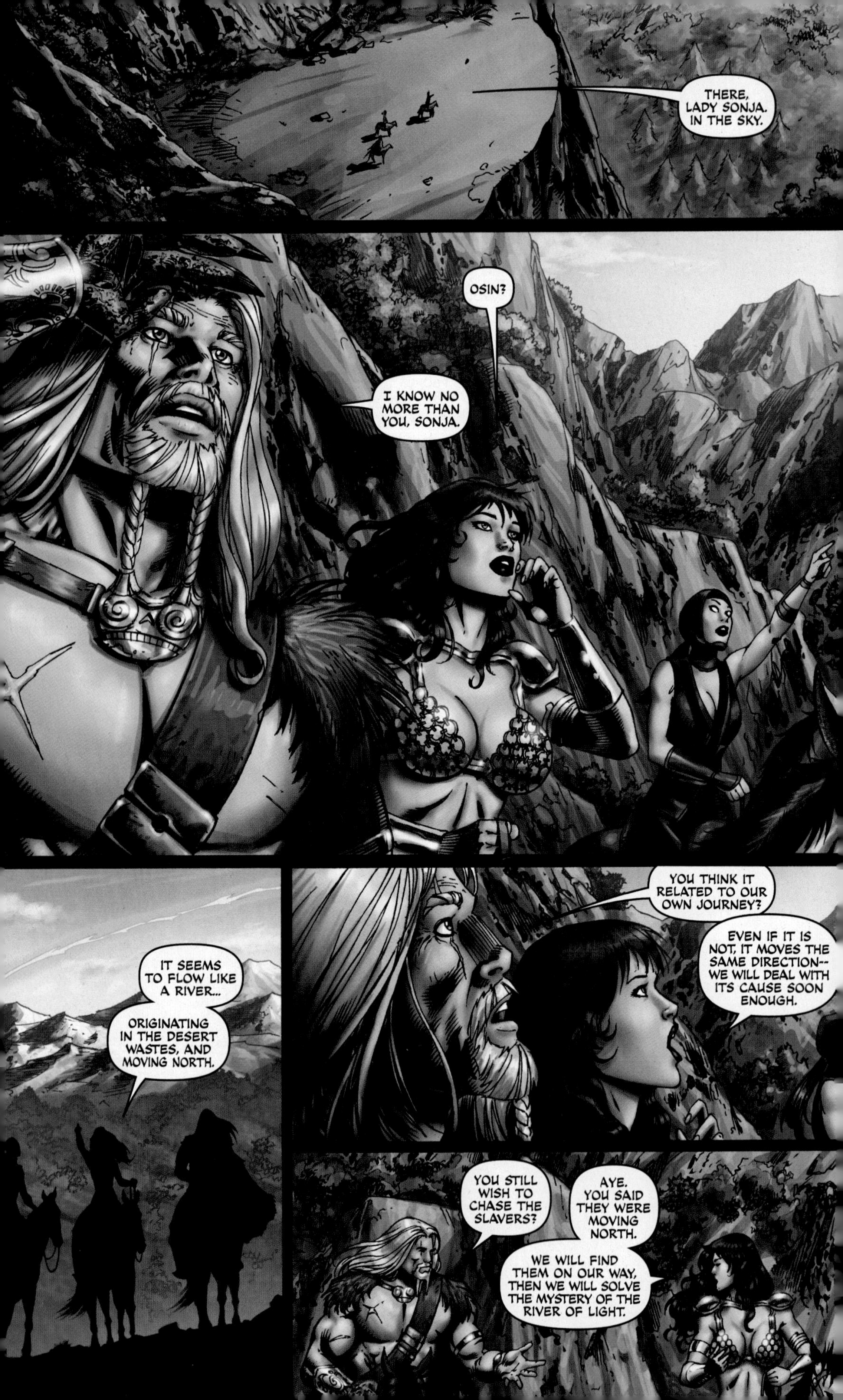
THERE, LADY SONJA. IN THE SKY.
OSIN?
I KNOW NO MORE THAN YOU, SONJA.
IT SEEMS TO FLOW LIKE A RIVER...
ORIGINATING IN THE DESERT WASTES, AND MOVING NORTH.
YOU THINK IT RELATED TO OUR OWN JOURNEY?
EVEN IF IT IS NOT, IT MOVES THE SAME DIRECTION-- WE WILL DEAL WITH ITS CAUSE SOON ENOUGH.
YOU STILL WISH TO CHASE THE SLAVERS?
AYE. YOU SAID THEY WERE MOVING NORTH.
WE WILL FIND THEM ON OUR WAY, THEN WE WILL SOLVE THE MYSTERY OF THE RIVER OF LIGHT.

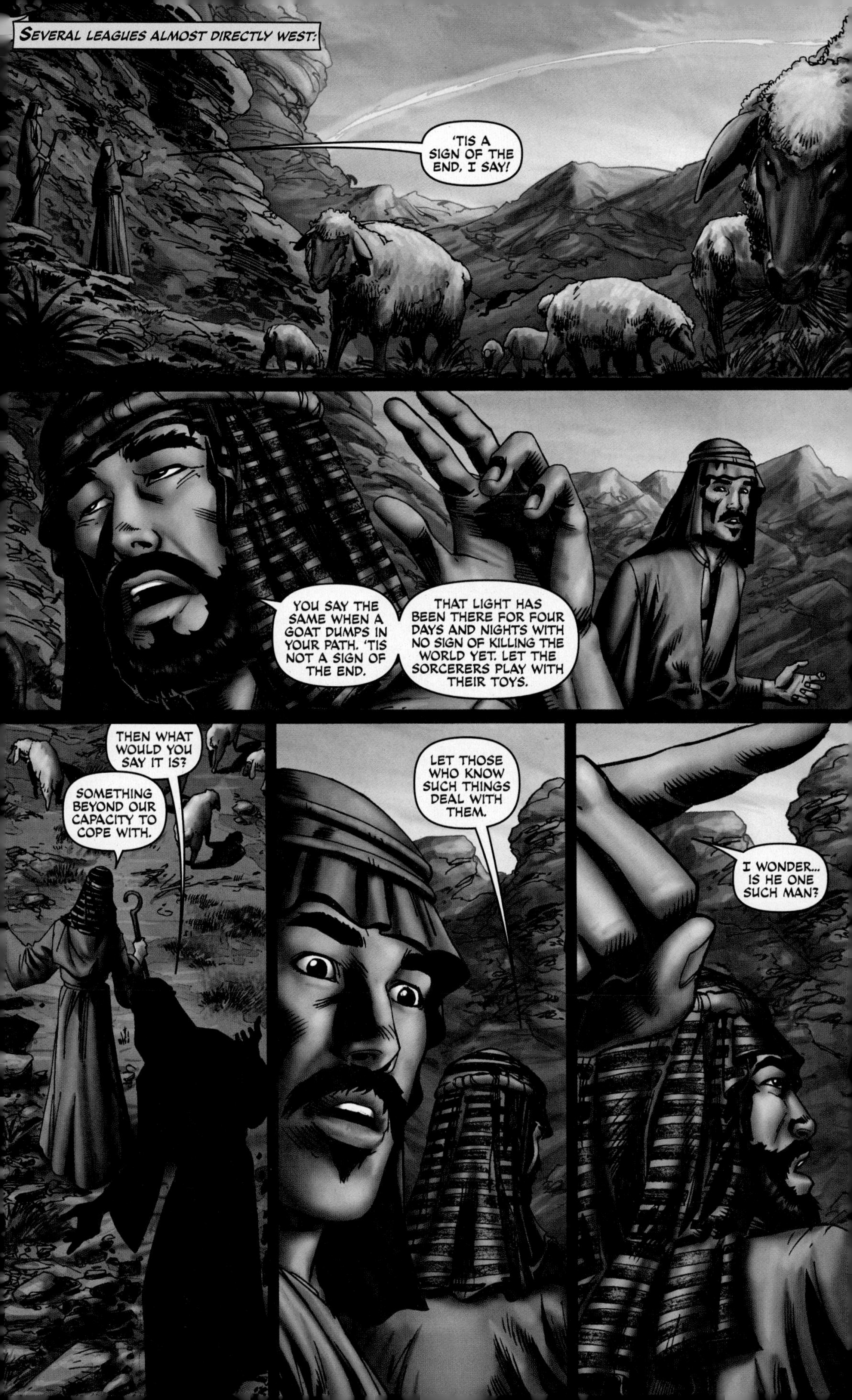
SEVERAL LEAGUES ALMOST DIRECTLY WEST:
'TIS A SIGN OF THE END, I SAY!
YOU SAY THE SAME WHEN A GOAT DUMPS IN YOUR PATH. 'TIS NOT A SIGN OF THE END.
THAT LIGHT HAS BEEN THERE FOR FOUR DAYS AND NIGHTS WITH NO SIGN OF KILLING THE WORLD YET. LET THE SORCERERS PLAY WITH THEIR TOYS.
THEN WHAT WOULD YOU SAY IT IS?
SOMETHING BEYOND OUR CAPACITY TO COPE WITH.
LET THOSE WHO KNOW SUCH THINGS DEAL WITH THEM.
I WONDER... IS HE ONE SUCH MAN?

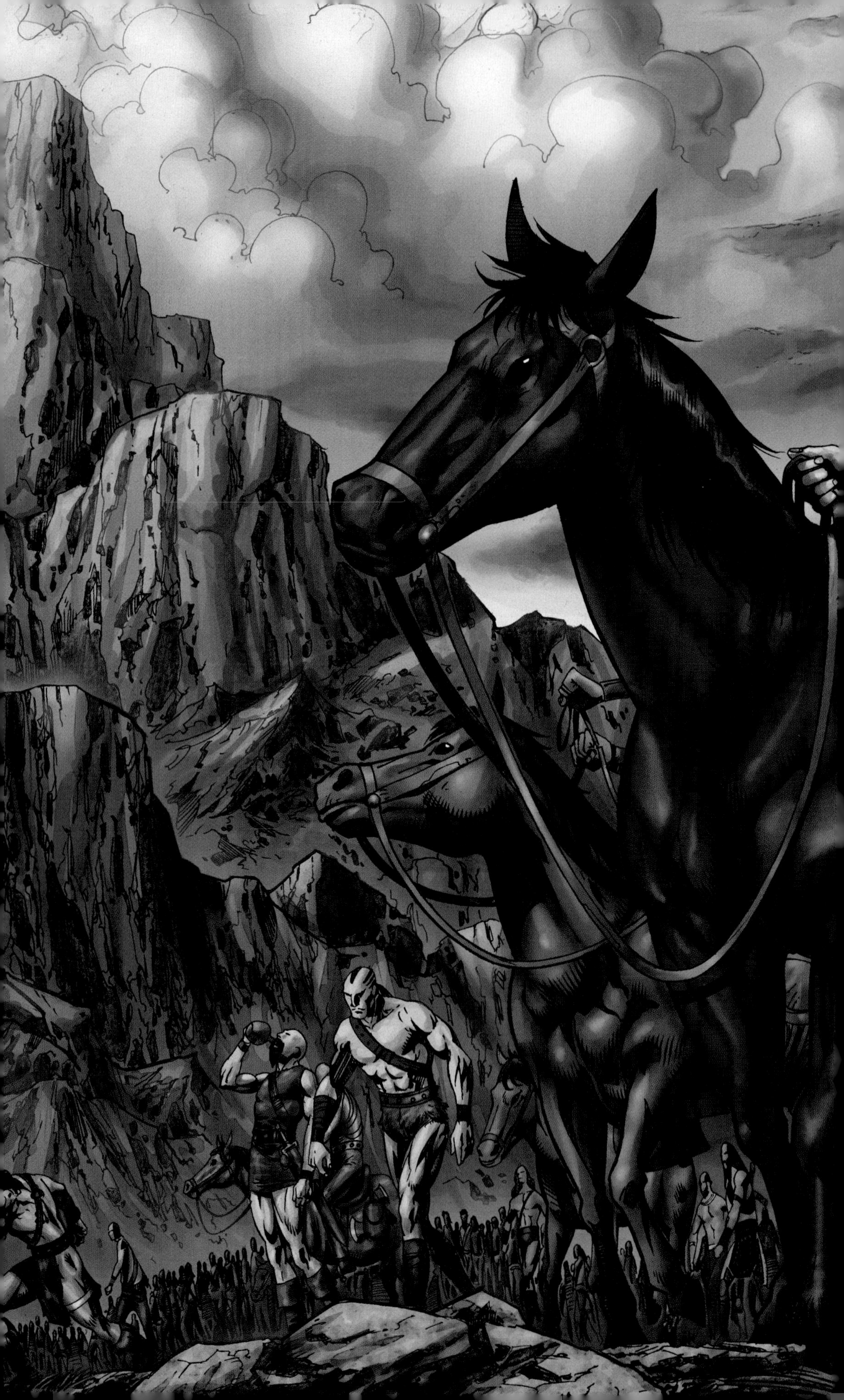

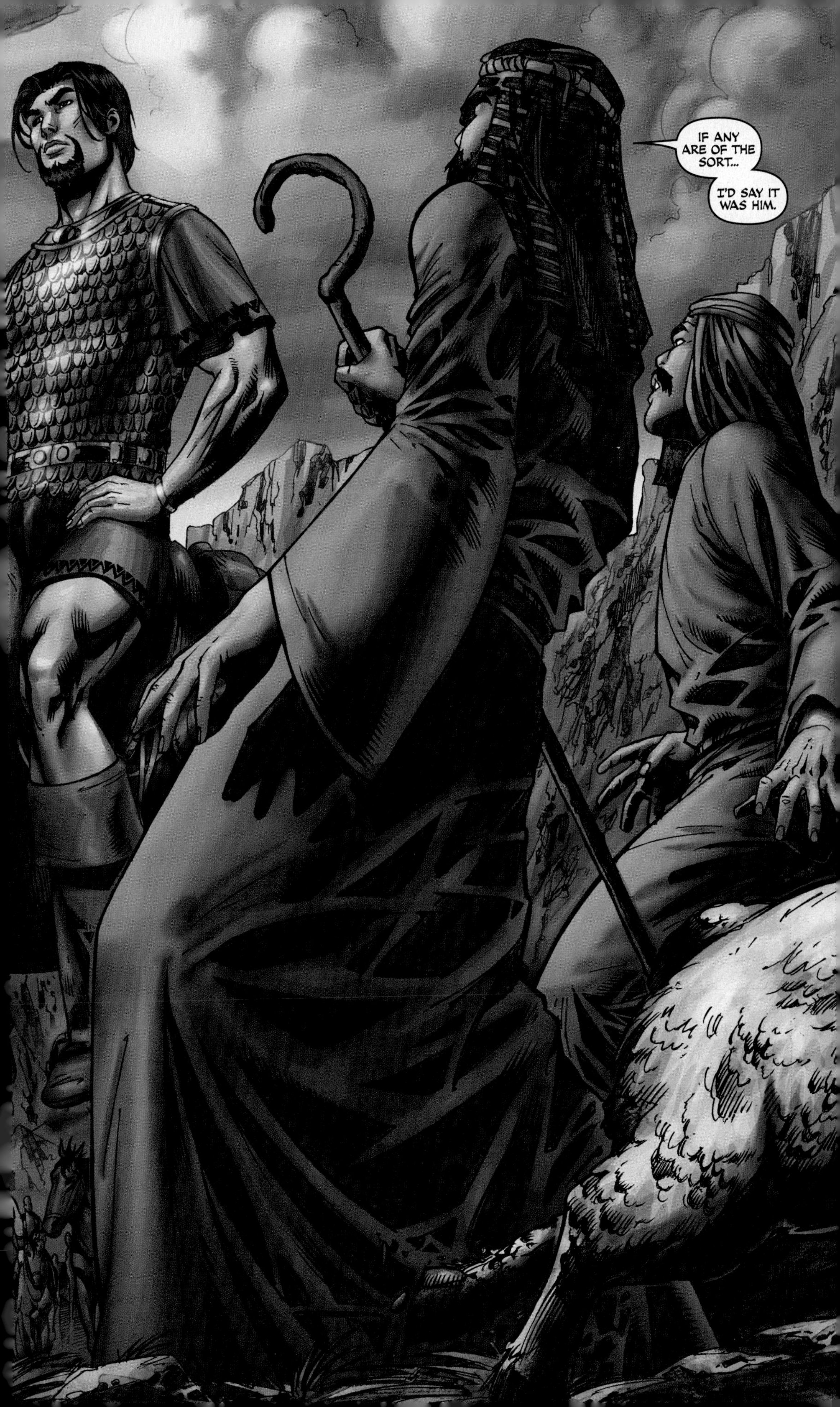
IF ANY ARE OF THE SORT...
I'D SAY IT WAS HIM.

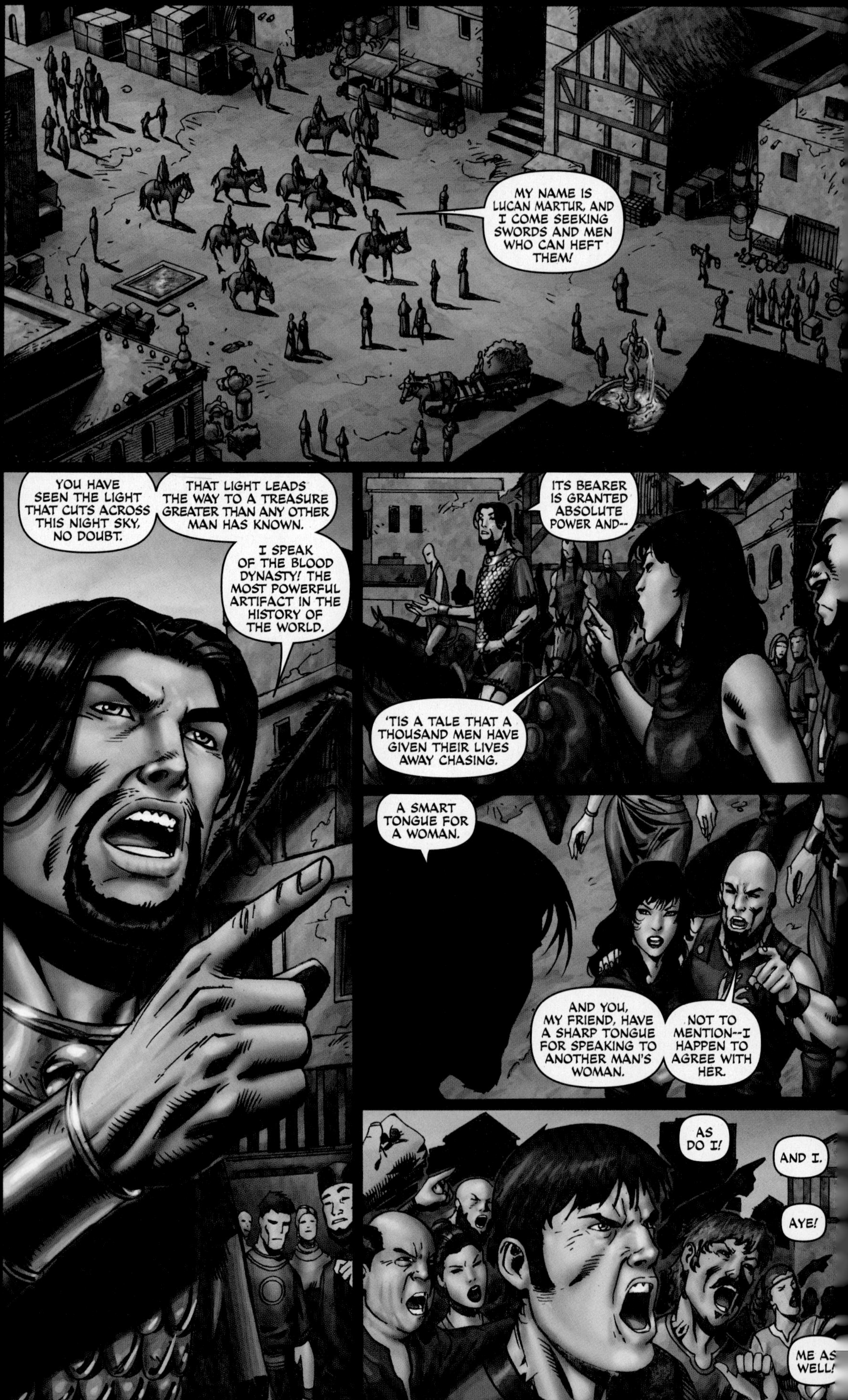
MY NAME IS LUCAN MARTUR, AND I COME SEEKING SWORDS AND MEN WHO CAN HEFT THEM!
YOU HAVE SEEN THE LIGHT THAT CUTS ACROSS THIS NIGHT SKY, NO DOUBT.
THAT LIGHT LEADS THE WAY TO A TREASURE GREATER THAN ANY OTHER MAN HAS KNOWN.
I SPEAK OF THE BLOOD DYNASTY! THE MOST POWERFUL ARTIFACT IN THE HISTORY OF THE WORLD.
ITS BEARER IS GRANTED ABSOLUTE POWER AND--
'TIS A TALE THAT A THOUSAND MEN HAVE GIVEN THEIR LIVES AWAY CHASING.
A SMART TONGUE FOR A WOMAN.
AND YOU, MY FRIEND, HAVE A SHARP TONGUE FOR SPEAKING TO ANOTHER MAN'S WOMAN.
NOT TO MENTION--I HAPPEN TO AGREE WITH HER.
AS DO I!
AND I.
AYE!
ME AS WELL!

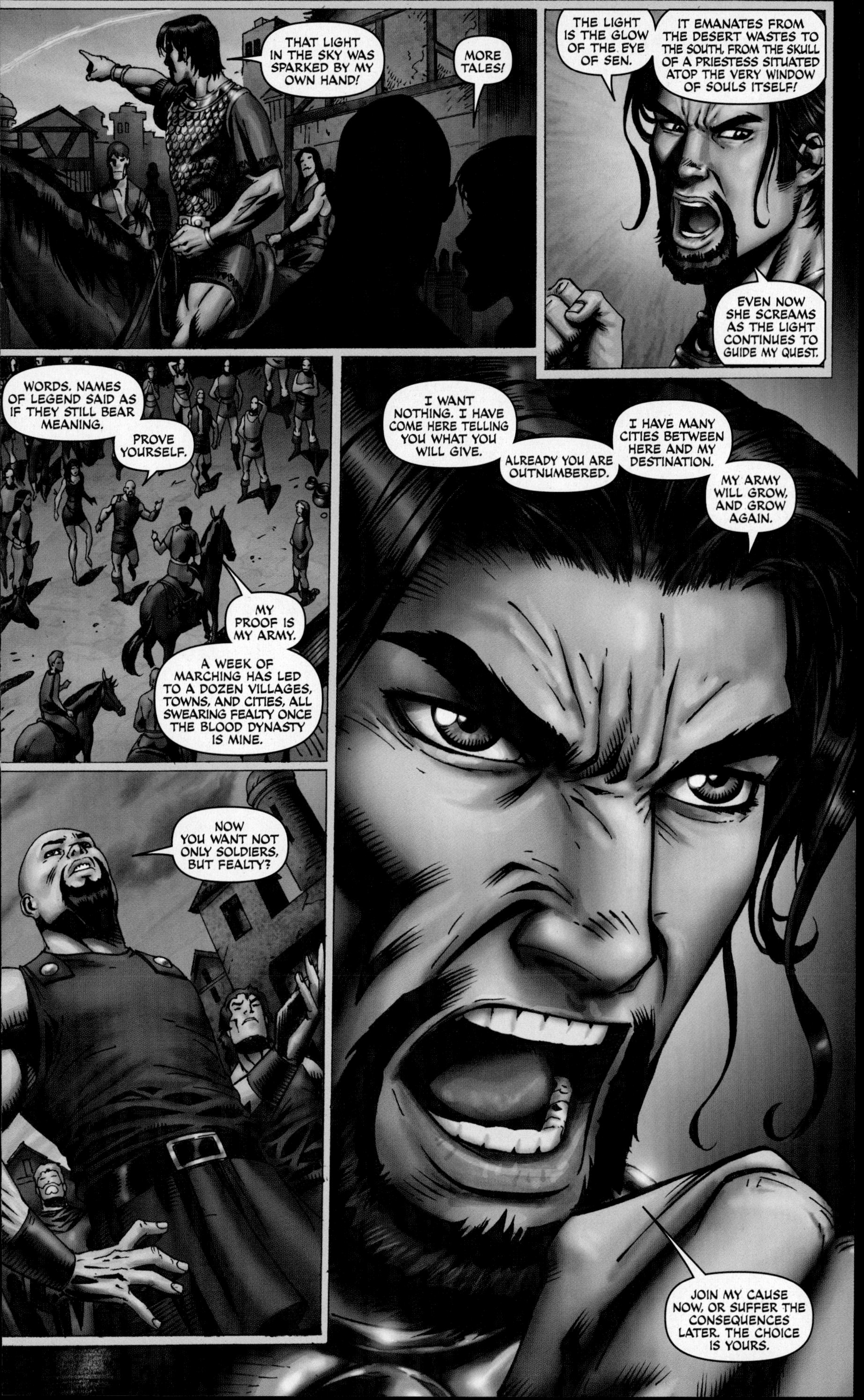
THAT LIGHT IN THE SKY WAS SPARKED BY MY OWN HAND!
MORE TALES!
THE LIGHT IS THE GLOW OF THE EYE OF SEN.
IT EMANATES FROM THE DESERT WASTES TO THE SOUTH, FROM THE SKULL OF A PRIESTESS SITUATED ATOP THE VERY WINDOW OF SOULS ITSELF!
EVEN NOW SHE SCREAMS AS THE LIGHT CONTINUES TO GUIDE MY QUEST.
WORDS. NAMES OF LEGEND SAID AS IF THEY STILL BEAR MEANING.
PROVE YOURSELF.
MY PROOF IS MY ARMY.
A WEEK OF MARCHING HAS LED TO A DOZEN VILLAGES, TOWNS, AND CITIES, ALL SWEARING FEALTY ONCE THE BLOOD DYNASTY IS MINE.
NOW YOU WANT NOT ONLY SOLDIERS, BUT FEALTY?
I WANT NOTHING. I HAVE COME HERE TELLING YOU WHAT YOU WILL GIVE.
ALREADY YOU ARE OUTNUMBERED.
I HAVE MANY CITIES BETWEEN HERE AND MY DESTINATION.
MY ARMY WILL GROW, AND GROW AGAIN.
JOIN MY CAUSE NOW, OR SUFFER THE CONSEQUENCES LATER. THE CHOICE IS YOURS.

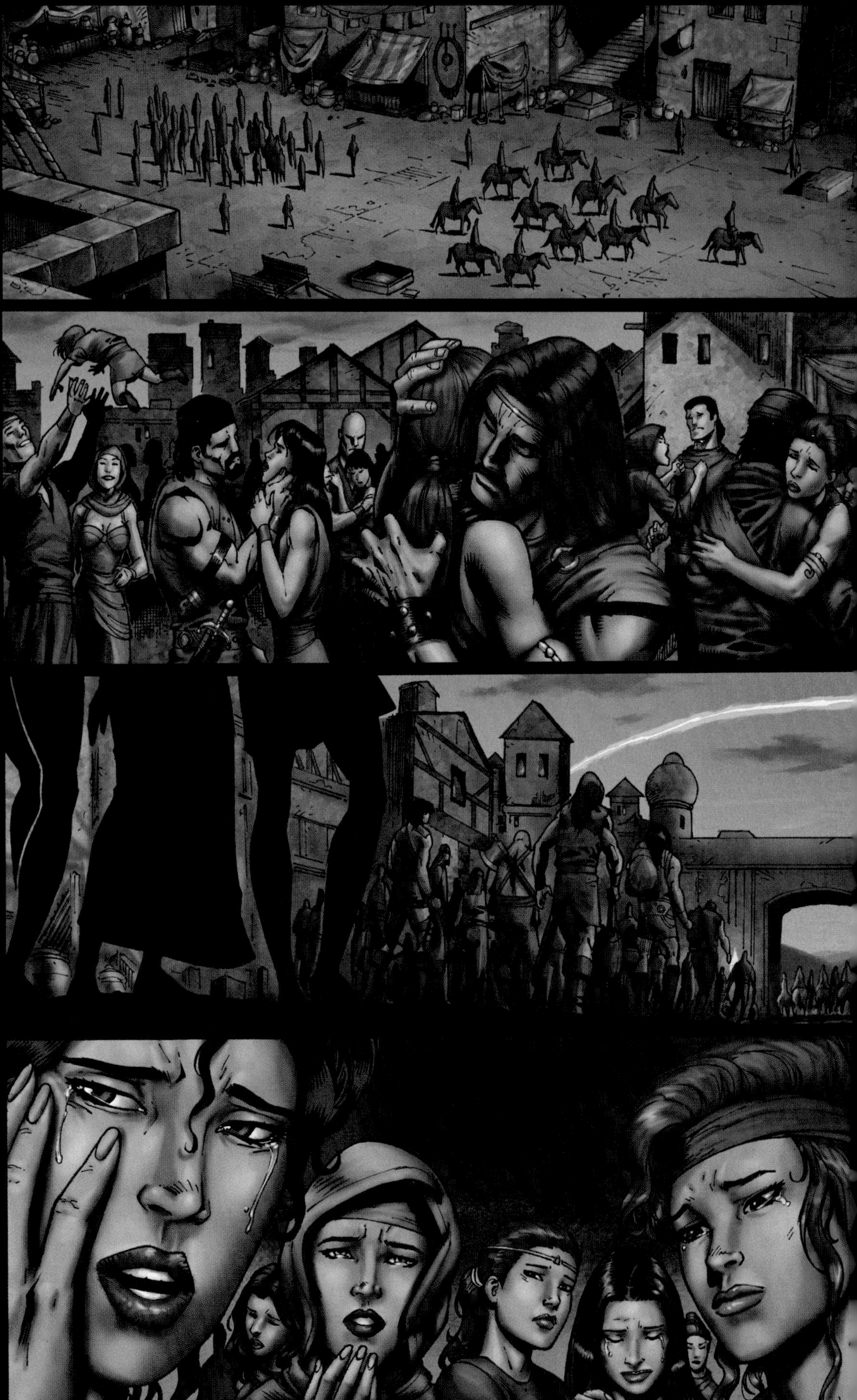

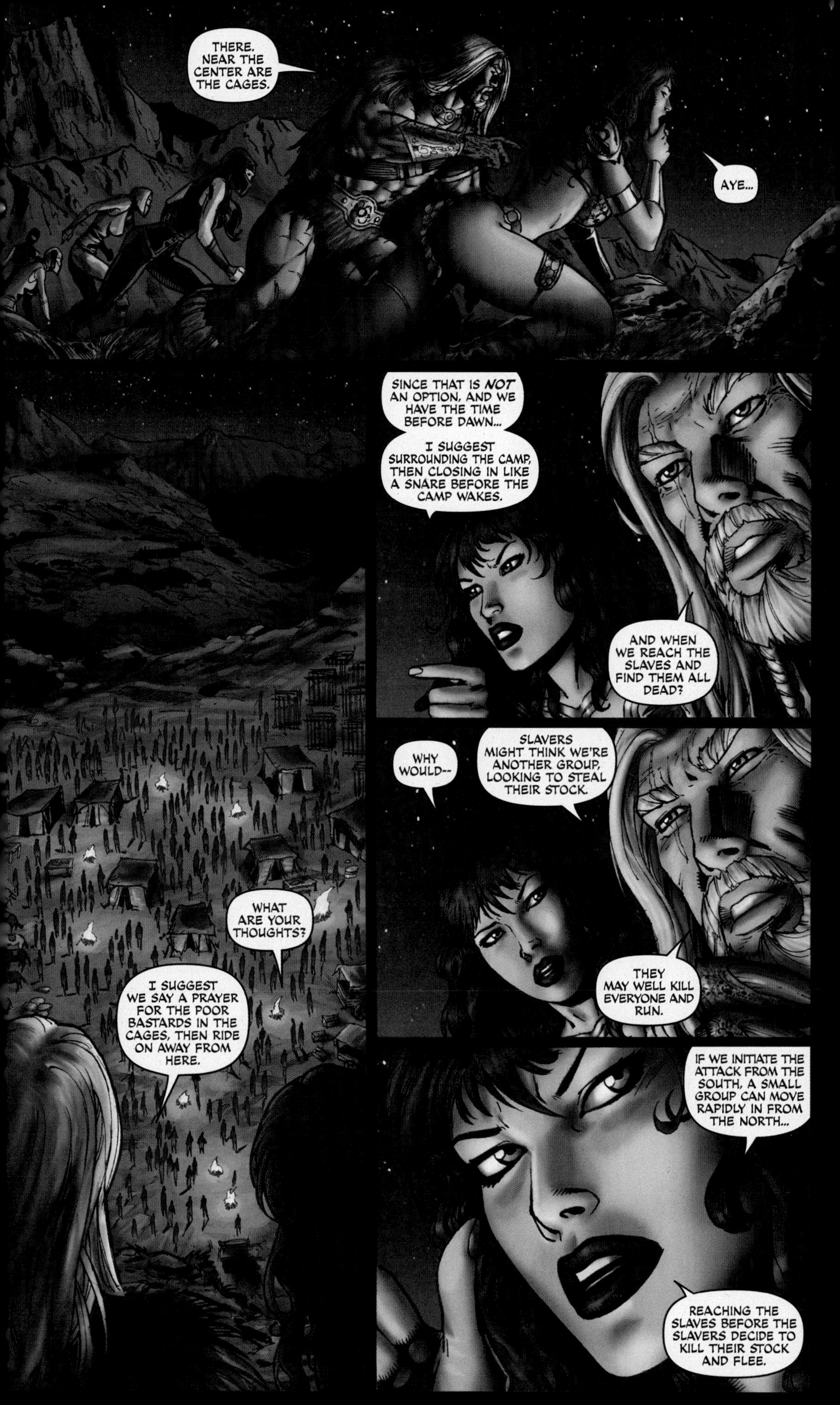
THERE. NEAR THE CENTER ARE THE CAGES.
AYE...
WHAT ARE YOUR THOUGHTS?
I SUGGEST WE SAY A PRAYER FOR THE POOR BASTARDS IN THE CAGES, THEN RIDE ON AWAY FROM HERE.
SINCE THAT IS NOT AN OPTION, AND WE HAVE THE TIME BEFORE DAWN...
I SUGGEST SURROUNDING THE CAMP, THEN CLOSING IN LIKE A SNARE BEFORE THE CAMP WAKES.
AND WHEN WE REACH THE SLAVES AND FIND THEM ALL DEAD?
WHY WOULD--
SLAVERS MIGHT THINK WE'RE ANOTHER GROUP, LOOKING TO STEAL THEIR STOCK.
THEY MAY WELL KILL EVERYONE AND RUN.
IF WE INITIATE THE ATTACK FROM THE SOUTH, A SMALL GROUP CAN MOVE RAPIDLY IN FROM THE NORTH...
REACHING THE SLAVES BEFORE THE SLAVERS DECIDE TO KILL THEIR STOCK AND FLEE.

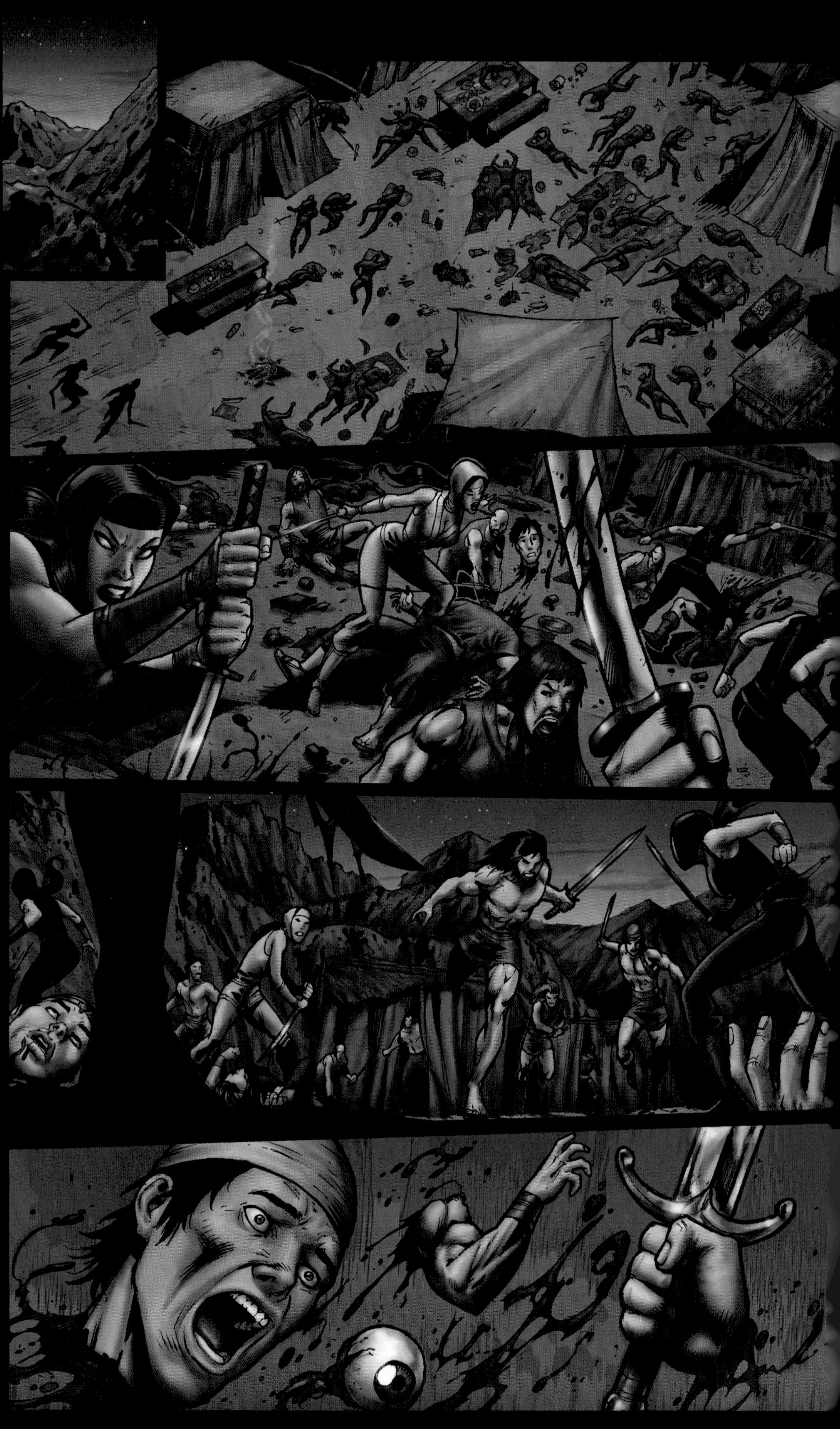

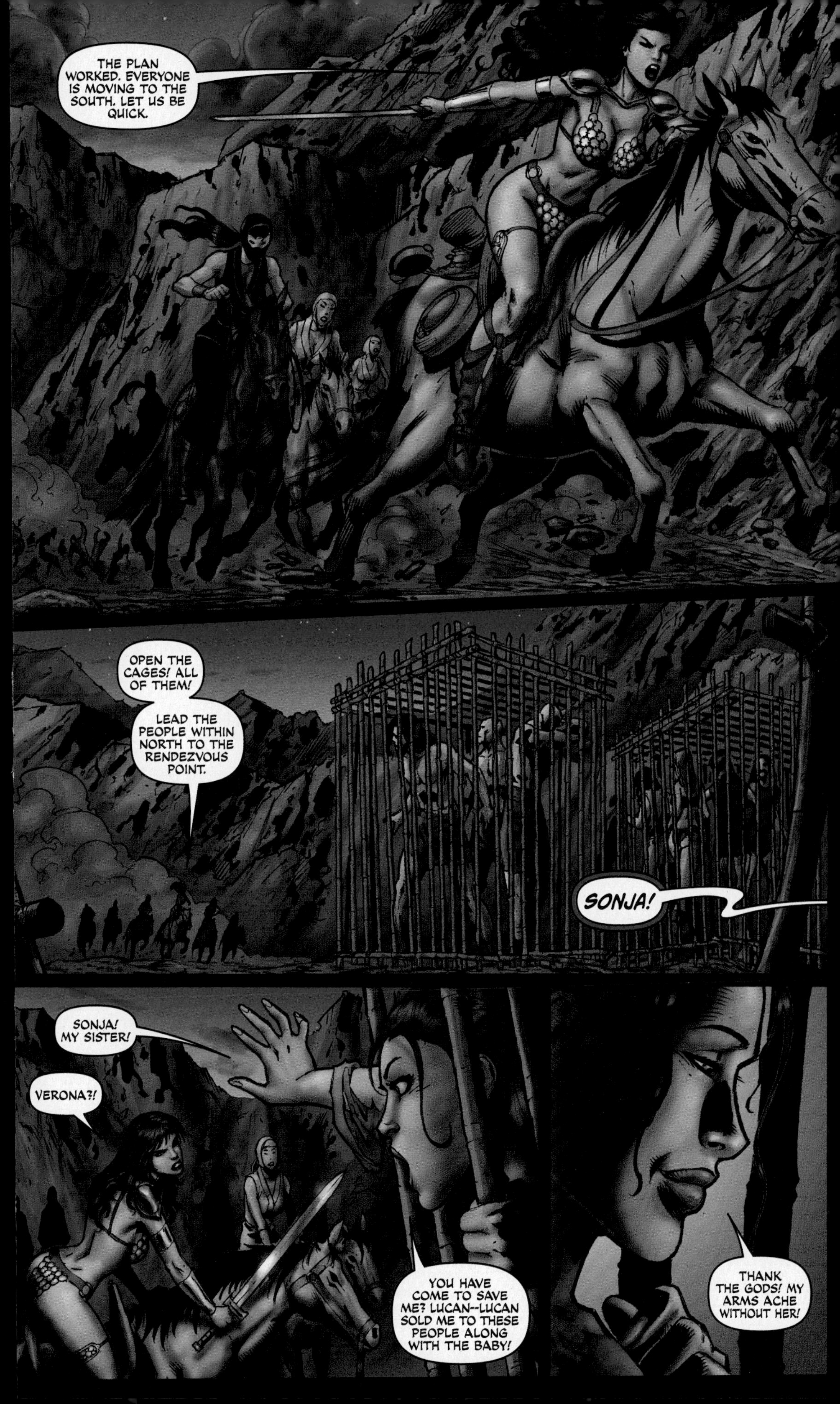
THE PLAN WORKED. EVERYONE IS MOVING TO THE SOUTH. LET US BE QUICK.
OPEN THE CAGES! ALL OF THEM!
LEAD THE PEOPLE WITHIN NORTH TO THE RENDEZVOUS POINT.
SONJA!
SONJA! MY SISTER!
VERONA?!
YOU HAVE COME TO SAVE ME? LUCAN--LUCAN SOLD ME TO THESE PEOPLE ALONG WITH THE BABY!
THANK THE GODS! MY ARMS ACHE WITHOUT HER!

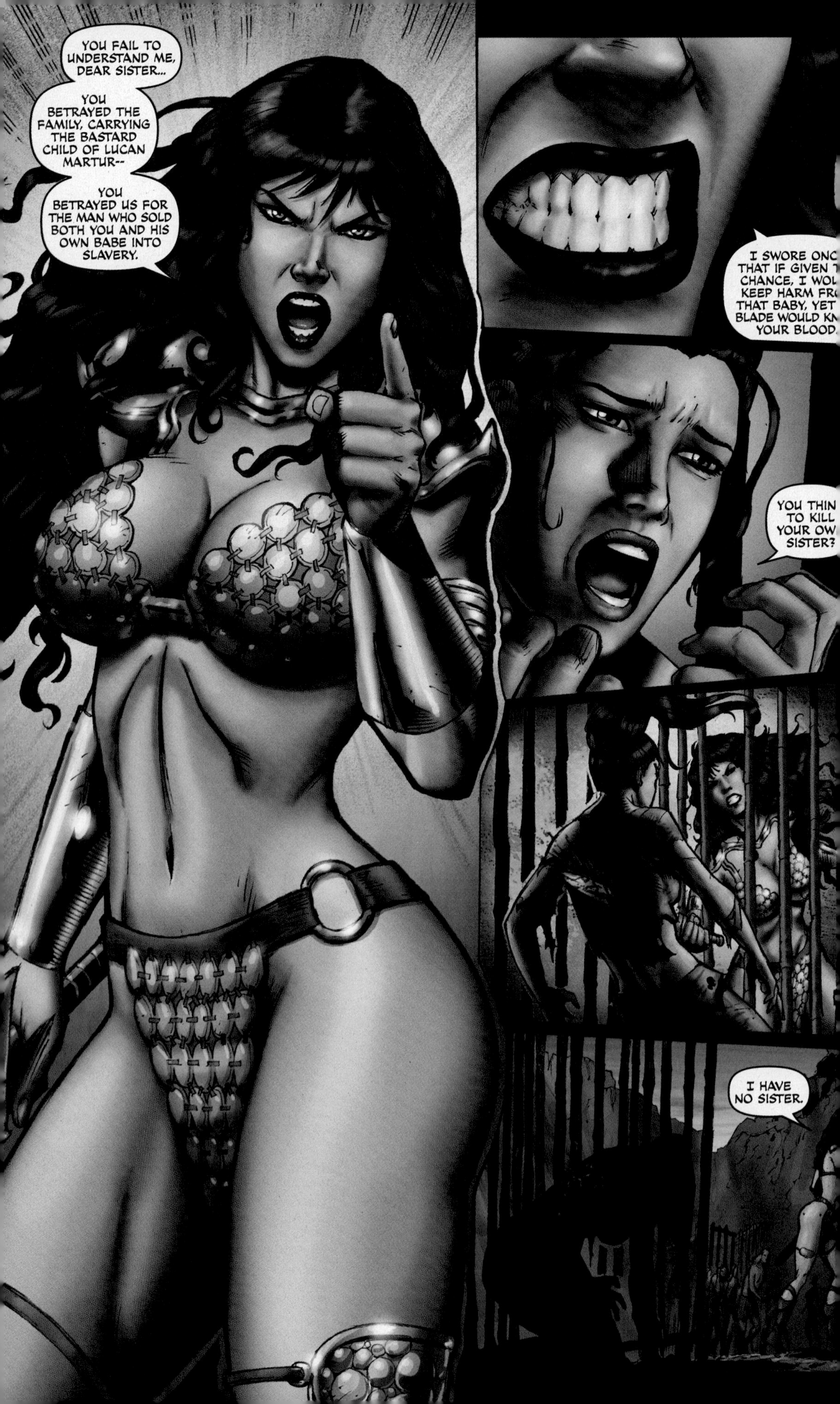

YOU FAIL TO UNDERSTAND ME, DEAR SISTER...
YOU BETRAYED THE FAMILY, CARRYING THE BASTARD CHILD OF LUCAN MARTUR--
YOU BETRAYED US FOR THE MAN WHO SOLD BOTH YOU AND HIS OWN BABE INTO SLAVERY.
I SWORE ONC THAT IF GIVEN T CHANCE, I WOU KEEP HARM FR THAT BABY, YET BLADE WOULD KN YOUR BLOOD.
YOU THIN TO KILL YOUR OW SISTER?
I HAVE NO SISTER.

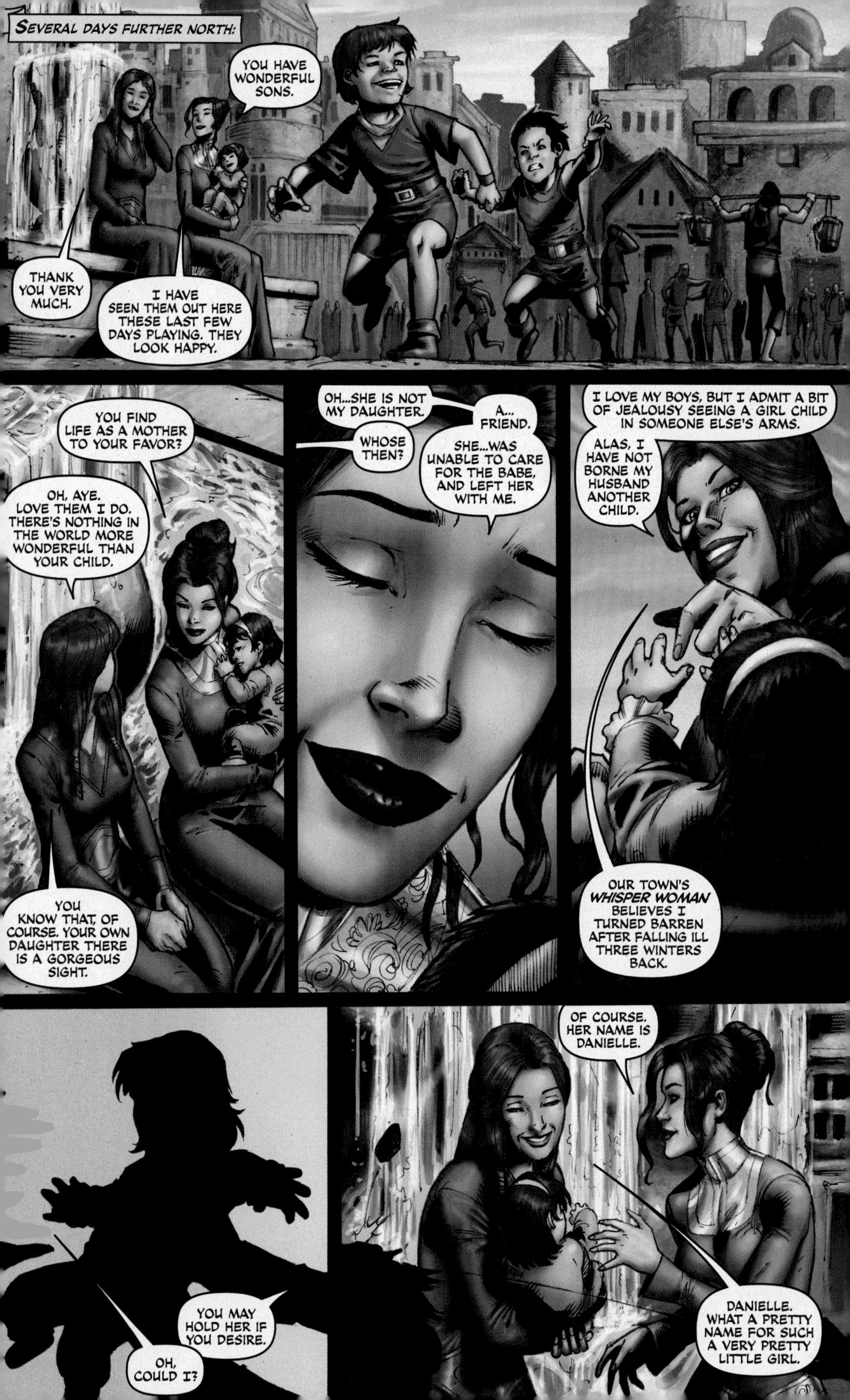
SEVERAL DAYS FURTHER NORTH:
YOU HAVE WONDERFUL SONS.
THANK YOU VERY MUCH.
I HAVE SEEN THEM OUT HERE THESE LAST FEW DAYS PLAYING. THEY LOOK HAPPY.
YOU FIND LIFE AS A MOTHER TO YOUR FAVOR?
OH, AYE. LOVE THEM I DO. THERE'S NOTHING IN THE WORLD MORE WONDERFUL THAN YOUR CHILD.
YOU KNOW THAT, OF COURSE. YOUR OWN DAUGHTER THERE IS A GORGEOUS SIGHT.
OH...SHE IS NOT MY DAUGHTER.
WHOSE THEN?
A... FRIEND.
SHE...WAS UNABLE TO CARE FOR THE BABE, AND LEFT HER WITH ME.
I LOVE MY BOYS, BUT I ADMIT A BIT OF JEALOUSY SEEING A GIRL CHILD IN SOMEONE ELSE'S ARMS.
ALAS, I HAVE NOT BORNE MY HUSBAND ANOTHER CHILD.
OUR TOWN'S WHISPER WOMAN BELIEVES I TURNED BARREN AFTER FALLING ILL THREE WINTERS BACK.
YOU MAY HOLD HER IF YOU DESIRE.
OH, COULD I?
OF COURSE. HER NAME IS DANIELLE.
DANIELLE. WHAT A PRETTY NAME FOR SUCH A VERY PRETTY LITTLE GIRL.

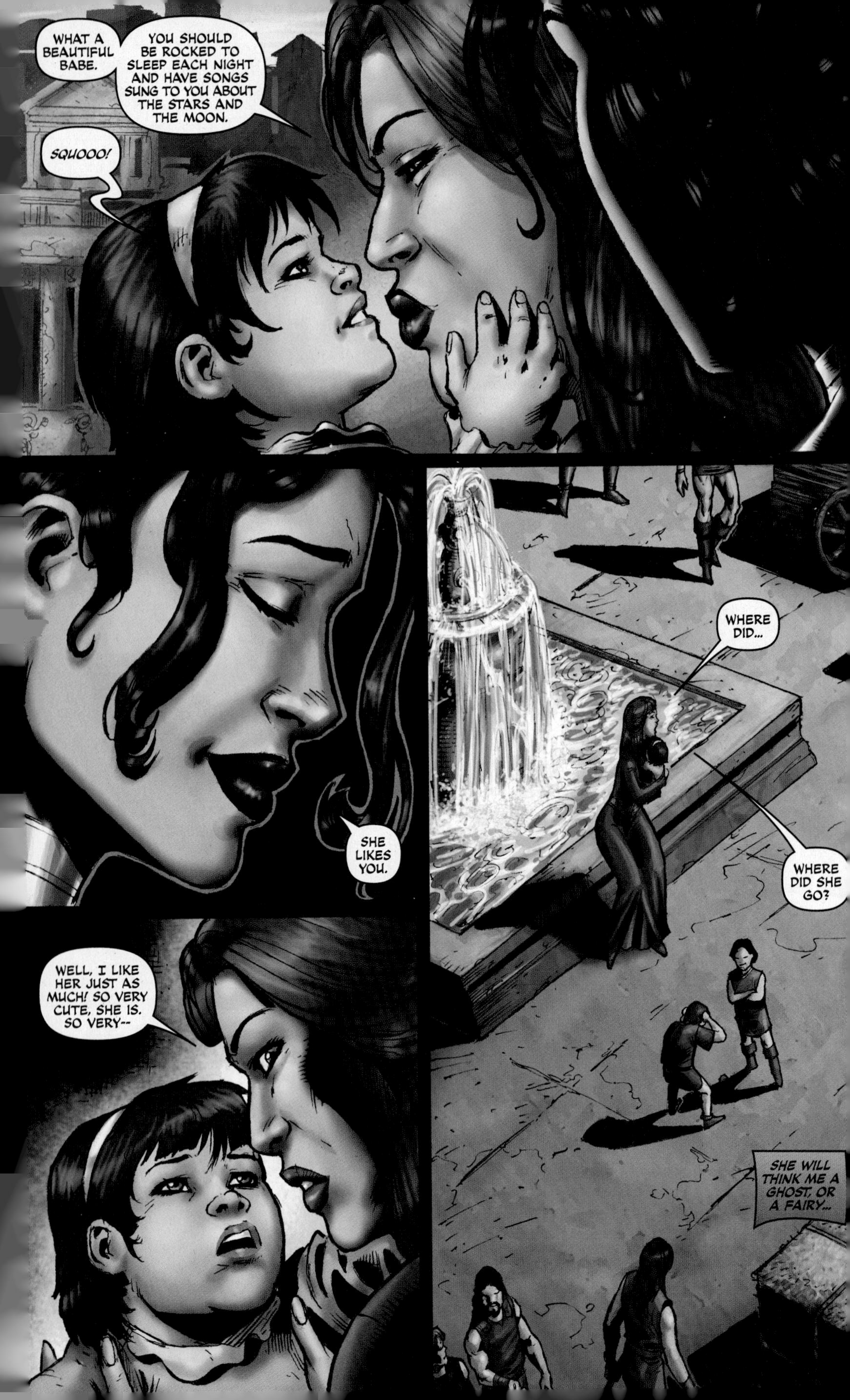
WHAT A BEAUTIFUL BABE.
YOU SHOULD BE ROCKED TO SLEEP EACH NIGHT AND HAVE SONGS SUNG TO YOU ABOUT THE STARS AND THE MOON.
SQUOOO!
SHE LIKES YOU.
WELL, I LIKE HER JUST AS MUCH! SO VERY CUTE, SHE IS. SO VERY--
WHERE DID...
WHERE DID SHE GO?
SHE WILL THINK ME A GHOST, OR A FAIRY...

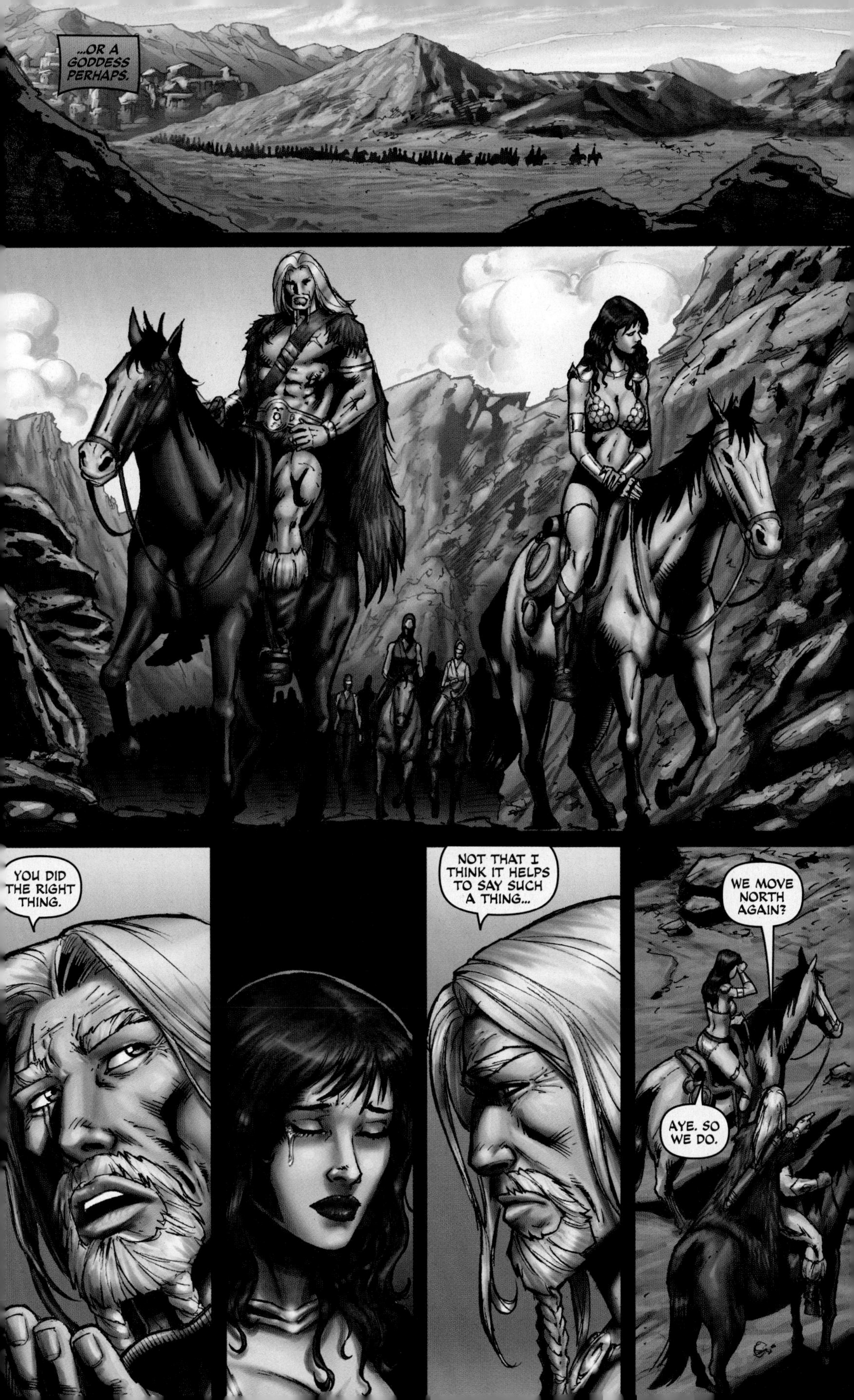
...OR A GODDESS PERHAPS.
YOU DID THE RIGHT THING.
NOT THAT I THINK IT HELPS TO SAY SUCH A THING...
WE MOVE NORTH AGAIN?
AYE. SO WE DO.

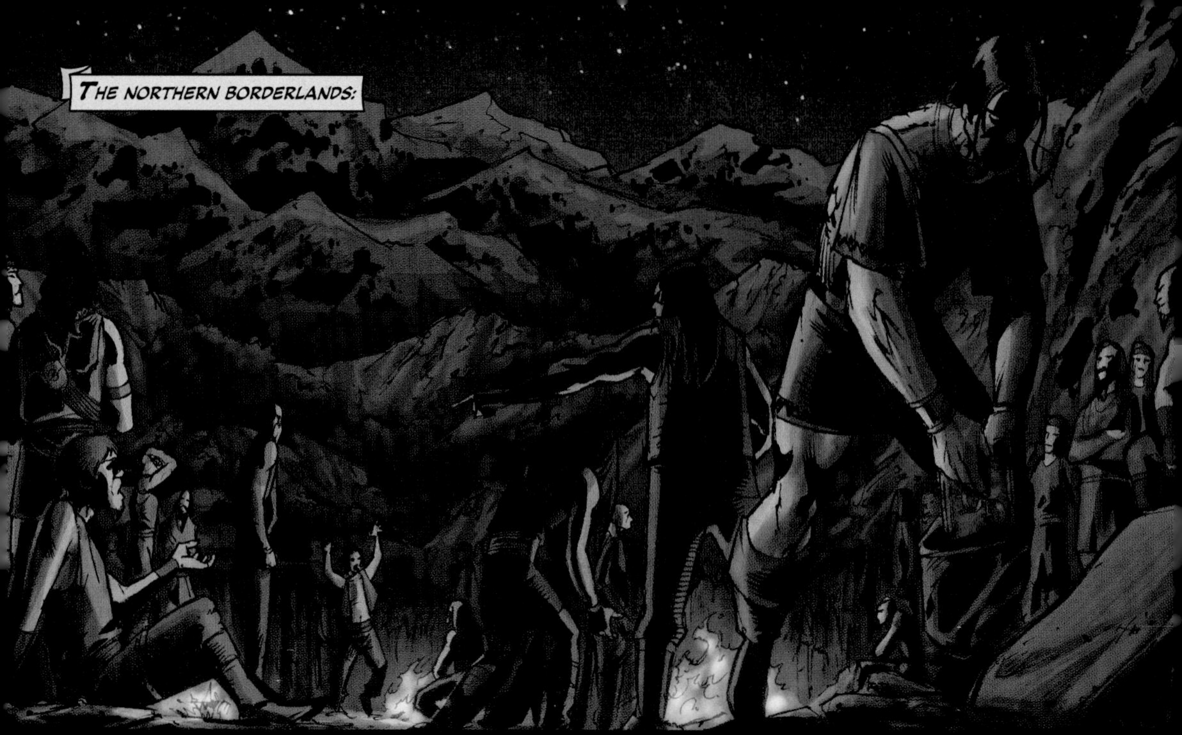
THE NORTHERN BORDERLANDS:

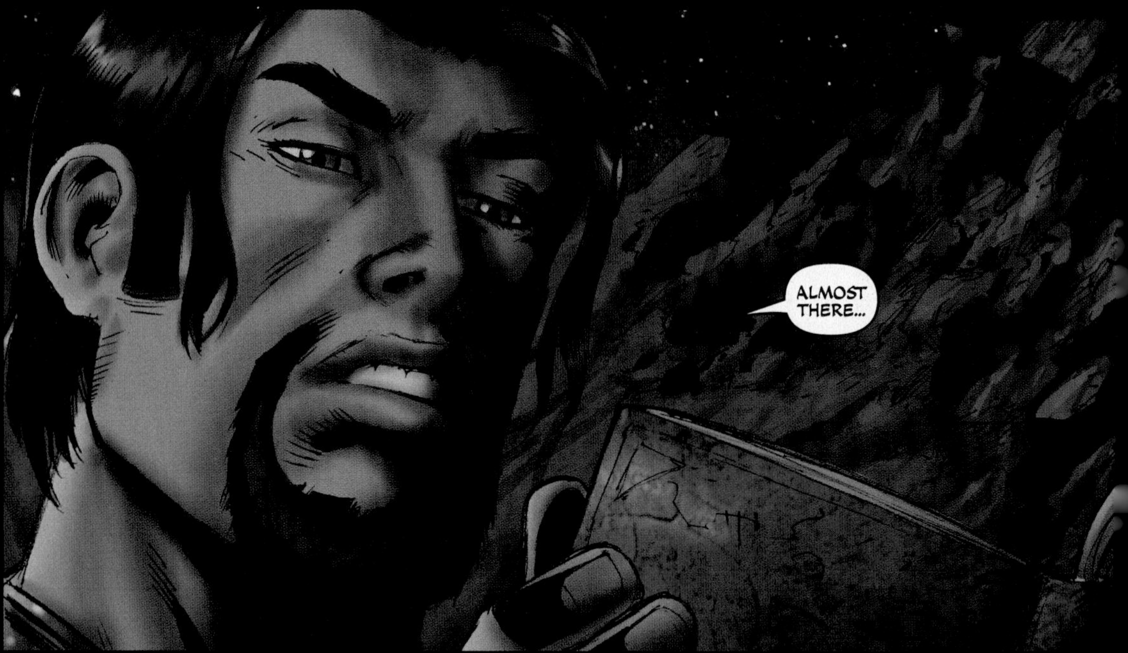
ALMOST THERE...

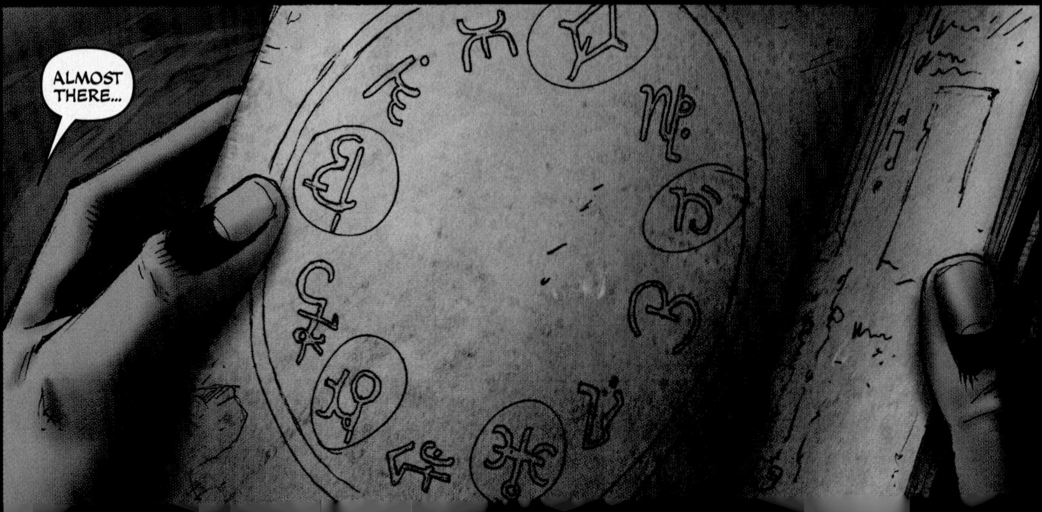
ALMOST THERE...

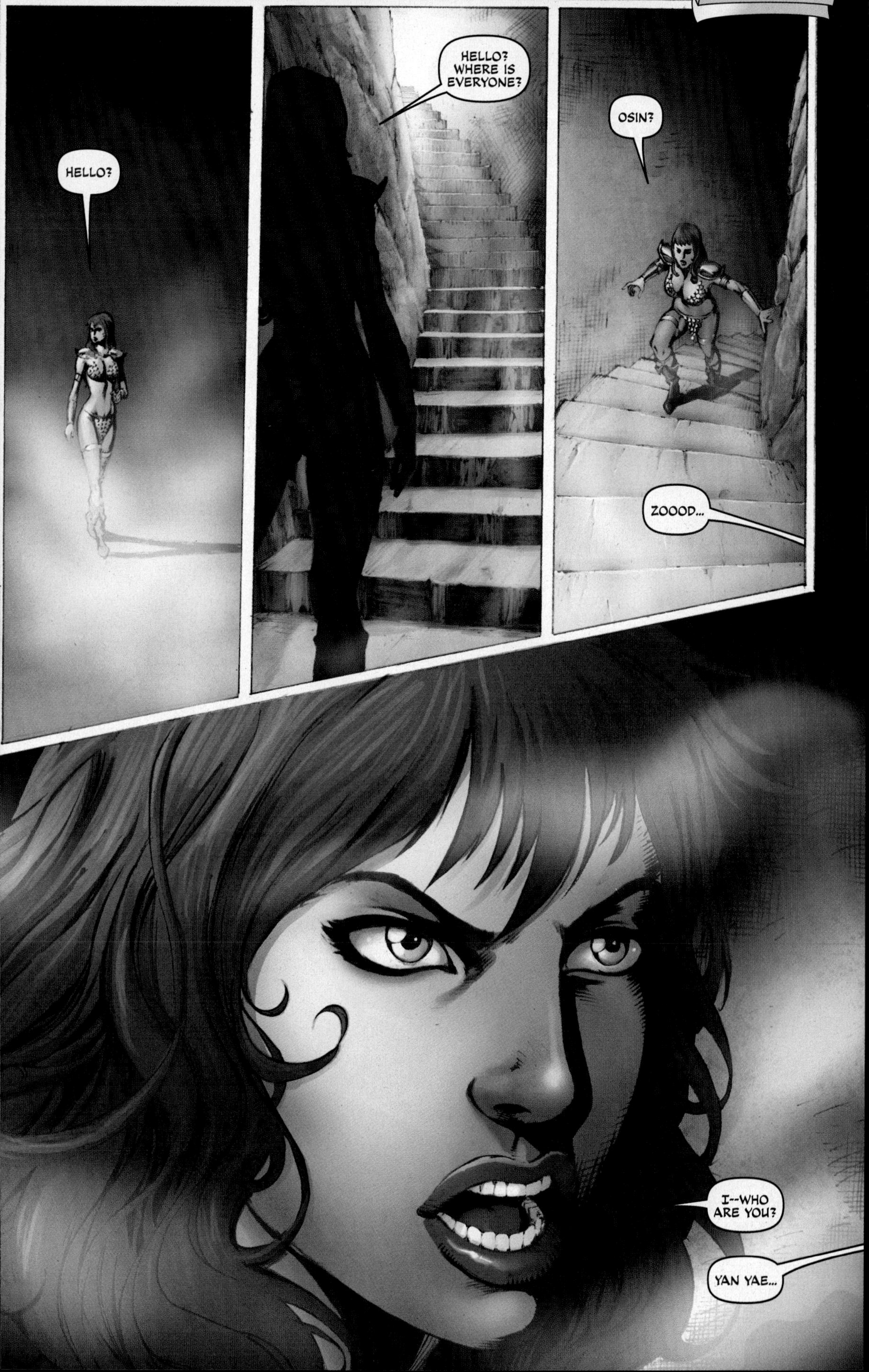
HELLO?
HELLO? WHERE IS EVERYONE?
OSIN?
ZOOOD...
I--WHO ARE YOU?
YAN YAE...

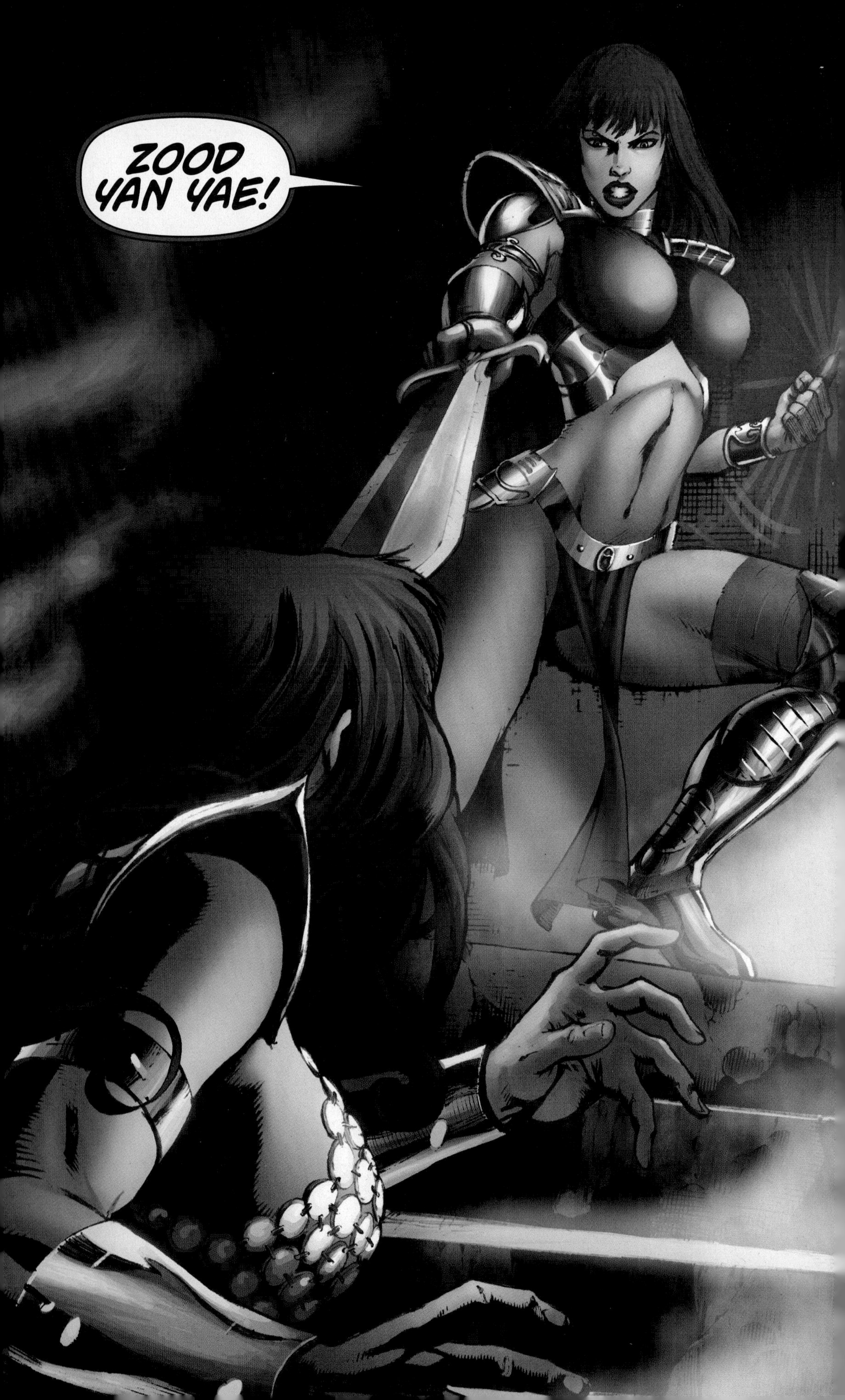
ZOOD YAN YAE!

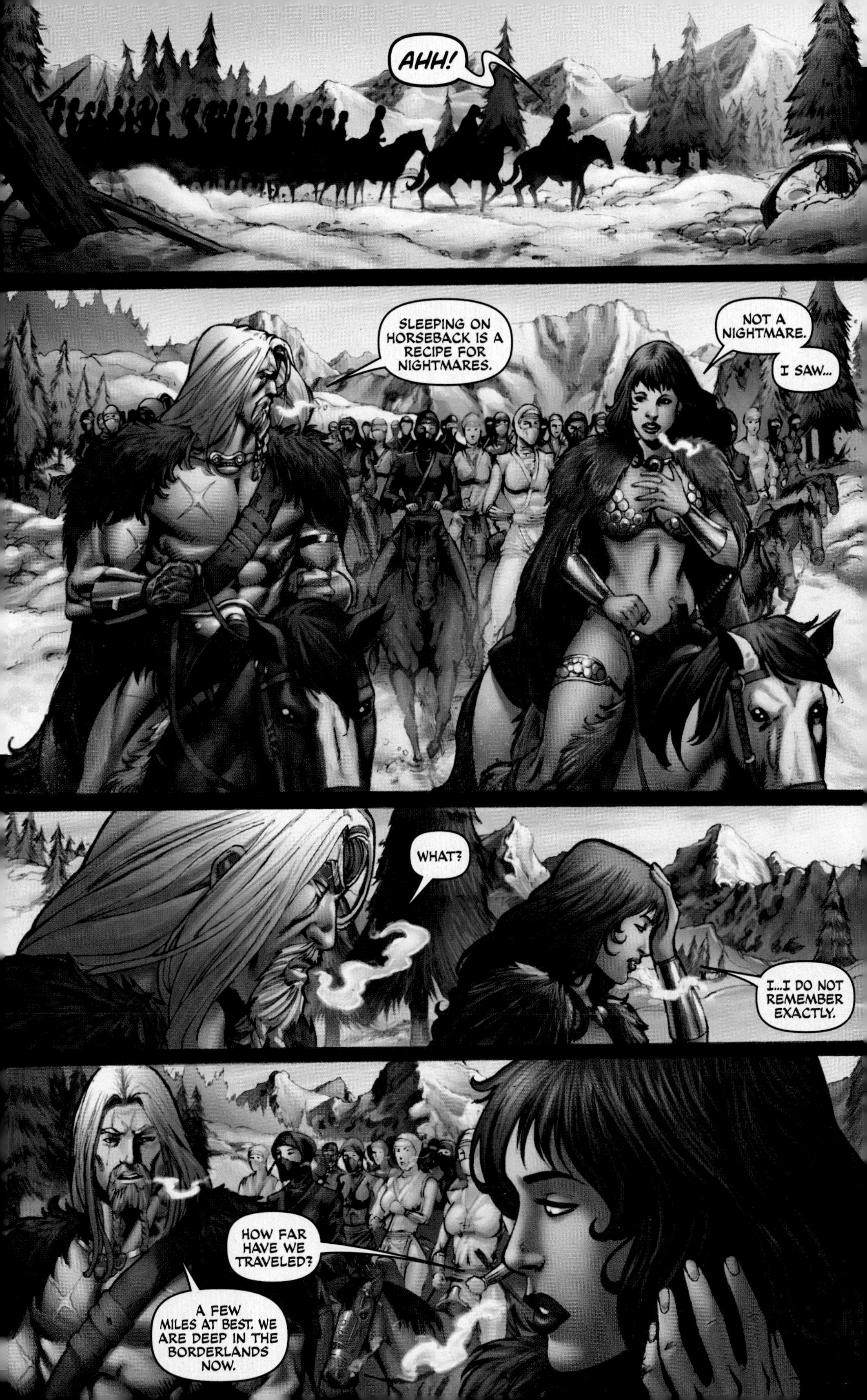
AHH!
SLEEPING ON HORSEBACK IS A RECIPE FOR NIGHTMARES.
NOT A NIGHTMARE.
I SAW...
WHAT?
I...I DO NOT REMEMBER EXACTLY.
HOW FAR HAVE WE TRAVELED?
A FEW MILES AT BEST. WE ARE DEEP IN THE BORDERLANDS NOW.

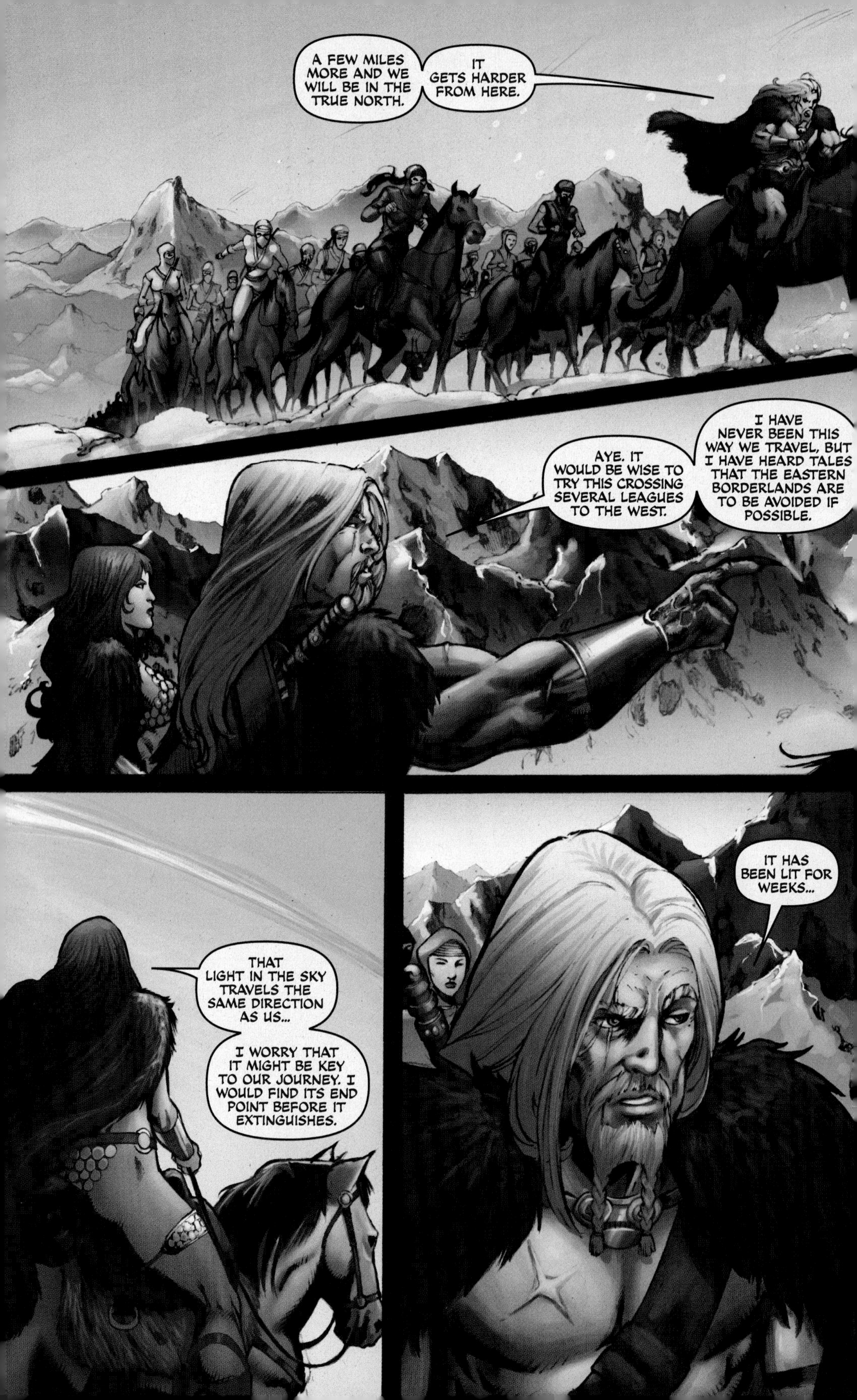
A FEW MILES MORE AND WE WILL BE IN THE TRUE NORTH.
IT GETS HARDER FROM HERE.
AYE. IT WOULD BE WISE TO TRY THIS CROSSING SEVERAL LEAGUES TO THE WEST.
I HAVE NEVER BEEN THIS WAY WE TRAVEL, BUT I HAVE HEARD TALES THAT THE EASTERN BORDERLANDS ARE TO BE AVOIDED IF POSSIBLE.
THAT LIGHT IN THE SKY TRAVELS THE SAME DIRECTION AS US...
I WORRY THAT IT MIGHT BE KEY TO OUR JOURNEY. I WOULD FIND ITS END POINT BEFORE IT EXTINGUISHES.
IT HAS BEEN LIT FOR WEEKS...

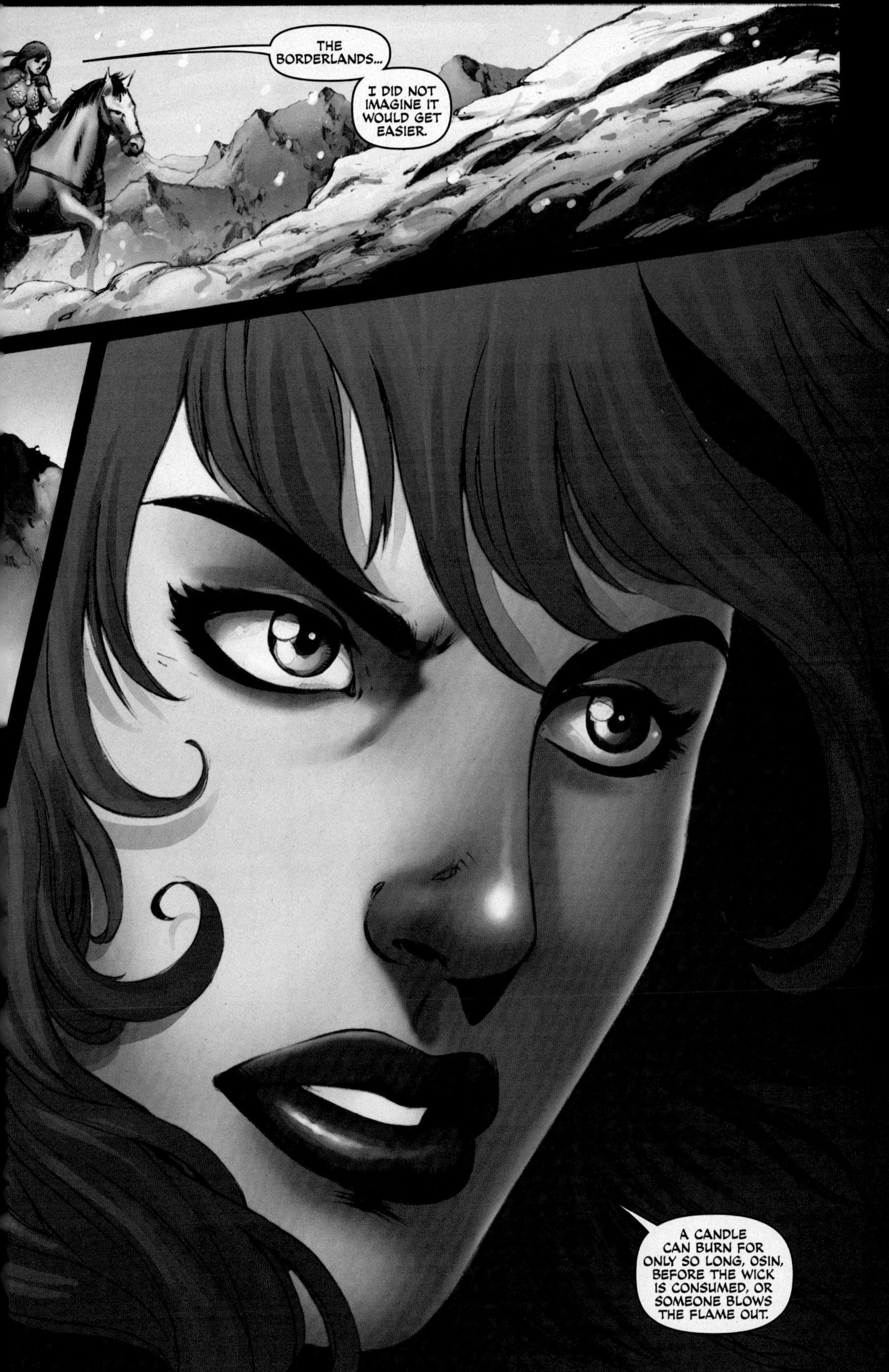
THE BORDERLANDS...
I DID NOT IMAGINE IT WOULD GET EASIER.
A CANDLE CAN BURN FOR ONLY SO LONG, OSIN, BEFORE THE WICK IS CONSUMED, OR SOMEONE BLOWS THE FLAME OUT.

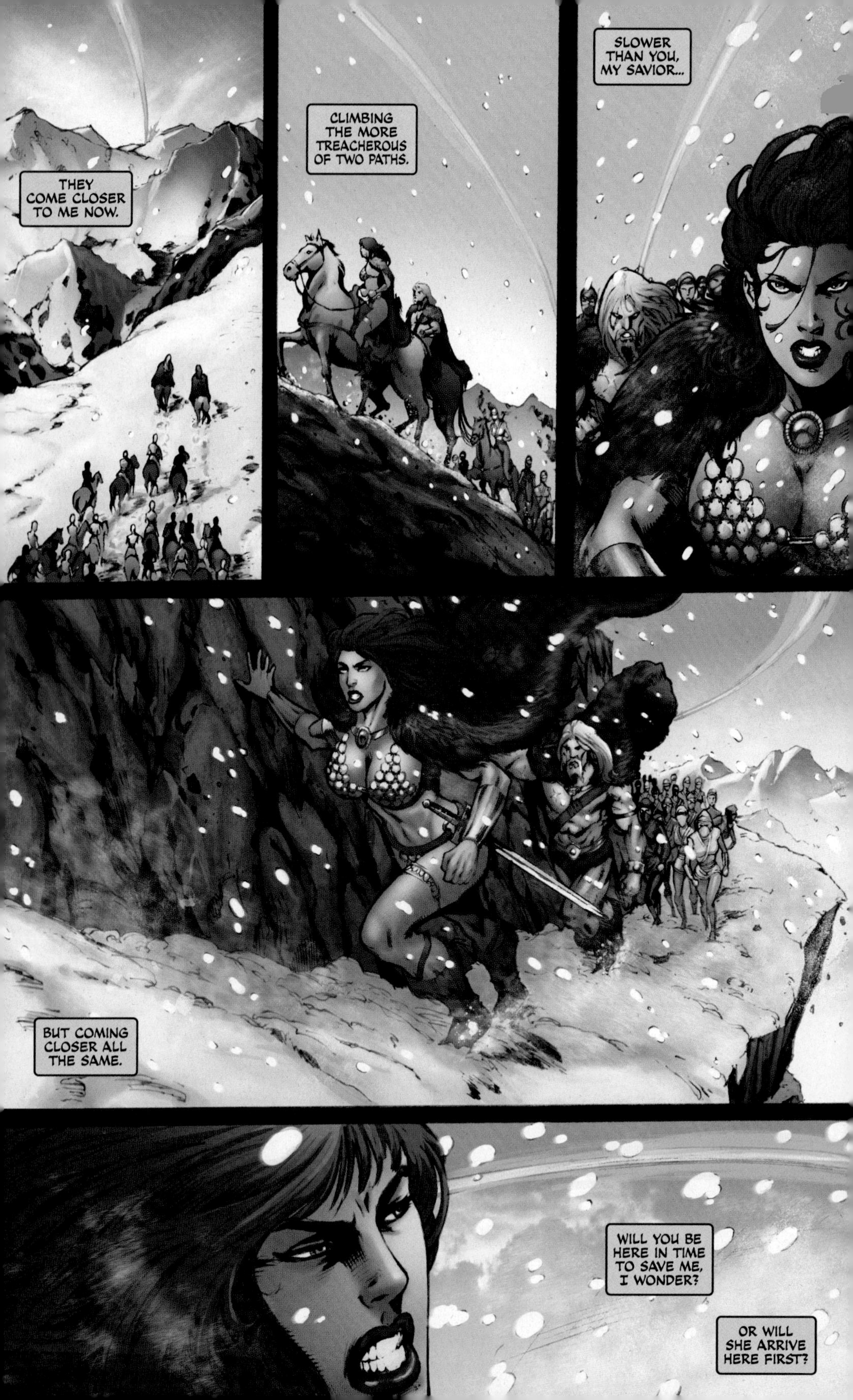
THEY COME CLOSER TO ME NOW.
CLIMBING THE MORE TREACHEROUS OF TWO PATHS.
SLOWER THAN YOU, MY SAVIOR...
BUT COMING CLOSER ALL THE SAME.
WILL YOU BE HERE IN TIME TO SAVE ME, I WONDER?
OR WILL SHE ARRIVE HERE FIRST?

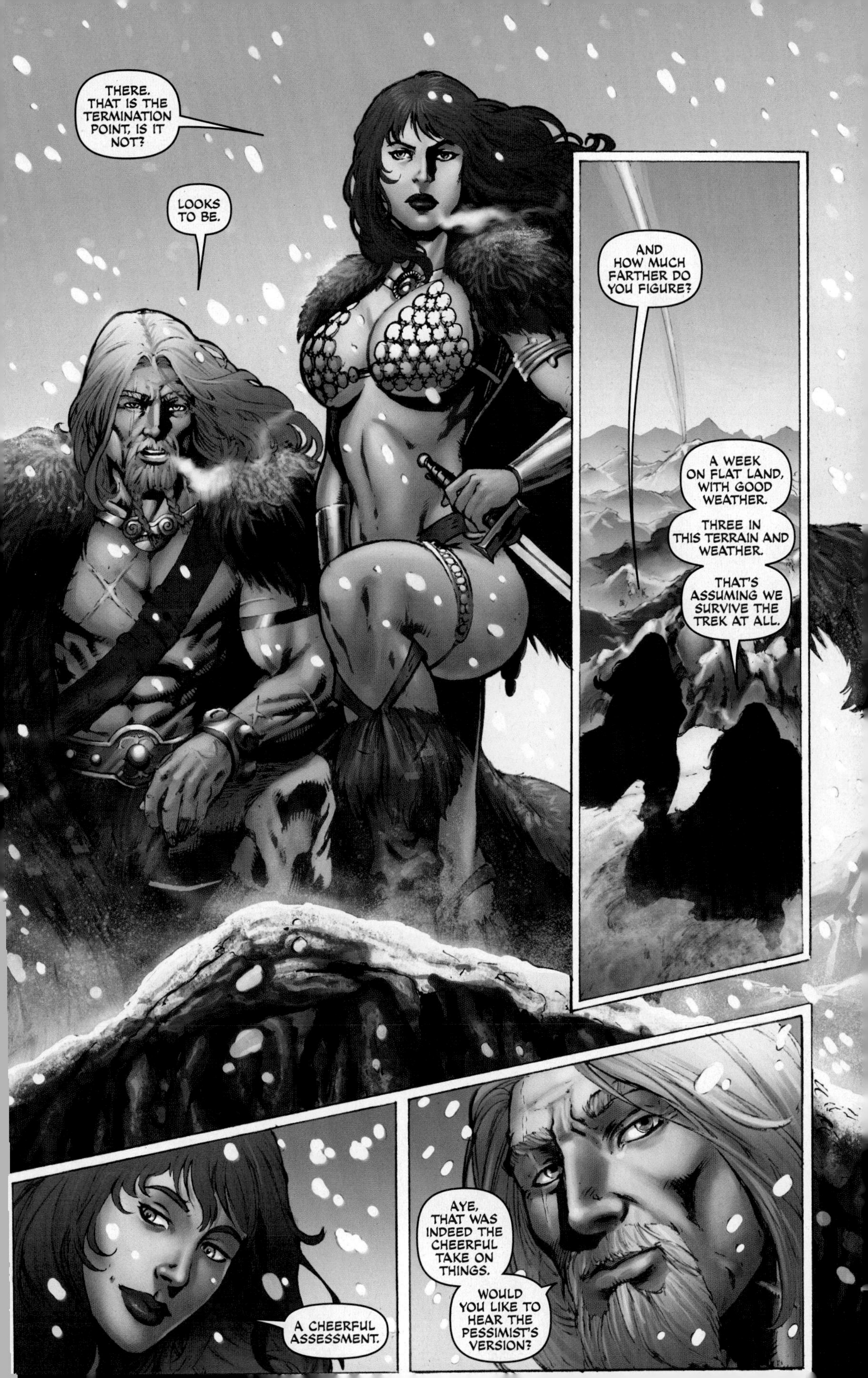
THERE. THAT IS THE TERMINATION POINT, IS IT NOT?
LOOKS TO BE.
AND HOW MUCH FARTHER DO YOU FIGURE?
A WEEK ON FLAT LAND, WITH GOOD WEATHER.
THREE IN THIS TERRAIN AND WEATHER.
THAT'S ASSUMING WE SURVIVE THE TREK AT ALL.
A CHEERFUL ASSESSMENT.
AYE, THAT WAS INDEED THE CHEERFUL TAKE ON THINGS.
WOULD YOU LIKE TO HEAR THE PESSIMIST'S VERSION?

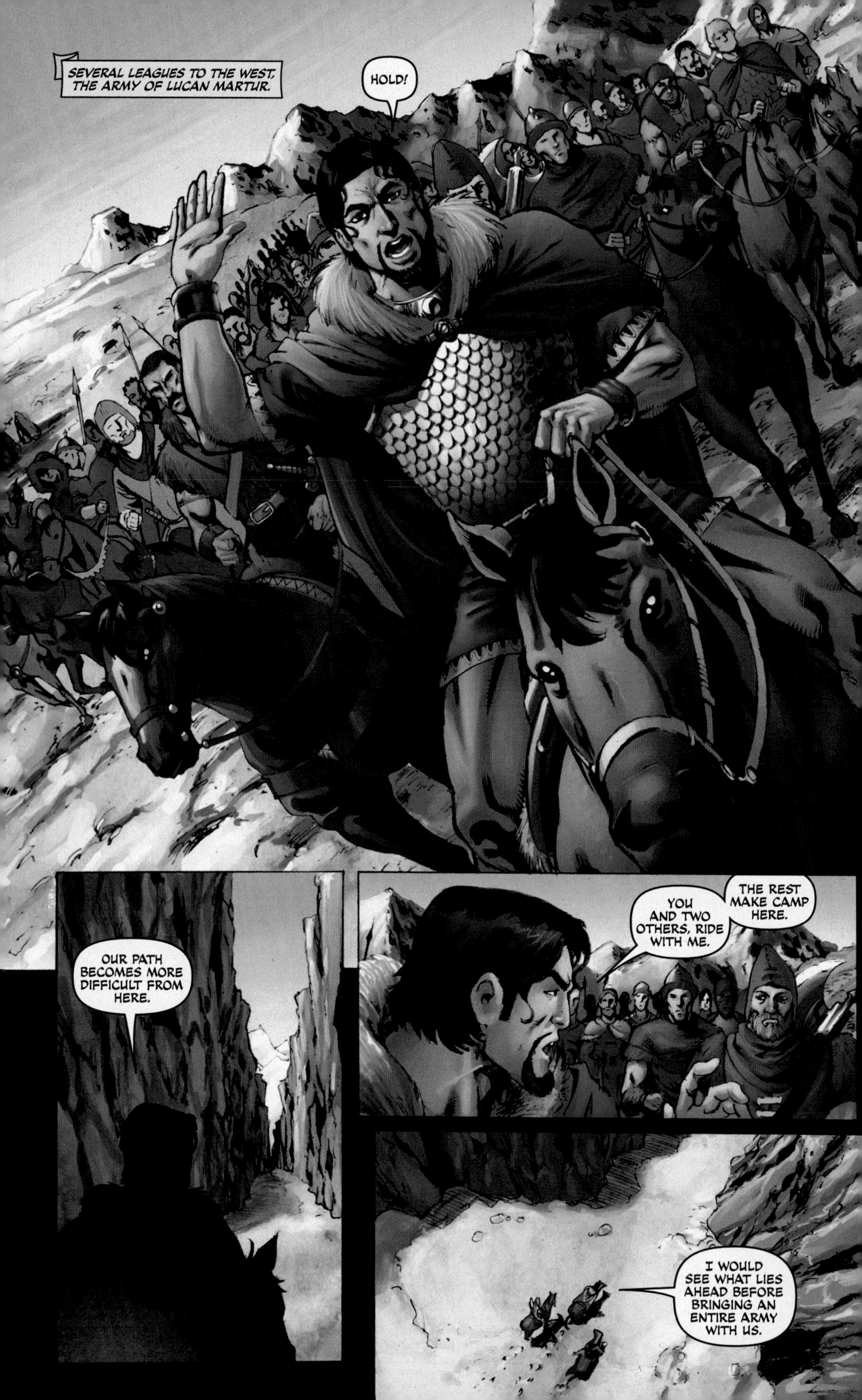
SEVERAL LEAGUES TO THE WEST, THE ARMY OF LUCAN MARTUR.
HOLD!
OUR PATH BECOMES MORE DIFFICULT FROM HERE.
YOU AND TWO OTHERS, RIDE WITH ME.
THE REST MAKE CAMP HERE.
I WOULD SEE WHAT LIES AHEAD BEFORE BRINGING AN ENTIRE ARMY WITH US.

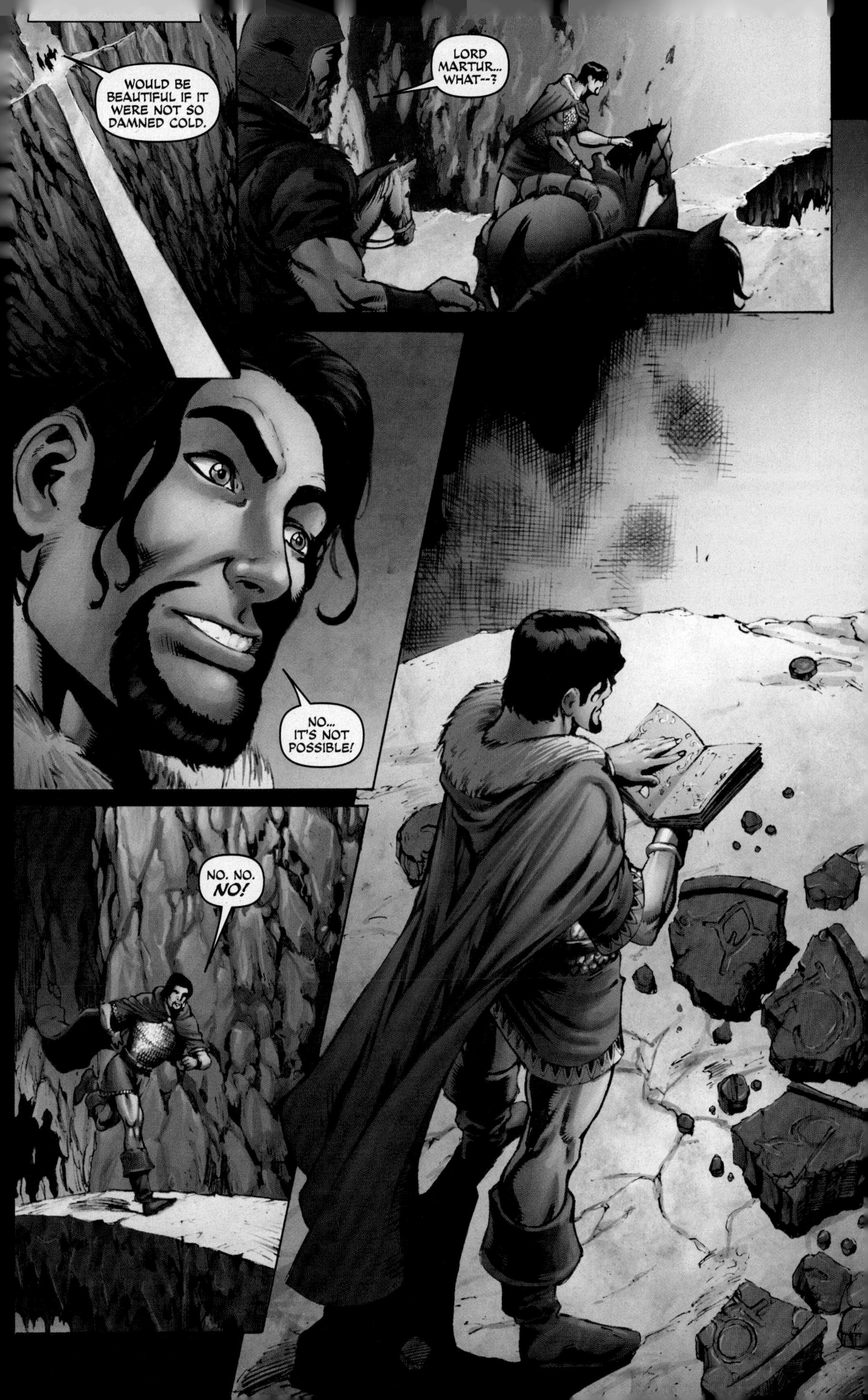
WOULD BE BEAUTIFUL IF IT WERE NOT SO DAMNED COLD.
LORD MARTUR... WHAT--?
NO... IT'S NOT POSSIBLE!
NO. NO. NO!

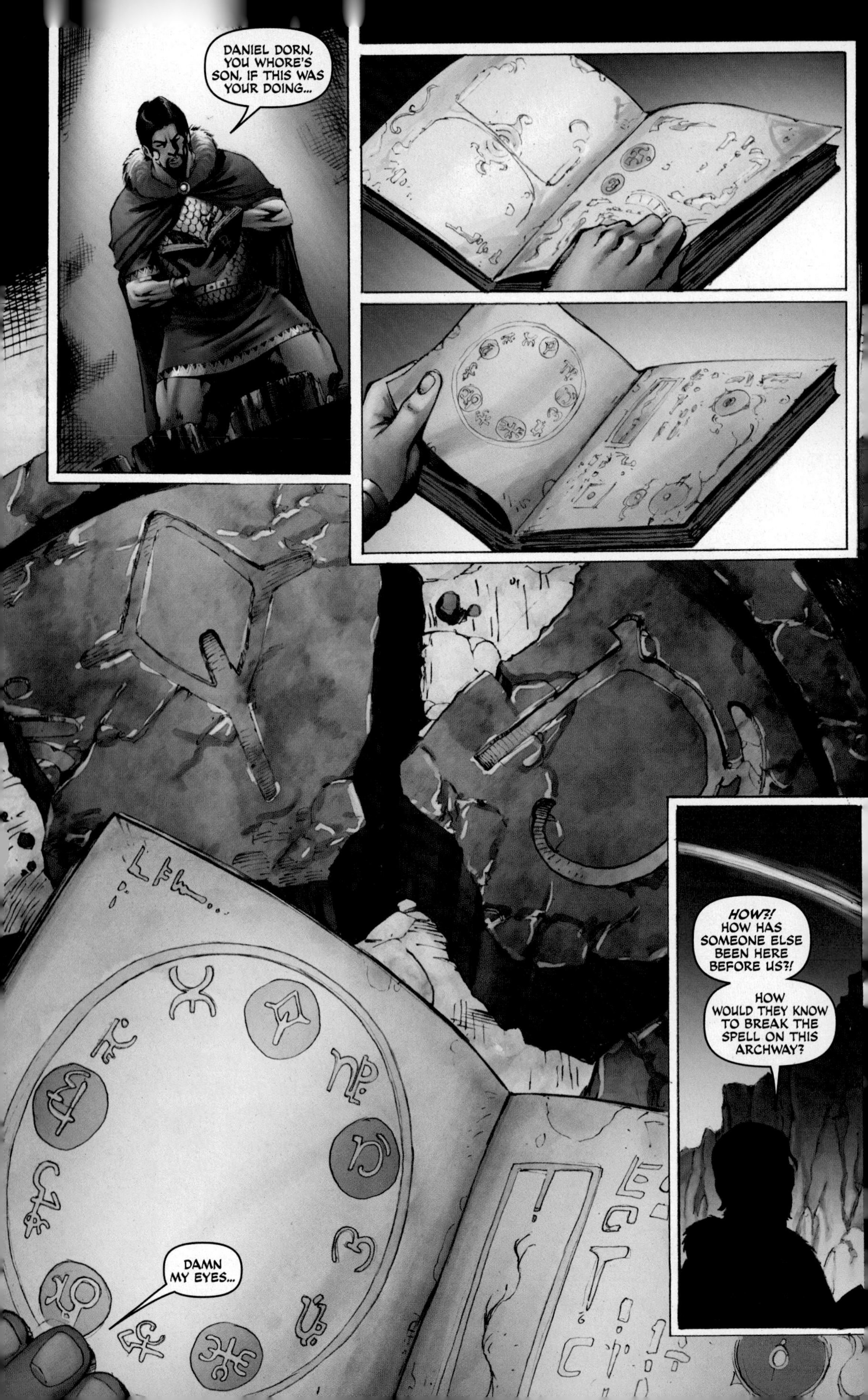
DANIEL DORN, YOU WHORE'S SON, IF THIS WAS YOUR DOING...
HOW?! HOW HAS SOMEONE ELSE BEEN HERE BEFORE US?!
HOW WOULD THEY KNOW TO BREAK THE SPELL ON THIS ARCHWAY?
DAMN MY EYES...

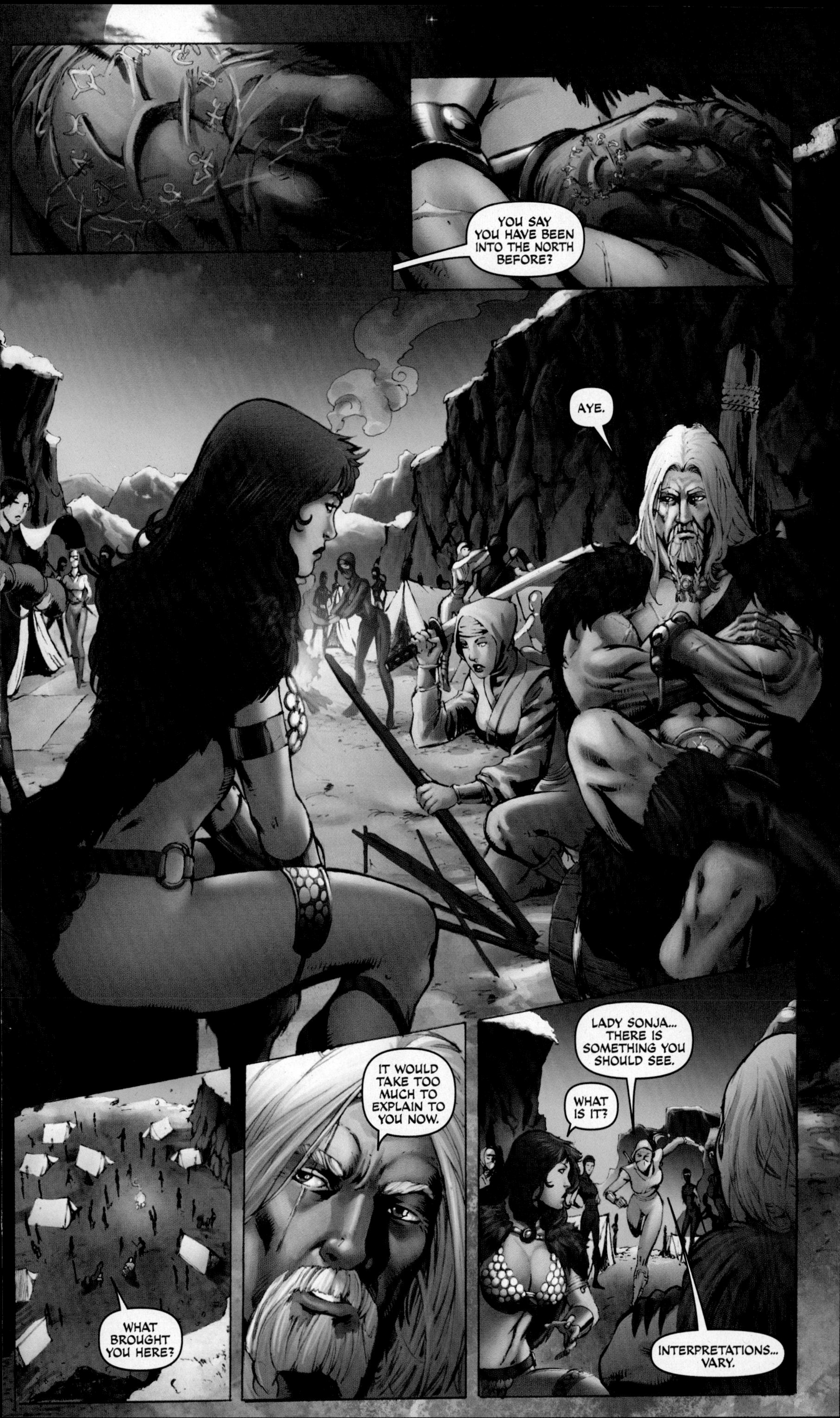
YOU SAY YOU HAVE BEEN INTO THE NORTH BEFORE?
AYE.
WHAT BROUGHT YOU HERE?
IT WOULD TAKE TOO MUCH TO EXPLAIN TO YOU NOW.
LADY SONJA... THERE IS SOMETHING YOU SHOULD SEE.
WHAT IS IT?
INTERPRETATIONS... VARY.

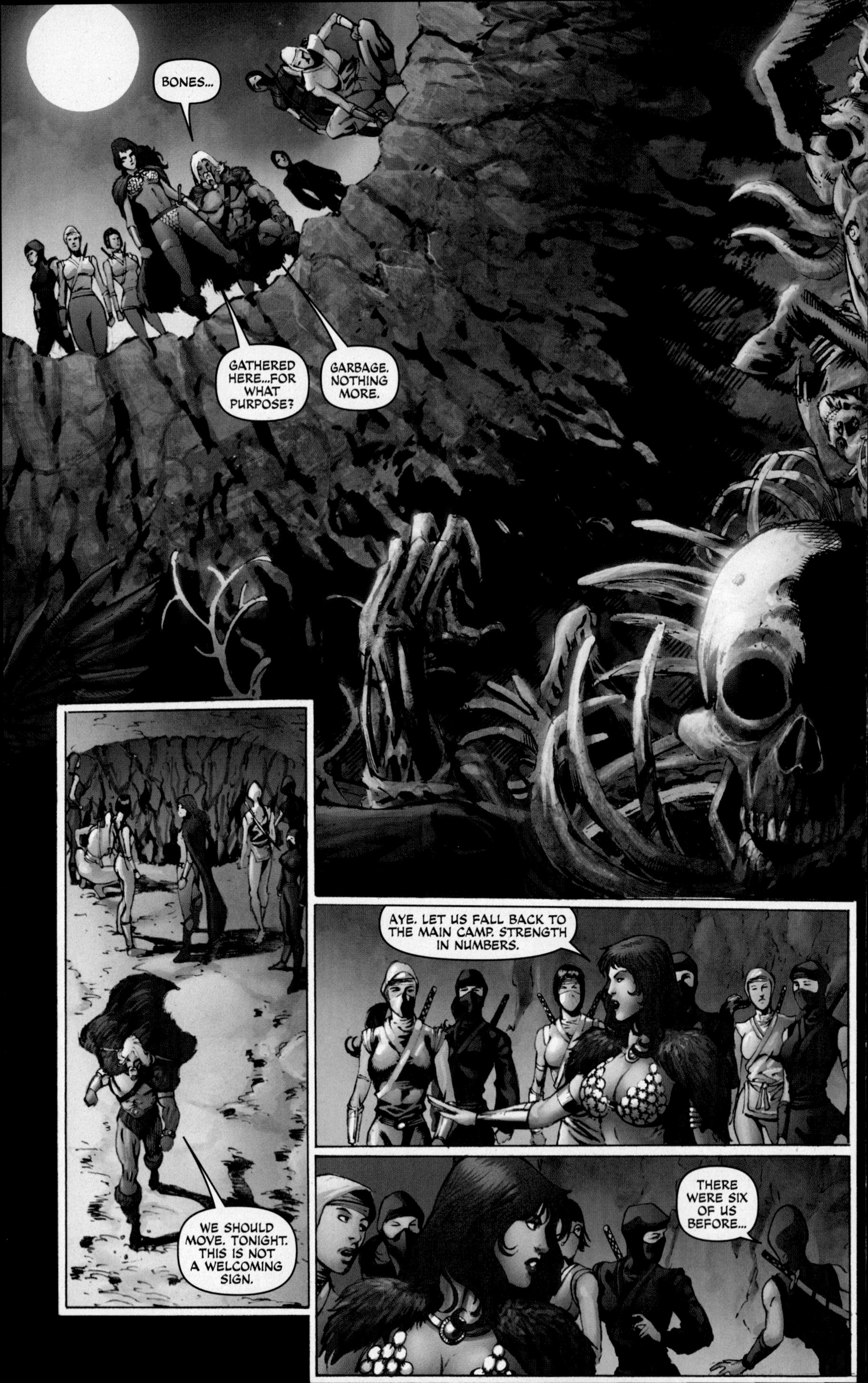
BONES...
GATHERED HERE...FOR WHAT PURPOSE?
GARBAGE. NOTHING MORE.
WE SHOULD MOVE. TONIGHT. THIS IS NOT A WELCOMING SIGN.
AYE. LET US FALL BACK TO THE MAIN CAMP. STRENGTH IN NUMBERS.
THERE WERE SIX OF US BEFORE...

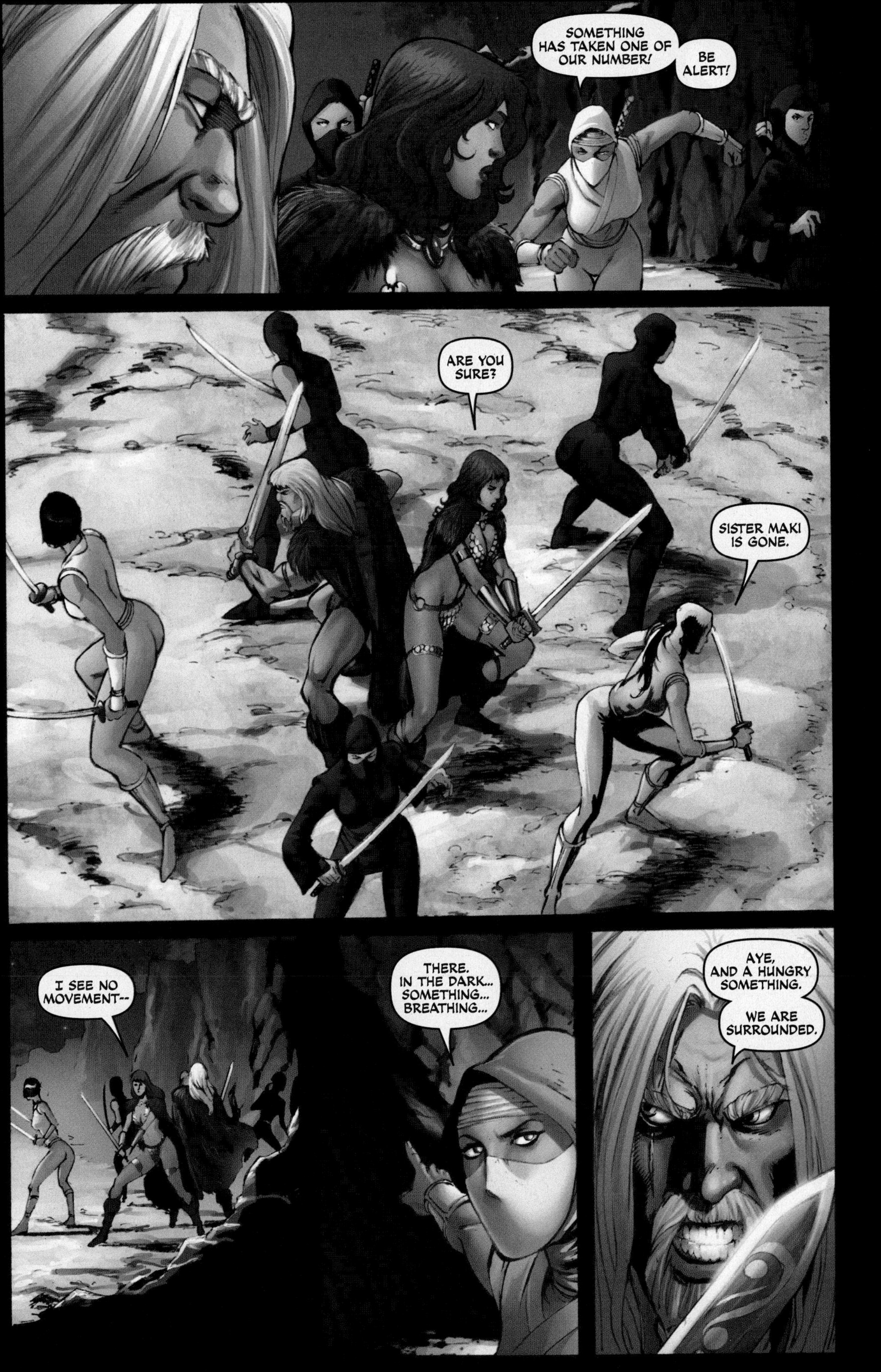

SOMETHING HAS TAKEN ONE OF OUR NUMBER!
BE ALERT!
ARE YOU SURE?
SISTER MAKI IS GONE.
I SEE NO MOVEMENT--
THERE. IN THE DARK... SOMETHING... BREATHING...
AYE, AND A HUNGRY SOMETHING.
WE ARE SURROUNDED.

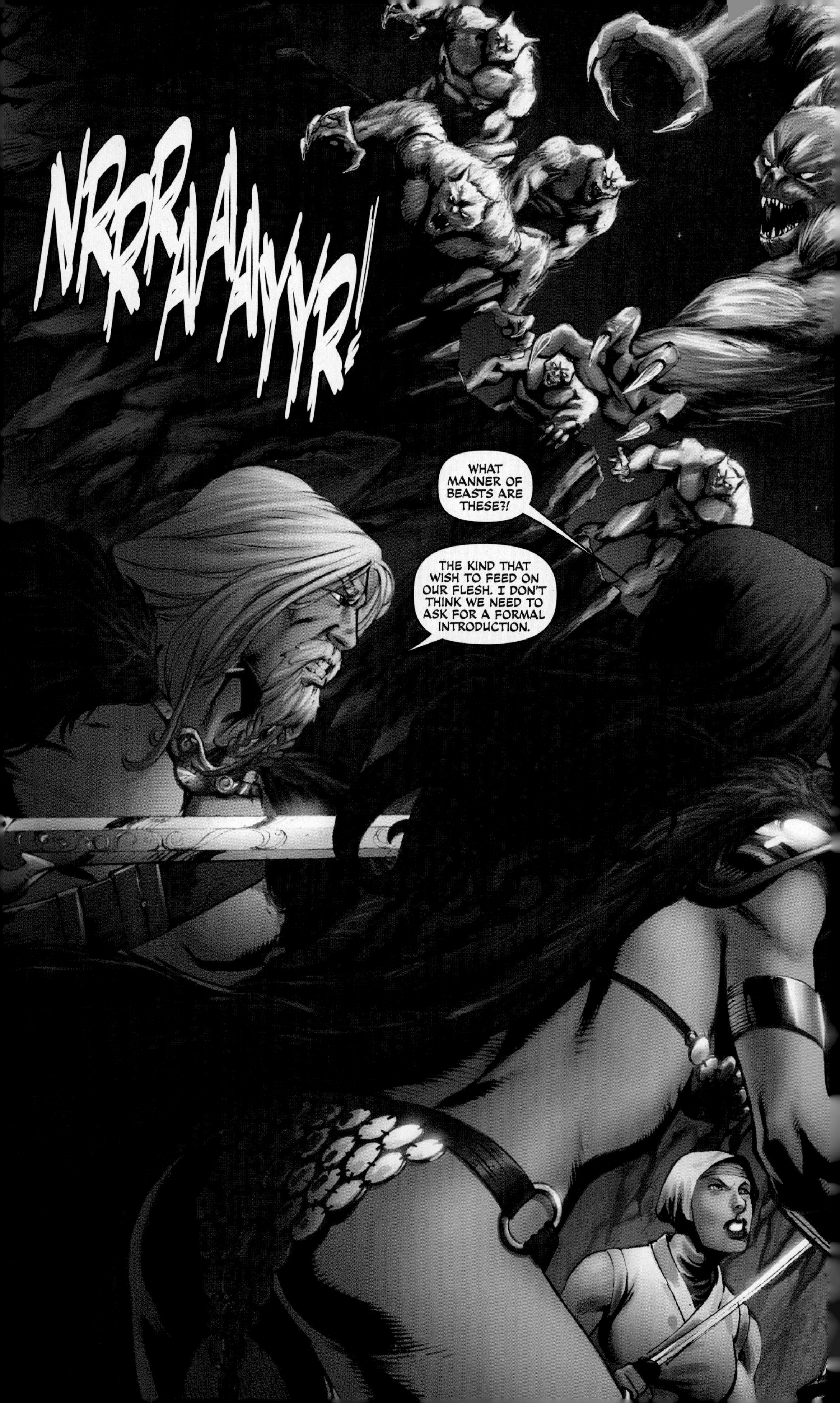
NRRRAAAYYR!
WHAT MANNER OF BEASTS ARE THESE?!
THE KIND THAT WISH TO FEED ON OUR FLESH. I DON'T THINK WE NEED TO ASK FOR A FORMAL INTRODUCTION.

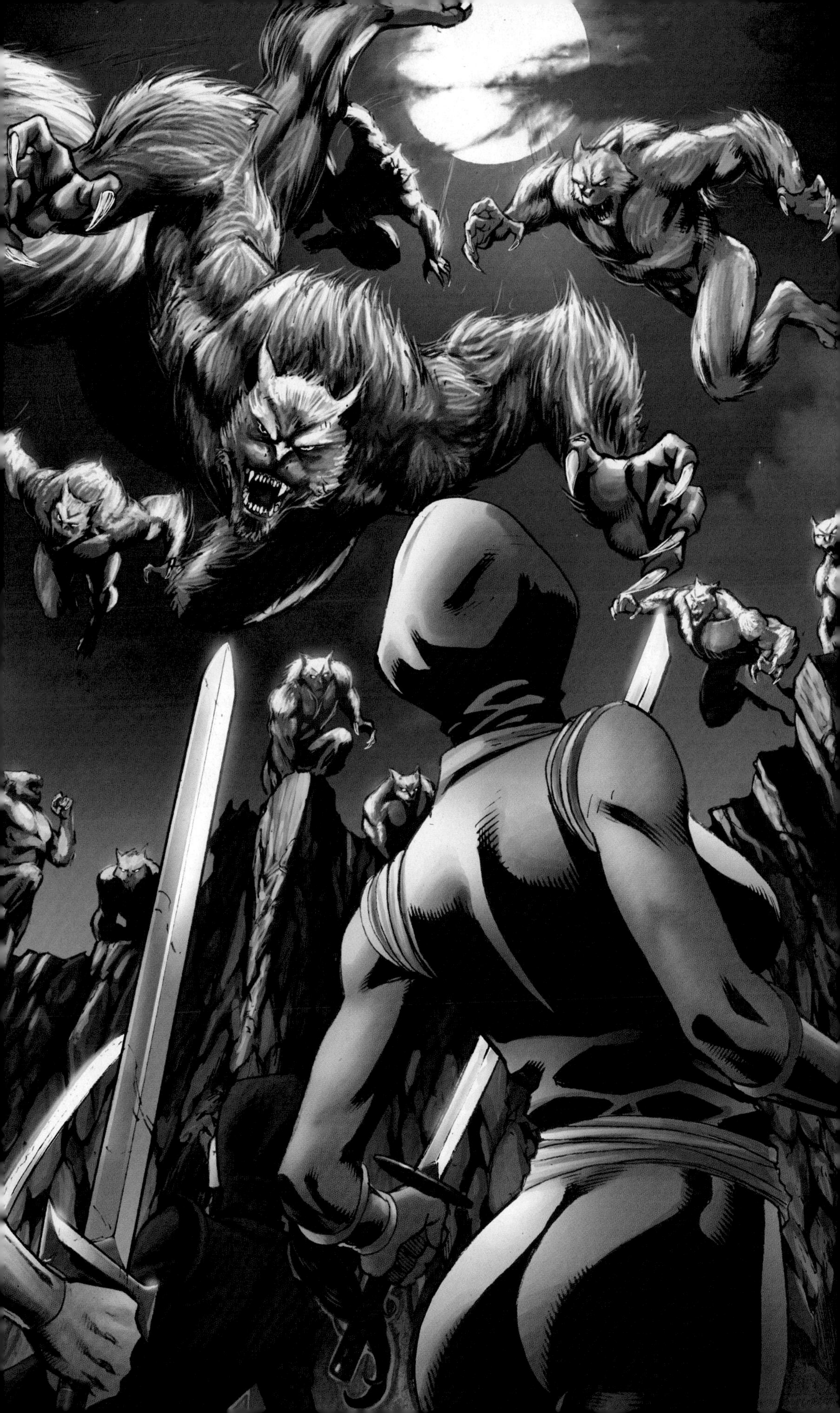

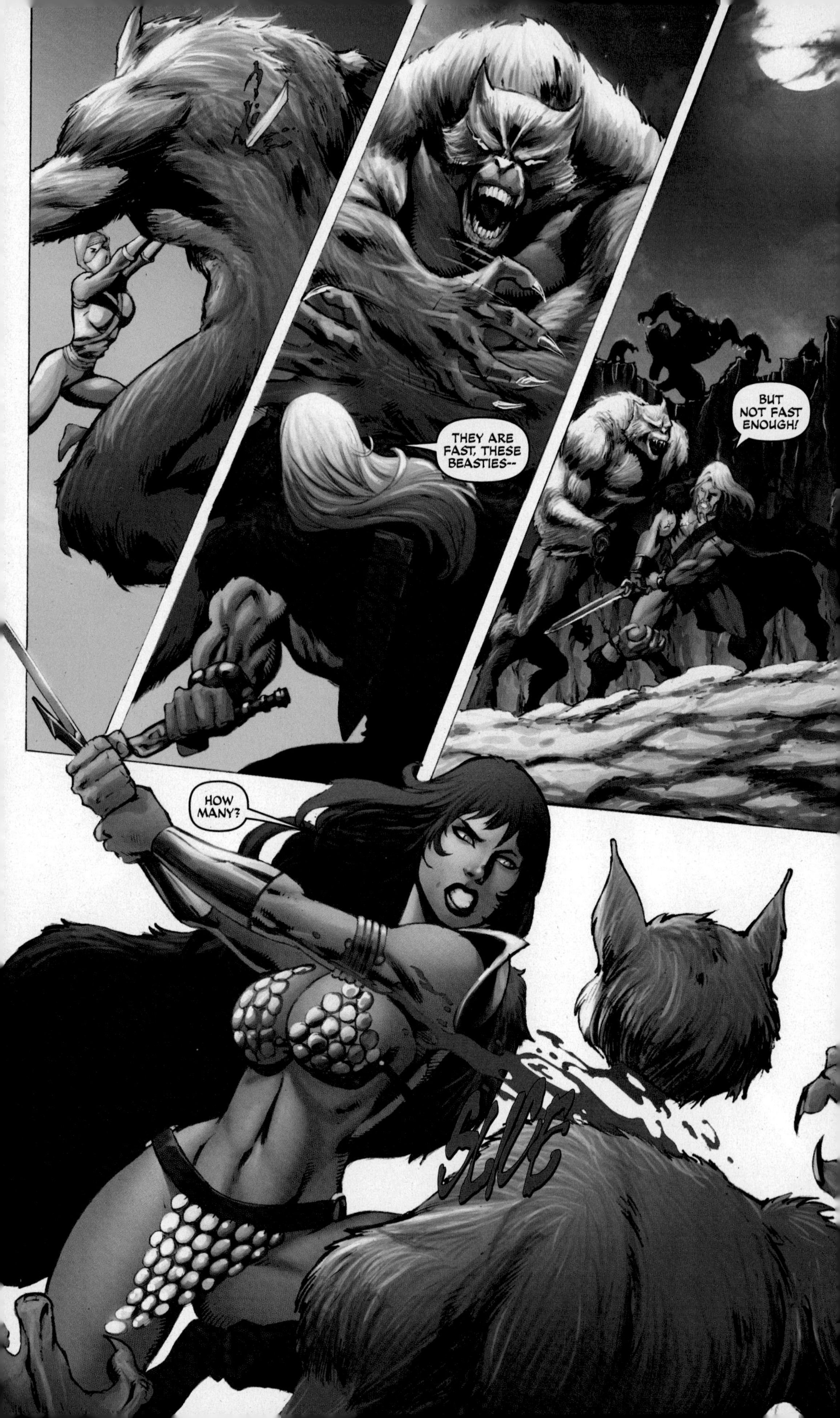
THEY ARE FAST, THESE BEASTIES--
BUT NOT FAST ENOUGH!
HOW MANY?
SLICE

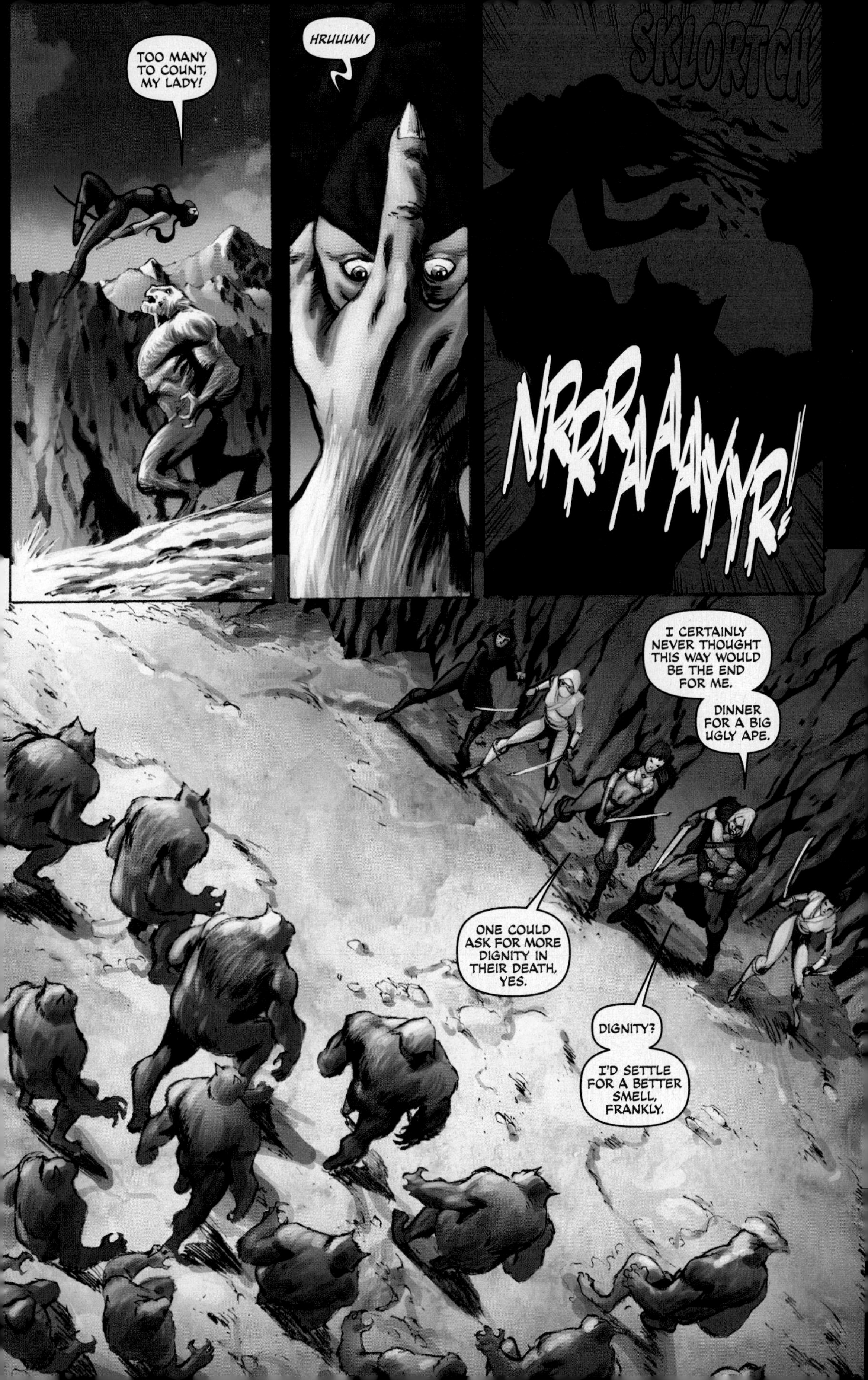
TOO MANY TO COUNT, MY LADY!
HRUUUM!
SKLORTCH
NRRRRAAAYYR!
I CERTAINLY NEVER THOUGHT THIS WAY WOULD BE THE END FOR ME.
DINNER FOR A BIG UGLY APE.
ONE COULD ASK FOR MORE DIGNITY IN THEIR DEATH, YES.
DIGNITY?
I'D SETTLE FOR A BETTER SMELL, FRANKLY.

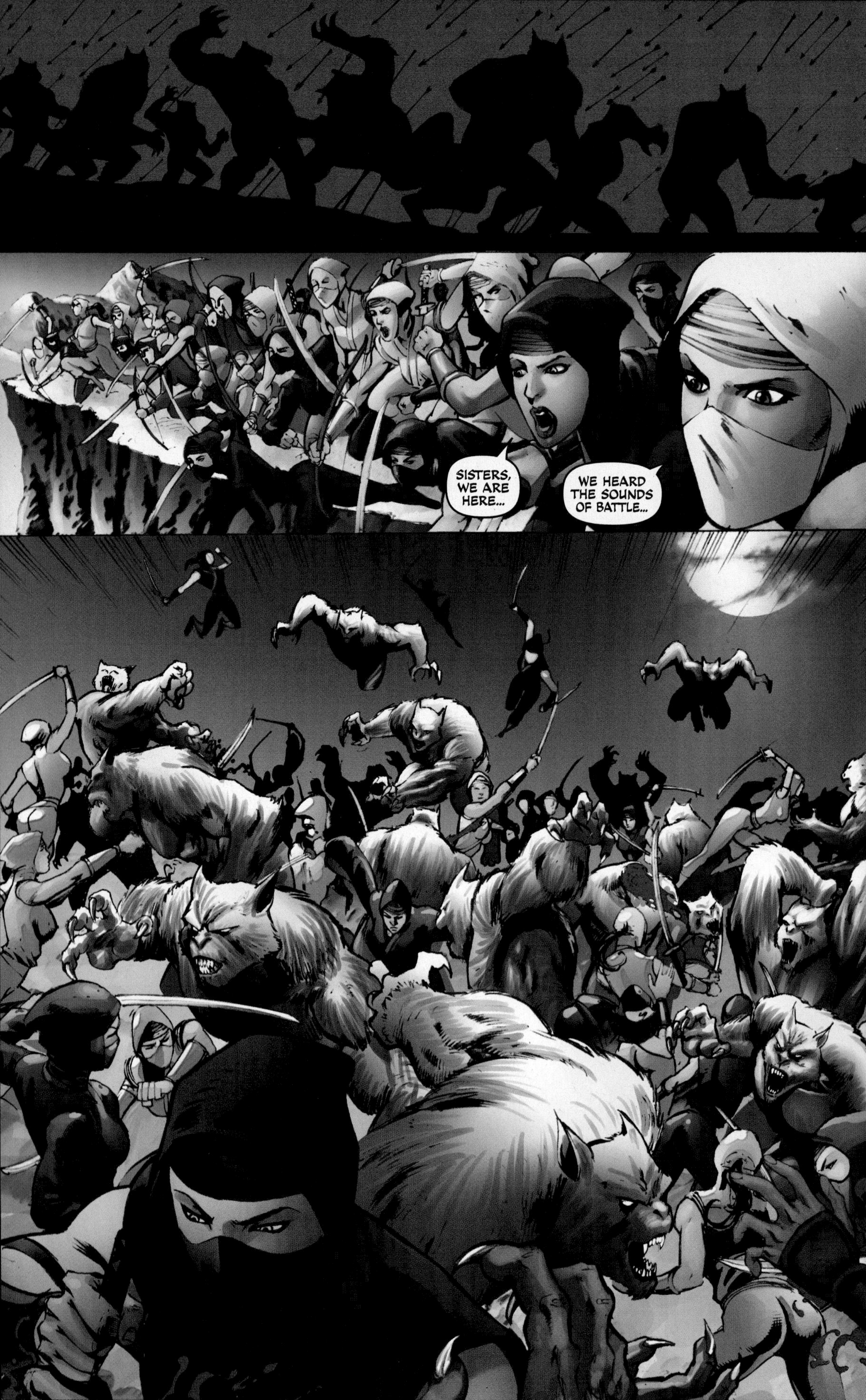

SISTERS, WE ARE HERE...
WE HEARD THE SOUNDS OF BATTLE...

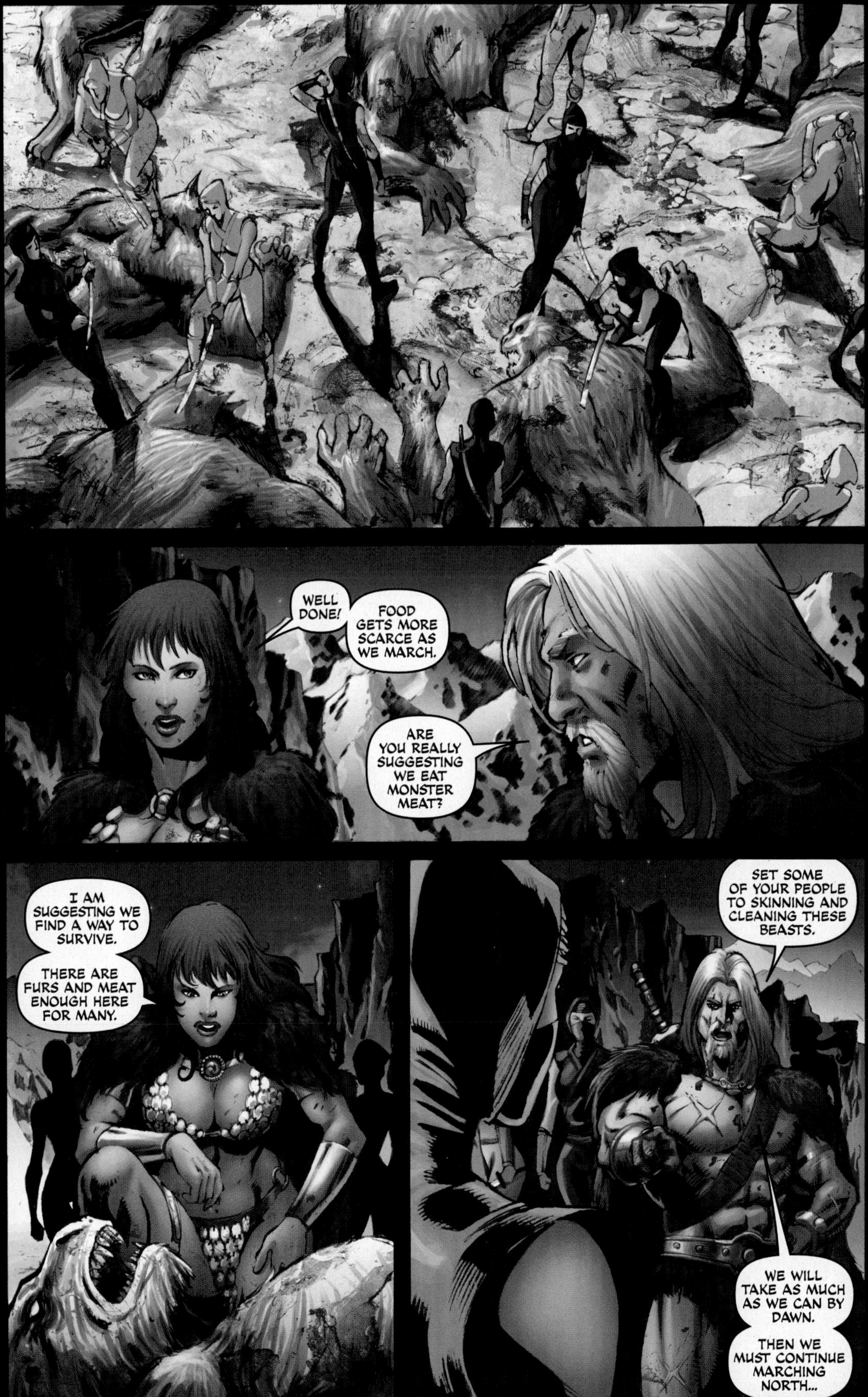
WELL DONE!
FOOD GETS MORE SCARCE AS WE MARCH.
ARE YOU REALLY SUGGESTING WE EAT MONSTER MEAT?
I AM SUGGESTING WE FIND A WAY TO SURVIVE.
THERE ARE FURS AND MEAT ENOUGH HERE FOR MANY.
SET SOME OF YOUR PEOPLE TO SKINNING AND CLEANING THESE BEASTS.
WE WILL TAKE AS MUCH AS WE CAN BY DAWN.
THEN WE MUST CONTINUE MARCHING NORTH...

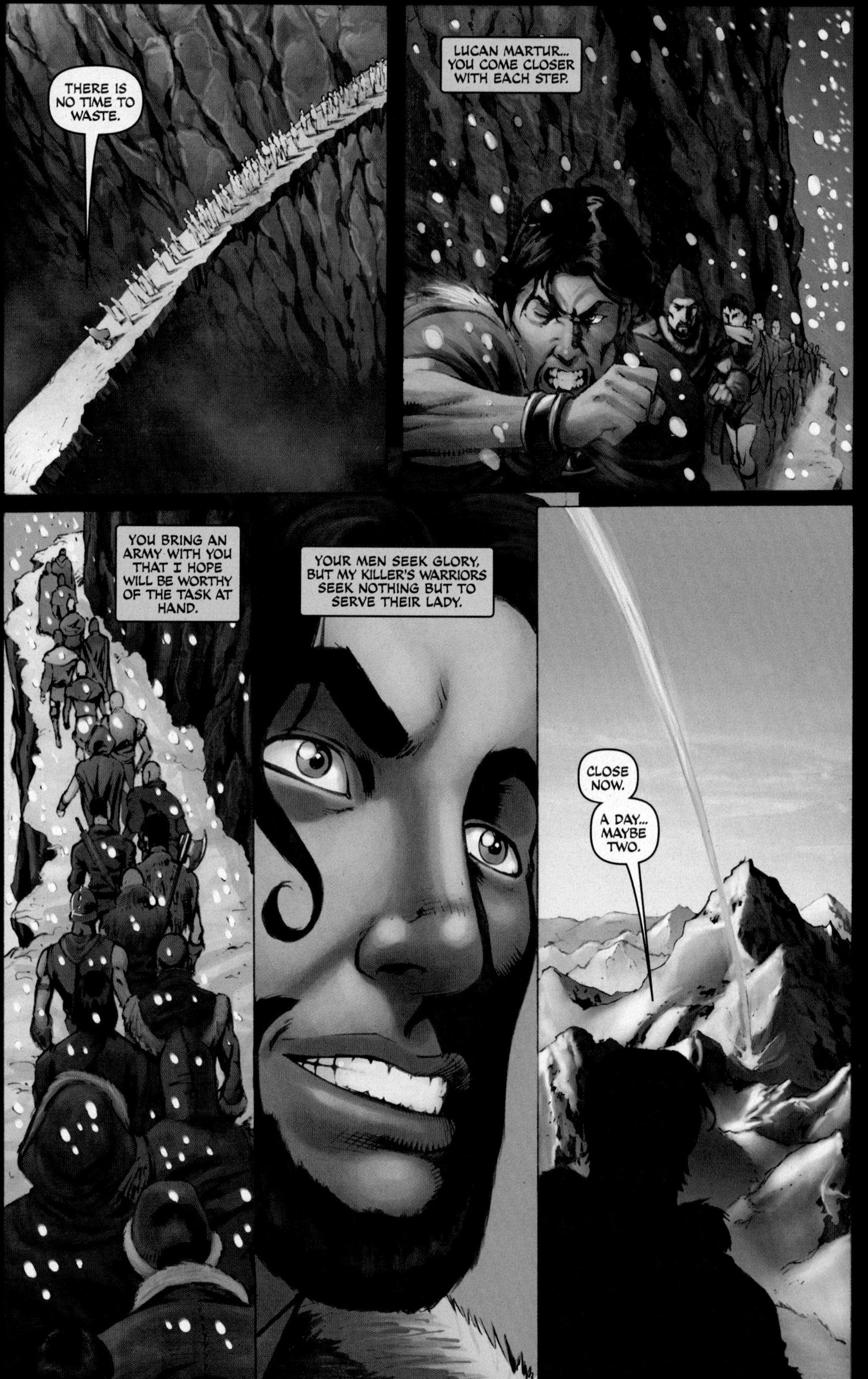
THERE IS NO TIME TO WASTE.
LUCAN MARTUR... YOU COME CLOSER WITH EACH STEP.
YOU BRING AN ARMY WITH YOU THAT I HOPE WILL BE WORTHY OF THE TASK AT HAND.
YOUR MEN SEEK GLORY, BUT MY KILLER'S WARRIORS SEEK NOTHING BUT TO SERVE THEIR LADY.
CLOSE NOW.
A DAY... MAYBE TWO.

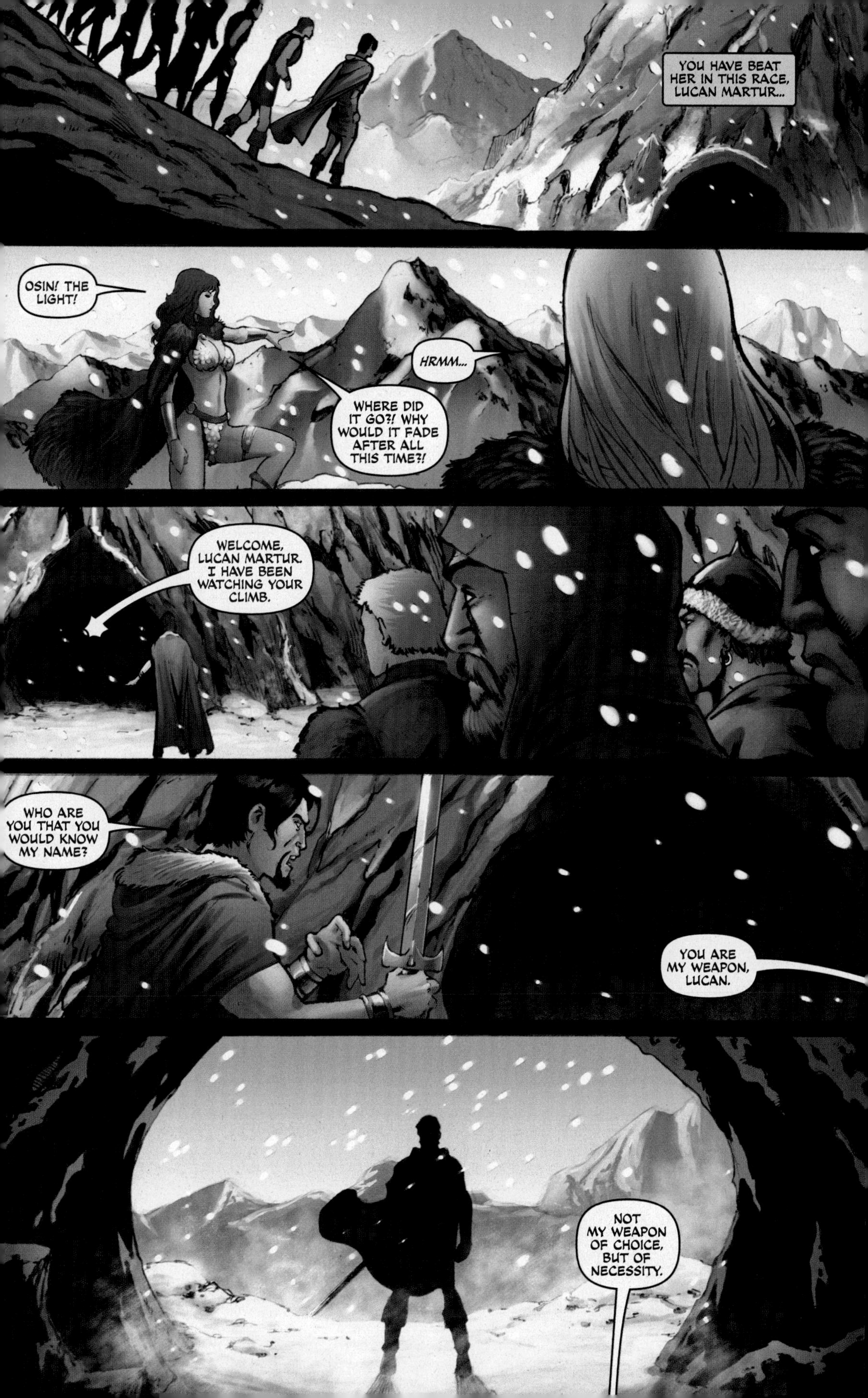
YOU HAVE BEAT HER IN THIS RACE, LUCAN MARTUR...
OSIN! THE LIGHT!
HRMM...
WHERE DID IT GO?! WHY WOULD IT FADE AFTER ALL THIS TIME?!
WELCOME, LUCAN MARTUR. I HAVE BEEN WATCHING YOUR CLIMB.
WHO ARE YOU THAT YOU WOULD KNOW MY NAME?
YOU ARE MY WEAPON, LUCAN.
NOT MY WEAPON OF CHOICE, BUT OF NECESSITY.

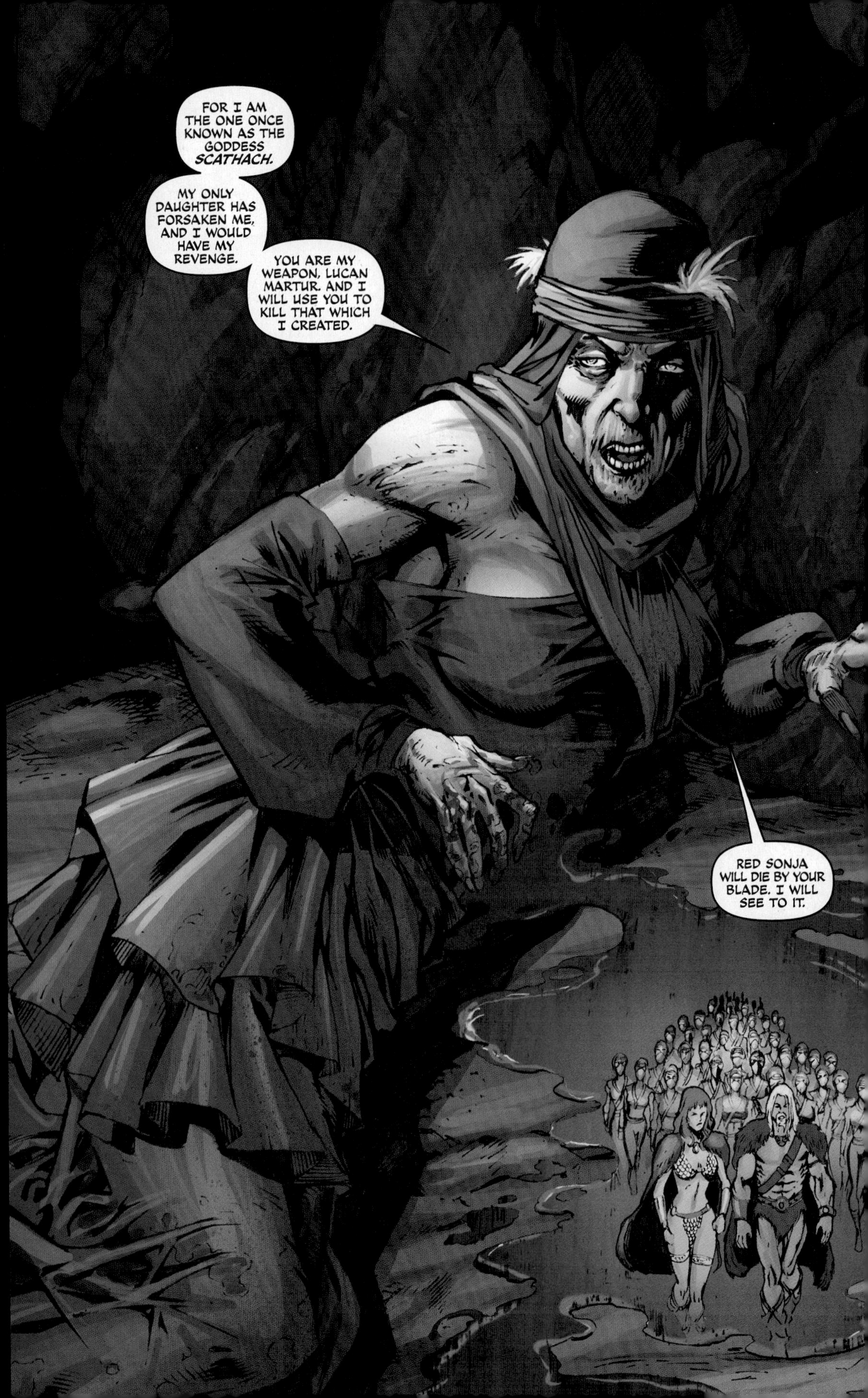
FOR I AM THE ONE ONCE KNOWN AS THE GODDESS *SCATHACH.*
MY ONLY DAUGHTER HAS FORSAKEN ME, AND I WOULD HAVE MY REVENGE.
YOU ARE MY WEAPON, LUCAN MARTUR. AND I WILL USE YOU TO KILL THAT WHICH I CREATED.
RED SONJA WILL DIE BY YOUR BLADE. I WILL SEE TO IT.

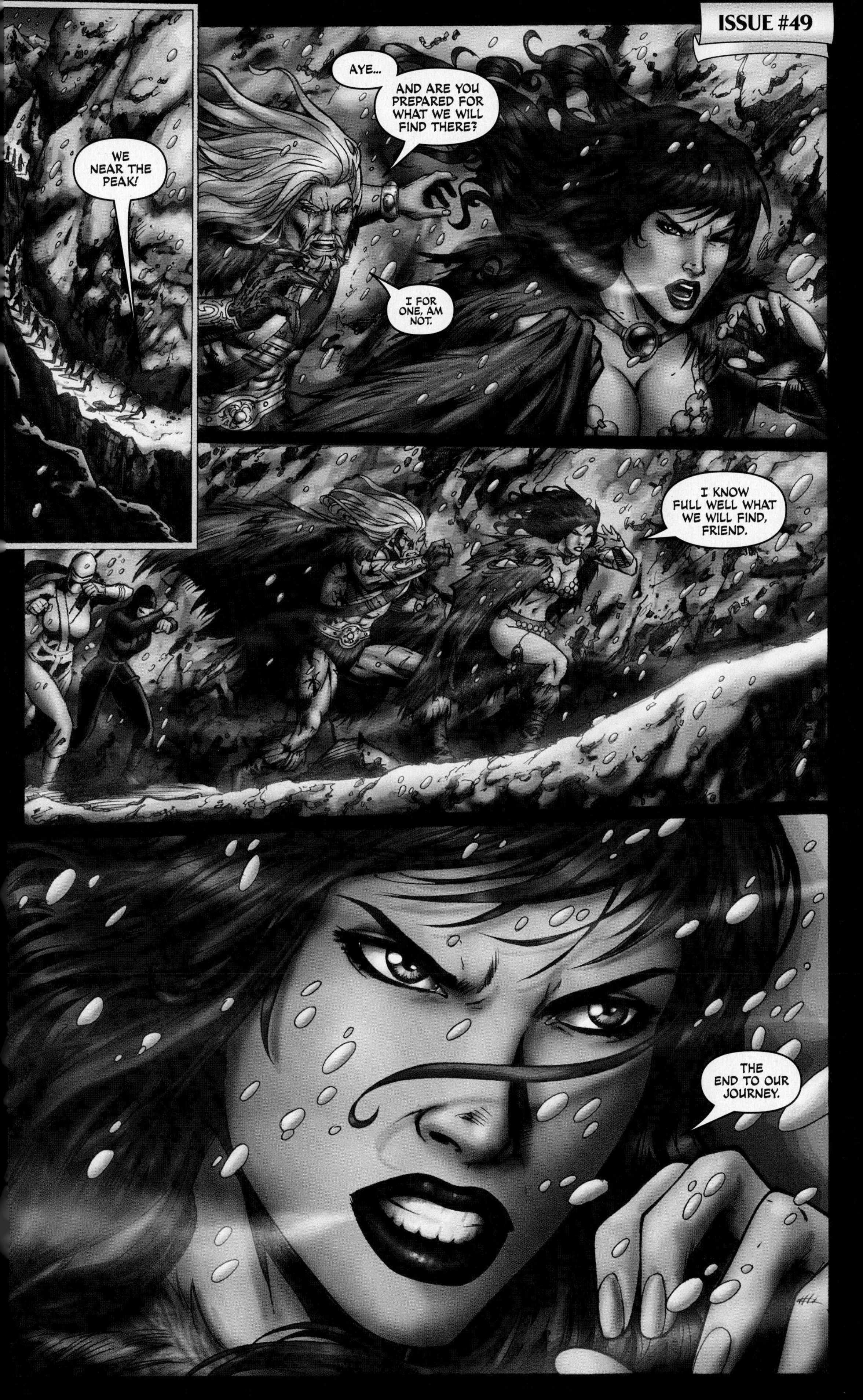
WE NEAR THE PEAK!
AYE...
AND ARE YOU PREPARED FOR WHAT WE WILL FIND THERE?
I FOR ONE, AM NOT.
I KNOW FULL WELL WHAT WE WILL FIND, FRIEND.
THE END TO OUR JOURNEY.

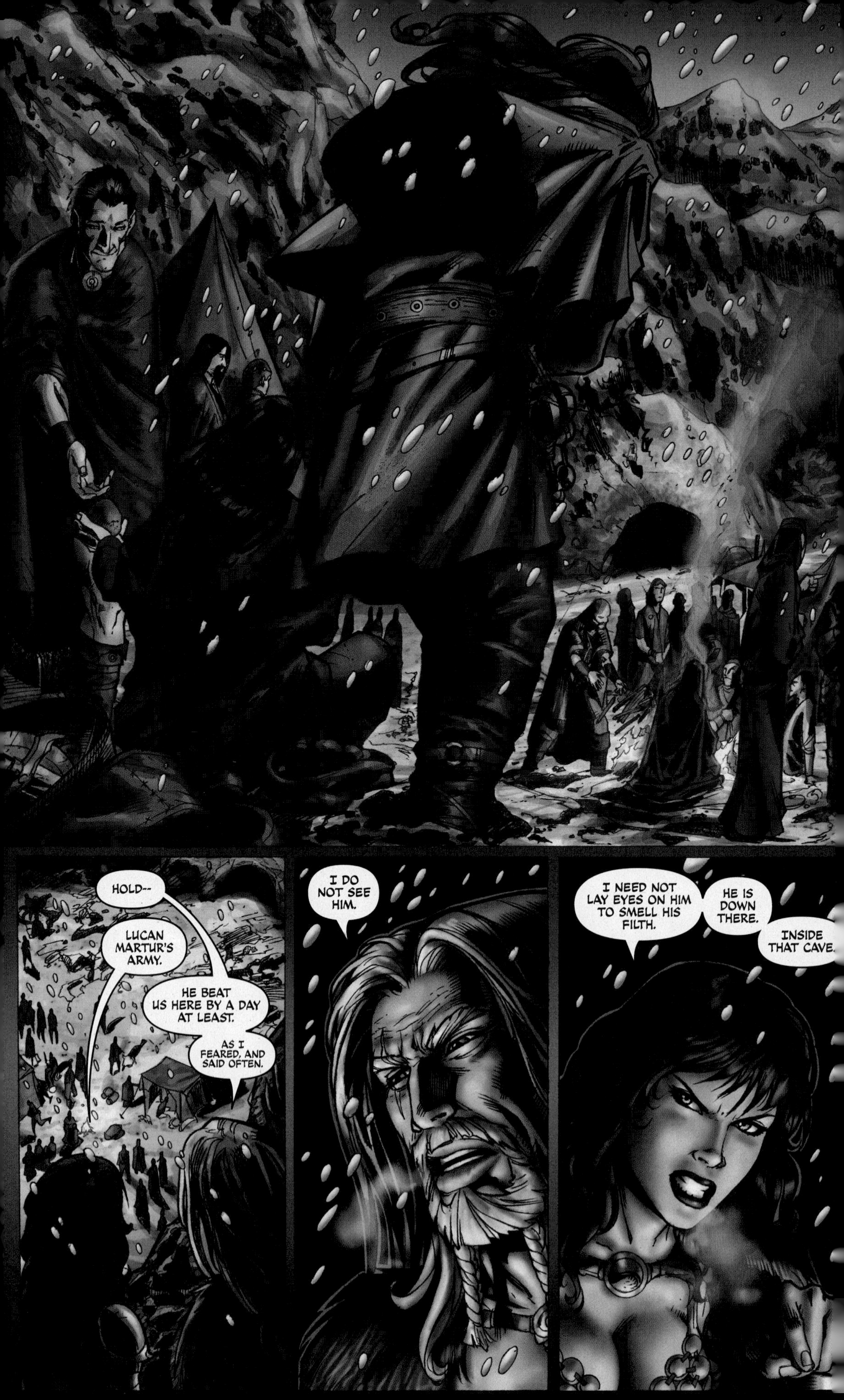
HOLD--
LUCAN MARTUR'S ARMY.
HE BEAT US HERE BY A DAY AT LEAST.
AS I FEARED, AND SAID OFTEN.
I DO NOT SEE HIM.
I NEED NOT LAY EYES ON HIM TO SMELL HIS FILTH.
HE IS DOWN THERE.
INSIDE THAT CAVE.

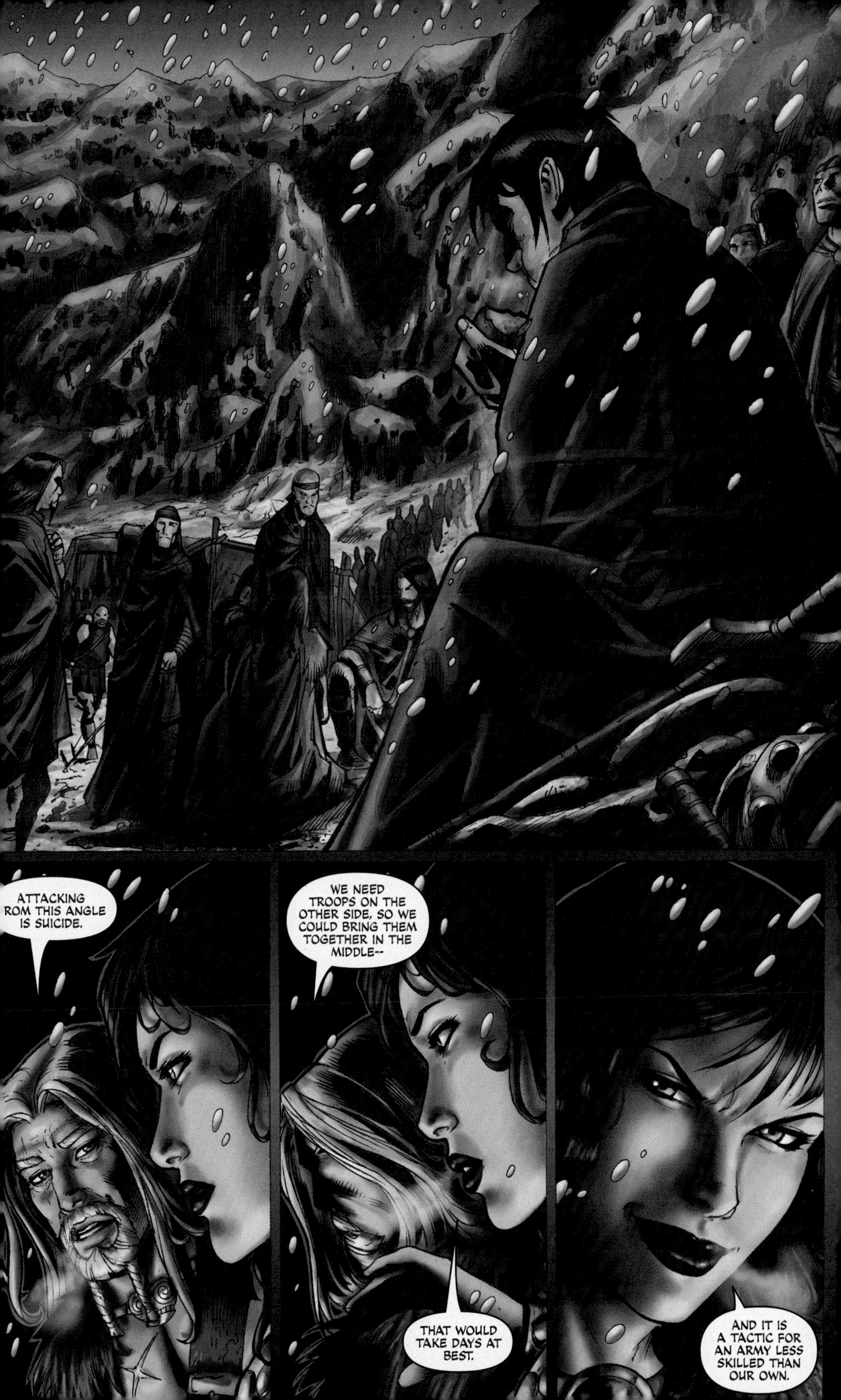
ATTACKING ROM THIS ANGLE IS SUICIDE.
WE NEED TROOPS ON THE OTHER SIDE, SO WE COULD BRING THEM TOGETHER IN THE MIDDLE--
THAT WOULD TAKE DAYS AT BEST.
AND IT IS A TACTIC FOR AN ARMY LESS SKILLED THAN OUR OWN.

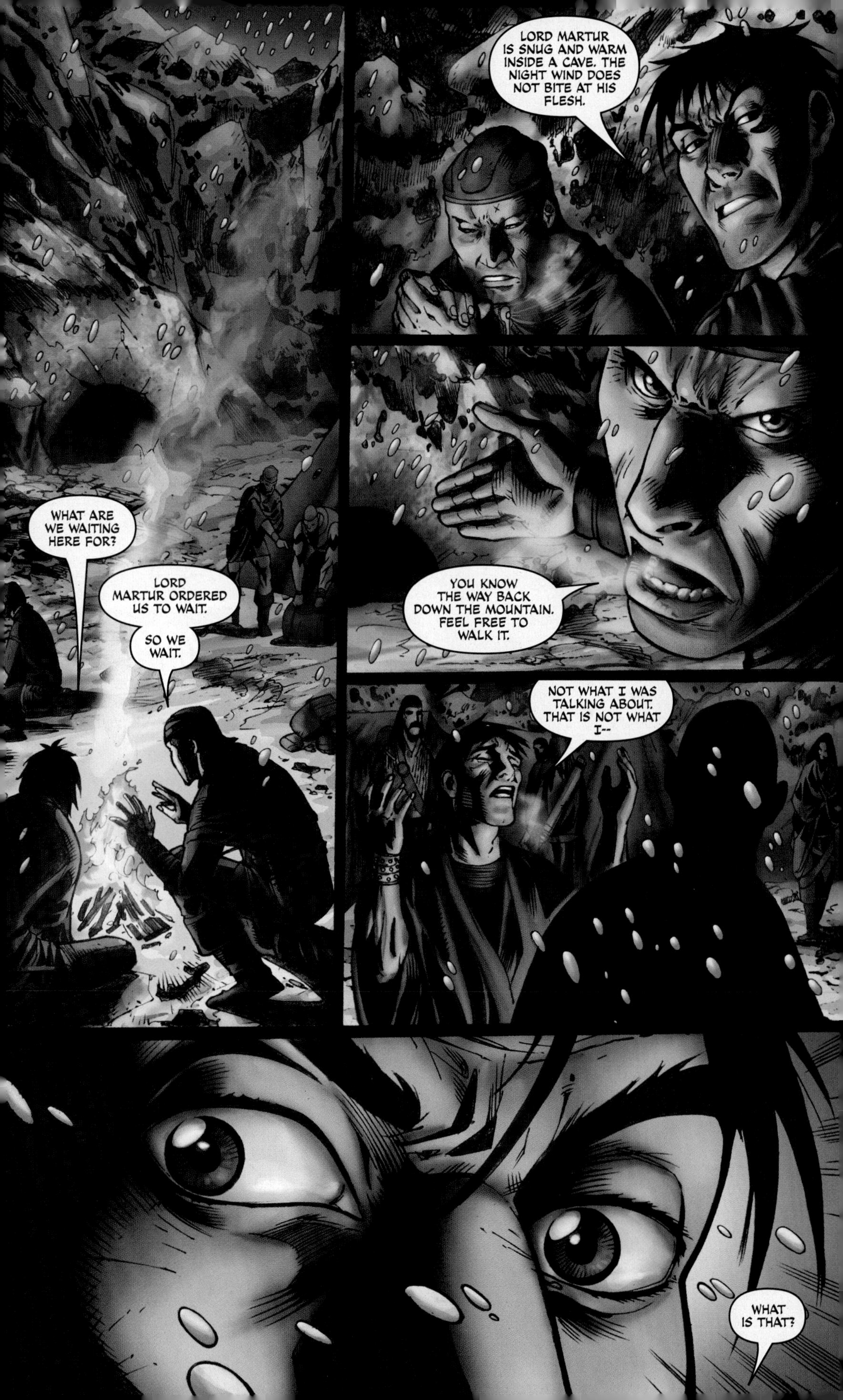
WHAT ARE WE WAITING HERE FOR?
LORD MARTUR ORDERED US TO WAIT.
SO WE WAIT.
LORD MARTUR IS SNUG AND WARM INSIDE A CAVE. THE NIGHT WIND DOES NOT BITE AT HIS FLESH.
YOU KNOW THE WAY BACK DOWN THE MOUNTAIN. FEEL FREE TO WALK IT.
NOT WHAT I WAS TALKING ABOUT. THAT IS NOT WHAT I--
WHAT IS THAT?

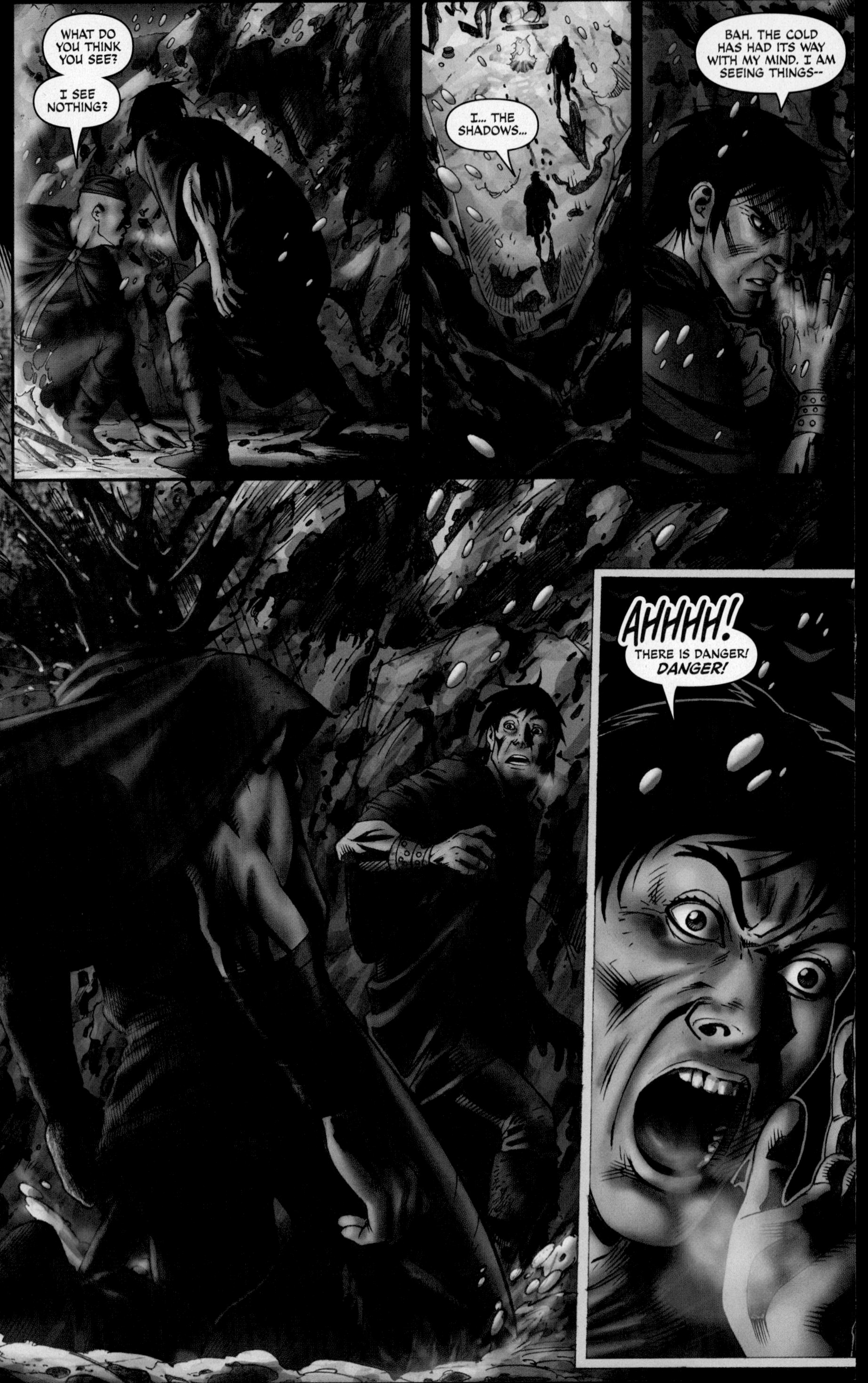
WHAT DO YOU THINK YOU SEE?
I SEE NOTHING?
I... THE SHADOWS...
BAH. THE COLD HAS HAD ITS WAY WITH MY MIND. I AM SEEING THINGS--
AHHHH!
THERE IS DANGER! DANGER!

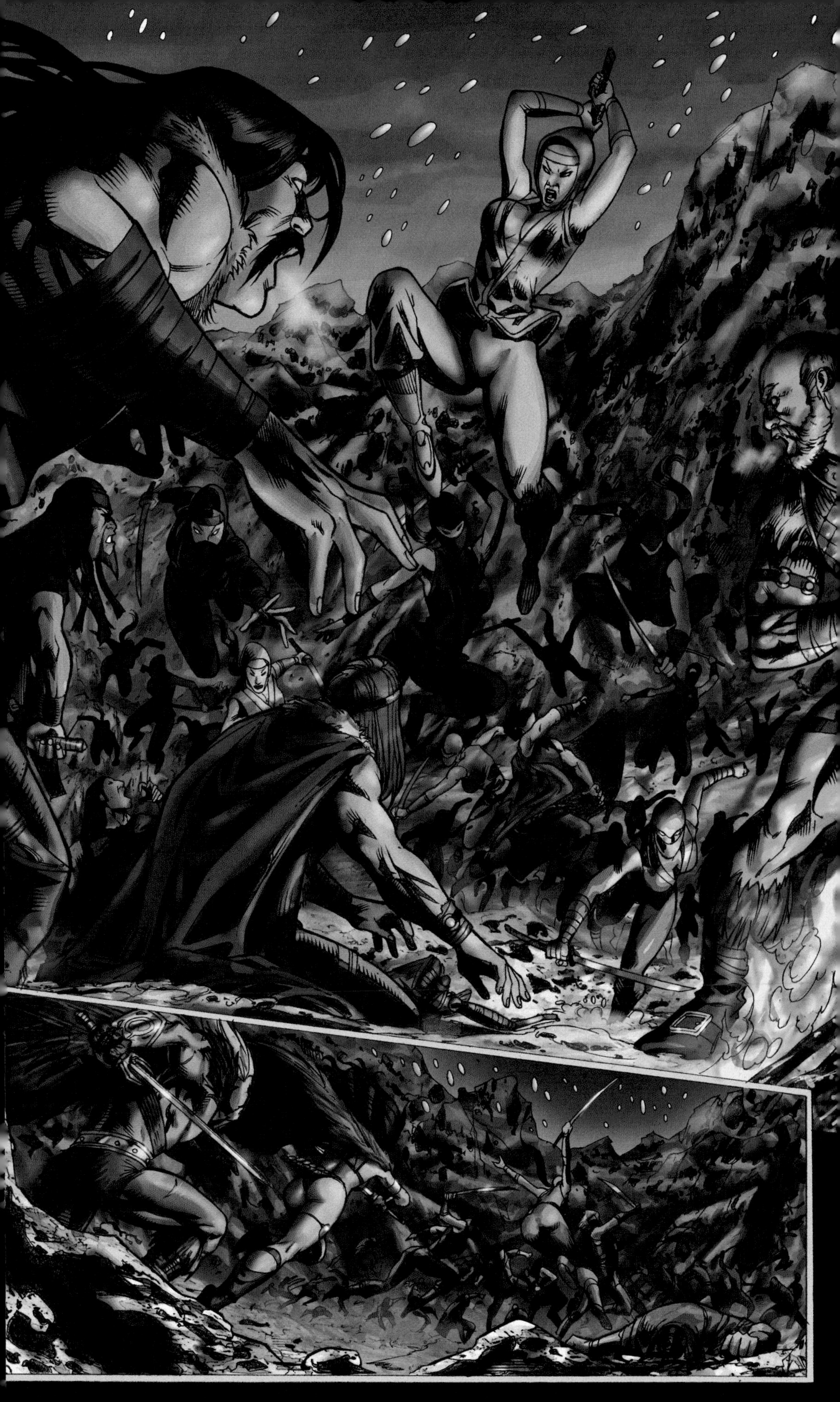

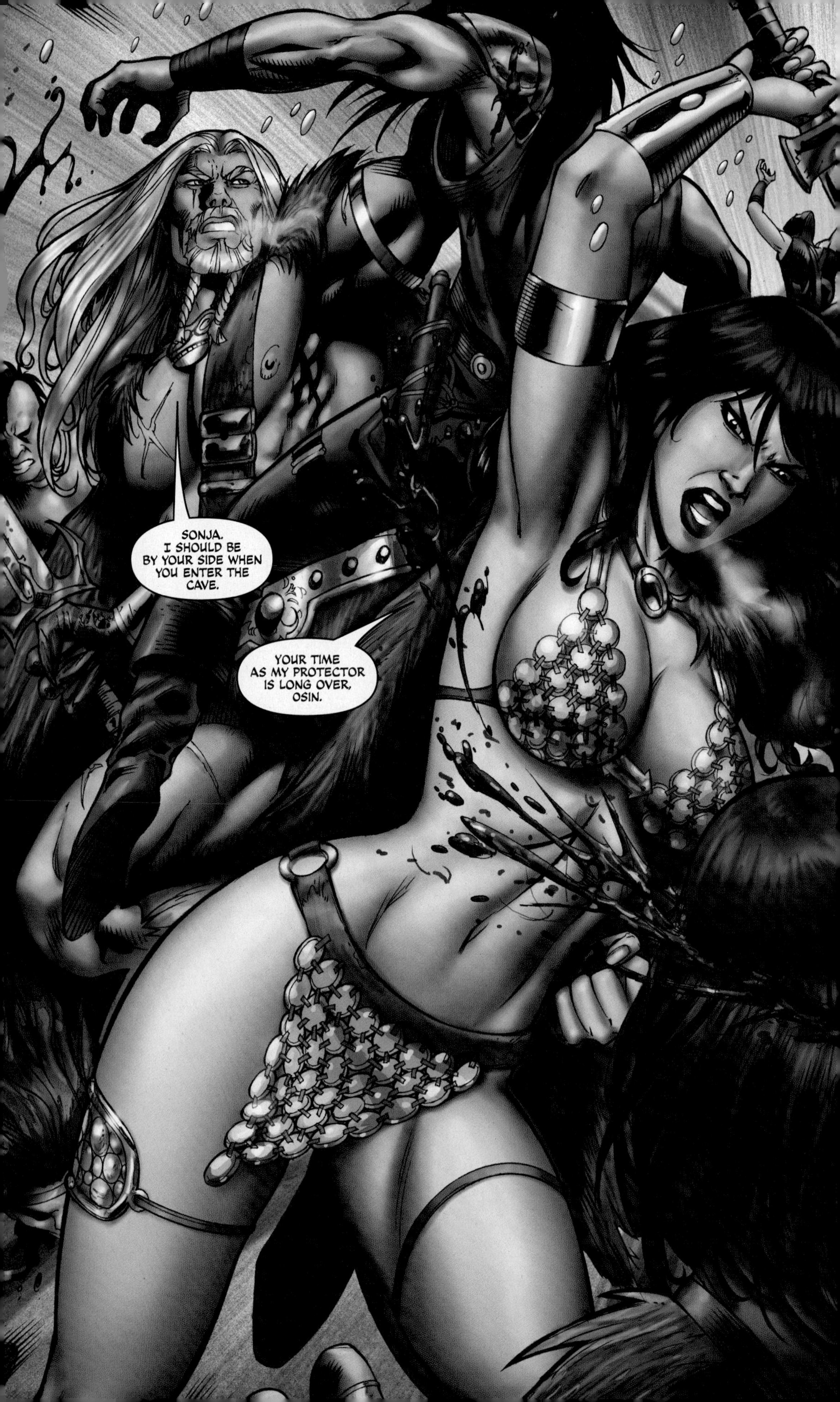
SONJA. I SHOULD BE BY YOUR SIDE WHEN YOU ENTER THE CAVE.
YOUR TIME AS MY PROTECTOR IS LONG OVER, OSIN.

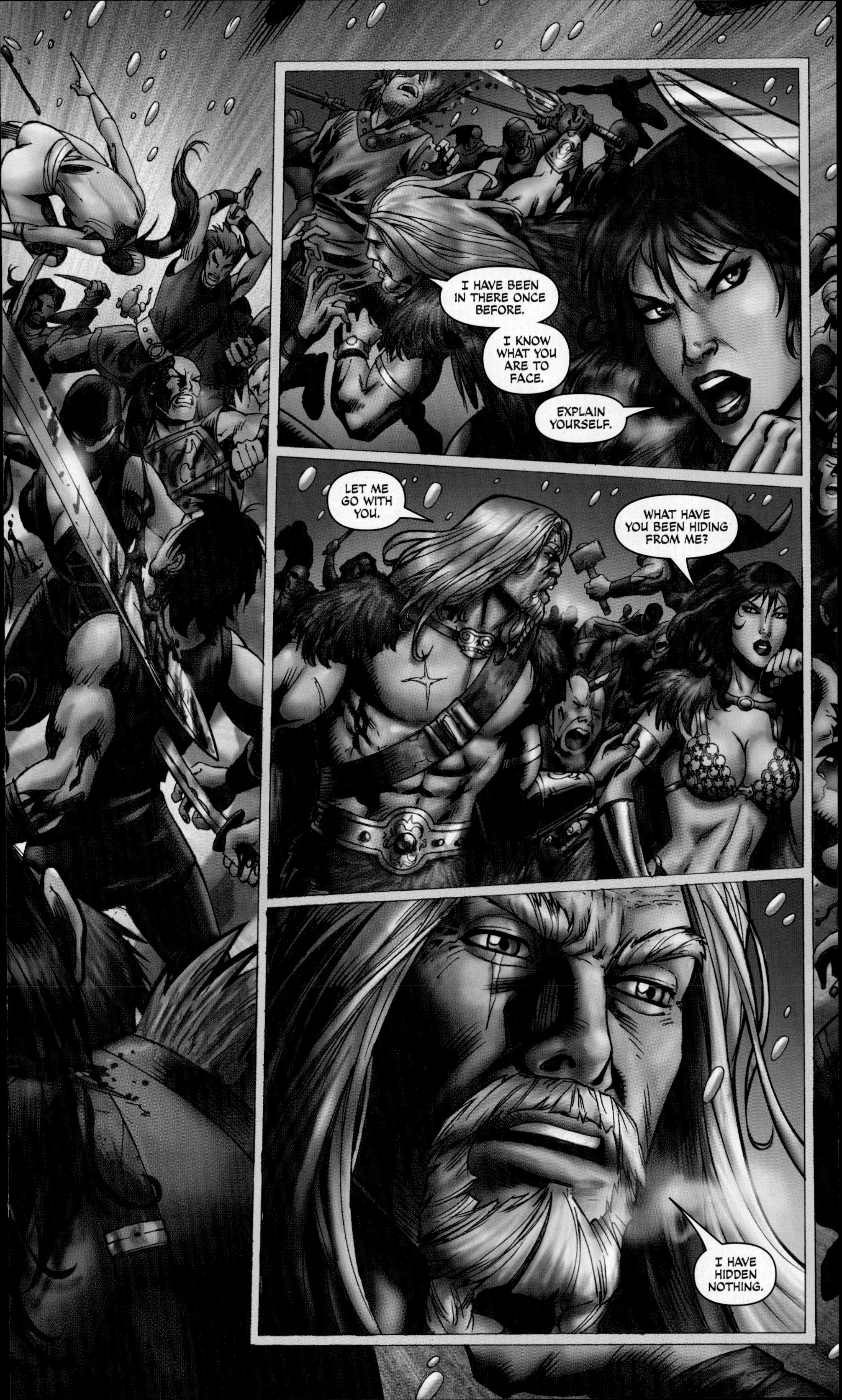
I HAVE BEEN IN THERE ONCE BEFORE.
I KNOW WHAT YOU ARE TO FACE.
EXPLAIN YOURSELF.
LET ME GO WITH YOU.
WHAT HAVE YOU BEEN HIDING FROM ME?
I HAVE HIDDEN NOTHING.

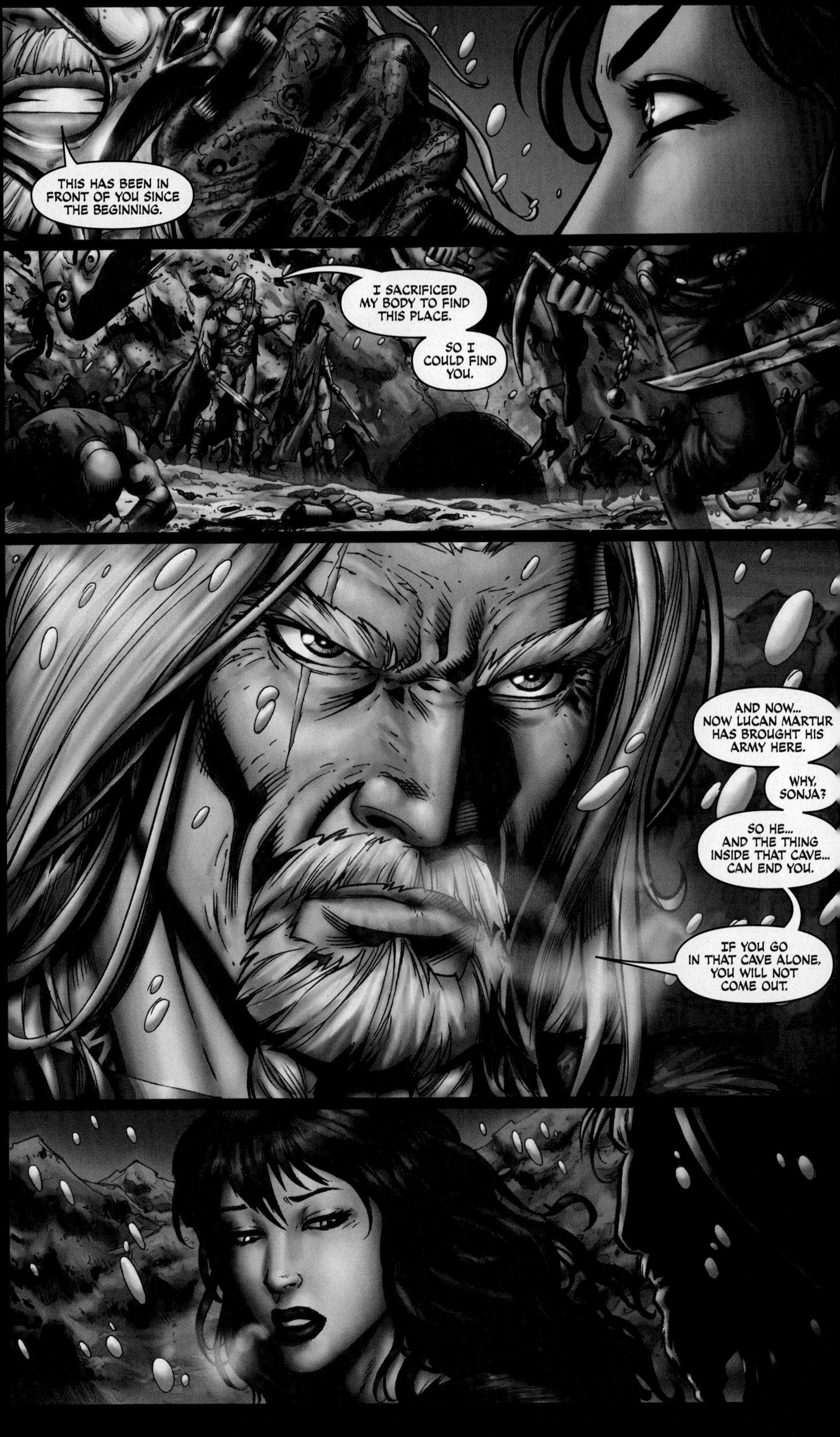

THIS HAS BEEN IN FRONT OF YOU SINCE THE BEGINNING.
I SACRIFICED MY BODY TO FIND THIS PLACE.
SO I COULD FIND YOU.
AND NOW... NOW LUCAN MARTUR HAS BROUGHT HIS ARMY HERE.
WHY, SONJA?
SO HE... AND THE THING INSIDE THAT CAVE... CAN END YOU.
IF YOU GO IN THAT CAVE ALONE, YOU WILL NOT COME OUT.

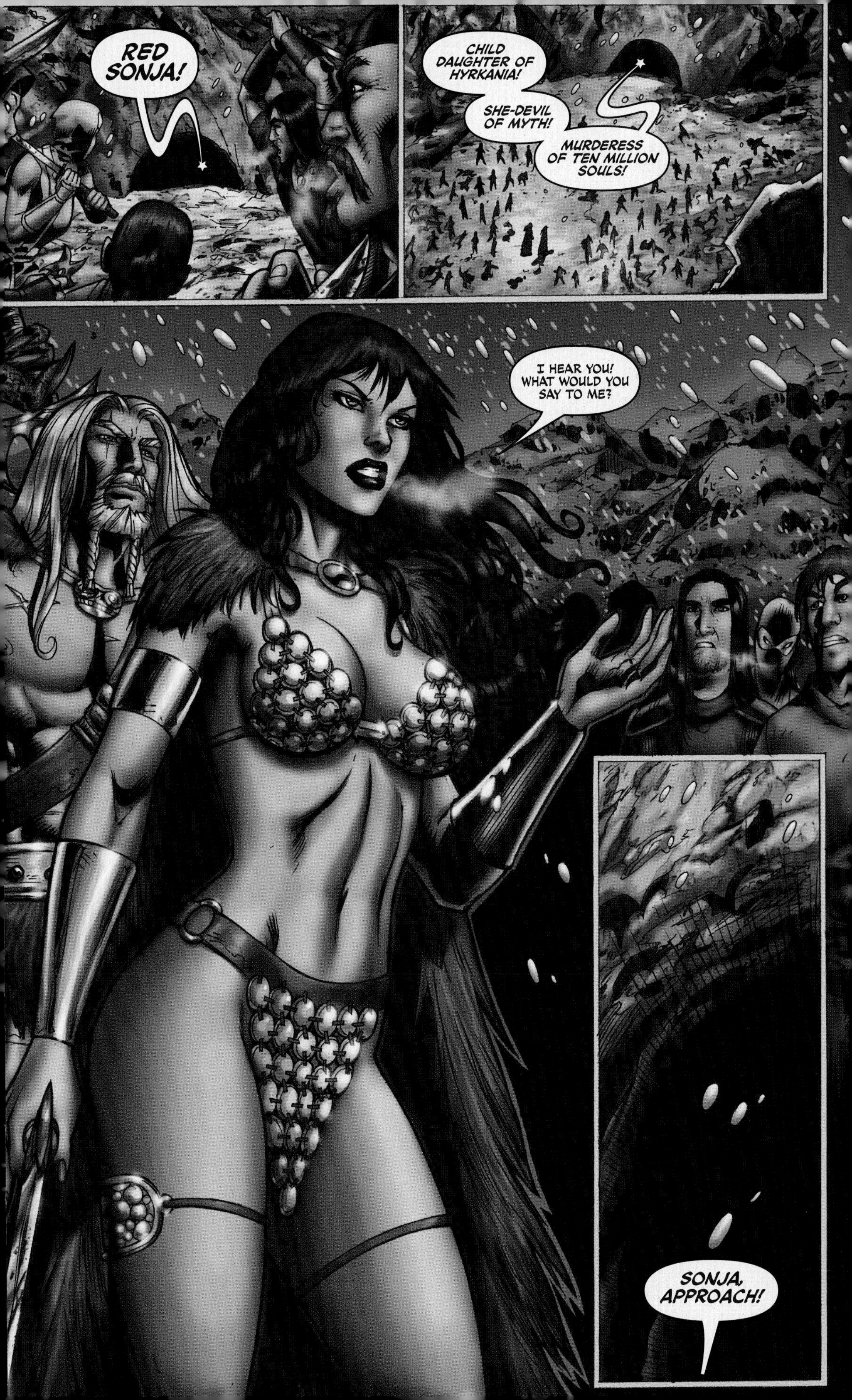
RED SONJA!
CHILD DAUGHTER OF HYRKANIA!
SHE-DEVIL OF MYTH!
MURDERESS OF TEN MILLION SOULS!
I HEAR YOU! WHAT WOULD YOU SAY TO ME?
SONJA, APPROACH!

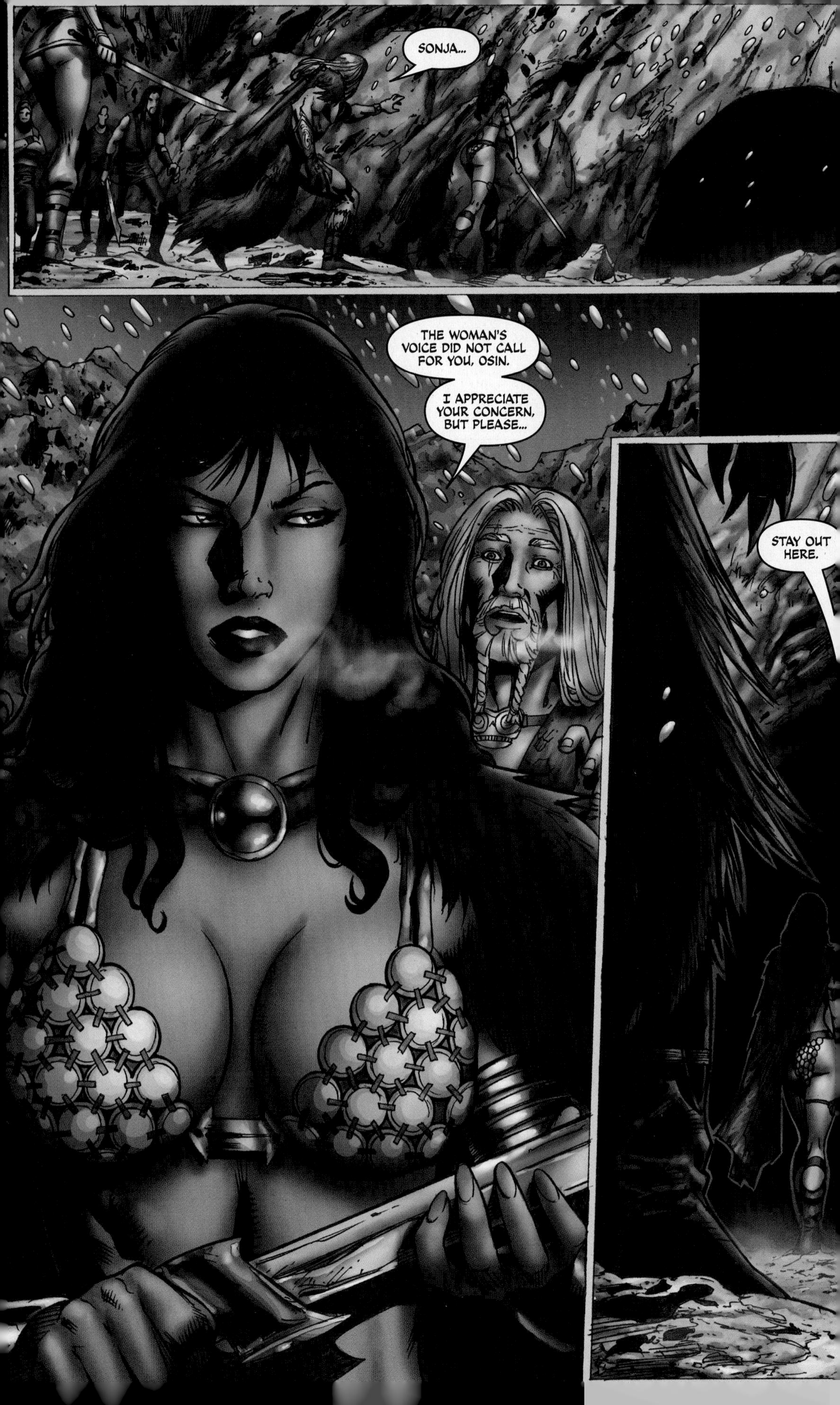
SONJA...
THE WOMAN'S VOICE DID NOT CALL FOR YOU, OSIN.
I APPRECIATE YOUR CONCERN, BUT PLEASE...
STAY OUT HERE.

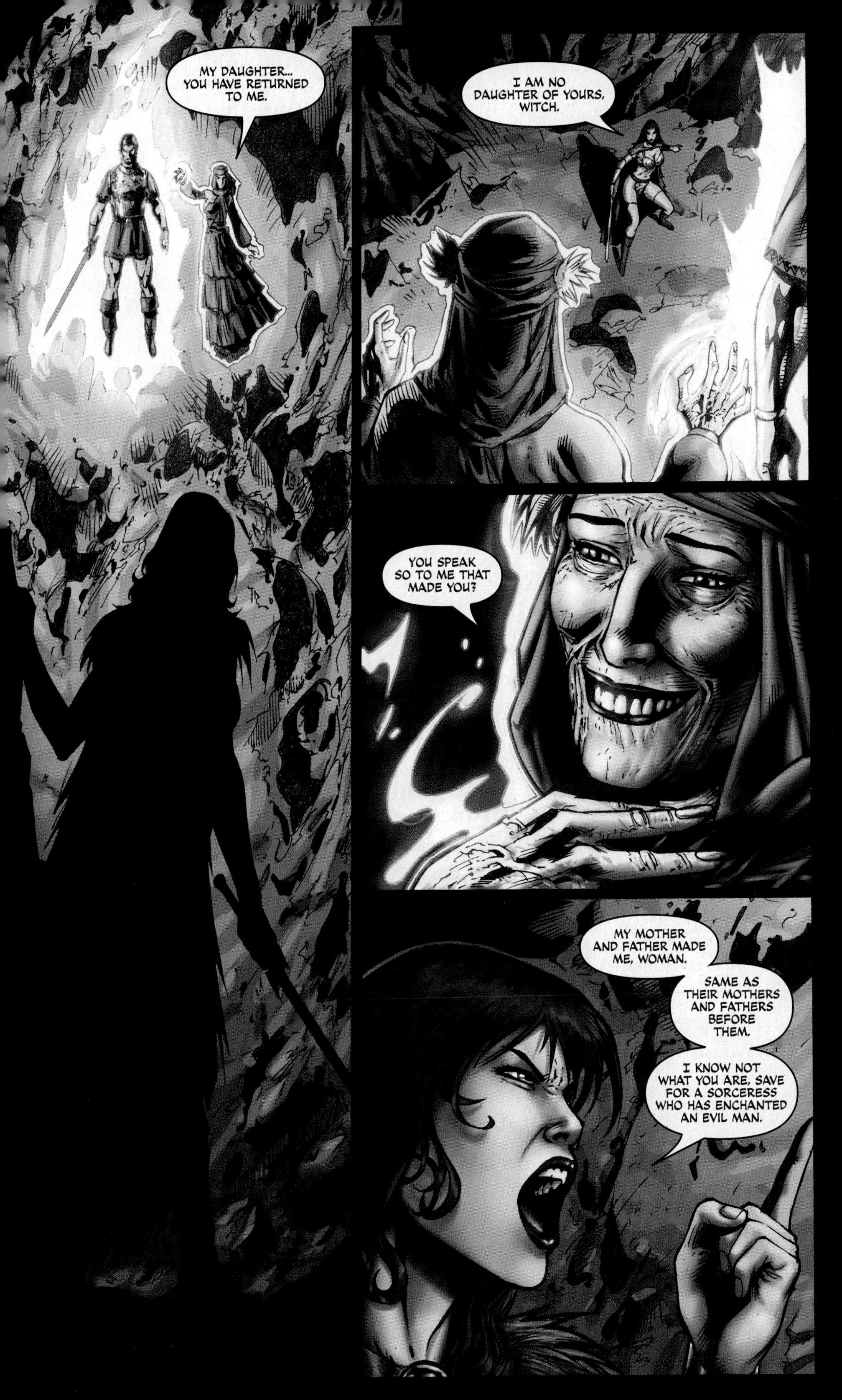
MY DAUGHTER... YOU HAVE RETURNED TO ME.
I AM NO DAUGHTER OF YOURS, WITCH.
YOU SPEAK SO TO ME THAT MADE YOU?
MY MOTHER AND FATHER MADE ME, WOMAN.
SAME AS THEIR MOTHERS AND FATHERS BEFORE THEM.
I KNOW NOT WHAT YOU ARE, SAVE FOR A SORCERESS WHO HAS ENCHANTED AN EVIL MAN.

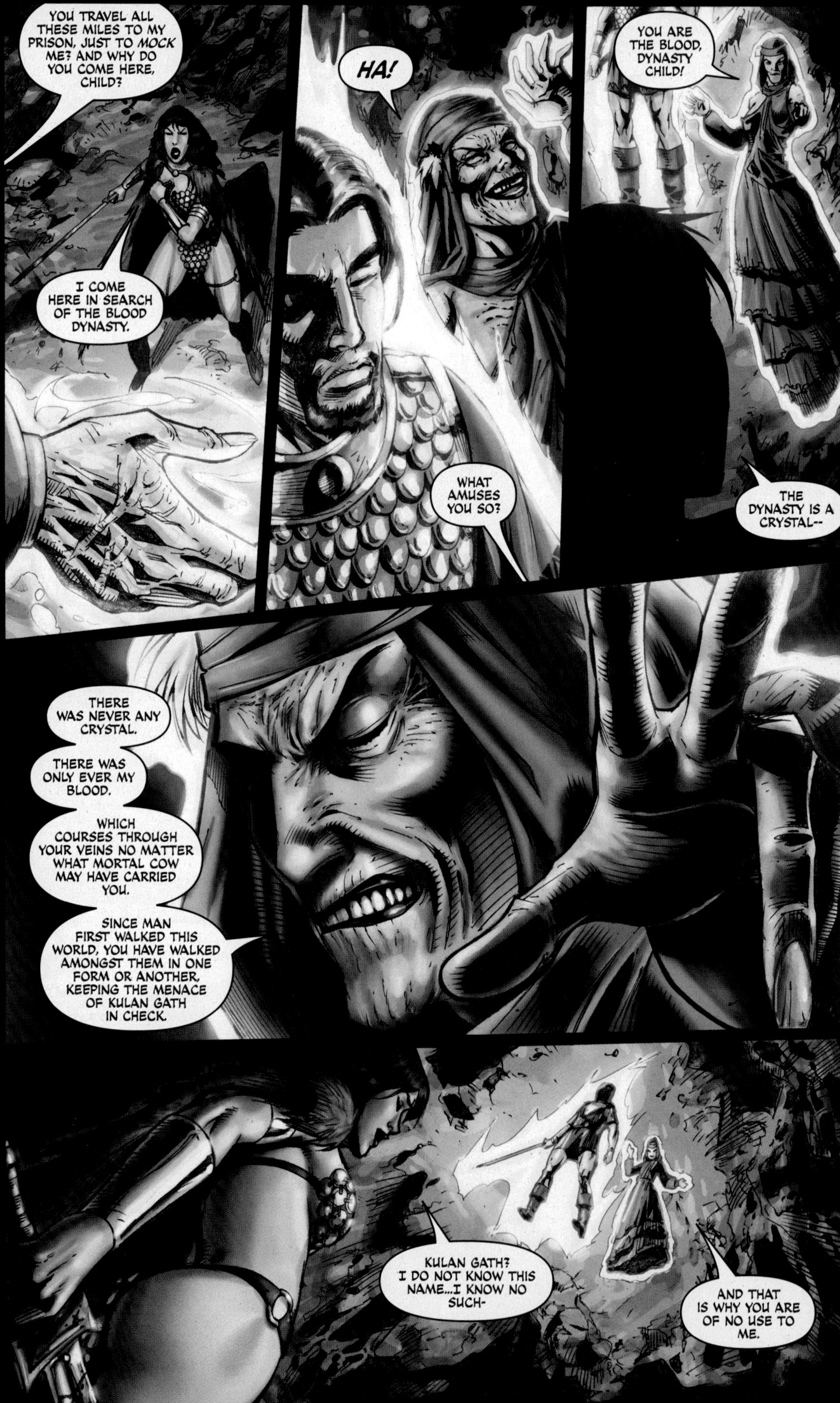
YOU TRAVEL ALL THESE MILES TO MY PRISON, JUST TO *MOCK* ME? AND WHY DO YOU COME HERE, CHILD?
I COME HERE IN SEARCH OF THE BLOOD DYNASTY.
HA!
WHAT AMUSES YOU SO?
YOU ARE THE BLOOD, DYNASTY CHILD!
THE DYNASTY IS A CRYSTAL--
THERE WAS NEVER ANY CRYSTAL.
THERE WAS ONLY EVER MY BLOOD.
WHICH COURSES THROUGH YOUR VEINS NO MATTER WHAT MORTAL COW MAY HAVE CARRIED YOU.
SINCE MAN FIRST WALKED THIS WORLD, YOU HAVE WALKED AMONGST THEM IN ONE FORM OR ANOTHER, KEEPING THE MENACE OF KULAN GATH IN CHECK.
KULAN GATH? I DO NOT KNOW THIS NAME...I KNOW NO SUCH-
AND THAT IS WHY YOU ARE OF NO USE TO ME.

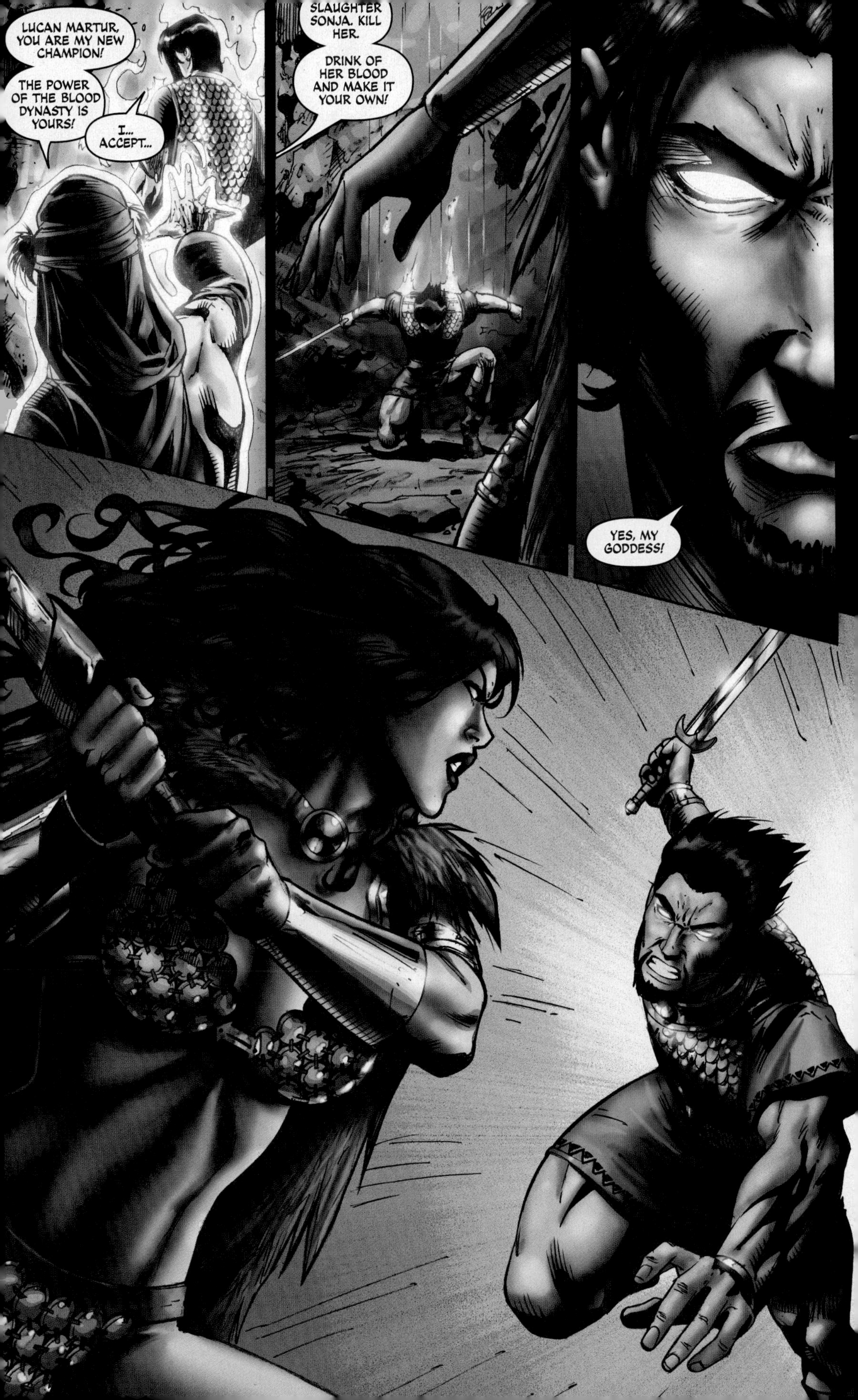
LUCAN MARTUR, YOU ARE MY NEW CHAMPION!
THE POWER OF THE BLOOD DYNASTY IS YOURS!
I... ACCEPT...
SLAUGHTER SONJA. KILL HER.
DRINK OF HER BLOOD AND MAKE IT YOUR OWN!
YES, MY GODDESS!

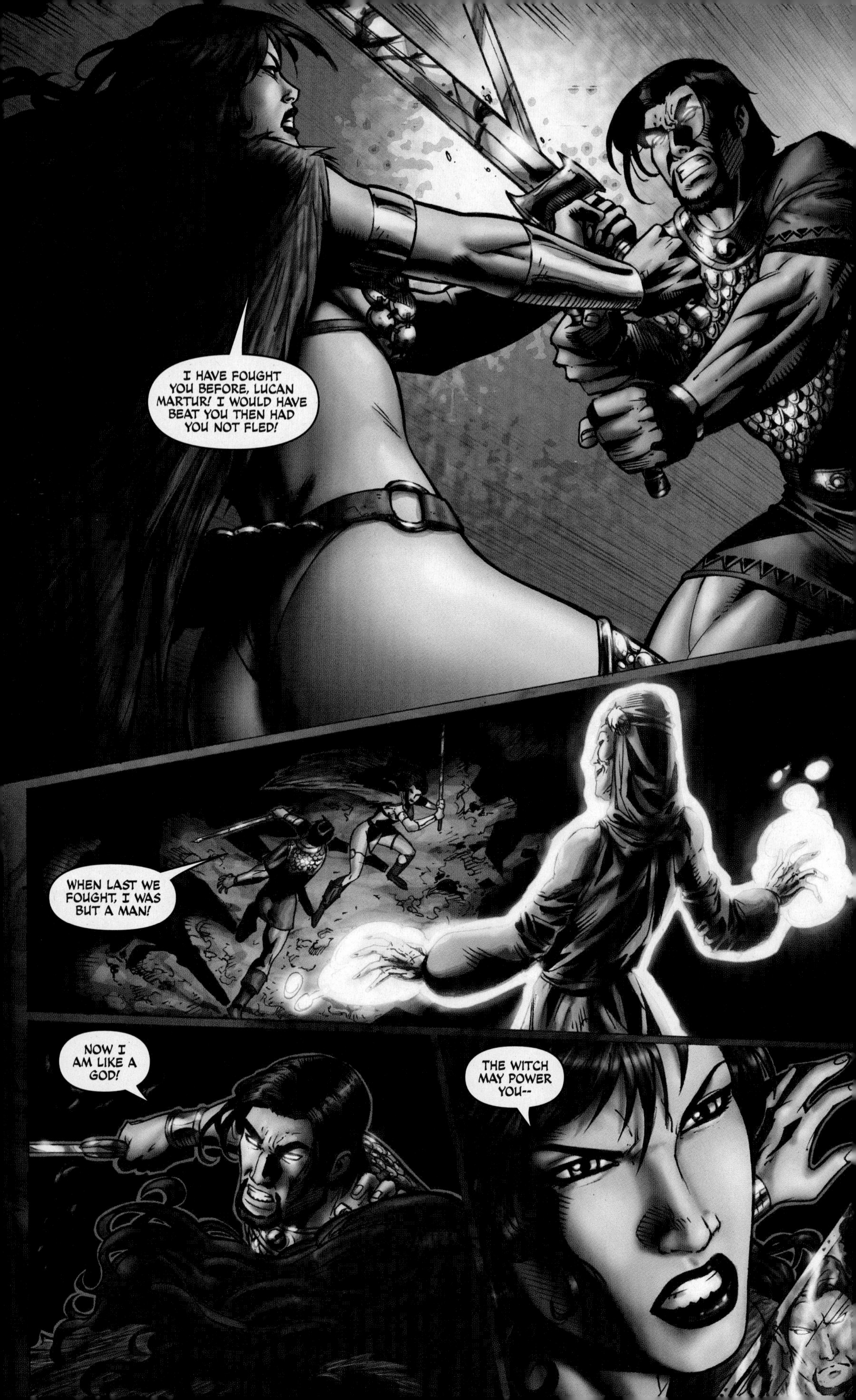

I HAVE FOUGHT YOU BEFORE, LUCAN MARTUR! I WOULD HAVE BEAT YOU THEN HAD YOU NOT FLED!
WHEN LAST WE FOUGHT, I WAS BUT A MAN!
NOW I AM LIKE A GOD!
THE WITCH MAY POWER YOU--

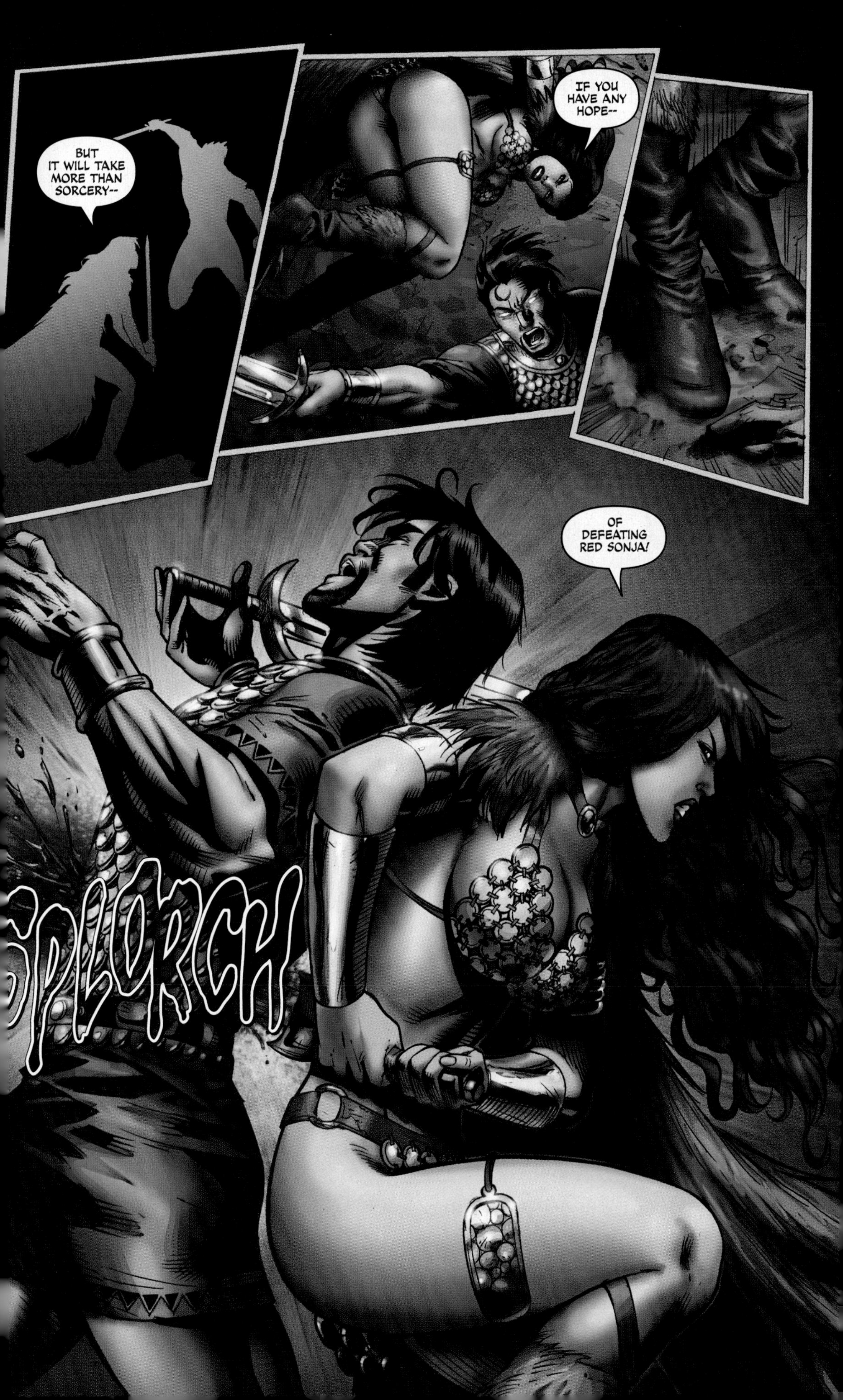
BUT IT WILL TAKE MORE THAN SORCERY--
IF YOU HAVE ANY HOPE--
OF DEFEATING RED SONJA!
SPLORCH

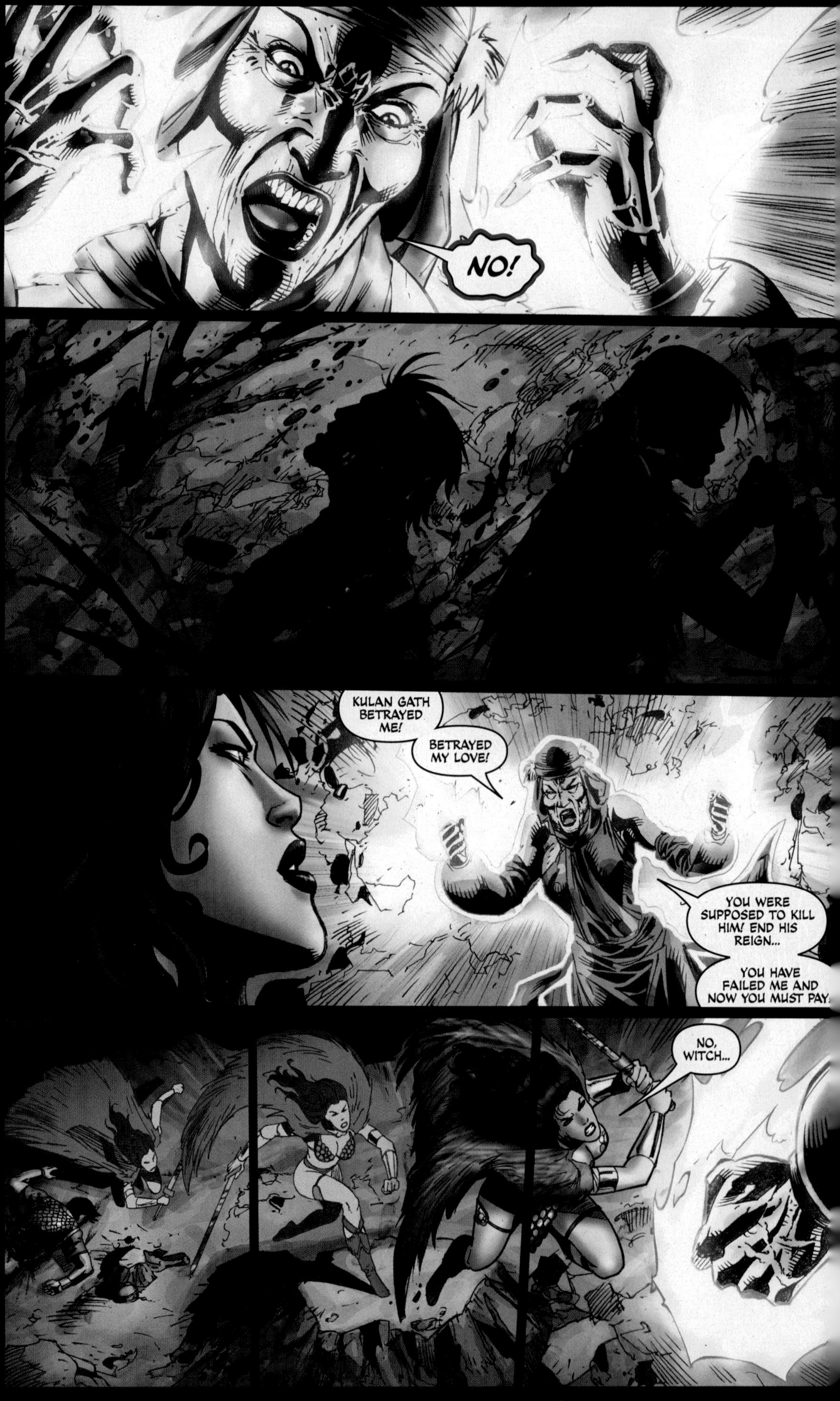
NO!
KULAN GATH BETRAYED ME!
BETRAYED MY LOVE!
YOU WERE SUPPOSED TO KILL HIM! END HIS REIGN...
YOU HAVE FAILED ME AND NOW YOU MUST PAY.
NO, WITCH...

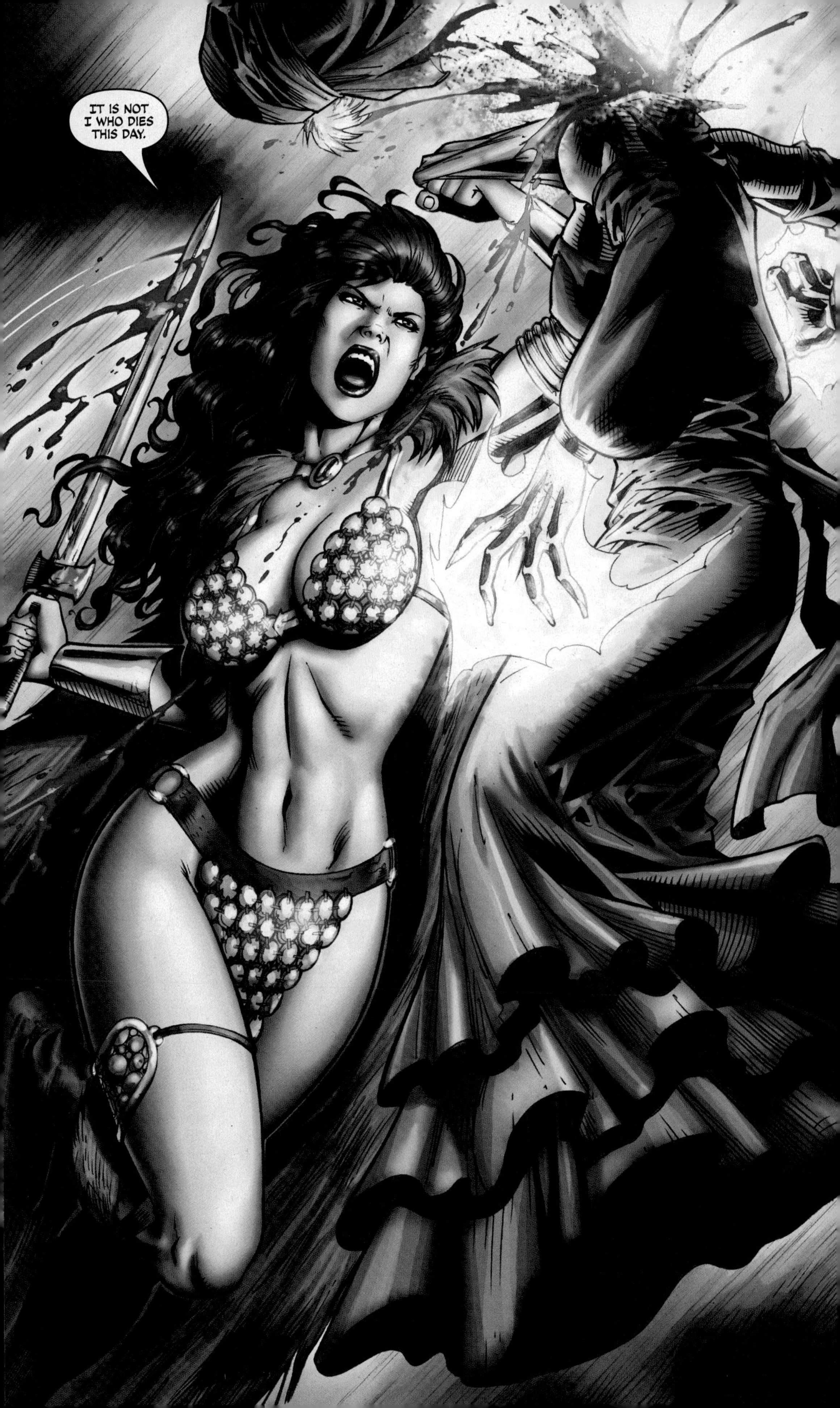
IT IS NOT
I WHO DIES
THIS DAY.

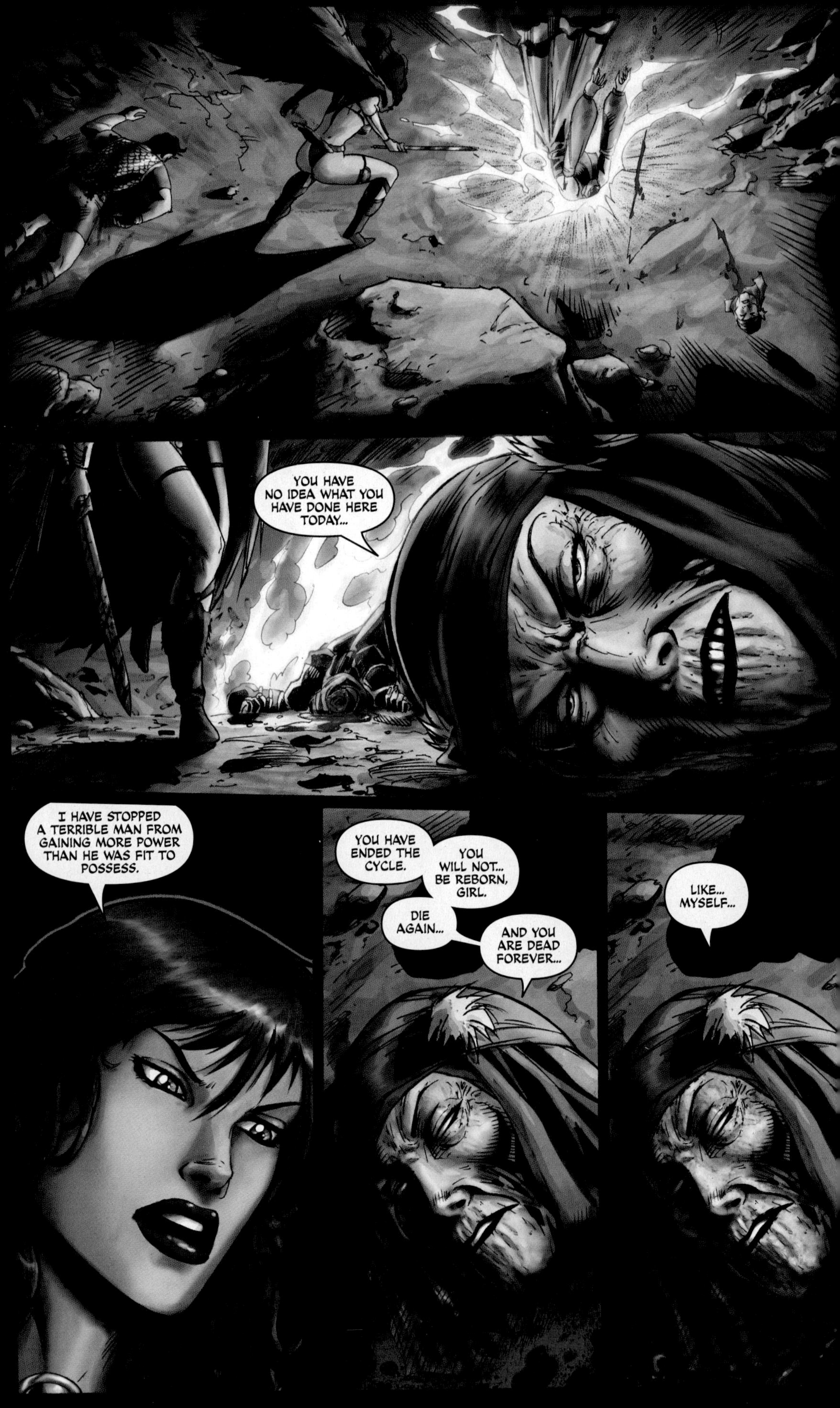
YOU HAVE NO IDEA WHAT YOU HAVE DONE HERE TODAY...
I HAVE STOPPED A TERRIBLE MAN FROM GAINING MORE POWER THAN HE WAS FIT TO POSSESS.
YOU HAVE ENDED THE CYCLE.
YOU WILL NOT... BE REBORN, GIRL.
DIE AGAIN...
AND YOU ARE DEAD FOREVER...
LIKE... MYSELF...

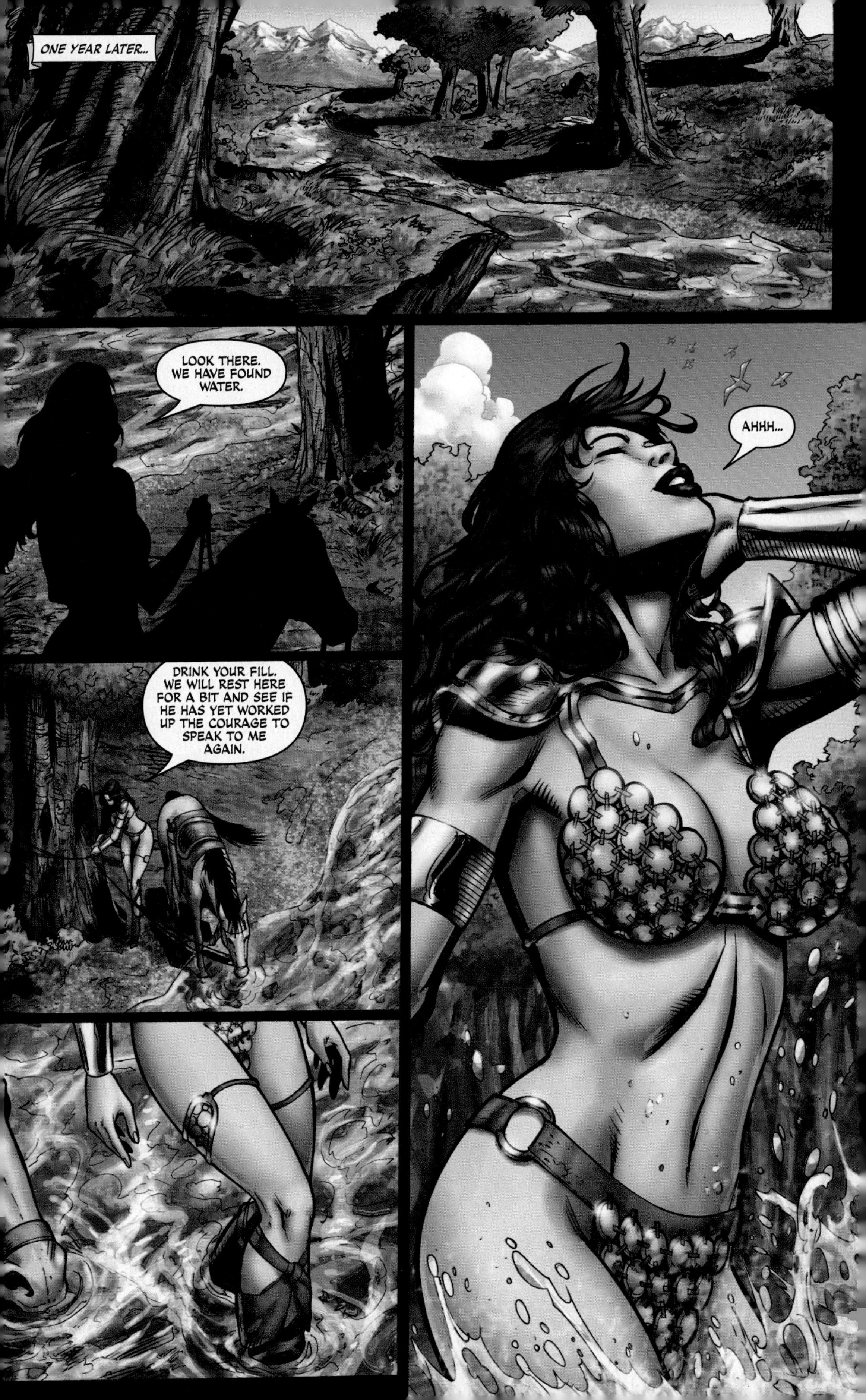
ONE YEAR LATER...
LOOK THERE. WE HAVE FOUND WATER.
DRINK YOUR FILL. WE WILL REST HERE FOR A BIT AND SEE IF HE HAS YET WORKED UP THE COURAGE TO SPEAK TO ME AGAIN.
AHHH...

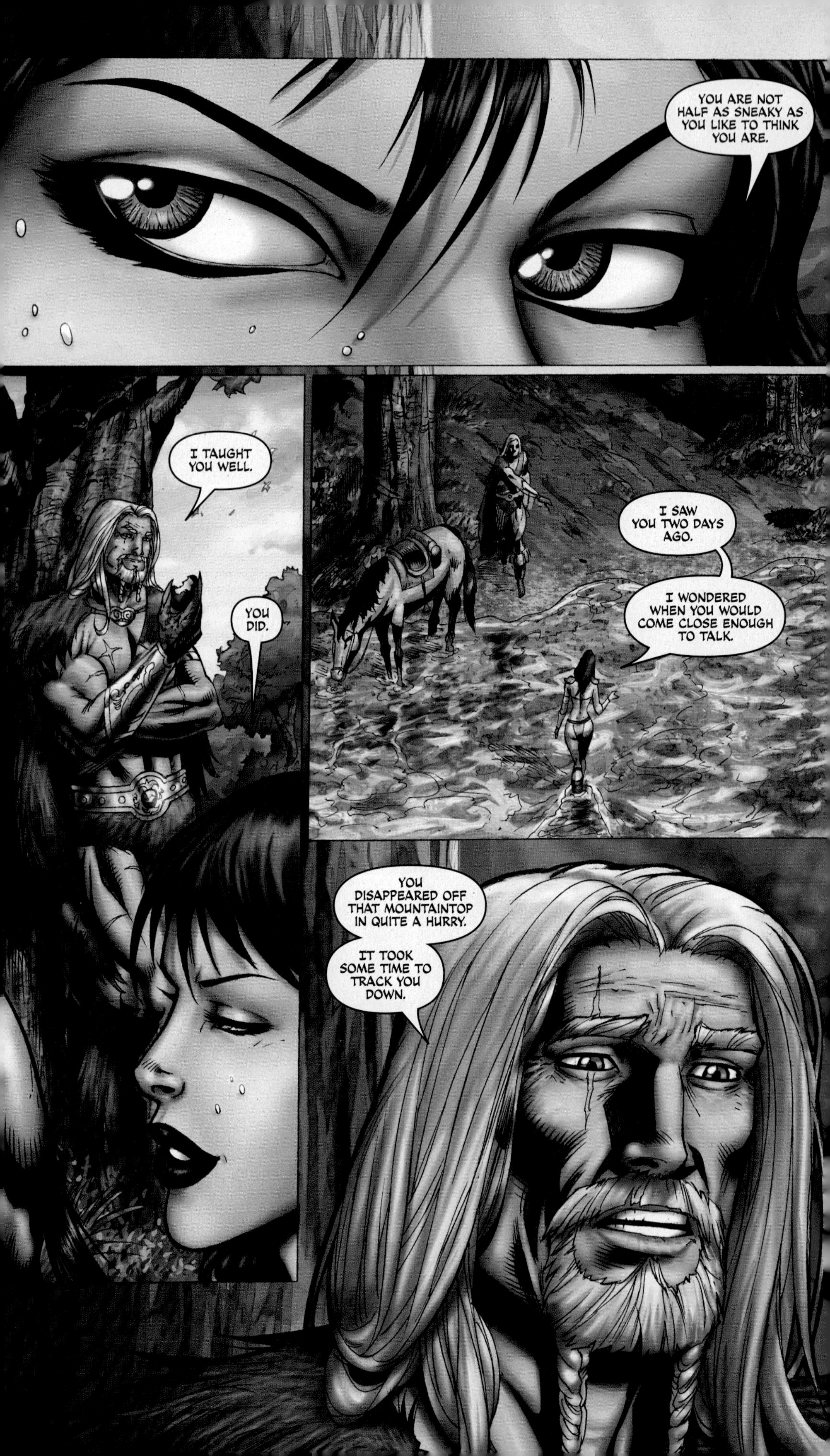
YOU ARE NOT HALF AS SNEAKY AS YOU LIKE TO THINK YOU ARE.
I TAUGHT YOU WELL.
YOU DID.
I SAW YOU TWO DAYS AGO.
I WONDERED WHEN YOU WOULD COME CLOSE ENOUGH TO TALK.
YOU DISAPPEARED OFF THAT MOUNTAINTOP IN QUITE A HURRY.
IT TOOK SOME TIME TO TRACK YOU DOWN.

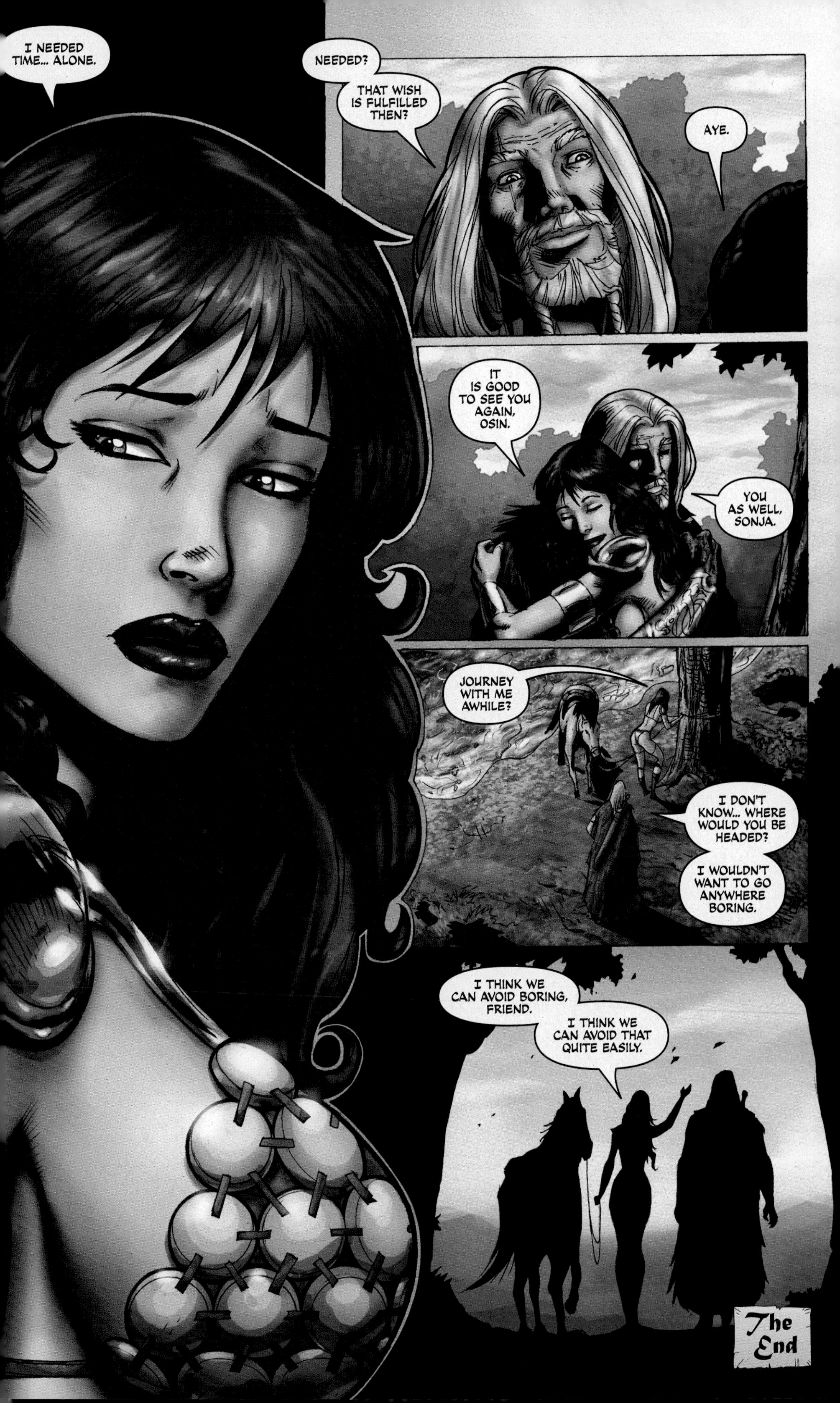
I NEEDED TIME... ALONE.
NEEDED?
THAT WISH IS FULFILLED THEN?
AYE.
IT IS GOOD TO SEE YOU AGAIN, OSIN.
YOU AS WELL, SONJA.
JOURNEY WITH ME AWHILE?
I DON'T KNOW... WHERE WOULD YOU BE HEADED?
I WOULDN'T WANT TO GO ANYWHERE BORING.
I THINK WE CAN AVOID BORING, FRIEND.
I THINK WE CAN AVOID THAT QUITE EASILY.
The End

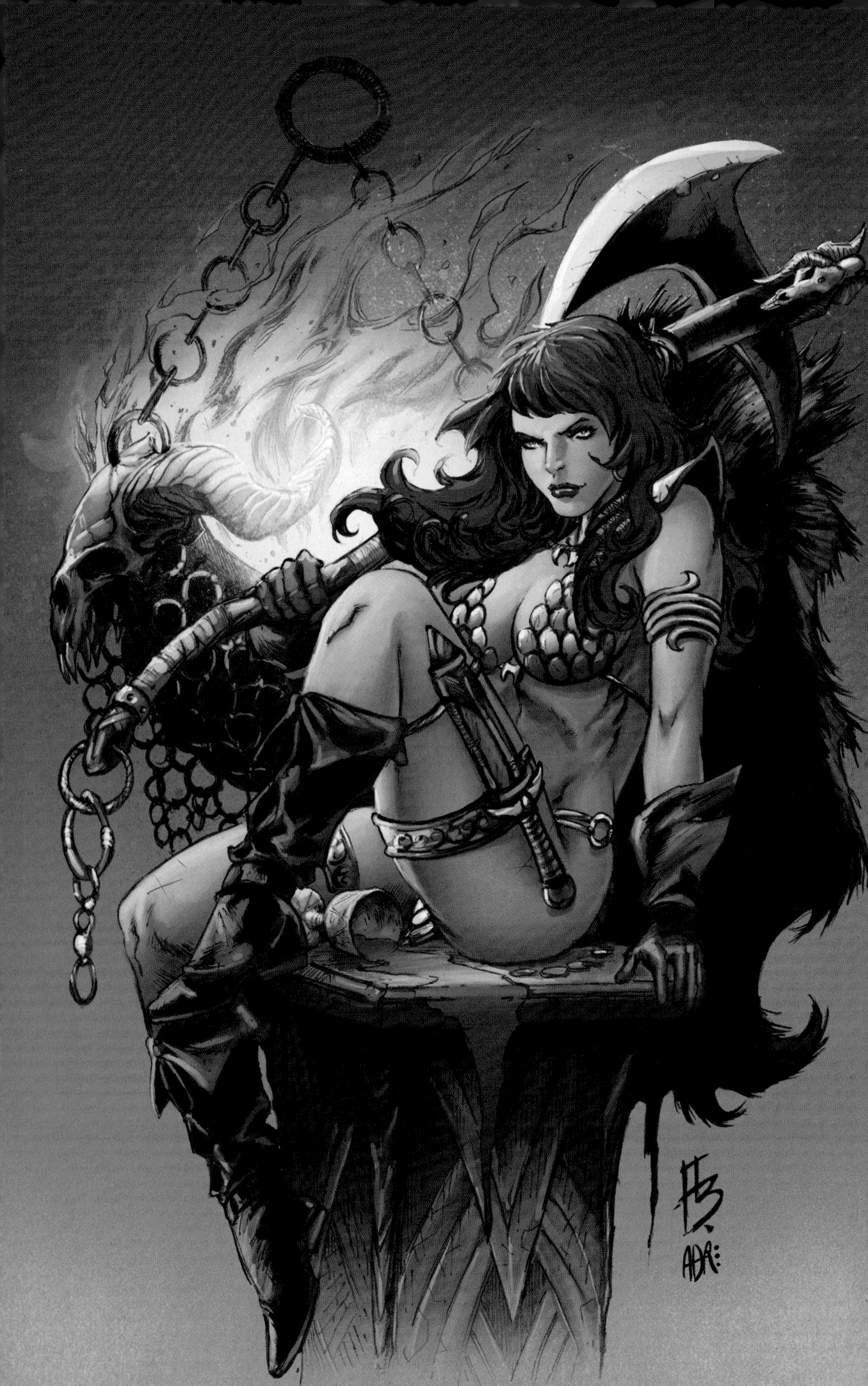

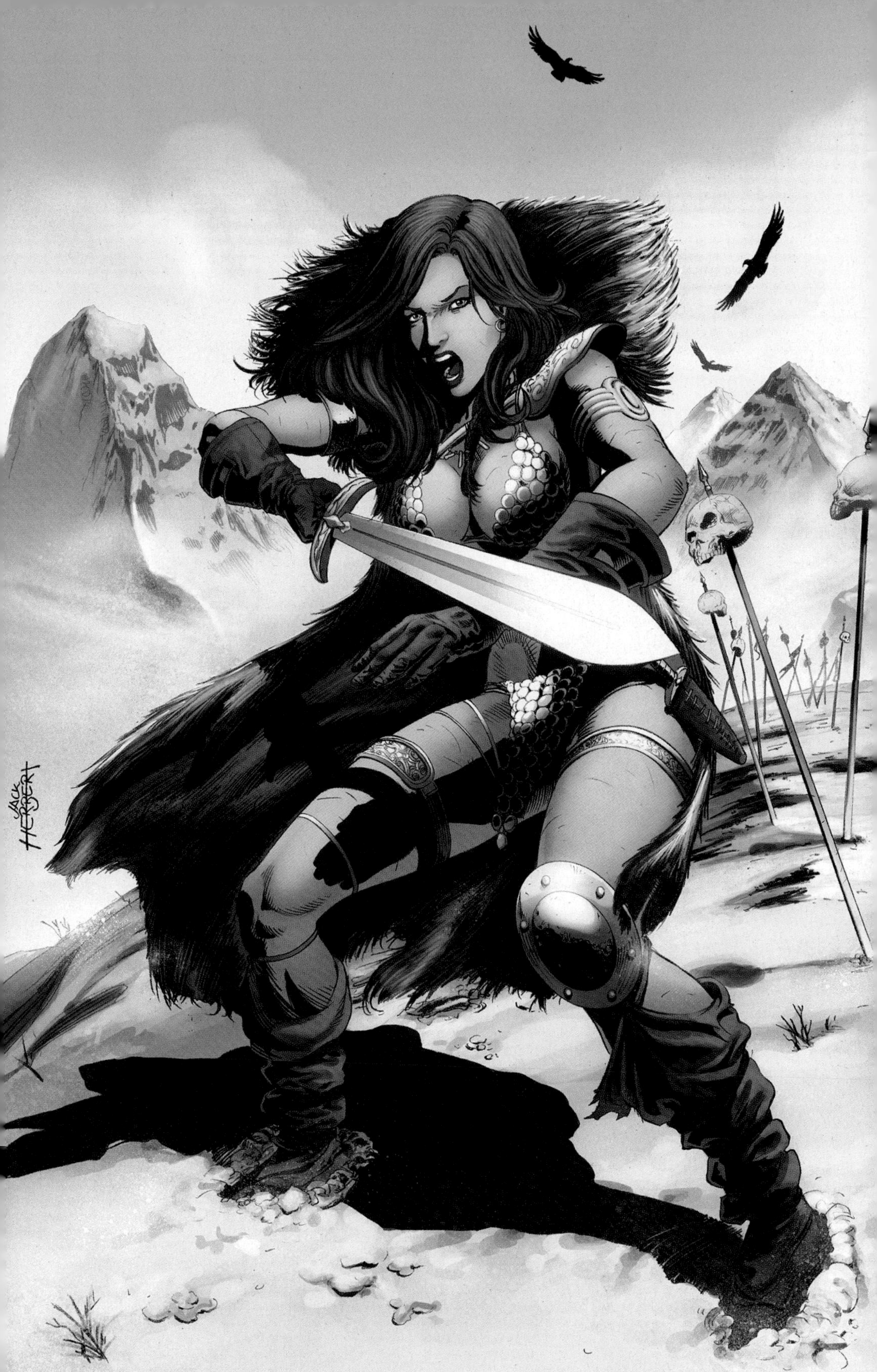
JACK HERBERT

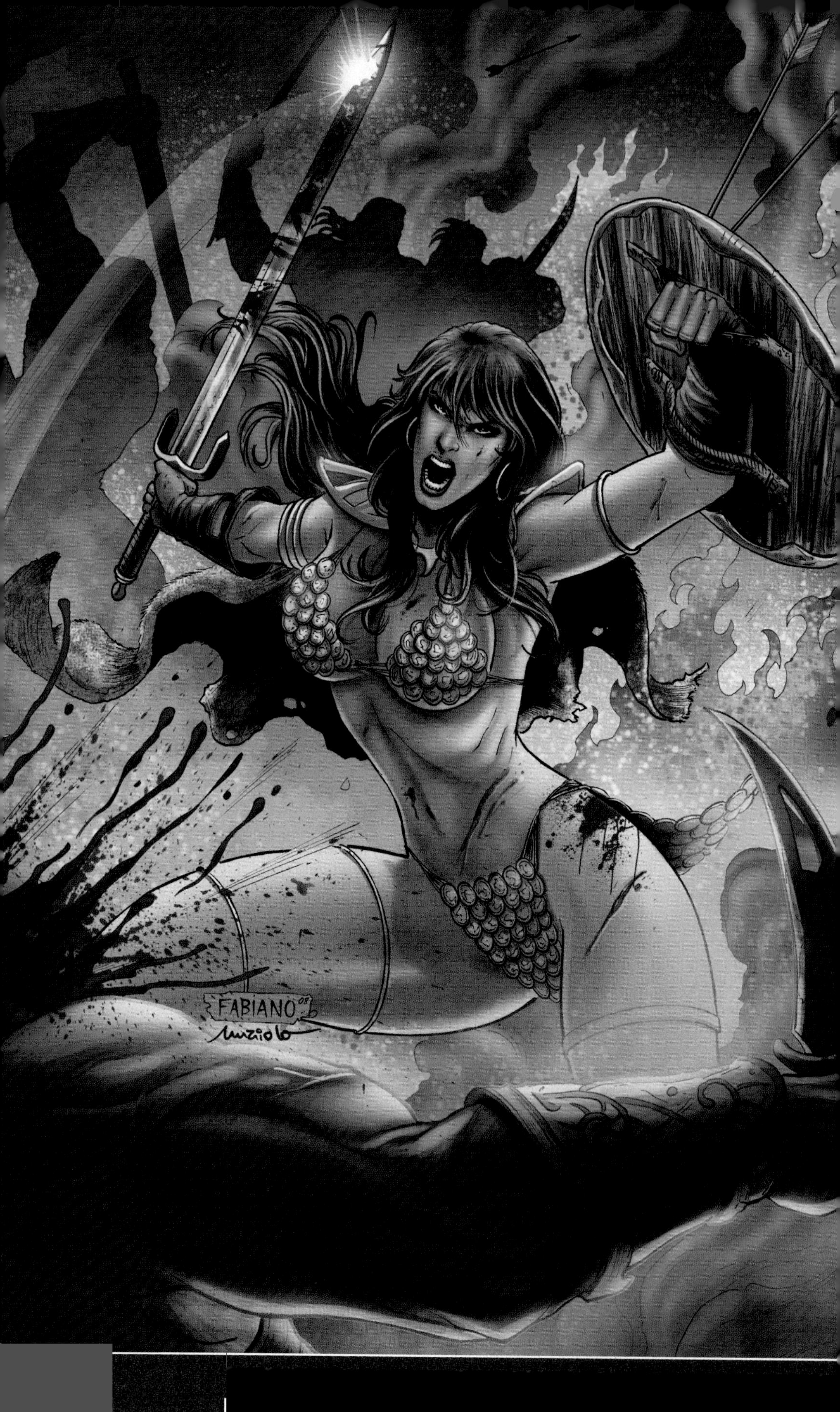
FABIANO

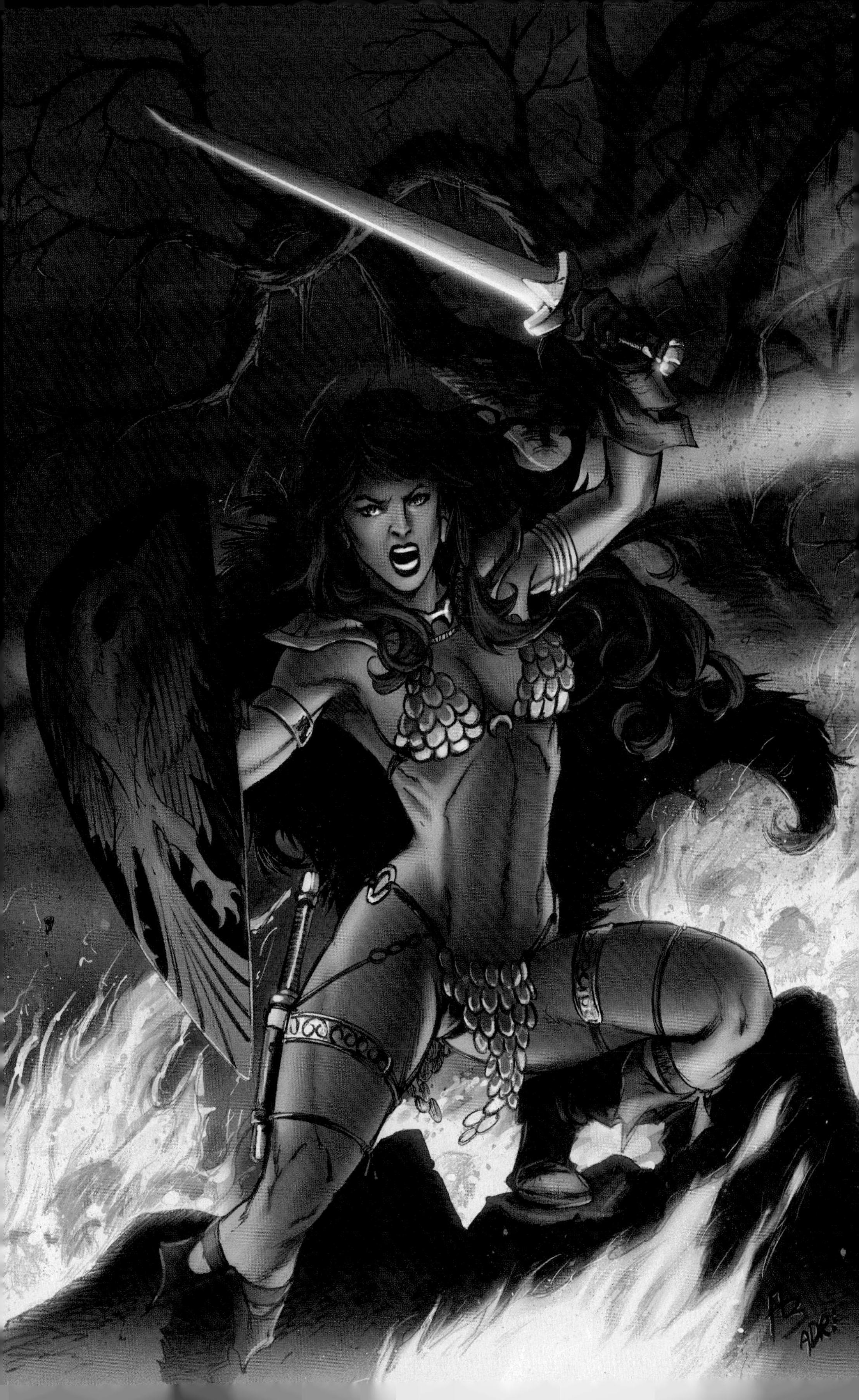

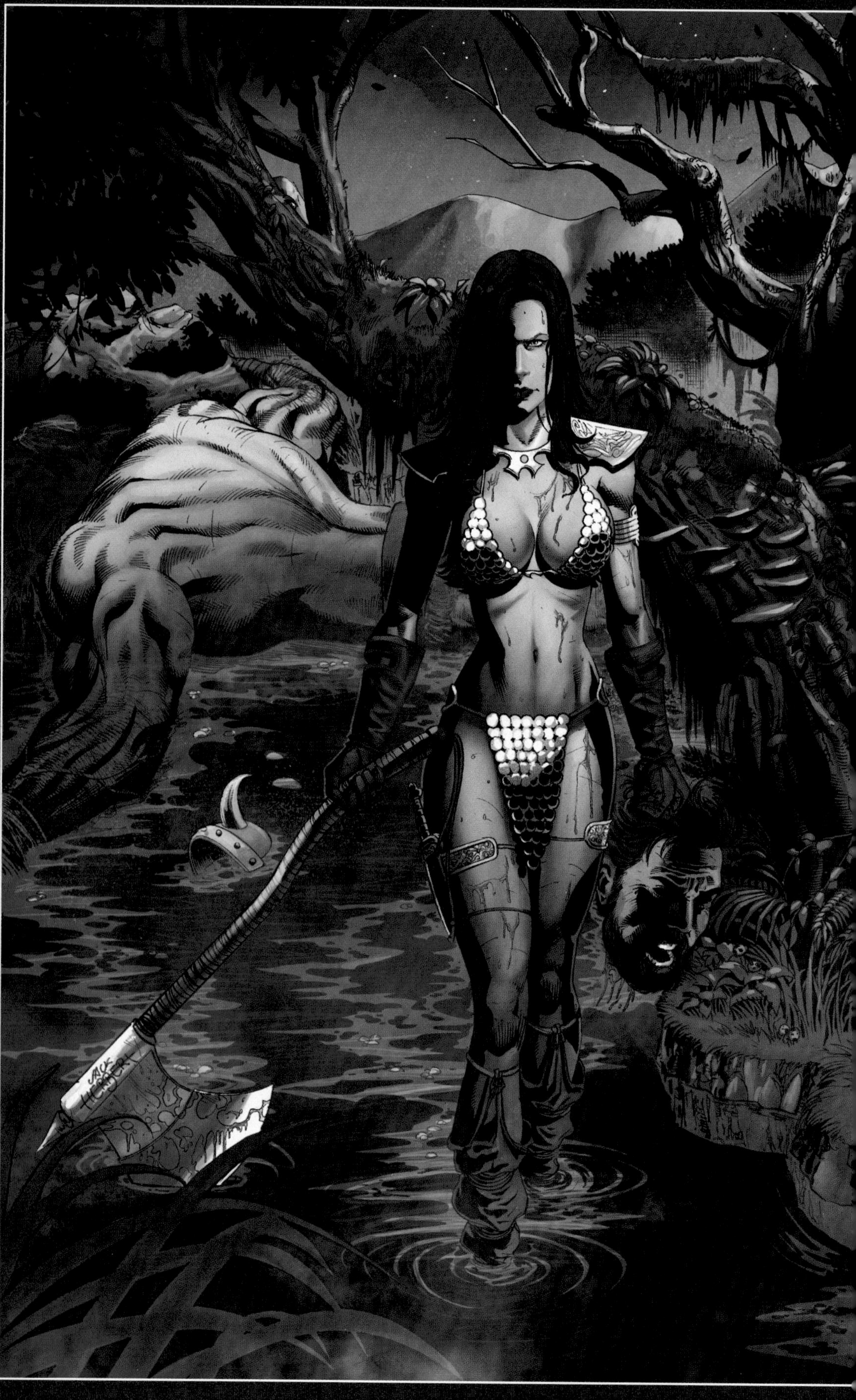
JACK HERBERT

Red Sonja #42 cover by JACK HERBERT

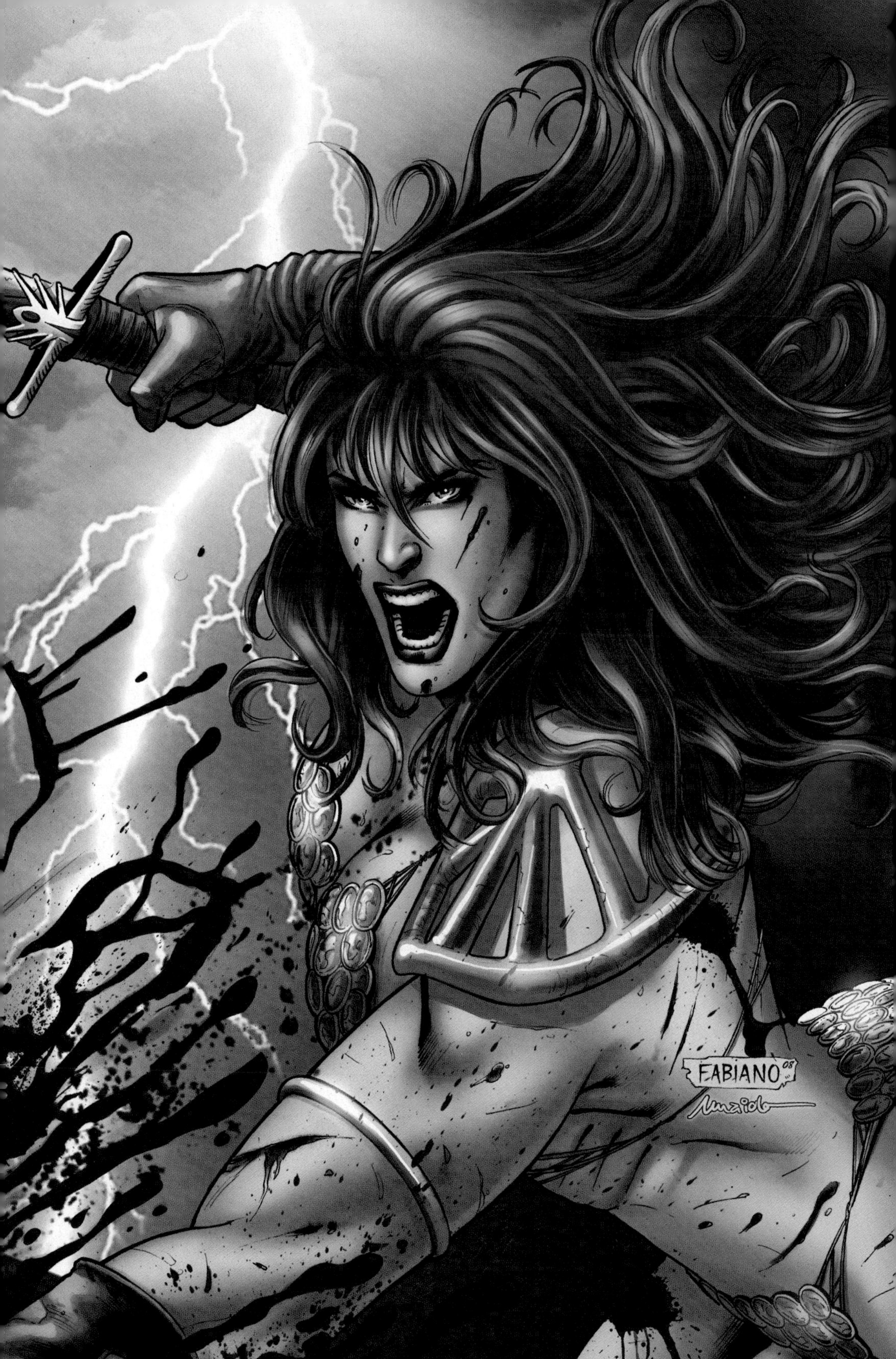
FABIANO 08

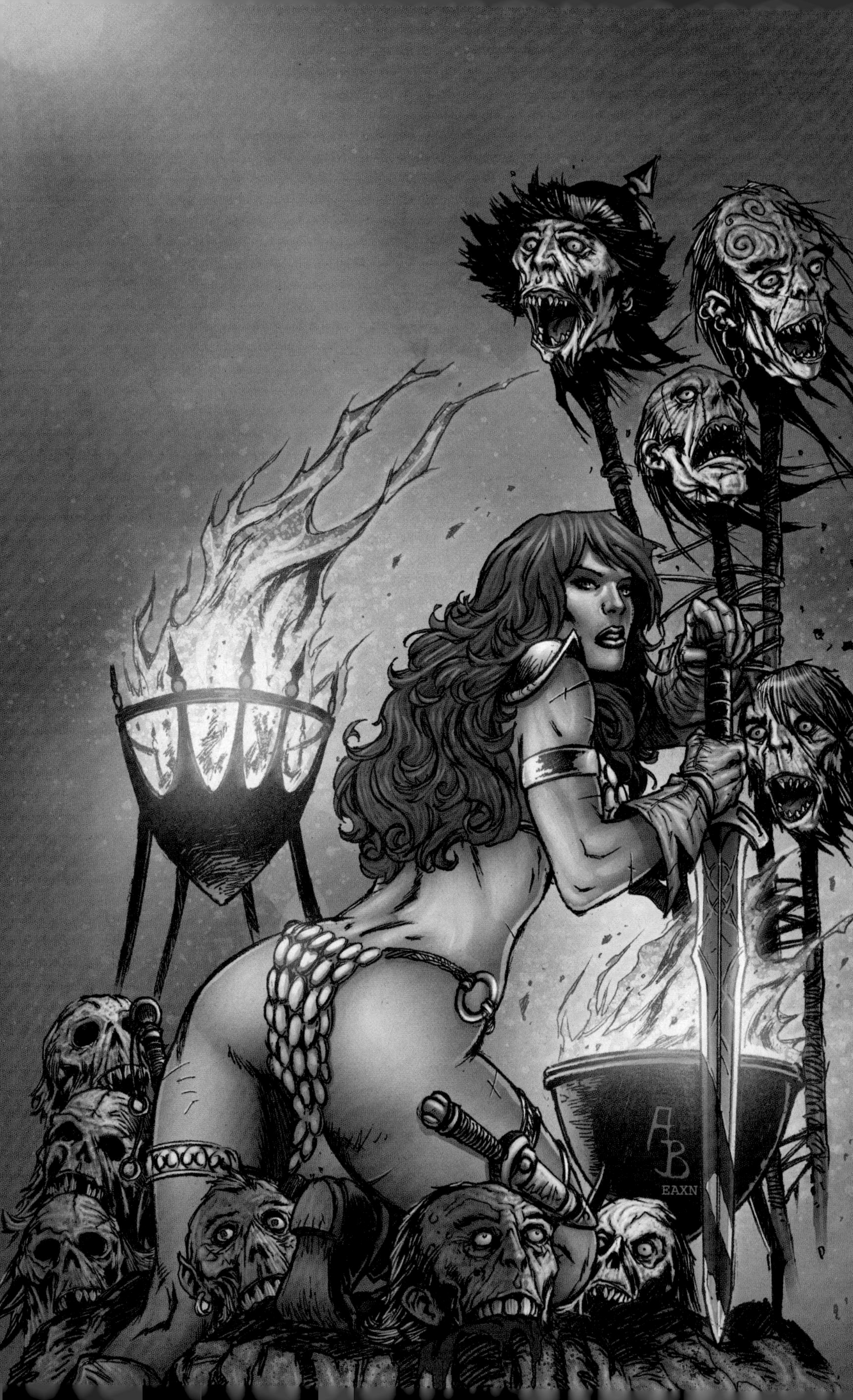

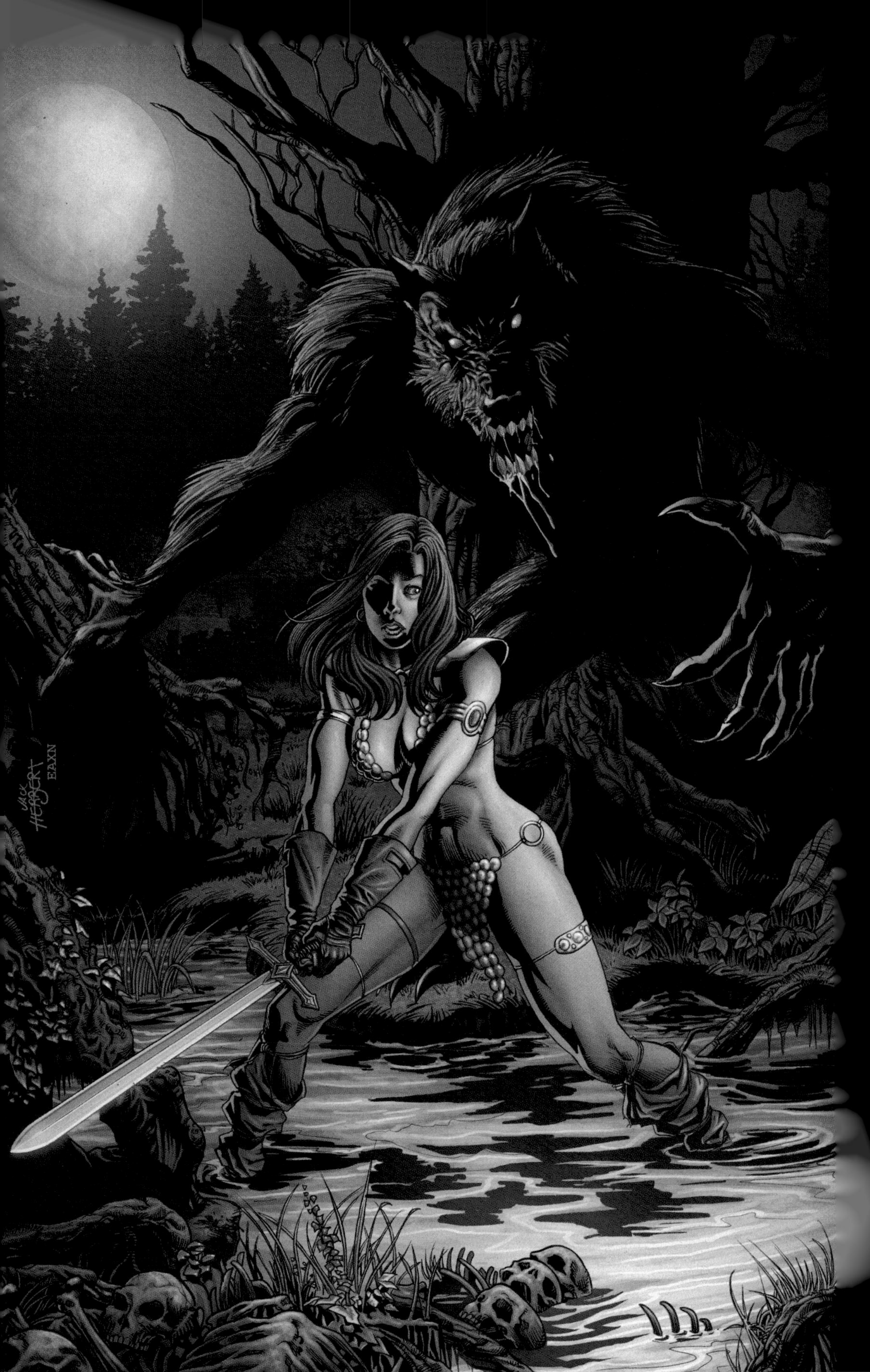
JACK HERBERT

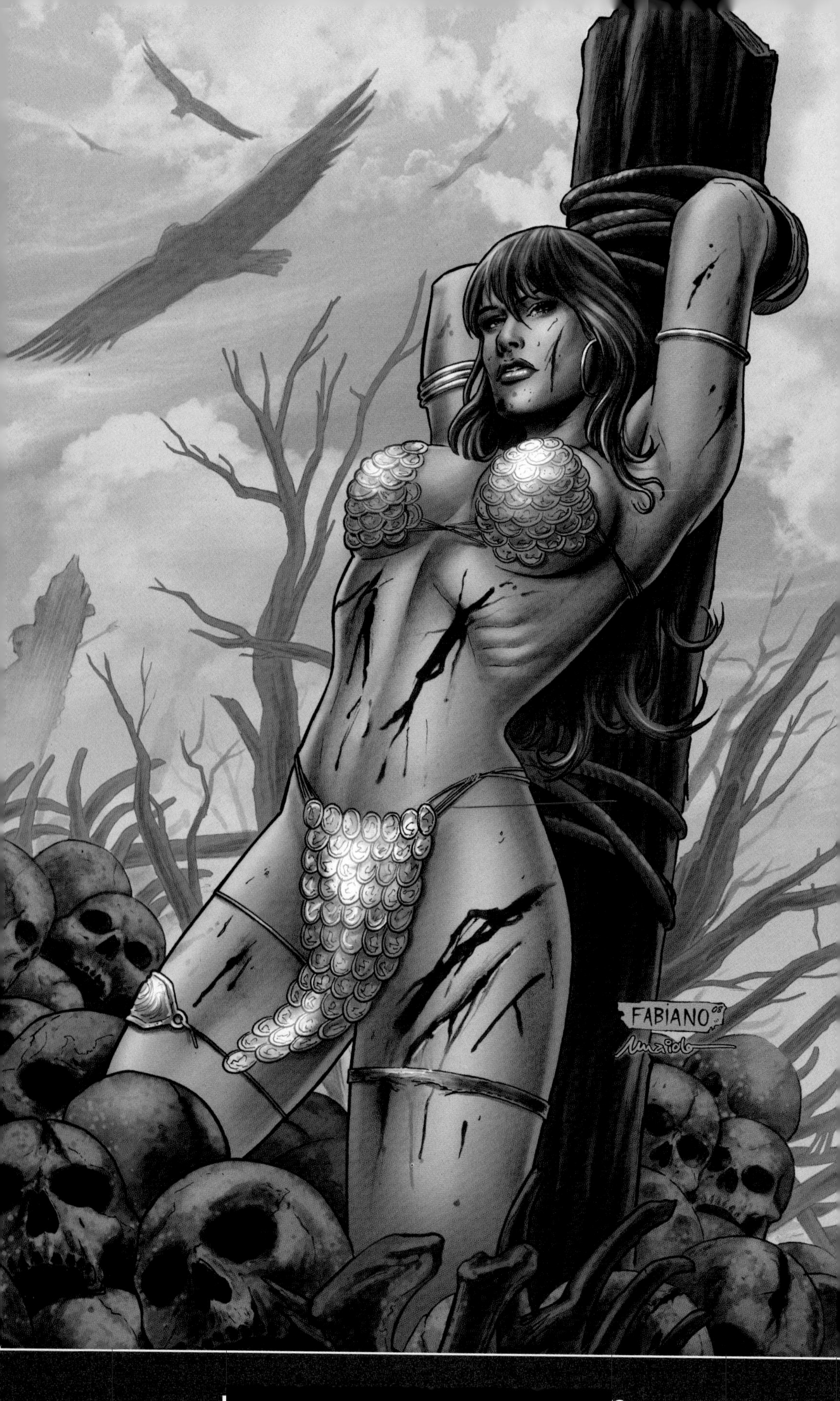
FABIANO 08

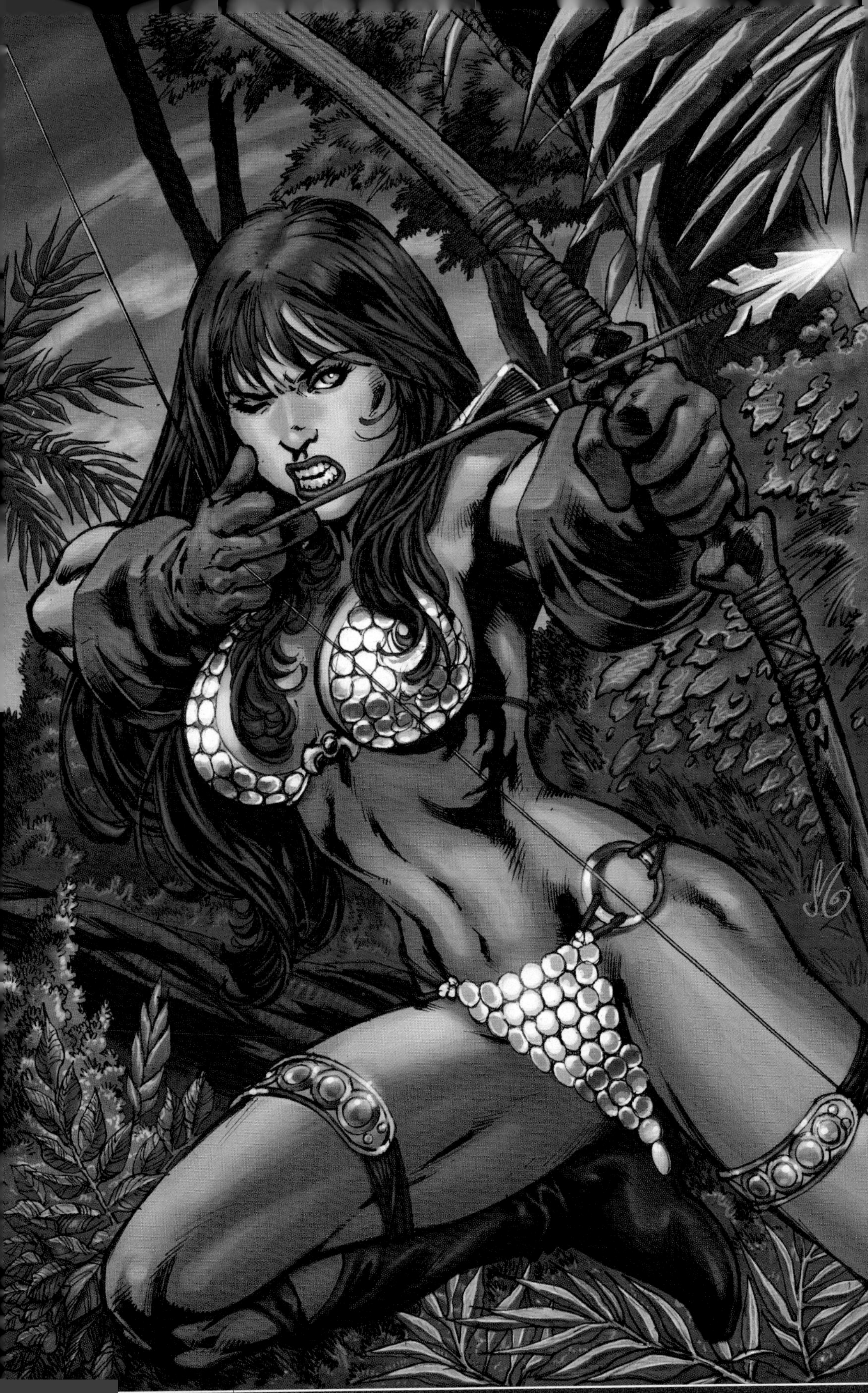

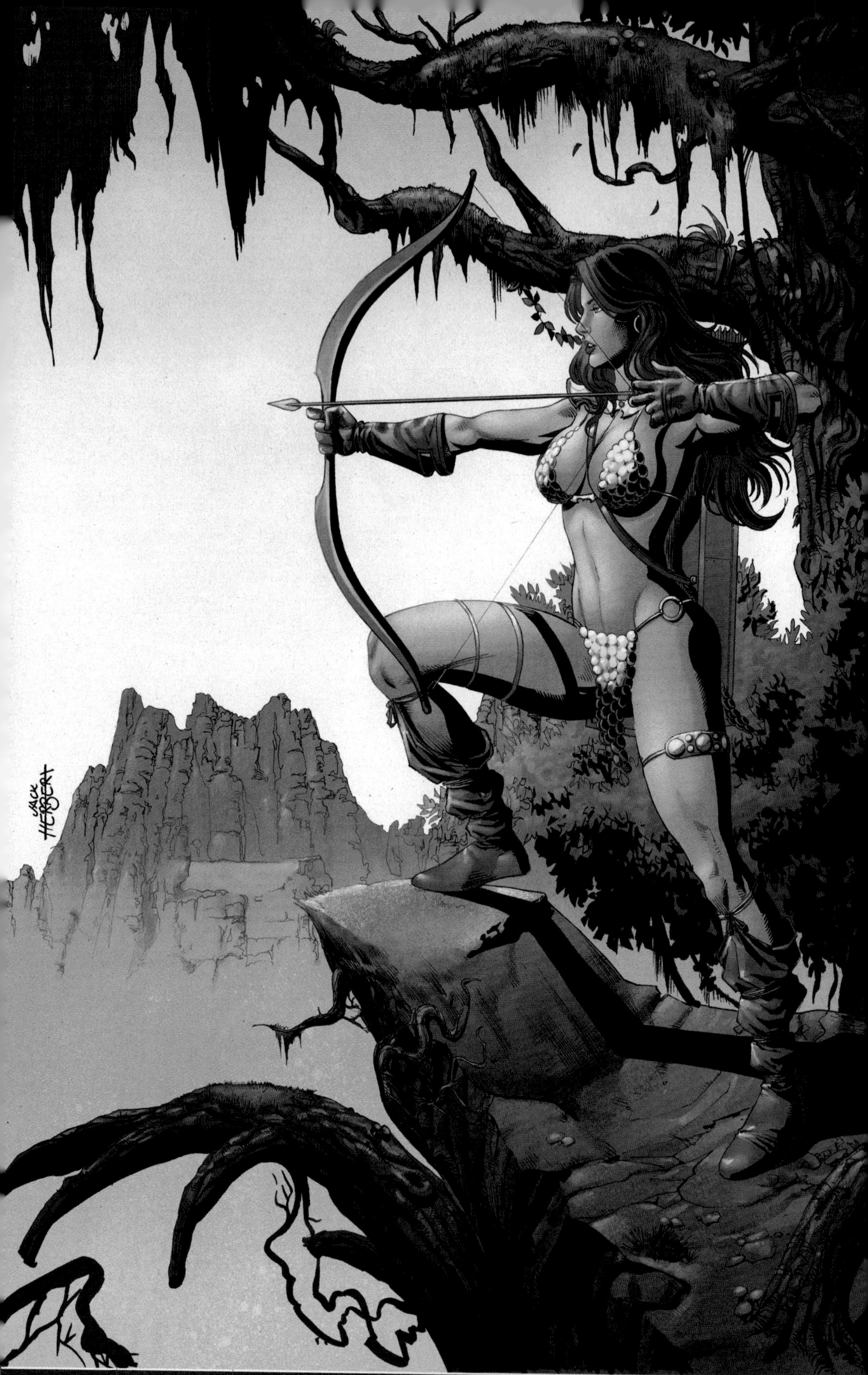
JACK HERBERT

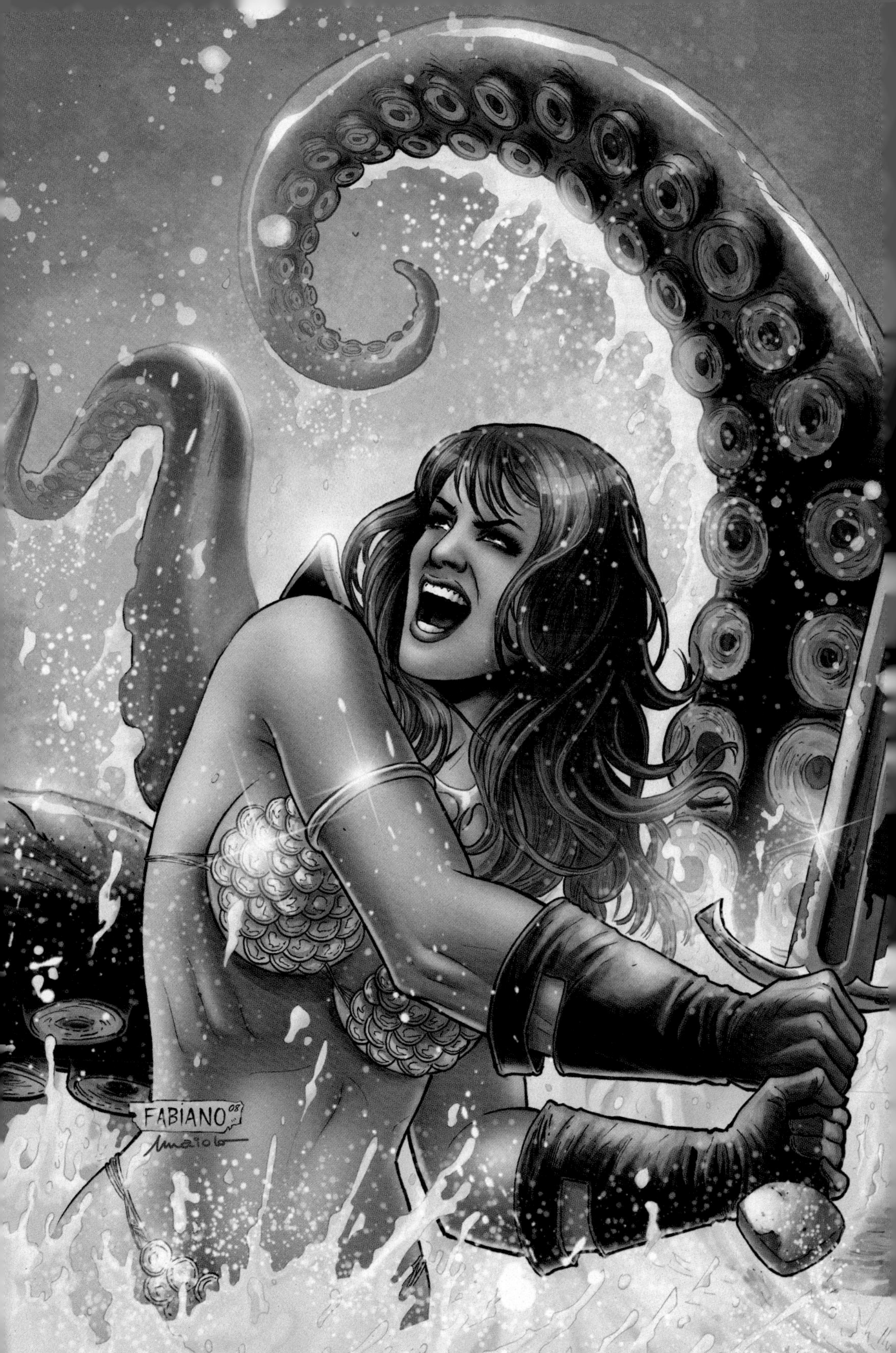
FABIANO 08

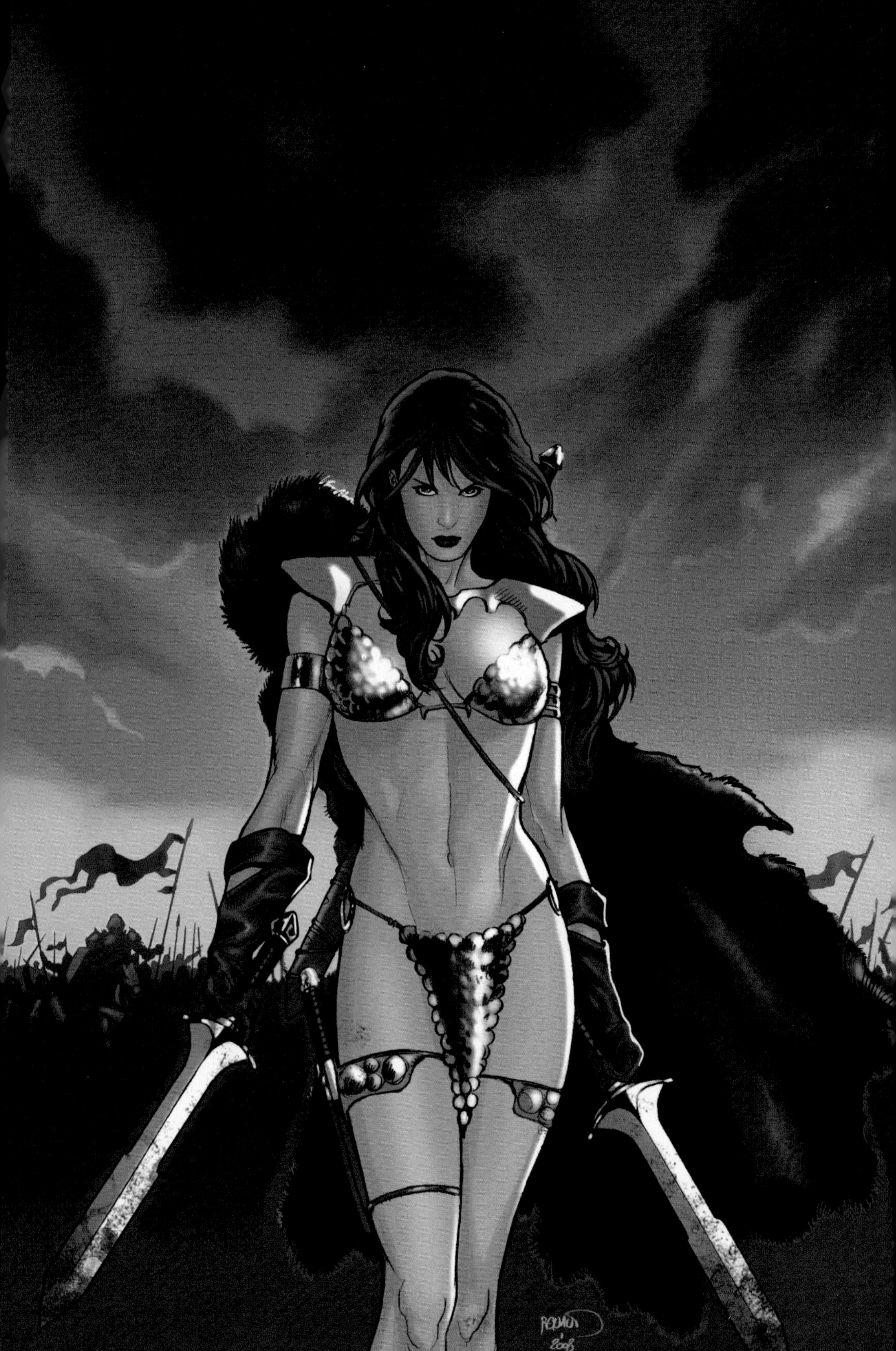

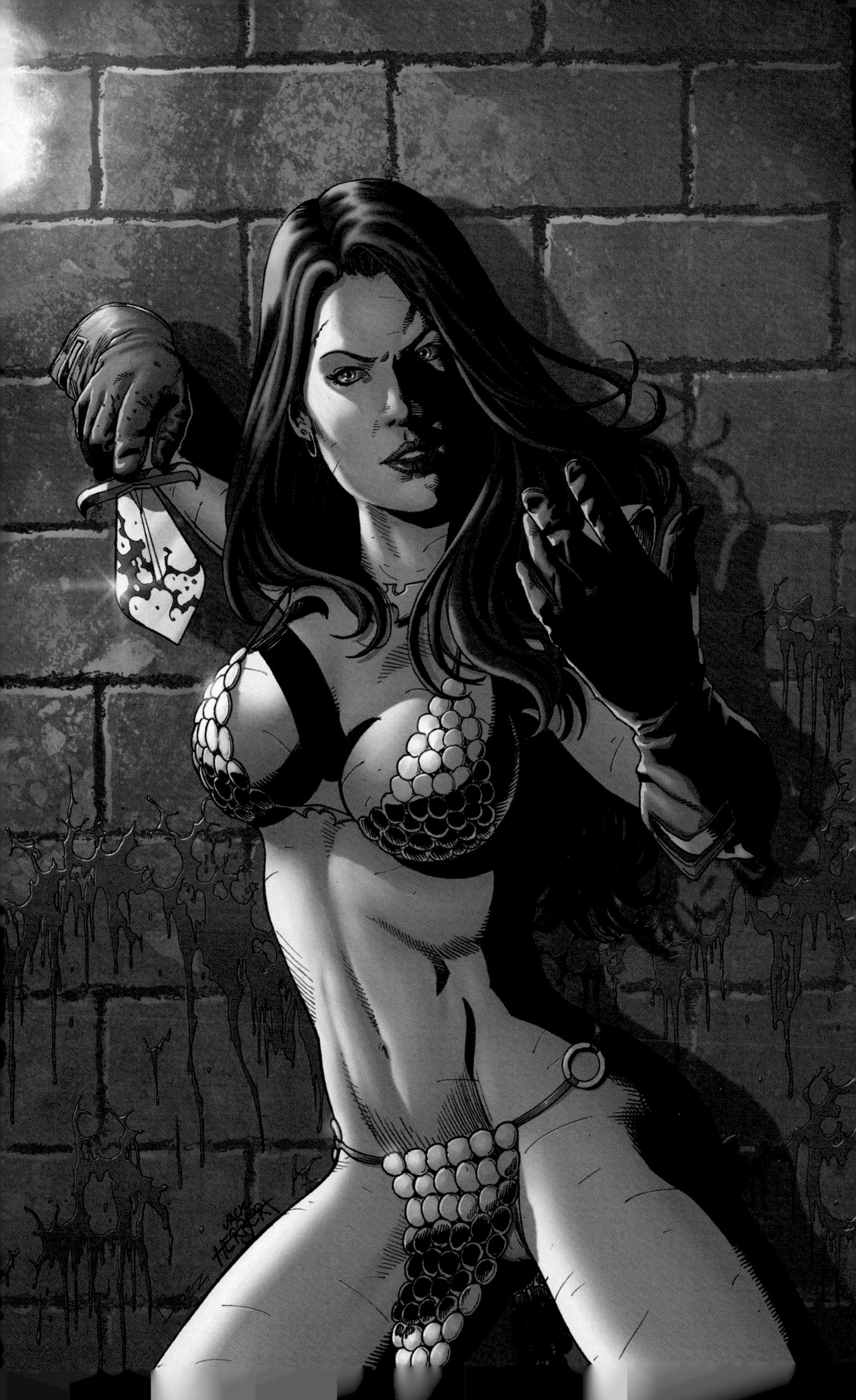
JACK HERBERT

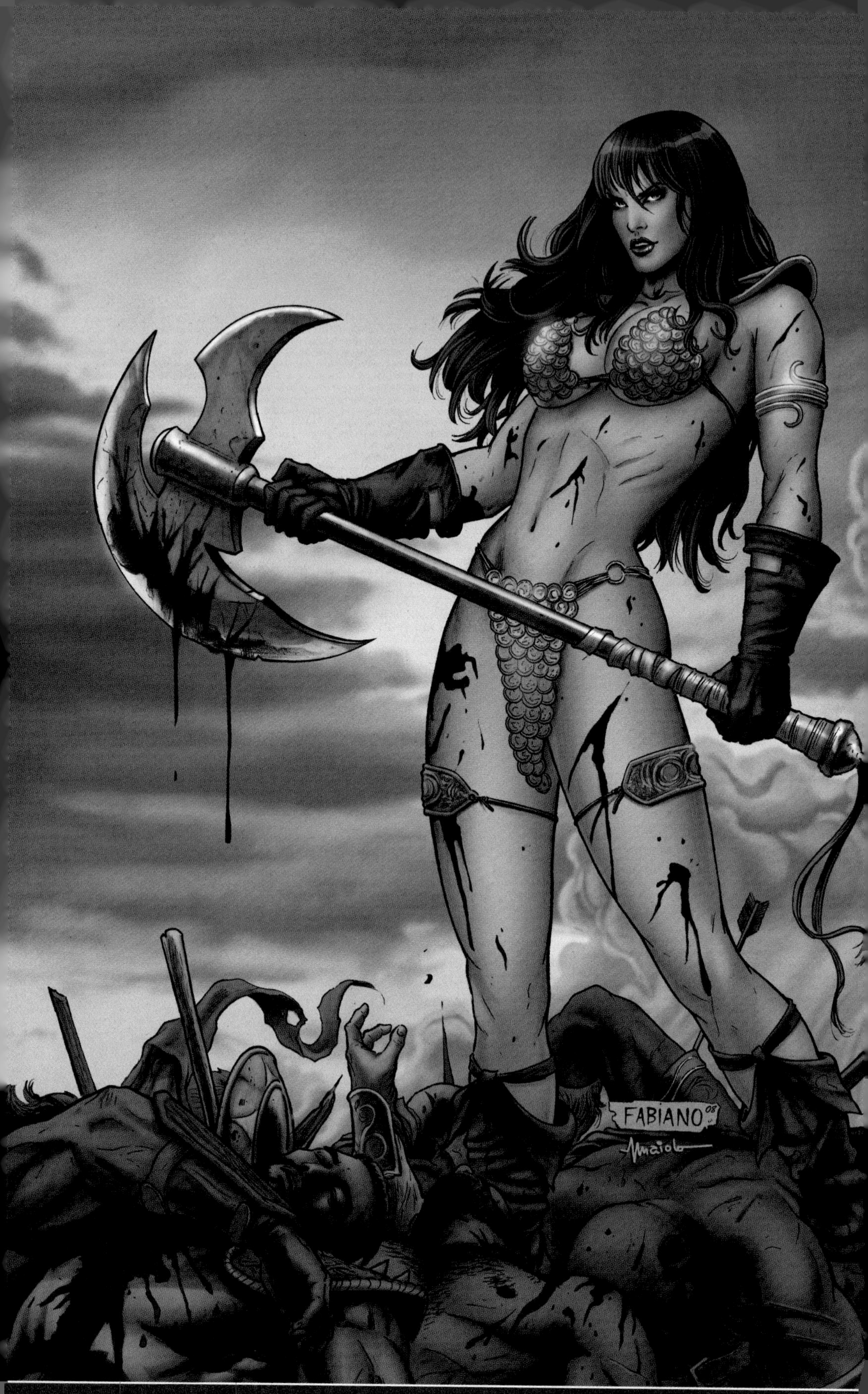
FABIANO 08

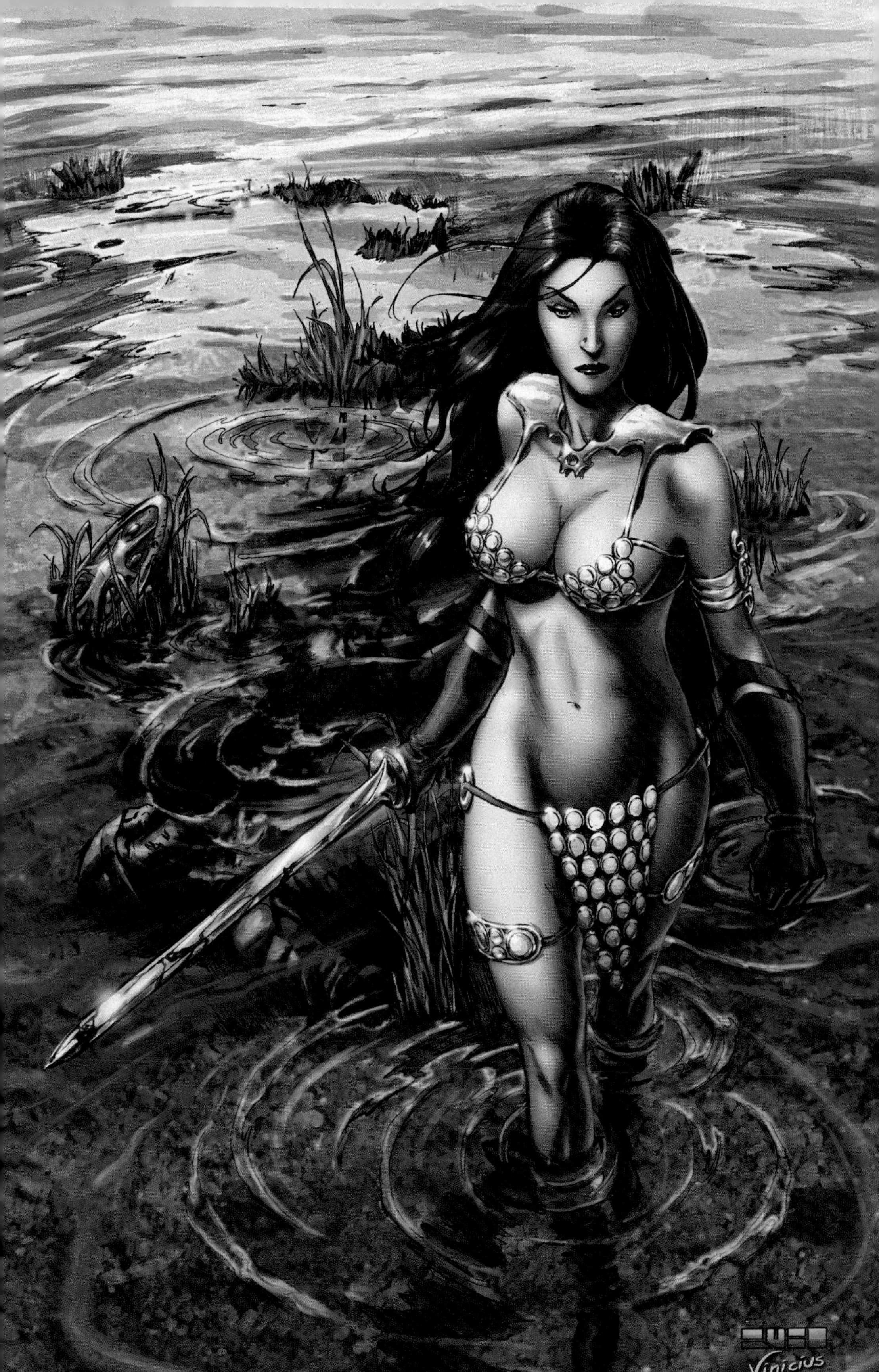
Vinicius
Andrade

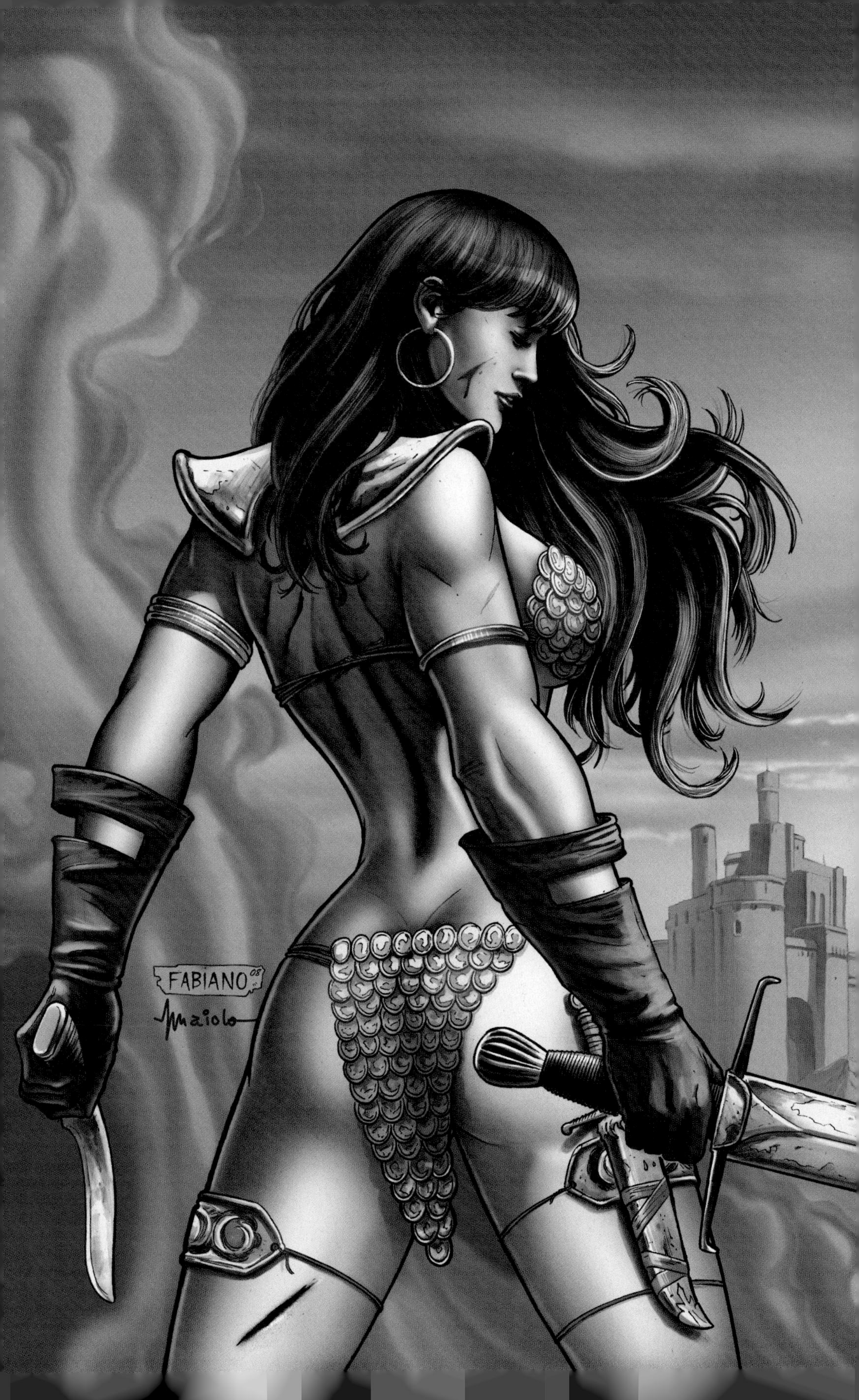
FABIANO 08

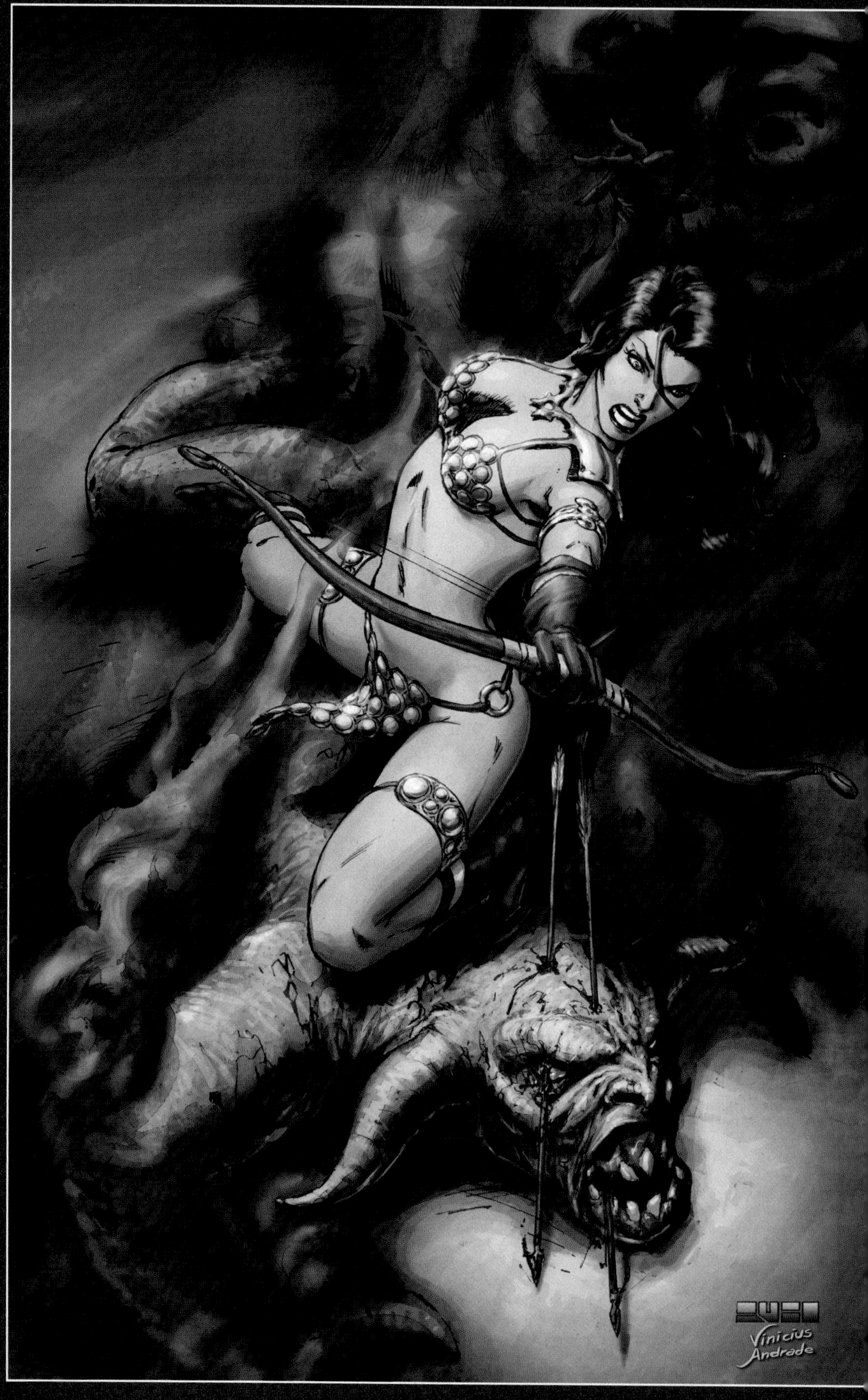
Vinicius
Andrade

Red Sonja #47 cover by MEL RUBI

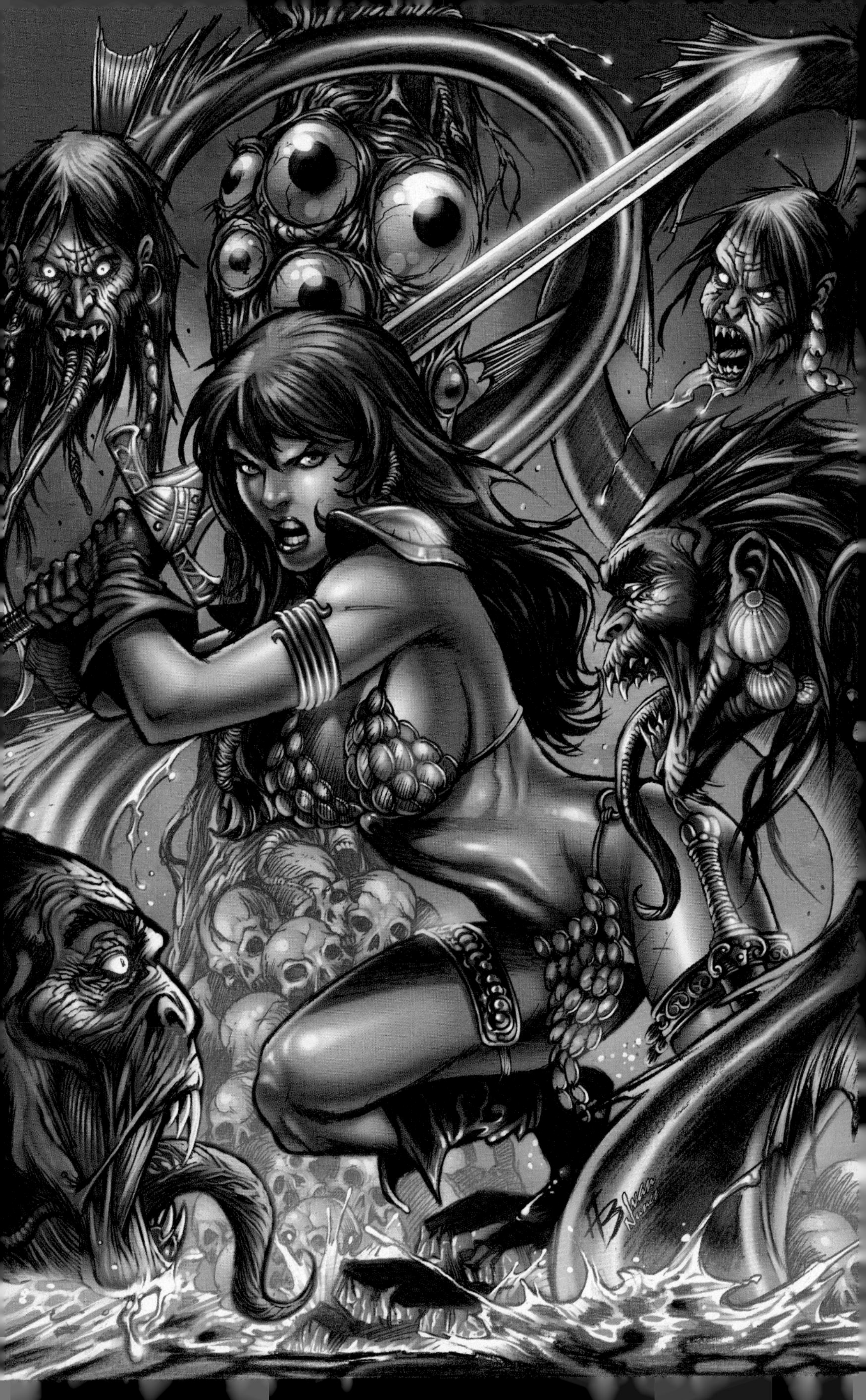

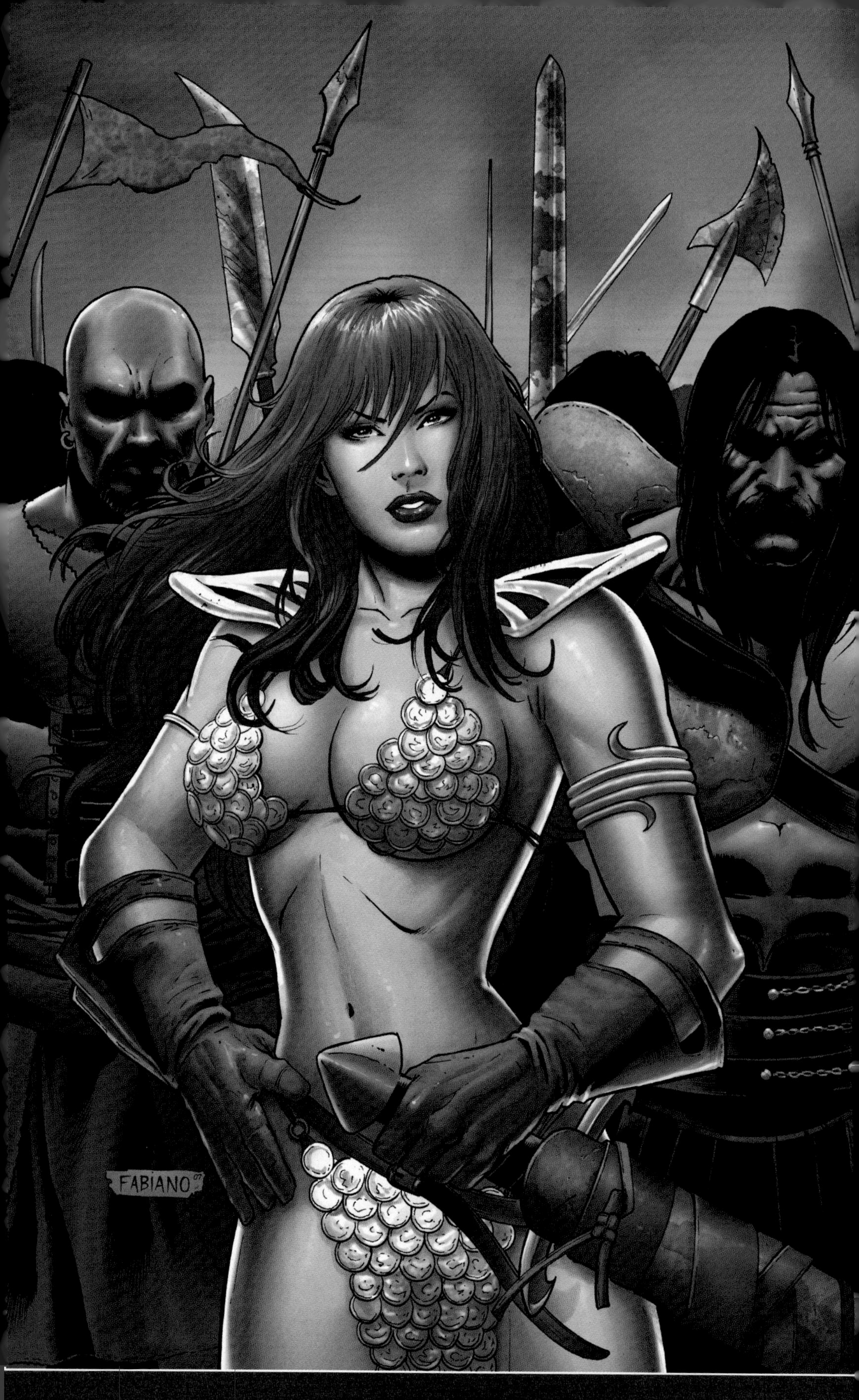
FABIANO 07

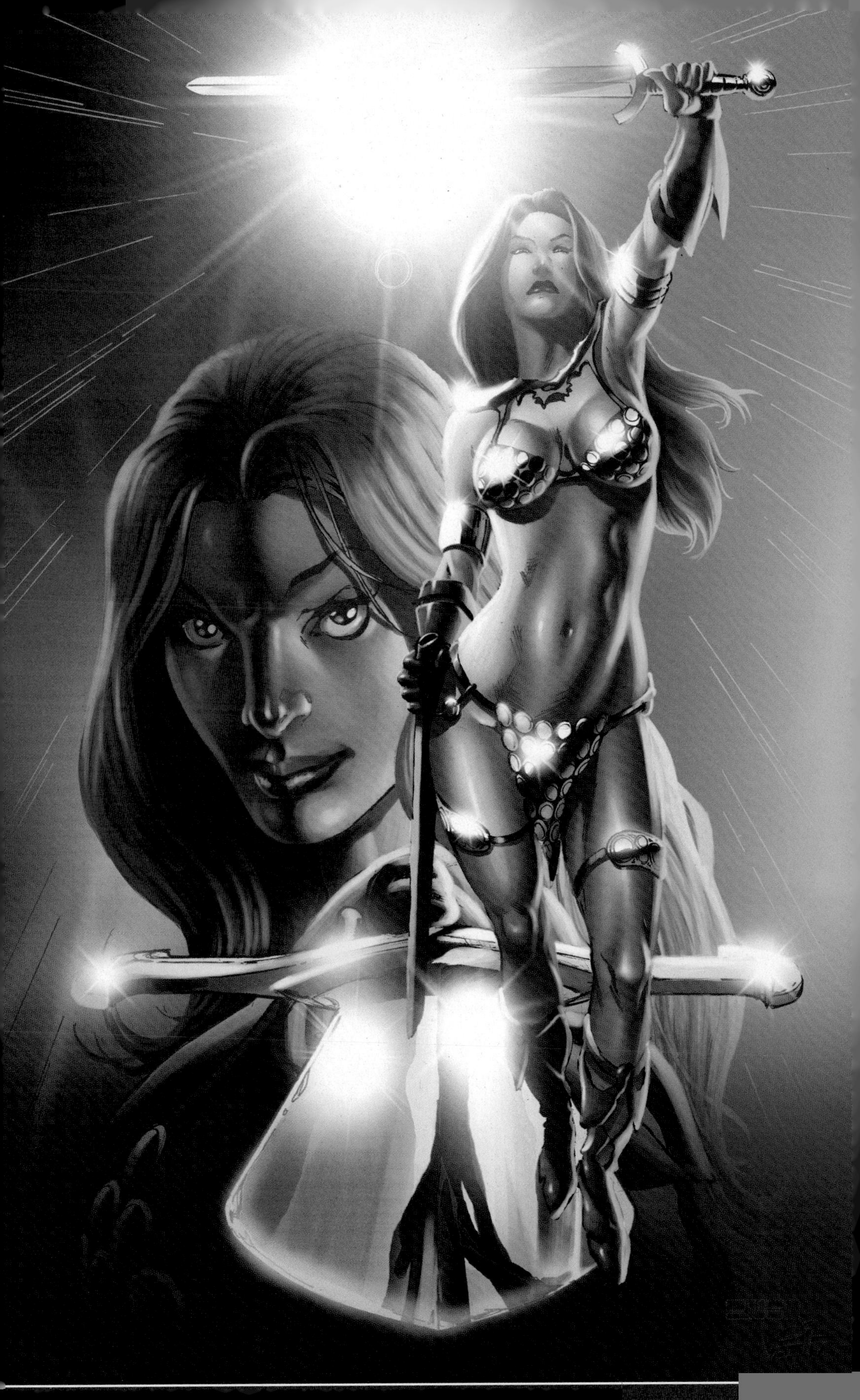

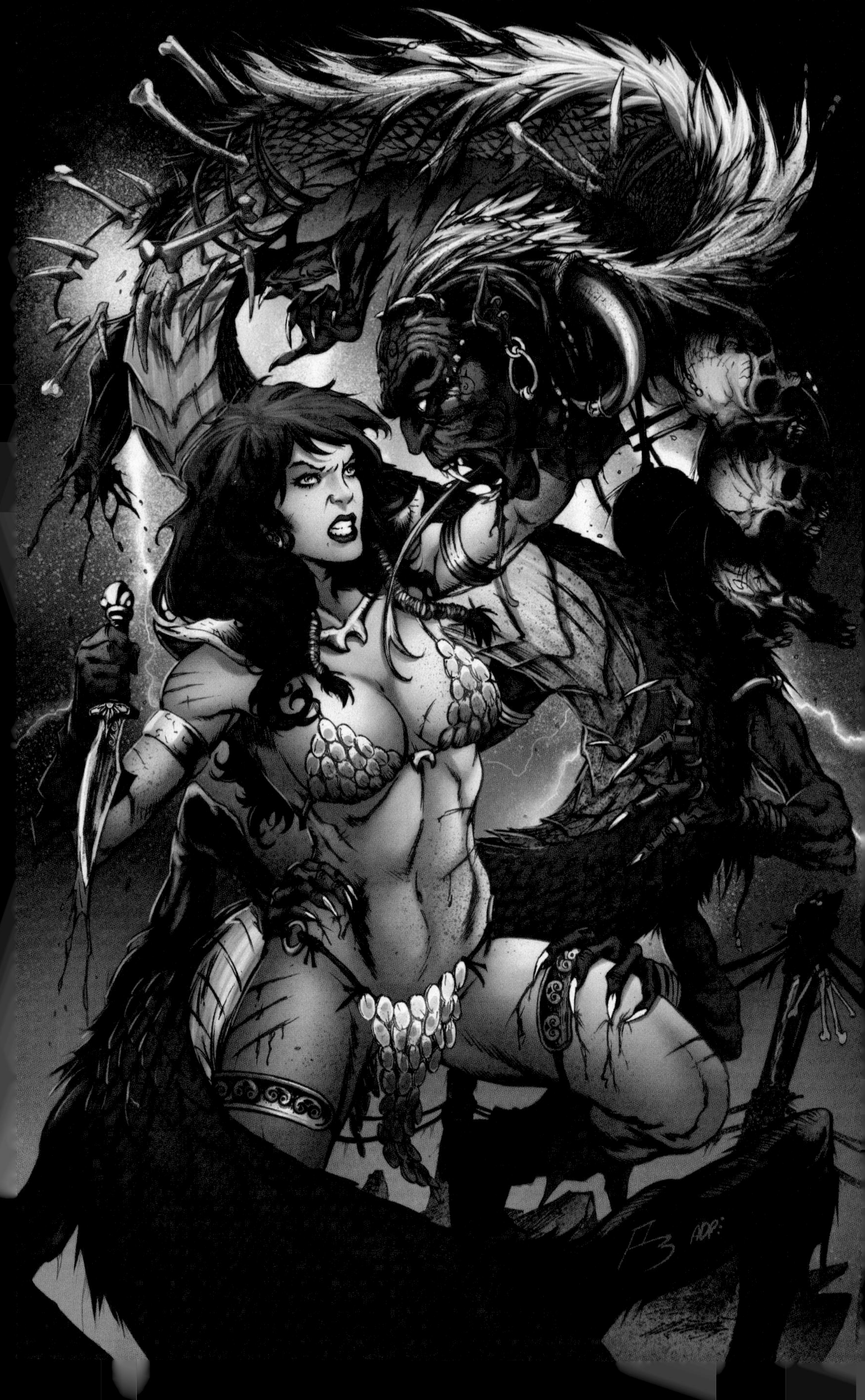

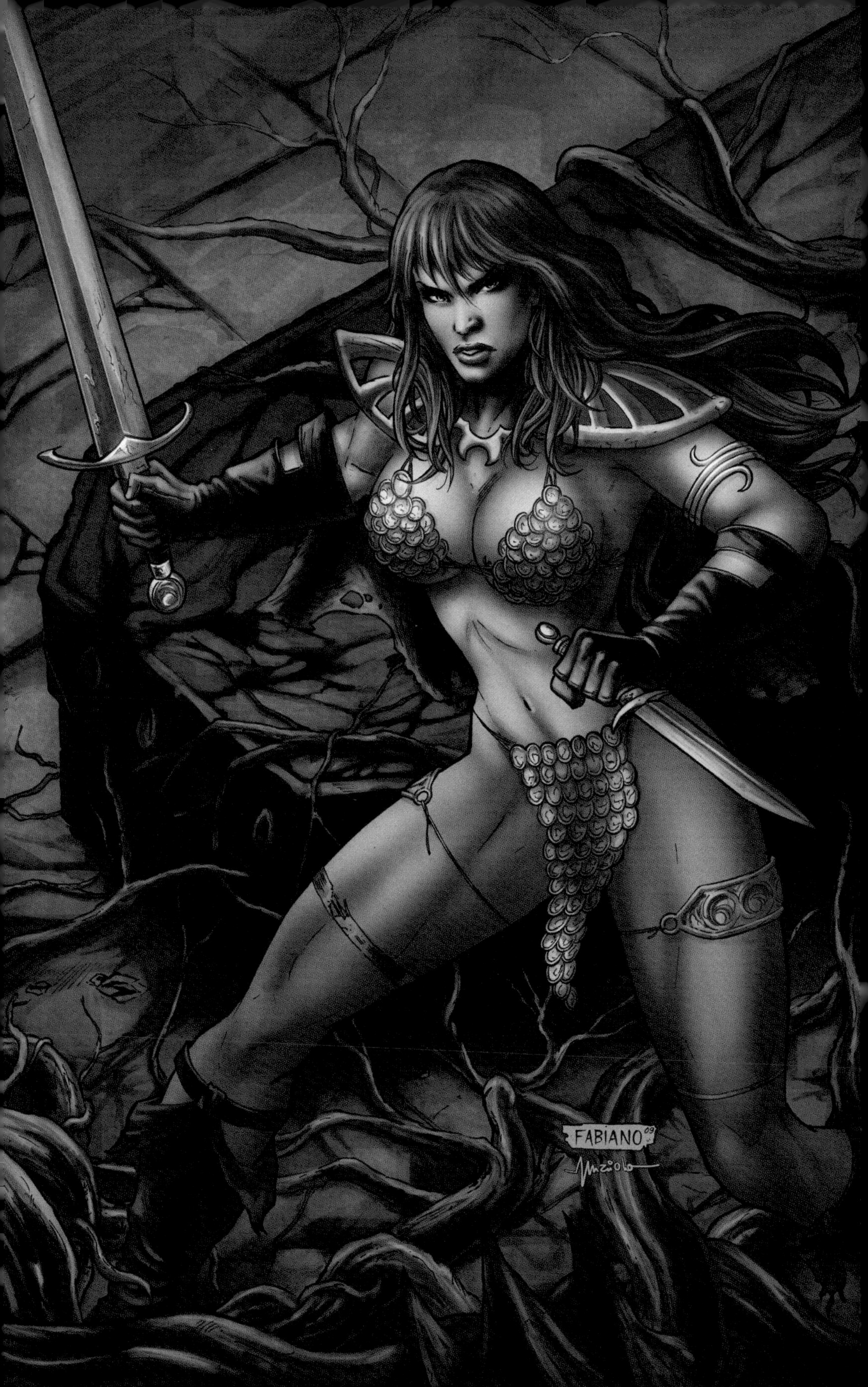
FABIANO 09

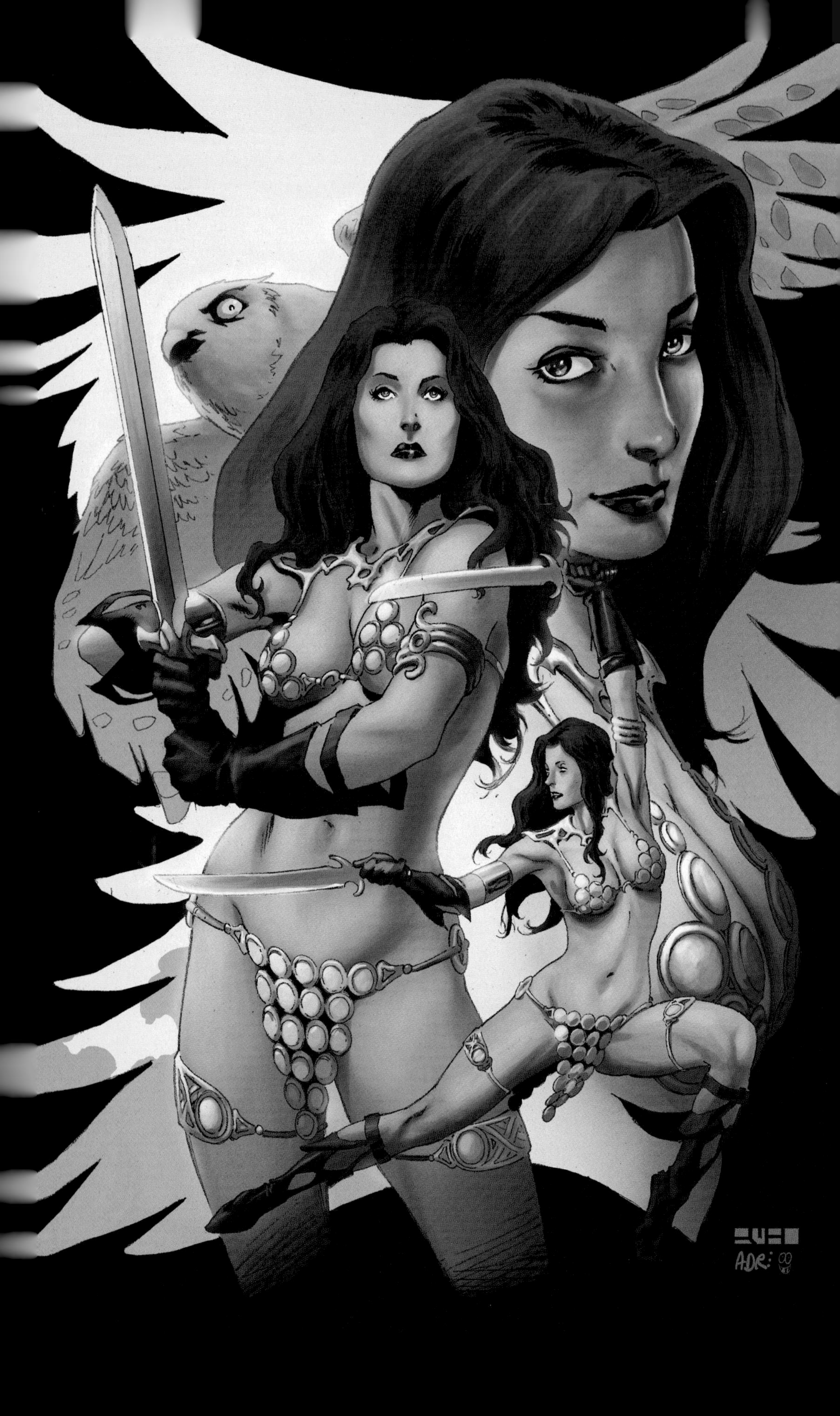

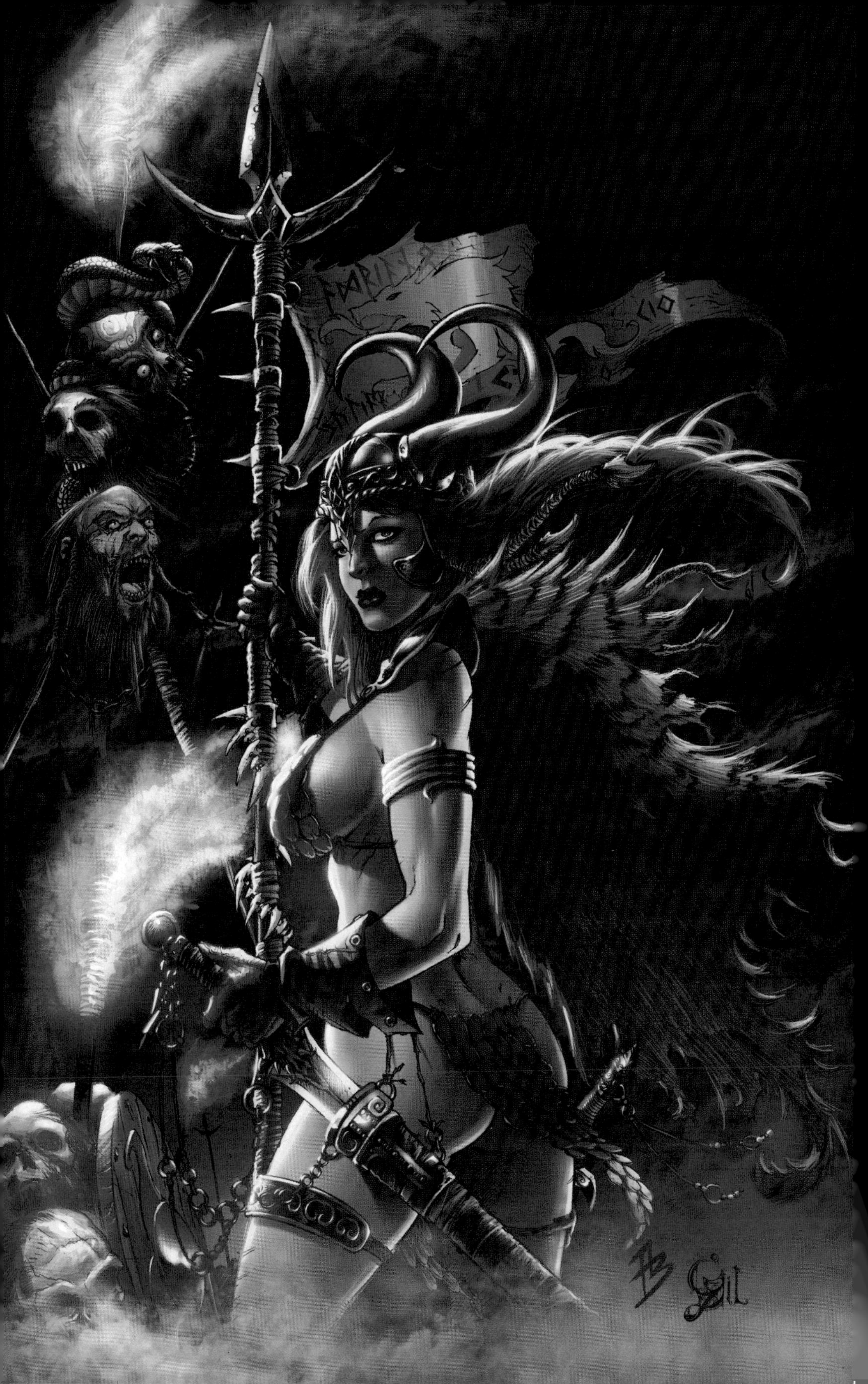

Rec[redacted]TA

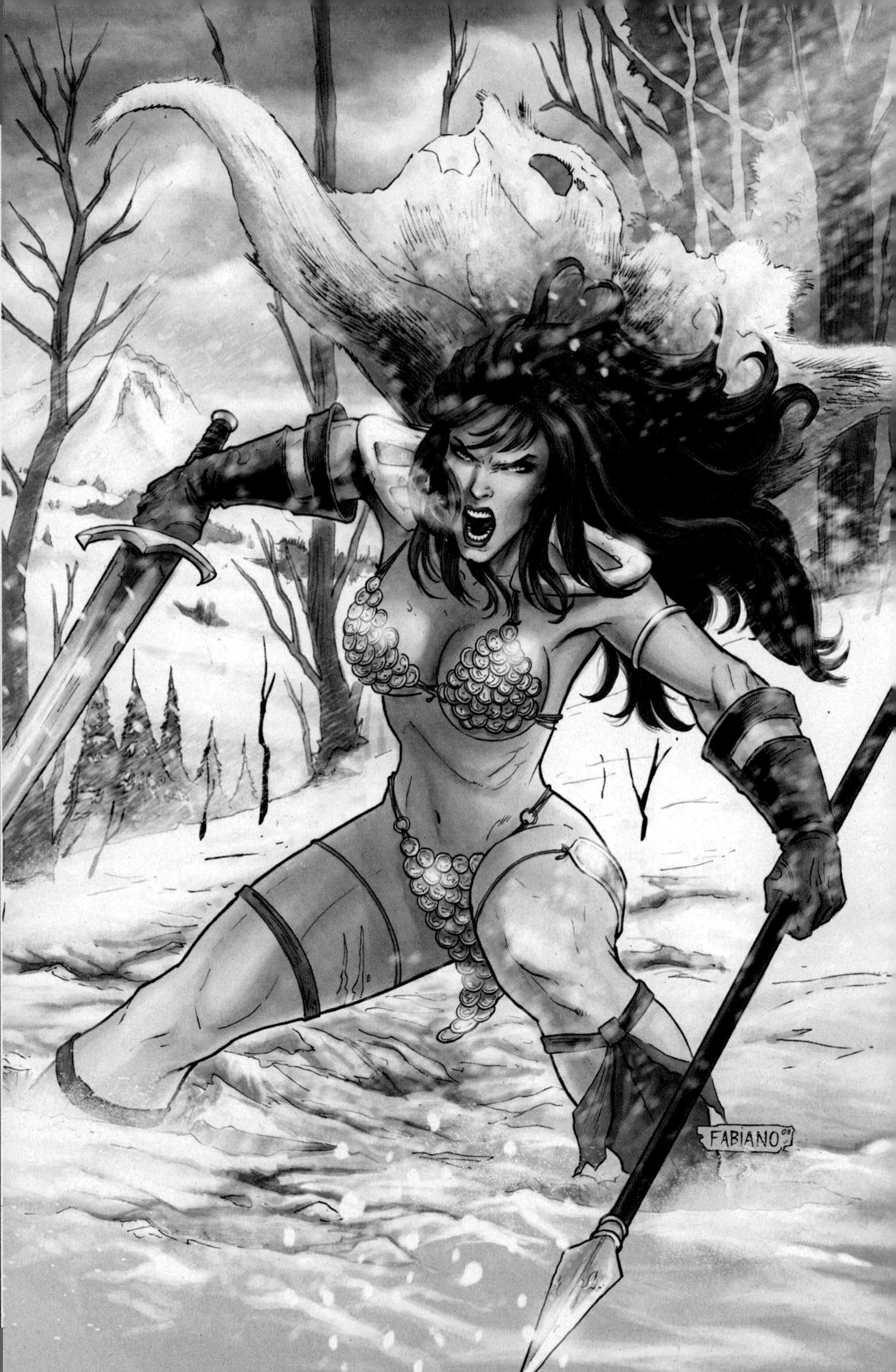
FABIANO 09

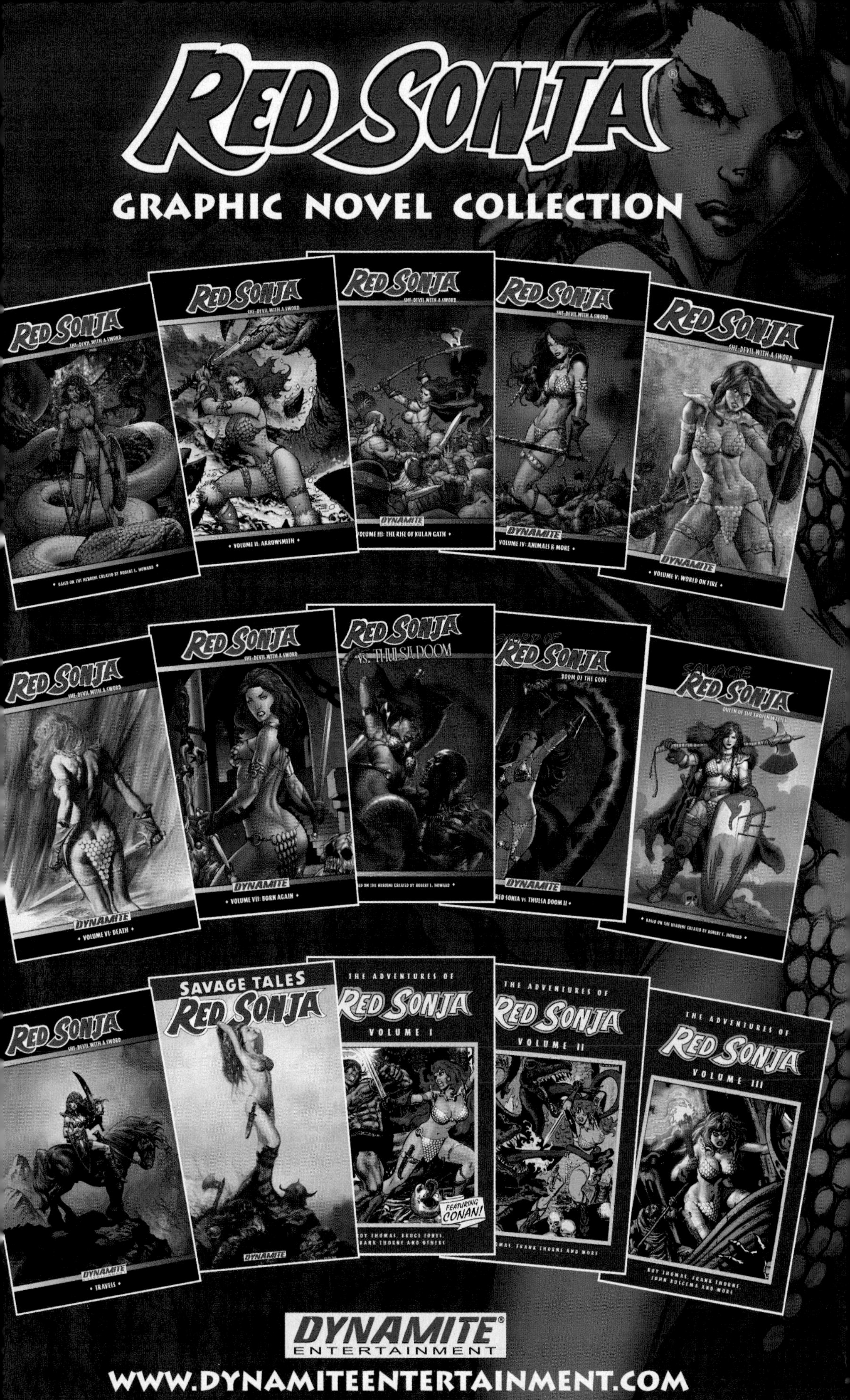

RED SONJA®
GRAPHIC NOVEL COLLECTION
RED SONJA
SHE-DEVIL WITH A SWORD
BASED ON THE HEROINE CREATED BY ROBERT E. HOWARD
RED SONJA
SHE-DEVIL WITH A SWORD
VOLUME II: ARROWSMITH
RED SONJA
SHE-DEVIL WITH A SWORD
DYNAMITE
VOLUME III: THE RISE OF KULAN GATH
RED SONJA
SHE-DEVIL WITH A SWORD
DYNAMITE
VOLUME IV: ANIMALS & MORE
RED SONJA
SHE-DEVIL WITH A SWORD
DYNAMITE
VOLUME V: WORLD ON FIRE
RED SONJA
SHE-DEVIL WITH A SWORD
DYNAMITE
VOLUME VI: DEATH
RED SONJA
SHE-DEVIL WITH A SWORD
DYNAMITE
VOLUME VII: BORN AGAIN
RED SONJA
VS. THULSA DOOM
BASED ON THE HEROINE CREATED BY ROBERT E. HOWARD
RED SONJA
DOOM OF THE GODS
DYNAMITE
RED SONJA VS. THULSA DOOM II
SAVAGE
RED SONJA
QUEEN OF THE FROZEN WASTES
BASED ON THE HEROINE CREATED BY ROBERT E. HOWARD
RED SONJA
SHE-DEVIL WITH A SWORD
DYNAMITE
TRAVELS
SAVAGE TALES
RED SONJA
DYNAMITE
THE ADVENTURES OF
RED SONJA
VOLUME I
FEATURING CONAN!
ROY THOMAS, BRUCE JONES, FRANK THORNE AND OTHERS
THE ADVENTURES OF
RED SONJA
VOLUME II
THOMAS, FRANK THORNE AND MORE
THE ADVENTURES OF
RED SONJA
VOLUME III
ROY THOMAS, FRANK THORNE JOHN BUSCEMA AND MORE
DYNAMITE® ENTERTAINMENT
WWW.DYNAMITEENTERTAINMENT.COM

CURRENTLY AVAILABLE AND UPCOMING COLLECTIONS FROM DYNAMITE ENTERTAINMENT
For a complete list, visit us online at www.dynamiteentertainment.com

Adventures of Red Sonja Vol. 1
Thomas, Thorne, More

Adventures of Red Sonja Vol. 2
Thomas, Thorne, More

Adventures of Red Sonja Vol. 3
Thomas, Thorne, More

American Flagg! Definitive Collection Vol. 1
Chaykin

Army of Darkness: Movie Adaptation
Raimi, Raimi, Bolton

Army of Darkness: Ashes to Ashes
Hartnell, Bradshaw

Army of Darkness: Shop 'Till You Drop Dead
Kuhoric, Bradshaw, Greene

Army of Darkness vs. Re-Animator
Kuhoric, Bradshaw, Greene

Army of Darkness: Old School & More
Kuhoric, Sharpe

Army of Darkness: Ash vs. The Classic Monsters
Kuhoric, Sharpe, Blanco

Army of Darkness: From The Ashes
Kuhoric, Blanco

Army of Darkness: The Long Road Home
Kuhoric, Raicht, Blanco

Army of Darkness: Home Sweet Hell
Kuhoric, Raicht, Perez

Army of Darkness: Hellbillies & Deadnecks
Kuhoric, Raicht, Cohn

Army of Darkness: League of Light Assemble!
Raicht, Cohn

Army of Darkness Omnibus Vol. 1
Hartnell, Kuhoric, Kirkman, more

Army of Darkness: Ash Saves Obama
Serrano, Padilla

Army of Darkness vs. Xena Vol. 1: Why Not?
Layman, Jerwa, Montenegro

Xena vs. Army of Darkness Vol. 2: What...Again?!
Jerwa, Serrano, Montenegro

Bad Boy 10th Anniv. Edition
Miller, Bisley

Borderline Vol. 1
Risso, Trillo

Borderline Vol. 2
Risso, Trillo1

Borderline Vol. 3
Risso, Trillo

The Boys Vol. 1 The Name of the Game
Ennis, Robertson

The Boys Vol. 2 Get Some
Ennis, Robertson, Snejbjerg

The Boys Vol. 3 Good For The Soul
Ennis, Robertson

The Boys Vol. 4 We Gotta Go Now
Ennis, Robertson

The Boys Vol. 5 Herogasm
Ennis, McCrea
Ennis, Robertson

The Boys Vol. 6 The Self-Preservation Society
Ennis, Robertson, Ezquerra

The Boys Definitive Edition Vol. 1
Ennis, Robertson

The Boys Definitive Edition Vol. 2
Ennis, Robertson

Buck Rogers Vol. 1: Future Shock
Beatty, Rafael

Classic Battlestar Galactica Vol. 1
Remender, Rafael

Classic Battlestar Galactica Vol. 2: Cylon Apocalypse
Grillo-Marxuach, Rafael

The Complete Dracula
Stoker, Moore, Reppion, Worley

Dan Dare Omnibus
Ennis, Erskine

Darkman vs. Army of Darkness
Busiek, Stern, Fry

Darkness vs. Eva Vol. 1
Moore, Reppion, Salazar

Dead Irons
Kuhoric, Alexander, Lee

Dreadstar The Definitive Collection
Starlin

Dreadstar: The Beginning
Starlin

Eduardo Risso's Tales of Terror
Risso, Trillo

Garth Ennis' Battlefields Vol. 1: The Night Witches
Ennis, Braun

Garth Ennis' Battlefields Vol. 2: Dear Billy
Ennis, Snejbjerg

Garth Ennis' Battlefields Vol. 3: The Tankies
Ennis, Ezquerra

Garth Ennis' The Complete Battlefields Vol. 1
Ennis, Braun, Snejbjerg, Ezquerra

Garth Ennis' Battlefields Vol. 4: Happy Valley
Ennis, Holden

The Good, The Bad and the Ugly Vol. 1
Dixon, Polls

Hellshock
Lee, Chung

Highlander Vol. 1: The Coldest War
Oeming, Jerwa, Moder, Sharpe

Highlander Vol. 2: Dark Quickening
Jerwa, Laguna

Highlander Vol. 3: Armageddon
Jerwa, Rafael

Highlander Way Of The Sword
Krul, Rafael

Jungle Girl Vol. 1
Cho, Murray, Batista

Jungle Girl Season 2
Cho, Murray, Batista

Just A Pilgrim
Ennis, Ezquerra

Kevin Smith's Green Hornet Vol. 1: Sins of the Father
Smith, Lau

Kid Kosmos: Cosmic Guard
Starlin

Kid Kosmos: Kidnapped
Starlin

The Lone Ranger Vol. 1: Now & Forever
Matthews, Cariello, Cassaday

The Lone Ranger Vol. 2: Lines Not Crossed
Matthews, Cariello, Cassaday, Pope

The Lone Ranger Vol. 3: Scorched Earth
Matthews, Cariello, Cassaday

The Lone Ranger Definitive Edition Vol. 1
Matthews, Cariello, Cassaday

The Man With No Name Vol. 1: Saints and Sinners
Gage, Dias

The Man With No Name Vol. 2: Holliday in the Sun
Lieberman, Wolpert, Bernard

Masquerade Vol. 1
Ross, Hester, Paul

Mercenaries Vol. 1
Reed, Salazar

Monster War
Golden, Chin, more

New Battlestar Galactica Vol. 1
Pak, Raynor

New Battlestar Galactica Vol. 2
Pak, Raynor

New Battlestar Galactica Vol. 3
Pak, Raynor, Lau

New Battlestar Galactica Complete Omnibus V1
Pak, Raynor, Jerwa, Lau

New Battlestar Galactica: Zarek
Jerwa, Batista

New Battlestar Galactica: Season Zero Vol. 1
Jerwa, Herbert

New Battlestar Galactica: Season Zero Vol. 2
Jerwa, Herbert

New Battlestar Galactica Origins: Baltar
Fahey, Lau

New Battlestar Galactica Origins: Adama
Napton, Lau

New Battlestar Galactica Origins: Starbuck & Helo
Fahey, Lau

New Battlestar Galactica: Ghosts
Jerwa, Lau

New Battlestar Galactica: Cylon War
Ortega, Nylund, Raynor

New Battlestar Galactica: The Final Five
Fahey, Reed, Raynor

Essential Painkiller Jane Vol. 1
Quesada, Palmiotti, Leonardi, more

Painkiller Jane Vol. 1: The Return
Quesada, Palmiotti, Moder

Painkiller Jane Vol. 2: Everything Explodes
Quesada, Palmiotti, Moder

Painkiller Jane vs. Terminator
Palmiotti, Raynor

Power & Glory
Chaykin

Project Superpowers Chapter 1
Ross, Krueger, Paul, Sadowski

Project Superpowers Chapter 2 Vol. 1
Ross, Krueger, Salazar

Project Superpowers: Meet The Bad Guys
Ross, Casey, Lilly, Lau, Paul, Herbert

Raise The Dead
Moore, Reppion, Petrus

Red Sonja She-Devil With a Sword Vol. 1
Oeming, Carey, Rubi

Red Sonja She-Devil With a Sword Vol. 2: Arrowsmiths
Oeming, Rubi, more

Red Sonja She-Devil With a Sword Vol. 3: The Rise of Kulan Gath
Oeming, Rubi, more

Red Sonja She-Devil With a Sword Vol. 4: Animals & More
Oeming, Homs, more

Red Sonja She-Devil With a Sword Vol. 5: World On Fire
Oeming, Reed, Homs

Red Sonja She-Devil With a Sword Vol. 6: Death
Marz, Ortega, Reed, more

Red Sonja She-Devil With a Sword Vol. 7: Born Again
Reed, Geovani

Red Sonja She-Devil With a Sword Vol. 8: Blood Dynasty
Reed, Geovani

Red Sonja She-Devil With a Sword Omnibus Vol. 1
Oeming, Carey, Rubi, more

Red Sonja vs. Thulsa Doom Vol. 1
David, Lieberman, Conrad

Savage Red Sonja: Queen of the Frozen Wastes
Cho, Murray, Homs

Red Sonja: Travels
Marz, Ortega, Thomas, more

Sword of Red Sonja: Doom of the Gods (Red Sonja vs. Thulsa Doom 2)
Lieberman, Antonio

Savage Tales of Red Sonja
Marz, Gage, Ortega, more

Robert E. Howard Presents: ThulsaDoom Vol. 1
Nelson, Antonio

Robocop Vol. 1: Revolution
Williams, Neves

Scout Vol. 1
Truman

Scout Vol. 2
Truman

Sherlock Holmes Vol. 1: The Trial of Sherlock Holmes
Moore, Reppion, Campbell

Six From Sirius
Moench, Gulacy

Street Magik
Lieberman, McCarthy, Buchemi

Super Zombies
Guggenheim, Gonzales, Rubi

Terminator: Infinity
Furman, Raynor

Terminator: Revolution
Furman, Antonio

Witchblade: Shades of Gray
Moore, Reppion, Segovia, Geovani

Xena Vol. 1: Contest of Pantheons
Layman, Neves

Xena Vol. 2: Dark Xena
Layman, Champagne, Salonga

Zorro Vol. 1: Year One Trail of the Fox
Wagner, Francavilla

Zorro Vol. 2: Clashing Blades
Wagner, Razek